S0-BSF-629

Penguin Books

Joe Wilson's Mates

Henry Lawson was born in 1867 on the Grenfell
goldfields in central west New South Wales. When
he was sixteen his parents separated and he moved
to Sydney with his formidable mother, Louisa, who
was a dedicated feminist and republican, and a major
influence on her son.

At the age of twenty Lawson submitted his first poem
to the *Bulletin*, and it was accepted, thus beginning
a lifelong association with that journal. By 1896 Lawson's growing reputation was confirmed with the
publication of an anthology of verse, *In the Days
When the World Was Wide*, and a collection of short
stories, *While the Billy Boils*. In 1900 he went to
England where he had three books published.

A complex, contradictory man, Lawson's writing and
personality deteriorated badly towards the end of his
life, despite his friends' efforts to help him. He had
been struggling against alcoholism for many years.
He died aged fifty-five in 1922.

AW

JOE WILSON'S
Mates

HENRY LAWSON

PENGUIN BOOKS

Penguin Books Australia Ltd
487 Maroondah Highway, PO Box 257
Ringwood, Victoria 3134, Australia
Penguin Books Ltd
Harmondsworth, Middlesex, England
Viking Penguin Inc.
40 West 23rd Street, New York, N.Y. 10010, U.S.A.
Penguin Books Canada Ltd
2801 John Street, Markham, Ontario, Canada L3R 1B4
Penguin Books (N.Z.) Ltd
182-190 Wairau Road, Auckland 10, New Zealand

First published by Remington, London, 1888
This edition published by Lloyd O'Neil Pty Ltd 1984
Published by Penguin Books Australia Ltd 1988

Produced by Viking O'Neil
56 Claremont Street, South Yarra, Victoria 3141, Australia
A division of Penguin Books Australia Ltd

Made and printed in Australia by Griffen Press

CIP

National Library of Australia
Cataloguing-in-Publication data

Lawson, Henry, 1867-1922.
Joe Wilson's mates.

Includes index.
ISBN 0 14 011225 1.

I. Title.

A823' .2

JOE WILSON'S COURTSHIP

There are many times in this world when a healthy boy is happy. When he is put into knickerbockers, for instance, and "comes a man to-day," as my little Jim used to say. When they're cooking something at home that he likes. When the "sandy blight" or measles breaks out amongst the children, or the teacher or his wife falls dangerously ill—or dies, it doesn't matter which—"and there ain't no school." When a boy is naked and in his natural state for a warm climate like Australia, with three or four of his schoolmates, under the shade of the creek-oaks in the bend where there's a good clear pool with a sandy bottom. When his father buys him a gun, and he starts out after kangaroos or possums. When he gets a horse, saddle, and bridle of his own. When he has his arm in splints or a stitch in his head—he's proud then, the proudest boy in the district.

I wasn't a healthy-minded, average boy; I reckon I was born for a poet by mistake, and grew up to be a bushman, and didn't know what was the matter with me—or the world—but that's got nothing to do with it.

There are times when a man is happy. When he finds out that the girl loves him. When he's just married. When he's a lawful father for the first time, and everything's going on all right: some men make fools of themselves then—I know I did. I'm happy to-night because I'm out of debt and can see clear ahead, and because I haven't been easy for a long time.

But I think that the happiest time in a man's life is when he's courting a girl, and finds out for sure that she loves him, and hasn't a thought for anyone else. Make the most of your courting days, you young chaps, and keep them clean, for they're about the only days when there's a chance of poetry and beauty coming into this life. Make the best of them, and you'll never regret it the longest day you live. They're the days that the wife will look back to, anyway, in the brightest of times as well as in the blackest; and there shouldn't be anything in those days that might hurt her when she looks back. Make the most of your courting days, you young chaps, for they will never come again.

A married man knows all about it—after a while; he sees the woman world through the eyes of his wife; he knows what an extra moment's pressure of the hand means, and, if he has had a hard life, and is inclined to be cynical, the knowledge does him no good. It leads him into awful messes sometimes, for a married man, if he's inclined that way, has three times the chance with a woman that a single man has—because the married man knows. He is privileged; he can guess pretty closely what a woman means when she says something else; he knows just how far he can go; he can go farther in five minutes towards coming to the point with a woman than an innocent young man dares go in three weeks. Above all, the married man is more decided with women; he takes them and things for granted. In short he is—well, he is a married man. And, when he knows all this, how much better or happier is he for it? Mark Twain says that he lost all the beauty of the river when he saw it with a pilot's eye—and there you have it.

But it's all new to a young chap, provided he hasn't been a young blackguard. It's all wonderful, new, and strange to him. He's a different man. He finds that he never knew anything about women. He sees none of woman's little ways and tricks in his girl. He is in heaven one day and down near the other place the next; and that's the sort of thing that makes life interesting. He takes his new world for granted. And, when she says she'll be his wife——!

Make the most of your courting days, you young chaps, for they've got a lot of influence on your married life afterwards—a lot more than you'd think. Make the best of them, for they'll never come any more, unless we do our courting over again in another world. If we do, I'll make the most of mine.

But, looking back, I didn't do so badly after all. I never told you about the days I courted Mary. The more I look back the more I come to think that I made the most of them, and if I had no more to regret in married life than I have in my courting days, I wouldn't walk to and fro in the room, or up and down the yard in the dark sometimes, or lie awake some nights thinking.... Ah, well!

I was between twenty-one and thirty then: birthdays had never been any use to me, and I'd left off counting them. You don't take much stock in birthdays in the bush. I'd knocked about the country for a few years, shearing and fencing and droving a little, and wasting my life without getting anything for it. I drank now and then, and made a fool of myself. I was reckoned "wild;" but I only drank because I felt less sensitive, and the world seemed a lot saner and better and kinder when I had a few drinks: I loved my fellow-man then and felt nearer to him. It's better to be thought "wild" than to be considered eccentric or ratty. Now, my old mate, Jack Barnes, drank—as far as I could see—first because he'd inherited the gambling habit from his father along with his father's luck; he'd the habit of being cheated and losing very bad, and when he lost he drank. Till drink got a hold on him. Jack was sentimental too, but in a different way. I was sentimental about other people—more fool I!—whereas Jack was sentimental about himself. Before he was married, and when he was recovering from a spree, he'd write rhymes about "Only a boy, drunk by the roadside," and that sort of thing; and he'd call 'em poetry, and talk about signing them and sending them to the *Town and Country Journal*. But he generally tore them up when he got better. The bush is breeding a race of poets, and I don't know what the country will come to in the end.

Well. It was after Jack and I had been out shearing at Beenaway Shed in the big scrubs. Jack was living in the little farming town of Solong, and I was hanging round. Black, the squatter, wanted some fencing done, and a new stable built, or buggy and harness-house, at his place at Haviland, a few miles out of Solong. Jack and I were good bush carpenters, so we took the job to keep us going till something else turned up. "Better than doing nothing," said Jack.

"There's a nice little girl in service at Black's," he said. "She's more like an adopted daughter, in fact, than a servant. She's a real good little girl, and good-looking into the bargain. I hear that young Black is sweet on her, but they say she won't have anything to do with him. I know a lot of chaps that have tried for her, but they've never had any luck. She's a regular little dumpling, and I like dumplings. They call her Possum. You ought to try a bear up in that direction, Joe."

I was always shy with women—except perhaps some that I should have fought shy of; but Jack wasn't—he was afraid of no woman, good, bad, or indifferent. I haven't time to explain why, but somehow, whenever a girl took any notice of me I took it for granted that she was only playing with me, and felt nasty about it. I made one or two mistakes, but—ah well!

"My wife knows little Possum," said Jack. "I'll get her to ask her out to our place, and let you know."

I reckoned that he wouldn't get me there then, and made a note to be on the watch for tricks. I had a hopeless little love-story behind me, of course. I suppose most married men can look back to their lost love; few marry the first flame. Many a married man looks back and thinks it was damned lucky that he didn't get the girl he couldn't have. Jack had been my successful rival, only he didn't know it—I don't think his wife knew it either. I used to think her the prettiest and sweetest little girl in the district.

But Jack was mighty keen on fixing me up with the little girl at Haviland. He seemed to take it for granted that I was going to fall in love with her at first sight. He took too many things for granted as far as I was concerned, and got me into awful tangles sometimes.

"You let me alone, and I'll fix you up, Joe," he said, as we rode up to the station. "I'll make it all right with the girl. You're rather a good-looking chap. You've got the sort of eyes that take with girls, only you don't know it; you haven't got the go. If I had your eyes along with my other attractions, I'd be in trouble on account of a woman about once a week."

"For God's sake shut up, Jack," I said.

Do you remember the first glimpse you got of your wife? Perhaps not in England, where so many couples grow up together from childhood; but it's different in Australia, where you may hail from two thousand miles away from where your wife was born, and yet she may be a countrywoman of yours, and a countrywoman in ideas and politics too. I remember the first glimpse I got of Mary.

It was a two-storey brick house with wide balconies and verandas all round, and a double row of pines down to the front gate. Parallel at the back was an old slab-and-shingle place, one room deep, and about eight rooms long, with a row of skillions at the back: the place was used for kitchen, laundry and servants' rooms. This was the old homestead before the new house was built. There was a wide, old-fashioned brick-floored veranda in front, with an open end; there was ivy climbing up the veranda-post on one side and a baby-rose on the other, and a grape-vine near the chimney. We rode up to the end of the veranda, and Jack called to see if there was anyone at home, and Mary came trotting out; so it was in the frame of vines that I first saw her.

More than once since then I've had a fancy to wonder whether the rose-bush killed the grape-vine or the ivy smothered 'em both in the end. I used to have a vague idea of riding that way some day to see. You do get strange fancies at odd times.

Jack asked her if the boss was in. He did all the talking. I saw a little girl, rather plump, with a complexion like a New England or Blue Mountain girl, or a girl from Tasmania, or from Gippsland in Victoria. Red and white girls were very scarce in the Solong district.

She had the biggest and brightest eyes I'd seen round there, dark hazel eyes, as I found out afterwards, and bright as a possum's. No wonder they called her "Possum." I forgot at once that Mrs Jack Barnes was the prettiest girl in the district. I felt a sort of comfortable satisfaction in the fact that I was on horseback; most bushmen look better oh horseback. It was a black filly, a fresh young thing, and she seemed as shy of girls as I was myself. I noticed Mary glanced in my direction once or twice to see if she knew me; but, when she looked, the filly took all my attention. Mary trotted in to tell old Black he was wanted, and after Jack had seen him and arranged to start work next day, we started back to Solong.

I expected Jack to ask me what I thought of Mary—but he didn't. He squinted at me sideways once or twice, and didn't say anything for a long time, and then he started talking of other things. I began to feel wild at him. He seemed so damnably satisfied with the way things were going. He seemed to reckon that I was a gone case now; but as he didn't say so, I had no way of getting at him. I felt sure he'd go home and tell his wife that Joe Wilson was properly gone on little Possum at Haviland. That was all Jack's way.

Next morning we started to work. We were to build the buggy-house at the back near the end of the old house, but first we had to take down a rotten old place that might have been the original hut in the bush before the old house was built. There was a window in it, opposite the laundry window in the old place, and the first thing I did was to take out the sash. I'd noticed Jack yarning with Possum before he started work. While I was at work at the window he called me round to the other end of the hut to help him lift a grindstone out of the way; and when we'd done it, he took the tip of my ear between his fingers and thumb and stretched it and whispered into it:

"Don't hurry with that window, Joe; the strips are hardwood and hard to get off—you'll have to take the sash out very carefully so as not to break the glass." Then he stretched my ear a little more and put his mouth closer:

"Make a looking-glass of that window, Joe," he said.

I was used to Jack, and when I went back to the window I started to puzzle out what he meant, and presently I saw it by chance.

That window reflected the laundry window: the room was dark inside, and there was a good clear reflection; and presently I saw Mary come to the laundry window and stand with her hands behind her back, thoughtfully watching me. The laundry window had an old-fashioned hinged sash, and I like that sort of window—there's more romance about it, I think. There was a thick dark-green ivy all round the window, and Mary looked prettier than a picture. I squared up my shoulders and put my heels together, and put as much style as I could into my work. I couldn't have turned round to save my life.

Presently Jack came round, and Mary disappeared.

"Well?" he whispered.

"You're a fool, Jack," I said. "She's only interested in the old house being pulled down."

"That's all right," he said. "I've been keeping an eye on the business round the corner, and she ain't interested when *I'm* round this end."

"You seem mighty interested in the business," I said.

"Yes," said Jack. "This sort of thing just suits a man of my rank in times of peace."

"What made you think of the window?" I asked.

"Oh, that's as simple as striking matches. I'm up to all those dodges. Why, where there wasn't a window, I've fixed up a piece of looking-glass to see if a girl was taking any notice of me when she thought I wasn't looking."

He went away and presently Mary was at the window again, and this time she had a tray with cups of tea and a plate of cake and bread-and-butter. I was prizing off the strips that held the sash, very carefully, and my heart suddenly commenced to gallop, without any reference to me. I'd never felt like that before, except once or twice. It was just as if I'd swallowed some clock-work arrangement, unconsciously, and it had started to go, without warning. I reckon it was all on account of that blarsted Jack working me up. He had a quiet way of working you up to a thing, that made you want to hit him sometimes—after you'd made an ass of yourself.

I didn't hear Mary at first. I hoped Jack would come round and help me out of the fix, but he didn't.

"Mr—Mr Wilson!" said Mary. She had a sweet voice.

I turned round.

"I thought you and Mr Barnes might like a cup of tea."

"Oh, thank you!" I said, and I made a dive for the window, as if hurry would help it. I trod on an old cask-hoop; it sprang up and dinted my skin and I stumbled—and that didn't help matters much.

"Oh! did you hurt yourself, Mr Wilson?" cried Mary.

"Hurt myself! Oh no, not at all, thank you," I blurted out. "It takes more than that to hurt me."

I was about the reddest shy lanky fool of a bushman that ever was taken at a disadvantage on foot, and when I took the tray my hands shook so that a lot of the tea was spilt into the saucers. I embarrassed her too, like the damned fool I was, till she must have been as red as I was, and it's a wonder we didn't spill the whole lot between us. I got away from the window in as much of a hurry as if Jack had cut his leg with a chisel and fainted, and I was running with whisky for him. I blundered round to where he was, feeling like a man feels when he has just made an ass of himself in public. The memory of that sort of thing hurts you worse and makes you jerk your head more impatiently than the thought of a past crime would, I think.

I pulled myself together when I got to where Jack was.

"Here, Jack!" I said. "I've struck something all right; here's some tea and brownie—we'll hang out here all right."

Jack took a cup of tea and a piece of cake and sat down to enjoy it, just as if he'd paid for it and ordered it to be sent out about that time.

He was silent for a while, with the sort of silence that always made me wild at him. Presently he said, as if he'd just thought of it:

"That's a very pretty little girl, Possum, isn't she, Joe? Do you notice how she dresses?—always fresh and trim. But she's got on her best bib-and-tucker to-day, and a pinafore with frills to it. And it's ironing-day, too. It can't be on your account. If it was Saturday or Sunday afternoon, or some holiday, I could understand it. But perhaps one of her admirers is going to take her to the church bazaar in Solong tonight. That's what it is."

He gave me time to think over that.

"But yet she seems interested in you, Joe," he said. "Why didn't you offer to take her to the bazaar instead of letting another chap get in ahead of you? You miss all your chances, Joe."

Then a thought struck me. I ought to have known Jack well enough to have thought of it before.

"Look here, Jack," I said. "What have you been saying to that girl about me?"

"Oh, not much," said Jack. "There isn't much to say about you."

"What did you tell her?"

"Oh, nothing in particular. She'd heard all about you before."

"She hadn't heard much good, I suppose," I said.

"Well, that's true, as far as I could make out. But you've only got yourself to blame. I didn't have the breeding and rearing of you. I smoothed over matters with her as much as I could."

"What did you tell her?" I said. "That's what I want to know."

"Well, to tell the truth, I didn't tell her anything much. I only answered questions."

"And what questions did she ask?"

"Well, in the first place, she asked if your name wasn't Joe Wilson; and I said it was, as far as I knew. Then she said she heard that you wrote poetry, and I had to admit that that was true."

"Look here, Jack," I said, "I've two minds to punch your head."

"And she asked me if it was true that you were wild," said Jack, "and I said you was, a bit. She said it seemed a pity. She asked me if it was true that you drank, and I drew a long face and said that I was sorry to say it was true. She asked me if you had any friends, and I said none that I knew of, except me. I said that you'd lost all your friends; they stuck to you as long as they could, but they had to give you best, one after the other."

"What next?"

"She asked me if you were delicate, and I said no, you were as tough as fencing-wire. She said you looked rather pale and thin, and asked me if you'd had an illness lately. And I said no—it was all on account of the wild dissipated life you'd led. She said it was a pity you hadn't a mother or a sister to look after you—it was a pity that something couldn't be done for you, and I said it was, but I was afraid that nothing could be done. I told her that I was doing all I could to keep you straight."

I knew enough of Jack to know that most of this was true. And so she only pitied me after all. I felt as if I'd been courting her for six months and she'd thrown me over—but I didn't know anything about women yet.

"Did you tell her I was in jail?" I growled.

"No, by gum! I forgot that. But never mind, I'll fix that up all right. I'll tell her that you got two years' hard for horse-stealing. That ought to make her interested in you, if she isn't already."

We smoked a while.

"And was that all she said?" I asked.

"Who?—Oh! Possum," said Jack, rousing himself. "Well—no; let me think—we got chatting of other things—you know a married man's privileged, and can say a lot more to a girl than a single man can. I got talking nonsense about sweethearts, and one thing led to another till at last she said, 'I suppose Mr Wilson's got a sweetheart, Mr Barnes?' "

"And what did you say?" I growled.

"Oh, I told her that you were a holy terror amongst the girls," said Jack. "You'd better take back that tray, Joe, and let us get to work."

I wouldn't take back the tray—but that didn't mend matters, for Jack took it back himself.

I didn't see Mary's reflection in the window again, so I took the window out. I reckoned that she was just a big-hearted, impulsive little thing, as many Australian girls are, and I reckoned that I was a fool for thinking for a moment that she might give me a second thought, except by way of kindness. Why! young Black and half a dozen better men than me were sweet on her, and young Black was to get his father's station and the money—or rather his mother's money, for she held the stuff (she kept it close, too, by all accounts). Young Black was away at the time, and his mother was dead against him about Mary, but that didn't make any difference, as far as I could see. I reckoned that it was only just going to be a hopeless, heart-breaking, stand-far-off-and-worship affair, as far as I was concerned—like my first love affair, that I haven't told you about yet. I was tired of being pitied by good girls. You see, I didn't know women then. If I had known, I think I might have made more than one mess of my life.

Jack rode home to Solong every night. I was staying at a pub some distance out of town, between Solong and Haviland. There were three or four wet days, and we didn't get on with the work. I fought shy of Mary till one day she was hanging out clothes and the line broke. It was the old-style sixpenny clothes-line. The clothes were all down, but it was clean grass, so it didn't matter much. I looked at Jack.

"Go and help her, you capital idiot!" he said, and I made the plunge.

"Oh, thank you, Mr Wilson!" said Mary, when I came to help. She had the broken end of the line, and was trying to hold some of the clothes off the ground, as if she could pull it an inch with the heavy wet sheets and table-cloths and things on it, or as if it would do any good if she did. But that's the way with women—especially little women—some of 'em would try to pull a store bullock if they got the end of the rope on the right side of the fence. I took the line from Mary and accidentally touched her soft, plump little hand as I did so: it sent a thrill right through me. She seemed a lot cooler than I was.

Now, in cases like this, especially if you lose your head a bit, you get hold of the loose end of the rope that's hanging from the post with one hand, and the end of the line with the clothes on with the other, and try to pull 'em far enough together to make a knot. And that's about all you do for the present, except look like a fool. Then I took off the post end, spliced the line, took it over the fork, and pulled, while Mary helped me with the prop. I thought Jack might have come and taken the prop from her, but he didn't; he just went on with his work as if nothing was happening inside the horizon.

She'd got the line about two-thirds full of clothes, it was a bit short now, so she had to jump and catch it with one hand and hold it down while she pegged a sheet she'd thrown over. I'd made the plunge now, so I volunteered to help her. I held down the line while she threw the things over and pegged out. As we got near the post and higher I straightened out some ends and pegged myself. Bushmen are handy at most things. We laughed, and now and again Mary would say, "No, that's not the way, Mr Wilson; that's not right; the sheet isn't far enough over; wait till I fix it." I'd a reckless idea once of holding her up while she pegged, and I was glad afterwards that I hadn't made such a fool of myself.

"There's only a few more things in the basket, Miss Brand," I said. "You can't reach—I'll fix 'em up."

She seemed to give a little gasp.

"Oh, those things are not ready yet," she said, "they're not rinsed," and she grabbed the basket and held it away from me. The things looked the same to me as the rest on the line; they looked rinsed enough and blued too. I reckoned that she didn't want me to take the trouble, or thought that I mightn't like to be seen hanging out clothes, and was only doing it out of kindness.

"Oh, it's no trouble," I said, "let me hang 'em out. I like it. I've hung out clothes at home on a windy day," and I made a reach into the basket. But she flushed red, with temper, I thought, and snatched the basket away.

"Excuse me, Mr Wilson," she said, "but those things are not ready yet!" and she marched into the wash-house.

"Ah, well! you've got a little temper of your own," I thought to myself.

When I told Jack, he said that I'd made another fool of myself. He said I'd both disappointed and offended her. He said that my line was to stand off a bit and be serious and melancholy in the background.

That evening when we'd started home, we stopped some time yarning with a chap we met at the gate; and I happened to look back and saw Mary hanging out the rest of the things—she thought that we were out of sight. Then I understood why those things weren't ready while we were round.

For the next day or two Mary didn't take the slightest notice of me, and I kept out of her way. Jack said I'd disillusioned her—and hurt her dignity—which was a thousand times worse. He said I'd spoilt the thing altogether. He said that she'd got an idea that I was shy and poetic, and I'd only shown myself the usual sort of bushwhacker.

I noticed her talking and chatting with other fellows once or twice, and it made me miserable. I got drunk two evenings running, and then, as it appeared afterwards, Mary consulted Jaek, and at last she said to him, when we were together:

"Do you play draughts, Mr Barnes?"

"No," said Jack.

"Do you, Mr Wilson?" she asked, suddenly turning her big bright eyes on me, and speaking to me for the first time since last washing-day.

"Yes," I said, "I do a little." Then there was a silence, and I had to say something else.

"Do you play draughts, Miss Brand?" I asked.

"Yes," she said, "but I can't get anyone to play with me here of an evening, the men are generally playing cards or reading." Then she said, "It's very dull these long winter evenings when you've got nothing to do. Young Mr Black used to play draughts, but he's away."

I saw Jack winking at me urgently.

"I'll play a game with you, if you like," I said, "but I ain't much of a player."

"Oh, thank you, Mr Wilson! When shall you have an evening to spare?"

We fixed it for that same evening. We got chummy over the draughts. I had a suspicion even then that it was a put-up job to keep me away from the pub.

Perhaps she found a way of giving a hint to old Black without committing herself. Women have ways—or perhaps Jack did it. Anyway, next day the boss came round and said to me:

"Look here, Joe, you've got no occasion to stay at the pub. Bring along your blankets and camp in one of the spare rooms of the old house. You can have your tucker here."

He was a good sort, was Black the squatter: a squatter of the old school, who'd shared the early hardships with his men, and couldn't see why he should not shake hands and have a smoke and a yarn over old times with any of his old station-hands that happened to come along. But he'd married an Englishwoman after the hardships were over, and she'd never got any Australian notions.

Next day I found one of the skillion rooms scrubbed out and a bed fixed up for me. I'm not sure to this day who did it, but I suppose that good-natured old Black had given one of the women a hint. After tea I had a yarn with Mary, sitting on a log of the wood-heap. I don't remember exactly how we came to be there, or who sat down first. There was about two feet between us. We got very chummy and confidential. She told me about her childhood and her father.

He'd been an old mate of Black's, a younger son of a well-to-do English family (with blue blood in it, I believe), and sent out to Australia with a thousand pounds to make his way, as many younger sons are, with more or less. They think they're hard done by; they blue their thousand pounds in Melbourne or Sydney, and they don't make any more nowadays, for the Roarin' Days have been dead these thirty years. I wish I'd had a thousand pounds to start on!

Mary's mother was the daughter of a German immigrant, who selected up there in the old days. She had a will of her own as far as I could understand, and bossed the home till the day of her death. Mary's father made money, and lost it, and drank—and died. Mary remembered him sitting on the veranda one evening with his hand on her head, and singing a German song (the "Lorelei," I think it was) softly, as if to himself. Next day he stayed in bed, and the children were kept out of the room; and, when he died, the children were adopted round (there was a little money coming from England).

Mary told me all about her girlhood. She went first to live with a sort of cousin in town, in a house where they took cards in on a tray, and then she came to live with Mrs Black, who took a fancy to her at first. I'd had no boyhood to speak of, so I gave her some of my ideas on what the world ought to be, and she seemed interested.

Next day there were sheets on my bed, and I felt pretty cocky until I remembered that I'd told her I had no one to care for me; then I suspected pity again.

But next evening we remembered that both our fathers and mothers were dead, and discovered that we had no friends except Jack and old Black, and things went on very satisfactorily.

And next day there was a little table in my room with a crocheted cover and a looking-glass.

I noticed the other girls began to act mysterious and giggle when I was round, but Mary didn't seem aware of it.

We got very chummy. Mary wasn't comfortable at Haviland. Old Black was very fond of her and always took her part, but she wanted to be independent. She had a great idea of going to Sydney and getting into the hospital as a nurse. She had friends in Sydney, but she had no money. There was a little money coming to her when she was twenty-one—a few pounds—and she was going to try and get it before that time.

"Look here, Miss Brand," I said, after we'd watched the moon rise. "I'll lend you the money. I've got plenty—more than I know what to do with."

But I saw I'd hurt her. She sat up very straight for a while, looking before her; then she said it was time to go in, and said, "Good night, Mr Wilson."

I reckoned I'd done it that time; but Mary told me afterwards that she was only hurt because it struck her that what she said about money might have been taken for a hint. She didn't understand me yet, and I didn't know human nature. I didn't say anything to Jack—in fact about this time I left off telling him about things. He didn't seem hurt; he worked hard and seemed happy.

I really meant what I said to Mary about the money. It was pure good nature. I'd be a happier man now, I think, and a richer man perhaps, if I'd never grown more selfish than I was that night on the wood-heap with Mary. I felt a great sympathy for her—but I got to love her. I went through all the ups and downs of it. One day I was having tea in the kitchen, and Mary and another girl, named Sarah, reached me a clean plate at the same time: I took Sarah's because she was first, and Mary seemed very nasty about it, and that gave me great hopes. But all next evening she played draughts with a drover that she'd chummed up with. I pretended to be interested in Sarah's talk, but it didn't seem to work.

A few days later a Sydney jackeroo visited the station. He had a good pea-rifle, and one afternoon he started to teach Mary to shoot at a target. They seemed to get very chummy. I had a nice time for three or four days, I can tell you. I was worse than a wall-eyed bullock with the pleuro. The other chaps had a shot out of the rifle. Mary called "Mr Wilson" to have a shot, and I made a worse fool of myself by sulking. If it hadn't been a blooming jackeroo I wouldn't have minded so much.

Next evening the jackeroo and one or two other chaps and the girls went out possum shooting. Mary went. I could have gone, but I

didn't. I mooched round all the evening like an orphan bandicoot on
a burnt ridge, and then I went up to the pub and filled myself up
with beer, and damned the world, and came home and went to bed.
I think that evening was the only time I ever wrote poetry down on a
piece of paper. I got so miserable that I enjoyed it.

I felt better next morning, and reckoned I was cured. I ran against
Mary accidentally, and had to say something.

"How did you enjoy yourself yesterday evening, Miss Brand?" I
asked.

"Oh, very well, thank you, Mr Wilson," she said. Then she asked,
"How did you enjoy yourself, Mr Wilson?"

I puzzled over that afterwards, but couldn't make anything out of
it. Perhaps she only said it for the sake of saying something. But
about this time my handkerchiefs and collars disappeared from the
room and turned up washed and ironed, and laid tidily on my table.
I used to keep an eye out, but could never catch anybody near my
room. I straightened up, and kept my room a bit tidy, and when my
handkerchief got too dirty, and I was ashamed of letting it go to the
wash, I'd slip down to the river after dark and wash it out, and dry it
next day, and rub it up to look as if it hadn't been washed, and leave
it on my table. I felt so full of hope and joy that I worked twice as
hard as Jack, till one morning he remarked casually:

"I see you've made a new mash, Joe. I saw the half-caste cook
tidying up your room this morning and taking your collars and
things to the wash-house."

I felt very much off colour all the rest of the day, and I had such a
bad night of it that I made up my mind next morning to look the
hopelessness square in the face and live the thing down.

It was the evening before Anniversary Day. Jack and I had put in
a good day's work to get the job finished, and Jack was having a
smoke and a yarn with the chaps before he started home. We sat on
an old log along by the fence at the back of the house. There was
Jimmy Nowlett the bullock-driver, and long Dave Regan the drover,
and Jim Bullock the fencer, and one or two others. Mary and the
station girls and one or two visitors were sitting under the old
veranda. The jackeroo was there too, so I felt happy. It was the girls
who used to bring the chaps hanging round. They were getting up a
dance party for Anniversary night. Along in the evening another
chap came riding up to the station: he was a big shearer, a dark,
handsome fellow, who looked like a gipsy; it was reckoned that there
was foreign blood in him. He went by the name of Romany. He was
supposed to be shook after Mary too. He had the nastiest temper

and the best violin in the district, and the chaps put up with him a lot because they wanted him to play at bush dances. The moon had risen over Pine Ridge, but it was dusky where we were. We saw Romany loom up, riding in from the gate; he rode round the end of the coach-house and across towards where we were—I suppose he was going to tie up his horse at the fence; but about half-way across the grass he disappeared. It struck me that there was something peculiar about the way he got down, and I heard a sound like a horse stumbling.

"What the hell's Romany trying to do?" said Jimmy Nowlett. "He couldn't have fell off his horse—or else he's drunk."

A couple of chaps got up and went to see. Then there was that waiting, mysterious silence that comes when something happens in the dark, and nobody knows what it is. I went over, and the thing dawned on me. I'd stretched a wire clothes-line across there during the day and had forgotten all about it for the moment. Romany had no idea of the line and, as he rode up, it caught him on a level with his elbows, and scraped him off his horse. He was sitting on the grass, swearing in a surprised voice, and the horse looked surprised too. Romany wasn't hurt, but the sudden shock had spoilt his temper. He wanted to know who'd put up that bloody line. He came over and sat on the log. The chaps smoked for a while.

"What did you git down so sudden for, Romany?" asked Jim Bullock, presently. "Did you hurt yerself on the pommel?"

"Why didn't you ask the horse to go round?" asked Dave Regan.

"I'd only like to know who put up that bleeding wire!" growled Romany.

"Well," said Jimmy Nowlett, "if we'd put up a sign to beware of the line you couldn't have seen it in the dark."

"Unless it was a transparency with a candle behind it," said Dave Regan. "But why didn't you get down on one end, Romany, instead of all along? It wouldn't have jolted yer so much."

All this with the bush drawl, and between the puffs of their pipes. But I didn't take any interest in it. I was brooding over Mary and the jackeroo.

"I've heard of men getting down over their horse's head," said Dave presently, in a reflective sort of way—"In fact, I've done it myself—but I never saw a man get off backwards over his horse's rump."

But they saw that Romany was getting nasty, and they wanted him to play the fiddle next night, so they dropped it.

Mary was singing an old song. I always thought she had a sweet voice, and I'd have enjoyed it if that damned jackeroo hadn't been listening too. We listened in silence until she'd finished.

"That gal's got a nice voice," said Jimmy Nowlett.

"Nice voice!" snarled Romany, who'd been waiting for a chance to be nasty. "Why, I've heard a tom-cat sing better."

I moved and Jack, he was sitting next me, nudged me to keep quiet. The chaps didn't like Romany's talk about Possum at all. They were all fond of her: she wasn't a pet or tomboy, for she wasn't built that way, but they were fond of her in such a way that they didn't like to hear anything said about her. They said nothing for a while, but it meant a lot. Perhaps the single men didn't care to speak for fear that it would be said that they were gone on Mary. But presently Jimmy Nowlett gave a big puff at his pipe and spoke:

"I suppose you got bit, too, in that quarter, Romany?"

"Oh, she tried it on, but it didn't go," said Romany. "I've met her sort before. She's setting her cap at that jackeroo now. Some girls will run after anything with trousers on," and he stood up.

Jack Barnes must have felt what was coming, for he grabbed my arm, and whispered, "Sit still, Joe, damn you! He's too good for you!" But I was on my feet and facing Romany as if a giant hand had reached down and wrenched me off the log and set me there.

"You're a damned crawler, Romany!" I said.

Little Jimmy Nowlett was between us, and the other fellows round us before a blow got home. "Hold on, you damned fools!" they said. "Keep quiet till we get away from the house!" There was a little clear flat down by the river, and plenty of light there, so we decided to go down there and have it out.

Now I never was a fighting man; I'd never learnt to use my hands. I scarcely knew how to put them up. Jack often wanted to teach me, but I wouldn't bother about it. He'd say, "You'll get into a fight some day, Joe, or out of one, and shame me;" but I hadn't the patience to learn. He'd wanted me to take lessons at the station after work, but he used to get excited, and I didn't want Mary to see him knocking me about. Before he was married, Jack was always getting into fights—he generally tackled a better man and got a hiding; but he didn't seem to care so long as he made a good show—though he used to explain the thing away from a scientific point of view for weeks after. To tell the truth, I had a horror of fighting; I had a horror of being marked about the face; I think I'd sooner stand off and fight a man with revolvers than fight him with fists; and then I think I would say, last thing, "Don't shoot me in the face!" Then

again I hated the idea of hitting a man. It seemed brutal to me. I
was too sensitive and sentimental, and that was what the matter
was. Jack seemed very serious on it as we walked down to the river,
and he couldn't help hanging out blue lights.

"Why didn't you let me teach you to use your hands?" he said.
"The only chance now is that Romany can't fight after all. If you'd
waited a minute I'd have been at him." We were a bit behind the
rest, and Jack started giving me points about lefts and rights, and
"half-arms," and that sort of thing. "He's left-handed, and that's
the worst of it," said Jack. "You must only make as good a show as
you can, and one of us will take him on afterwards."

But I just heard him and that was all. It was to be my first fight
since I was a boy, but somehow I felt cool about it—sort of dulled. If
the chaps had known all they would have set me down as a cur. I
thought of that, but it didn't make any difference with me then; I
knew it was a thing they couldn't understand. I knew I was
reckoned pretty soft. But I knew one thing that they didn't know. I
knew that it was going to be a fight to a finish, one way or the other.
I had more brains and imagination than the rest put together, and I
suppose that that was the real cause of most of my trouble. I kept
saying to myself, "You'll have to go through with it now, Joe, old
man! It's the turning point of your life." If I won the fight, I'd set to
work and win Mary; if I lost, I'd leave the district for ever. A man
thinks a lot in a flash sometimes; I used to get excited over little
things, because of the very paltriness of them, but I was mostly cool
in a crisis—Jack was the reverse. I looked ahead: I wouldn't be able
to marry a girl who could look back and remember when her
husband was beaten by another man—no matter what sort of brute
the other man was.

I never in my life felt so cool about a thing. Jack kept whispering
instructions, and showing with his hands, up to the last moment, but
it was all lost on me.

Looking back, I think there was a bit of romance about it: Mary
singing under the vines to amuse a jackeroo dude, and a coward
going down to the river in the moonlight to fight for her.

It was very quiet in the little moonlit flat by the river. We took off
our coats and were ready. There was no swearing or barracking. It
seemed an understood thing with the men that if I went out first
round Jack would fight Romany; and if Jack knocked him out
somebody else would fight Jack to square matters. Jim Bullock
wouldn't mind obliging for one; he was a mate of Jack's, but he

didn't mind who he fought so long as it was for the sake of fair play—or "peace and quietness," as he said. Jim was very good-natured. He backed Romany, and of course Jack backed me.

As far as I could see, all Romany knew about fighting was to jerk one arm up in front of his face and duck his head by way of a feint, and then rush and lunge out. But he had the weight and strength and length of reach, and my first lesson was a very short one. I went down early in the round. But it did me good; the blow and the look I'd seen in Romany's eyes knocked all the sentiment out of me. Jack said nothing—he seemed to regard it as a hopeless job from the first. Next round I tried to remember some things Jack had told me, and made a better show, but I went down in the end.

I felt Jack breathing quick and trembling as he lifted me up.

"How are you, Joe?" he whispered.

"I'm all right," I said.

"It's all right," whispered Jack in a voice as if I was going to be hanged, but it would soon be all over. "He can't use his hands much more than you can—take your time, Joe—try to remember something I told you, for God's sake!"

When two men fight who don't know how to use their hands, they stand a show of knocking each other about a lot. I got some awful thumps, but mostly on the body. Jimmy Nowlett began to get excited and jump round—he was an excitable little fellow.

"Fight! you ——!" he yelled. "Why don't you fight? That ain't fightin'. Fight, and don't try to murder each other. Use your crimson hands, or, by God, I'll chip you! Fight, or I'll blanky well bullock-whip the pair of you;" then his language got awful. They said we went like windmills, and that nearly every one of the blows we made was enough to kill a bullock if it had got home. Jimmy stopped us once, but they held him back.

Presently I went down pretty flat, but the blow was well up on the head, and didn't matter much—I had a good thick skull. And I had one good eye yet.

"For God's sake, hit him!" whispered Jack—he was trembling like a leaf. "Don't mind what I told you. I wish I was fighting him myself! Get a blow home, for God's sake! Make a good show this round and I'll stop the fight."

That showed how little even Jack, my old mate, understand me.

I had the bushman up in me now, and wasn't going to be beaten while I could think. I was wonderfully cool, and learning to fight. There's nothing like a fight to teach a man. I was thinking fast, and learning more in three seconds than Jack's sparring could have taught me in three weeks. People think that blows hurt in a fight, but they don't—not till afterwards. I fancy that a fighting man, if he isn't altogether an animal, suffers more mentally than he does physically.

While I was getting my wind I could hear through the moonlight and still air the sound of Mary's voice singing up at the house. I thought hard into the future, even as I fought. The fight only seemed something that was passing.

I was on my feet again and at it, and presently I lunged out and felt such a jar on my arm that I thought it was telescoped. I thought I'd put out my wrist and elbow. And Romany was lying on the broad of his back.

I heard Jack draw three breaths of relief in one. He said nothing as he straightened me up, but I could feel his heart beating. He said afterwards that he didn't speak because he thought a word might spoil it.

I went down again, but Jack told me afterwards that he *felt* I was all right when he lifted me.

Then Romany went down, then we fell together and the chaps separated us. I got another knock-down blow in, and was beginning to enjoy the novelty of it, when Romany staggered and limped.

"I've done," he said. "I've twisted my ankle." He'd caught his heel against a tuft of grass.

"Shake hands," yelled Jimmy Nowlett.

I stepped forward, but Romany took his coat, and limped to his horse.

"If yer don't shake hands with Wilson, I'll lam yer;" howled Jimmy; but Jack told him to let the man alone, and Romany got on his horse somehow and rode off.

I saw Jim Bullock stoop and pick up something from the grass, and heard him swear in surprise. There was some whispering, and presently Jim said:

"If I thought that, I'd kill him."

"What is it?" asked Jack.

Jim held up a butcher's knife. It was common for a man to carry a butcher's knife in a sheath fastened to his belt.

"Why did you let your man fight with a butcher's knife in his belt?" asked Jimmy Nowlett.

But the knife could easily have fallen out when Romany fell, and we decided it that way.

"Any way," said Jimmy Nowlett, "if he'd stuck Joe in hot blood before us all it wouldn't be so bad as if he sneaked up and stuck him in the back in the dark. But you'd best keep an eye over yer shoulder for a year or two, Joe. That chap's got Eye-talian blood in him somewhere. And now the best thing you chaps can do is to keep your mouth shut and keep all this dark from the gals."

Jack hurried me on ahead. He seemed to act queer, and when I glanced at him I could have sworn that there was water in his eyes. I said that Jack had no sentiment except for himself, but I forgot, and I'm sorry I said it.

"What's up, Jack?" I asked.

"Nothing," said Jack.

"What's up, you old fool?" I said.

"Nothing," said Jack, "except that I'm damned proud of you, Joe, you old ass!" and he put his arm round my shoulders and gave me a shake. "I didn't know it was in you, Joe—I wouldn't have said it before, or listened to any other man say it, but I didn't think you had the pluck—God's truth, I didn't. Come along and get your face fixed up."

We got into my room quietly, and Jack got a dish of water, and told one of the chaps to sneak a piece of fresh beef from somewhere.

Jack was as proud as a dog with a tin tail as he fussed round me. He fixed up my face in the best style he knew, and he knew a good many—he'd been mended himself so often.

While he was at work we heard a sudden hush and a scraping of feet amongst the chaps that Jack had kicked out of the room, and a girl's voice whispered. "Is he hurt? Tell me. I want to know—I might be able to help."

It made my heart jump, I can tell you. Jack went out at once, and there was some whispering. When he came back he seemed wild.

"What is it, Jack?" I asked.

"Oh, nothing," he said, "only that damned slut of a halfcaste cook overheard some of those blanky fools arguing as to how Romany's knife got out of the sheath, and she's put a nice yarn round amongst the girls. There's a regular bobbery, but it's all right now, Jimmy Nowlett's telling 'em lies at a great rate."

Presently there was another hush outside, and a saucer with vinegar and brown paper was handed in.

One of the chaps brought some beer and whisky from the pub, and we had a quiet little time in my room. Jack wanted to stay all night, but I reminded him that his little wife was waiting for him in

Solong, so he said he'd be round early in the morning, and went home.

I felt the reaction pretty bad. I didn't feel proud of the affair at all. I thought it was a low brutal business all round. Romany was a quiet chap after all, and the chaps had no right to chyack him. Perhaps he'd had a hard life, and carried a big swag of trouble that we didn't know anything about. He seemed a lonely man. I'd gone through enough myself to teach me not to judge men. I made up my mind to tell him how I felt about the matter next time we met. Perhaps I made my usual mistake of bothering about "feelings" in another party that hadn't any feelings at all—perhaps I didn't; but it's generally best to chance it on the kind side in a case like this. Altogether I felt as if I'd made another fool of myself, and been a weak coward. I drank the rest of the beer and went to sleep.

About daylight I woke and heard Jack's horse on the gravel. He came round the back of the buggy-shed and up to my door, and then, suddenly, a girl screamed out. I pulled on my trousers and 'lastic-side boots and hurried out. It was Mary herself, dressed, and sitting on an old stone step at the back of the kitchen with her face in her hands, and Jack was off his horse and stooping by her side with his hand on her shoulder. She kept saying, "I thought you were ——! I thought you were ——!" I didn't catch the name. An old single-barrel muzzle-loader shot-gun was lying in the grass at her feet. It was the gun they used to keep loaded and hanging in straps in a room off the kitchen ready for a shot at a cunning old hawk that they called "'Tarnal Death," and that used to be always after the chickens.

When Mary lifted her face it was as white as notepaper, and her eyes seemed to grow wilder when she caught sight of me.

"Oh, you did frighten me, Mr Barnes," she gasped. Then she gave a little ghost of a laugh and stood up, and some colour came back.

"Oh, I'm a little fool!" she said quickly. "I thought I heard old 'Tarnal Death at the chickens, and I thought it would be a great thing if I got the gun and brought him down; so I got up and dressed quietly so as not to wake Sarah. And then you came round the corner and frightened me. I don't know what you must think of me, Mr Barnes."

"Never mind," said Jack. "You go and have a sleep, or you won't be able to dance to-night. Never mind the gun—I'll put that away." And he steered her round to the door of her room off the brick veranda where she slept with one of the other girls.

"Well, that's a rum start!" I said.

"Yes, it is," said Jack; "it's very funny. Well, how's your face this morning, Joe?"

He seemed a lot more serious than usual.

We were hard at work all the morning cleaning out the big wool-shed and getting it ready for the dance, hanging hoops for the candles, and making seats. I kept out of sight of the girls as much as I could. One side of my face was a sight, and the other wasn't too classical. I felt as if I had been stung by a swarm of bees.

"You're a fresh, sweet-scented beauty now, and no mistake, Joe," said Jimmy Nowlett—he was going to play the accordion that night. "You ought to fetch the girls now, Joe. But never mind, your face'll go down in about three weeks. My lower jaw is crooked yet; but that fight straightened my nose, that had been knocked crooked when I was a boy—so I didn't lose much beauty by it."

When we'd done in the shed, Jack took me aside and said:

"Look here, Joe; if you won't come to the dance to-night—and I can't say you'd ornament it—I tell you what you'll do. You get little Mary away on the quiet and take her out for a stroll—and act like a man. The job's finished now, and you won't get another chance like this."

"But how am I to get her out?" I said.

"Never you mind. You be mooching round down by the big peppermint-tree near the river-gate, say about half-past ten."

"What good'll that do?"

"Never you mind. You just do as you're told, that's all you've got to do," said Jack, and he went home to get dressed and bring his wife.

After the dancing started that night I had a peep in once or twice. The first time I saw Mary dancing with Jack, and looking serious; and the second time she was dancing with the blarsted jackeroo dude, and looking excited and happy. I noticed that some of the girls, that I could see sitting on a stool along the opposite wall, whispered, and gave Mary black looks as the jackeroo swung her past. It struck me pretty forcibly that I should have taken fighting lessons from him instead of from poor Romany. I went away and walked about four miles down the river road, getting out of the way into the bush whenever I saw any chap riding along. I thought of poor Romany and wondered where he was, and thought that there wasn't much to choose between us as far as happiness was concerned. Perhaps he was walking by himself in the bush, and feeling like I did. I wished I could shake hands with him.

But somehow, about half-past ten, I drifted back to the river sliprails, and leant over them in the shadow of the peppermint-tree, looking at the rows of river-willows in the moonlight. I didn't expect anything, in spite of what Jack said.

I didn't like the idea of hanging myself: I'd been with a party who found a man hanging in the bush, and it was no place for a woman round where he was. And I'd helped drag two bodies out of the Cudgegong River in a flood, and they weren't sleeping beauties. I thought it was a pity that a chap couldn't lie down on a grassy bank in a graceful position in the moonlight, and die just by thinking of it—and die with his eyes and mouth shut. But then I remembered that I wouldn't make a beautiful corpse anyway it went, with the face I had on me.

I was just getting comfortably miserable when I heard a step behind me, and my heart gave a jump. And I gave a start, too.

"Oh, is that you, Mr Wilson?" said a timid little voice.

"Yes," I said. "Is that you, Mary?"

And she said yes. It was the first time I called her Mary, but she did not seem to notice it.

"Did I frighten you?" I asked.

"No—yes—just a little," she said. "I didn't know there was anyone——" then she stopped.

"Why aren't you dancing?" I asked her.

"Oh, I'm tired," she said. "It was too hot in the woolshed. I thought I'd like to come out, and get my head cool, and be quiet a little while."

"Yes," I said. "It must be hot in the wool-shed."

She stood looking out over the willows. Presently she said: "It must be very dull for you, Mr Wilson—you must feel lonely. Mr Barnes said——" Then she gave a little gasp and stopped—as if she was just going to put her foot in it.

"How beautiful the moonlight looks on the willows!" she said.

"Yes," I said, "doesn't it? Supposing we have a stroll by the river."

"Oh, thank you, Mr Wilson. I'd like it very much."

I didn't notice it then, but, now I come to think of it, it was a beautiful scene: there was a horse-shoe of high blue hills round behind the house, with the river running round under the slopes,

and in front was a rounded hill covered with pines, and pine ridges
and a soft blue peak away over the ridges, ever so far in the distance.

I had a handkerchief over the worst of my face, and kept the best
side turned to her. We walked down by the river, and didn't say
anything for a good while. I was thinking hard. We came to a white,
smooth log in a quiet place out of sight of the house.

"Suppose we sit down for a while, Mary," I said.

"If you like, Mr Wilson," she said.

There was about a foot of log between us.

"What a beautiful night!" she said.

"Yes," I said, "isn't it?"

Presently she said, "I suppose you know I'm going away next
month, Mr Wilson?"

I felt suddenly empty. "No," I said, "I didn't know that."

"Yes," she said, "I thought you knew. I'm going to try to get into
the hospital to be trained for a nurse, and if that doesn't come off I'll
get a place as assistant public-school teacher."

We didn't say anything for a good while.

"I suppose you won't be sorry to go, Miss Brand?" I said.

"I—I don't know," she said. "Everybody's been so kind to me
here."

She sat looking straight before her, and I fancied her eyes
glistened. I put my arm round her shoulders, but she didn't seem to
notice it. In fact, I scarcely noticed it myself at the time.

"So you think you'll be sorry to go away?" I said.

"Yes, Mr Wilson. I suppose I'll fret for a while. It's been my
home, you know."

I pressed my hand on her shoulder, just a little, so she couldn't
pretend not to know it was there. But she didn't seem to notice.

"Ah, well," I said, "I suppose I'll be on the wallaby again next
week."

"Will you, Mr Wilson?" she said. Her voice seemed very soft.

I slipped my arm round her waist, under her arm. My heart was
going like clockwork now.

Presently she said:

"Don't you think it's time to go back now, Mr Wilson?"

"Oh, there's plenty of time!" I said. I shifted up, and put my arm
further round, and held her closer. She sat straight up, looking right
in front of her, but she began to breathe hard.

"Mary," I said.

"Yes," she said.

"Call me Joe," I said.

"I—I don't like to," she said. "I don't think it would be right."

So I just turned her face round and kissed her. She clung to me and cried.

"What is it, Mary?" I asked.

She only held me tighter and cried.

"What is it, Mary?" I said. "Ain't you well? Ain't you happy?"

"Yes, Joe," she said, "I'm very happy." Then she said, "Oh, your poor face! Can't I do anything for it?"

"No," I said. "That's all right. My face doesn't hurt me a bit now."

But she didn't seem right.

"What is it, Mary?" I said. "Are you tired? You didn't sleep last night——" Then I got an inspiration.

"Mary," I said, "what were you doing out with the gun this morning?"

And after some coaxing it all came out, a bit hysterical.

"I couldn't sleep—I was frightened. Oh! I had such a terrible dream about you, Joe! I thought Romany came back and got into your room and stabbed you with his knife. I got up and dressed, and about daybreak I heard a horse at the gate; then I got the gun down from the wall—and—and Mr Barnes came round the corner and frightened me. He's something like Romany, you know."

Then I got as much of her as I could into my arms.

And, oh, but wasn't I happy walking home with Mary that night! She was too little for me to put my arm round her waist, so I put it round her shoulder, and that felt just as good. I remember I asked her who'd cleaned up my room and washed my things, but she wouldn't tell.

She wouldn't go back to the dance yet; she said she'd go into her room and rest a while. There was no one near the old veranda; and when she stood on the end of the floor she was just on a level with my shoulder.

"Mary," I whispered, "put your arms round my neck and kiss me."

She put her arms round my neck, but she didn't kiss me; she only hid her face.

"Kiss me, Mary!" I said.

"I—I don't like to," she whispered.

"Why not, Mary?"

Then I felt her crying or laughing, or half-crying and half-laughing. I'm not sure to this day which it was.

"Why won't you kiss me, Mary? Don't you love me?"

"Because," she said, "because—because I—I don't—I don't think it's right for—for a girl to—to kiss a man unless she's going to be his wife."

Then it dawned on me! I'd forgot all about proposing.

"Mary," I said, "would you marry a chap like me?"

And that was all right.

Next morning Mary cleared out my room and sorted out my things, and didn't take the slightest notice of the other girls' astonishment.

But she made me promise to speak to old Black, and I did the same evening. I found him sitting on the log by the fence, having a yarn on the quiet with an old bushman; and when the old bushman got up and went away, I sat down.

"Well, Joe," said Black, "I see somebody's been spoiling your face for the dance." And after a bit he said, "Well, Joe, what is it? Do you want another job? If you do, you'll have to ask Mrs Black, or Bob" (Bob was his eldest son); "they're managing the station for me now, you know." He could be bitter sometimes in his quiet way.

"No," I said; "it's not that, boss."

"Well, what is it, Joe?"

"I—well, the fact is, I want little Mary."

He puffed at his pipe for a long time, then I thought he spoke.

"What did you say, boss?" I said.

"Nothing, Joe," he said. "I was going to say a lot, but it wouldn't be any use. My father used to say a lot to me before I was married."

I waited a good while for him to speak.

"Well, boss," I said, "what about Mary?"

"Oh! I suppose that's all right, Joe," he said. "I—I beg your pardon. I got thinking of the days when I was courting Mrs Black."

BRIGHTEN'S SISTER-IN-LAW

Jim was born on Gulgong, New South Wales. We used to say "on" Gulgong—and old diggers still talked of being "on th' Gulgong"— though the goldfield there had been worked out for years, and the place was only a dusty little pastoral town in the scrubs. Gulgong was about the last of the great alluvial "rushes" of the "roaring days"—and dreary and dismal enough it looked when I was there. The expression "on" came from being on the "diggings" or goldfield—the workings or the goldfield was all underneath, of course, so we lived (or starved) on them—not in nor at 'em.

Mary and I had been married about two years when Jim came —— His name wasn't "Jim," by the way, it was "John Henry," after an uncle godfather; but we called him Jim from the first—(and before it)—because Jim was a popular bush name, and most of my old mates were Jims. The bush is full of good-hearted scamps called Jim.

We lived in an old weather-board shanty that had been a slygrog shop, and the Lord knows what else! in the palmy days of Gulgong; and I did a bit of digging ("fossicking," rather), a bit of shearing, a bit of fencing, a bit of bush-carpentering, tank-sinking—anything, just to keep the billy boiling.

We had a lot of trouble with Jim with his teeth. He was bad with every one of them, and we had most of them lanced—couldn't pull him through without. I remember we got one lanced and the gum healed over before the tooth came through, and we had to get it cut again. He was a plucky little chap, and after the first time he never whimpered when the doctor was lancing his gum: he used to say "tar" afterwards, and want to bring the lance home with him.

The first turn we got with Jim was the worst. I had had the wife and Jim camping with me in a tent at a dam I was making at Cattle Creek; I had two men working for me, and a boy to drive one of the tip-drays, and I took Mary out to cook for us. And it was lucky for us that the contract was finished and we got back to Gulgong, and within reach of a doctor, the day we did. We were just camping in the house, with our goods and chattels anyhow, for the night; and we were hardly back home an hour when Jim took convulsions for the first time.

Did you ever see a child in convulsions? You wouldn't want to see it again: it plays the devil with a man's nerves. I'd got the beds fixed up on the floor and the billies on the fire—I was going to make some tea, and put a piece of corned beef on to boil overnight—when Jim (he'd been queer all day, and his mother was trying to hush him to sleep)—Jim, he screamed out twice. He'd been crying a good deal, and I was dog-tired and worried (over some money a man owed me) or I'd have noticed at once that there was something unusual in the way the child cried out: as it was I didn't turn round till Mary screamed "Joe! Joe!" You know how a woman cries out when her child is in danger or dying—short, and sharp, and terrible. "Joe! Look! look! Oh, my God, our child! Get the bath, quick! quick! it's convulsions!"

Jim was bent back like a bow, stiff as a bullock-yoke, in his mother's arms, and his eyeballs were turned up and fixed—a thing I saw twice afterwards and don't want ever to see again.

I was falling over things getting the tub and the hot water, when the woman who lived next door rushed in. She called to her husband to run for the doctor, and before the doctor came she and Mary had got Jim into a hot bath and pulled him through.

The neighbour woman made me up a shake-down in another room, and stayed with Mary that night; but it was a long while before I got Jim and Mary's screams out of my head and fell asleep.

You may depend I kept the fire in, and a bucket of water hot over it for a good many nights after that; but (it always happens like this) there came a night, when the fright had worn off, when I was too tired to bother about the fire, and that night Jim took us by surprise. Our wood-heap was done, and I broke up a new chair to get a fire, and had to run a quarter of a mile for water; but this turn wasn't so bad as the first, and we pulled him through.

You never saw a child in convulsions? Well, you don't want to. It must be only a matter of seconds, but it seems long minutes; and half an hour afterwards the child might be laughing and playing with you, or stretched out dead. It shook me up a lot. I was always pretty high-strung and sensitive. After Jim took the first fit, every time he cried, or turned over, or stretched out in the night, I'd jump: I was always feeling his forehead in the dark to see if he was feverish, or feeling his limbs to see if he was "limp" yet. Mary and I often laughed about it—afterwards. I tried sleeping in another room, but for nights after Jim's first attack I'd just be dozing off into a sound sleep, when I'd hear him scream, as plain as could be, and I'd hear Mary cry, "Joe!—Joe!"—short, sharp, and terrible—and I'd be up and into their room like a shot, only to find them sleeping peacefully. Then I'd feel Jim's head and his breathing for signs of convulsions, see to the fire and water, and go back to bed and try to sleep. For the first few nights I was like that all night, and I'd feel relieved when daylight came. I'd be in first thing to see if they were all right; then I'd sleep till dinner-time if it was Sunday or I had no work. But then

I was run down about that time: I was worried about some money for a wool-shed I put up and never got paid for; and besides, I'd been pretty wild before I met Mary.

I was fighting hard then—struggling for something better. Both Mary and I were born to better things, and that's what made the life so hard for us.

Jim got on all right for a while: we used to watch him well, and have his teeth lanced in time.

It used to hurt and worry me to see how—just as he was getting fat and rosy and like a natural happy child, and I'd feel proud to take him out—a tooth would come along, and he'd get thin and white and pale and bigger-eyed and old-fashioned. We'd say, "He'll be safe when he gets his eye-teeth;" but he didn't get them till he was two; then. "He'll be safe when he gets his two-year-old teeth;" they didn't come till he was going on for three.

He was a wonderful little chap—Yes, I know all about parents thinking that their child is the best in the world. If your boy is small for his age, friends will say that small children make big men; that he's a very bright, intelligent child, and that it's better to have a bright, intelligent child than a big, sleepy lump of fat. And if your boy is dull and sleepy, they say that the dullest boys make the cleverest men—and all the rest of it. I never took any notice of that sort of clatter—took it for what it was worth; but, all the same, I don't think I ever saw such a child as Jim was when he turned two. He was everybody's favourite. They spoilt him rather. I had my own ideas about bringing up a child. I reckoned Mary was too soft with Jim. She'd say, "Put that" (whatever it was) "out of Jim's reach, will you, Joe?" and I'd say, "No! leave it there, and make him understand he's not to have it. Make him have his meals without any nonsense and go to bed at a regular hour," I'd say. Mary and I had many a breeze over Jim. She'd say that I forgot he was only a baby: but I held that a baby could be trained from the first week; and I believe I was right.

But, after all, what are you to do? You'll see a boy that was brought up strict turn out a scamp; and another that was dragged up anyhow (by the hair of the haid, as the saying is) turn out well. Then, again, when a child is delicate—and you might lose him any day—you don't like to spank him, though he might be turning out a little fiend, as delicate children often do. Suppose you gave a child a hammering, and the same night he took convulsions, or something, and died—how'd you feel about it? You never know what a child is going to take, any more than you can tell what some women are going to say or do.

I was very fond of Jim, and we were great chums. Sometimes I'd sit and wonder what the deuce he was thinking about, and often, the way he talked, he'd make me uneasy. When he was two he wanted a pipe above all things, and I'd get him a clean new clay and he'd sit by my side, on the edge of the veranda, or on a log of the wood-heap, in the cool of the evening, and suck away at his pipe, and try to spit when he saw me do it. He seemed to understand that a cold empty pipe wasn't quite the thing, yet to have the sense to know that he couldn't smoke tobacco yet: he made the best he could of things. And if he broke a clay pipe he wouldn't have a new one, and there'd be a row; the old one had to be mended up, somehow, with string or wire. If I got my hair cut, he'd want his cut too; and it always troubled him to see me shave—as if he thought there must be something wrong somewhere, else he ought to have to be shaved too. I lathered him one day, and pretended to shave him: he sat through it as solemn as an owl, but didn't seem to appreciate it—perhaps he had sense enough to know that it couldn't possibly be the real thing. He felt his face, looked very hard at the lather I scraped off, and whimpered, "No blood, daddy!"

I used to cut myself a good deal: I was always impatient over shaving.

Then he went in to interview his mother about it. She understood his lingo better than I did.

But I wasn't always at ease with him. Sometimes he'd sit looking into the fire, with his head on one side, and I'd watch him and wonder what he was thinking about (I might as well have wondered what a Chinaman was thinking about) till he seemed at least twenty years older than me: sometimes, when I moved or spoke, he'd glance round just as if to see what that old fool of a dadda of his was doing now.

I used to have a fancy that there was something Eastern, or Asiatic—something older than our civilization or religion—about old-fashioned children. Once I started to explain my idea to a woman I thought would understand—and as it happened she had an old-fashioned child, with very slant eyes—a little tartar he was too. I suppose it was the sight of him that unconsciously reminded me of my infernal theory, and set me off on it, without warning me. Anyhow it got me mixed up in an awful row with the woman and her husband—and all their tribe. It wasn't an easy thing to explain myself out of it, and the row hasn't been fixed up yet. There were some Chinamen in the district.

I took a good-size fencing contract, the frontage of a ten-mile paddock, near Gulgong, and did well out of it. The railway had got as far as the Cudgegong River—some twenty miles from Gulgong and two hundred from the coast—and "carrying" was good then. I had a couple of draught-horses, that I worked in the tip-drays when I was tank-sinking, and one or two others running in the bush. I bought a broken-down wagon cheap, tinkered it up myself—christened it "The Same Old Thing"—and started carrying from the railway terminus through Gulgong and along the bush roads and tracks that branch out fanlike through the scrubs to the one-pub towns and sheep and cattle stations out there in the howling wilderness. It wasn't much of a team. There were the two heavy horses for "shafters;" a stunted colt, that I'd bought out of the pound for thirty shillings; a light, spring-cart horse; an old grey mare, with points like a big red-and-white Australian store bullock, and with the grit of an old washerwoman to work; and a horse that had spanked along in Cobb & Co.'s mailcoach in his time. I had a couple there that didn't belong to me: I worked them for the feeding of them in the dry weather. And I had all sorts of harness, that I mended and fixed up myself. It was a mixed team, but I took light stuff, got through pretty quick, and freight rates were high. So I got along.

Before this, whenever I made a few pounds I'd sink a shaft somewhere, prospecting for gold; but Mary never let me rest till she had talked me out of that.

I made up my mind to take on a small selection farm—that an old mate of mine had fenced in and cleared, and afterwards chucked up—about thirty miles out west of Gulgong, at a place called Lahey's Creek. (The places were all called Lahey's Creek, or Spicer's Flat, or Murphy's Flat, or Ryan's Crossing, or some such name—round there.) I reckoned I'd have a run for the horses and be able to grow a bit of feed. I always had a dread of taking Mary and the children too far away from a doctor—or a good woman neighbour; but there were some people came to live on Lahey's Creek, and besides, there was a young brother of Mary's—a young scamp (his name was Jim, too, and we called him "Jimmy" at first to make room for our Jim—he hated the name "Jimmy" or James). He came to live with us—without asking—and I thought he'd find enough work at Lahey's Creek to keep him out of mischief. He wasn't to be depended on much—he thought nothing of riding off, five hundred miles or so, "to have a look at the country"—but he was fond of Mary, and he'd stay by her till I got someone else to keep her company while I was on the road. He would be a protection against "sundowners" or any shearers who happened to wander that way in the "d.t.'s" after a spree. Mary had a married sister come to live at Gulgong just before we left, and nothing would suit her and her husband but we must leave little Jim with them for a month or so—till we got settled down at Lahey's Creek. They were newly married.

Mary was to have driven into Gulgong, in the spring-cart, at the end of the month, and taken Jim home; but when the time came she wasn't too well—and besides, the tyres of the cart were loose, and I hadn't time to get them cut, so we let Jim's time run on a week or so longer, till I happened to come out through Gulgong from the river with a small load of flour for Lahey's Creek way. The roads were good, the weather grand—no chance of it raining, and I had a spare tarpaulin if it did—I would only camp out one night; so I decided to take Jim home with me.

Jim was turning three then, and he was a cure. He was so old-fashioned that he used to frighten me sometimes—I'd almost think that there was something supernatural about him; though of course, I never took any notice of that rot about some children being too old-fashioned to live. There's always the ghoulish old hag (and some not so old nor haggish either) who'll come round and shake up young parents with such croaks as, "You'll never rear that child—he's too bright for his age." To the devil with them! I say.

But I really thought that Jim was too intelligent for his age, and I often told Mary that he ought to be kept back, and not let talk too much to old diggers and long lanky jokers of bushmen who rode in and hung their horses outside my place on Sunday afternoons.

I don't believe in parents talking about their own children everlastingly—you get sick of hearing them; and their kids are generally little devils, and turn out larrikins as likely as not.

But, for all that, I really think that Jim, when he was three years old, was the most wonderful·little chap, in every way, that I ever saw.

For the first hour or so, along the road, he was telling me all about his adventures at his auntie's.

"But they spoilt me too much, dad," he said, as solemn as a native bear. "An' besides, a boy ought to stick to his parrans!"

I was taking out a cattle-pup for a drover I knew, and the pup took up a good deal of Jim's time.

Sometimes he'd jolt me the way he talked; and other times I'd have to turn away my head and cough, or shout at the horses, to keep from laughing outright. And once, when I was taken that way, he said:

"What are you jerking your shoulders and coughing, and grunting, and going on that way for, dad? Why don't you tell me something?"

"Tell you what, Jim?"

"Tell me some talk."

So I told him all the talk I could think of. And I had to brighten up, I can tell you, and not draw too much on my imagination—for Jim was a terror at cross-examination when the fit took him; and he didn't think twice about telling you when he thought you were talking nonsense. Once he said:

"I'm glad you took me home with you, dad. You'll get to know Jim."

"What!" I said.

"You'll get to know Jim."

"But don't I know you already?"

"No, you don't. You never has time to know Jim at home."

And, looking back, I saw that it was cruel true. I had known in my heart all along that this was the truth; but it came to me like a blow from Jim. You see, it had been a hard struggle for the last year or so; and when I was home for a day or two I was generally too busy, or too tired and worried, or full of schemes for the future to take much notice of Jim. Mary used to speak to me about it, sometimes. "You never take notice of the child," she'd say. "You could surely find a few minutes of an evening. What's the use of always worrying and brooding? Your brain will go with a snap some day, and, if you get over it, it will teach you a lesson. You'll be an old man, and Jim a young one, before you realize that you had a child once. Then it will be too late."

This sort of talk from Mary always bored me and made me impatient with her, because I knew it all too well. I never worried for myself—only for Mary and the children. And often, as the days went by, I said to myself, "I'll take more notice of Jim and give Mary

more of my time, just as soon as I can see things clear ahead a bit."
And the hard days went on, and the weeks, and the months, and the
years—— Ah, well!

Mary used to say, when things would get worse, "Why don't you
talk to me, Joe? Why don't you tell me your thoughts, instead of
shutting yourself up in yourself and brooding—eating your heart
out? It's hard for me: I get to think you're tired of me, and selfish. I
might be cross and speak sharp to you when you are in trouble. How
am I to know, if you don't tell me?"

But I didn't think she'd understand.

And so, getting acquainted, and chumming and dozing, with the
gums closing over our heads here and there, and the ragged patches
of sunlight and shade passing up, over the horses, over us, on the
front of the load, over the load, and down on to the white, dusty road
again—Jim and I got along the lonely bush road and over the ridges
some fifteen miles before sunset, and camped at Ryan's Crossing on
Sandy Creek for the night. I got the horses out and took the harness
off. Jim wanted badly to help me, but I made him stay on the load;
for one of the horses—a vicious, red-eyed chestnut—was a kicker:
he'd broken a man's leg. I got the feed-bags stretched across the
shafts, and the chaff-and-corn into them; and there stood the horses
all round with their rumps north, south, and west, and their heads
between the shafts, munching and switching their tails. We use
double shafts, you know, for horse-teams—two pairs side by
side—and prop them up, and stretch bags between them, letting the
bags sag to serve as feed boxes. I threw the spare tarpaulin over the
wheels on one side, letting about half of it lie on the ground in case of
damp, and so making a floor and a breakwind. I threw down bags
and the blankets and possum rug against the wheel to make a camp
for Jim and the cattle-pup, and got a gin-case we used for a
tucker-box, the frying-pan and billy down, and made a good fire at a
log close handy, and soon everything was comfortable. Ryan's
Crossing was a grand camp. I stood with my pipe in my mouth, my
hands behind my back, and my back to the fire, and took the
country in.

Reedy Creek came down along a western spur of the range: the
banks here were deep and green, and the water ran clear over the
granite bars, boulders, and gravel. Behind us was a dreary flat
covered with those gnarled, grey-barked, dry-rotted "native apple-
trees" (about as much like apple-trees as the native bear is like any

other), and a nasty bit of sand-dusty road that I was always glad to get over in wet weather. To the left on our side of the creek were reedy marshes, with frogs croaking, and across the creek the dark box-scrub-covered ridges ended in steep "sidings" coming down to the creek-bank, and to the main road that skirted them, running on west up over a "saddle" in the ridges and on towards Dubbo. The road by Lahey's Creek to a place called Cobborah branched off, through dreary apple-tree and stringy-bark flats to the left, just beyond the crossing: all these fanlike branch tracks from the Cudgegong were inside a big horse-shoe in the Great Western Line, and so they gave small carriers a chance, now that Cobb & Co.'s coaches and the big teams and vans had shifted out of the main western terminus. There were tall she-oaks all along the creek and a clump of big ones over a deep waterhole just above the crossing. The creek oaks have rough barked trunks, like English elms, but are much taller and higher to the branches—and the leaves are reedy; Kendall, the Australian poet, calls them the "she-oak harps Aeolian." Those trees are always sigh-sigh-sighing—more of a sigh than a sough or the "whoosh" of gum-trees in the wind. You always hear them sighing, even when you can't feel any wind. It's the same with telegraph wires: put your head against a telegraph-post on a dead, still day, and you'll hear and feel the far-away roar of the wires. But then the oaks are not connected with the distance, where there might be wind; and they don't *roar* in a gale, only sigh louder and softer according to the wind, and never seem to go above or below a certain pitch—like a big harp with all the strings the same. I used to have a theory that those creek oaks got the wind's voice telephoned to them, so to speak, through the ground.

I happened to look round and there was Jim (I thought he was on the tarpaulin playing with the pup): he was standing close beside me with his legs wide apart, his hands behind his back, and his back to the fire.

He held his head a little on one side, and there was such an old, old, wise expression in his big brown eyes—just as if he'd been a child for a hundred years or so, or as though he were listening to those oaks, and understanding them in a fatherly sort of way.

"Dad!" he said presently—"Dad! do you think I'll ever grow up to be a man?"

"Wh—why, Jim?" I gasped.

"Because I don't want to."

I couldn't think of anything against this. It made me uneasy. But I remember *I* used to have a childish dread of growing up to be a man.

"Jim," I said, to break the silence, "do you hear what the she-oaks say?"

"No, I don't. Is they talking?"

"Yes," I said, without thinking.

"What is they saying?" he asked.

I took the bucket and went down to the creek for some water for tea. I thought Jim would follow with a little tin billy he had, but he didn't: when I got back to the fire he was again on the possum rug, comforting the pup. I fried some bacon and eggs that I'd brought out with me. Jim sang out from the wagon:

"Don't cook too much, dad—I mightn't be hungry."

I got the tin plates, and pint-pots and things out on a clean new flour-bag, in honour of Jim, and dished up. He was leaning back on the rug looking at the pup in a listless sort of way. I reckoned he was tired out, and pulled the gin-case up close to him for a table and put his plate on it. But he only tried on a mouthful or two, and then he said:

"I ain't hungry, dad! You'll have to eat it all."

It made me uneasy—I never liked to see a child of mine turn from his food. They had given him some tinned salmon in Gulgong, and I was afraid that that was upsetting him. I was always against tinned muck.

"Sick, Jim?" I asked.

"No, dad, I ain't sick; I don't know what's the matter with me."

"Have some tea, sonny?"

"Yes, dad."

I gave him some tea, with some milk in it that I'd brought in a bottle from his aunt's for him. He took a sip or two and then put the pint-pot on the gin-case.

"Jim's tired, dad," he said.

I made him lie down while I fixed up a camp for the night. It had turned a bit chilly, so I let the big tarpaulin down all round—it was made to cover a high load, the flour in the wagon didn't come above the rail, so the tarpaulin came down well on to the ground. I fixed Jim up a comfortable bed under the tail-end of the wagon: when I went to lift him in he was lying back, looking up at the stars in a half-fascinated way that I didn't like. Whenever Jim was extra old-fashioned, or affectionate, there was danger.

"How do you feel now, sonny?"

It seemed a minute before he heard me and turned from the stars. "Jim's better, dad." Then he said something like, "The stars are looking at me." I thought he was half asleep. I took off his jacket and boots and carried him in under the wagon and made him comfortable for the night.

"Kiss me 'night-night, daddy," he said.

I'd rather he hadn't asked me—it was a bad sign. As I was going to the fire he called me back.

"What is it, Jim?"

"Get me my things and the cattle-pup, please, daddy."

I was scared now. His things were some toys and rubbish he'd brought from Gulgong, and I remembered, the last time he had convulsions, he took all his toys and a kitten to bed with him. And " 'night-night" and "daddy" were two-year-old language to Jim. I'd thought he'd forgotten those words—he seemed to be going back.

"Are you quite warm enough, Jim?"

"Yes, dad."

I started to walk up and down—I always did this when I was extra worried.

I was frightened now about Jim, though I tried to hide the fact from myself. Presently he called me again. "What is it, Jim?"

"Take the blankets off me, fahver—Jim's sick!" (They'd been teaching him to say father.)

I was scared now. I remembered a neighbour of ours had a little girl die (she swallowed a pin), and when she was going she said: "Take the blankets off me, muvver—I'm dying."

And I couldn't get that out of my head.

I threw back a fold of the possum rug, and felt Jim's head—he seemed cool enough.

"Where do you feel bad, sonny?"

No answer for a while; when he said suddenly, but in a voice as if he were talking in his sleep:

"Put my boots on, please, daddy. I want to go home to muvver!"

I held his hand, and comforted him for a while; then he slept—in a restless, feverish sort of way.

I got the bucket I used for water for the horses and stood it over the fire; I ran to the creek with the big kerosene-tin bucket and got it full of cold water and stood it handy. I got the spade (we always carried one to dig wheels out of bogs in wet weather) and turned a corner of the tarpaulin back, dug a hole, and trod the tarpaulin down into the hole to serve for a bath, in case of the worst. I had a tin of mustard, and meant to fight a good round for Jim, if death came along.

I stooped in under the tail-board of the wagon and felt Jim. His head was burning hot, and his skin parched and dry as a bone.

Then I lost nerve and started blundering backward and forward between the wagon and the fire, and repeating what I'd heard Mary say the last time we fought for Jim: "God! don't take my child! God! don't take my boy!" I'd never had much faith in doctors, but, my God! I wanted one then. The nearest was fifteen miles away.

I threw back my head and stared up at the branches in desperation; and—well, I don't ask you to take much stock in this, though most old bushmen will believe anything of the bush by night; and—now, it might have been that I was unstrung, or it might have been a patch of the sky outlined in the gently moving branches, or the blue smoke rising up. But I saw the figure of a woman, all white, come down, down, nearly to the limbs of the trees, point on up the main road, and then float up and up and vanish, still pointing. I thought Mary was dead! Then it flashed on me—

Four or five miles up the road, over the "saddle," was an old shanty that had been a half-way inn before the Great Western Line got round as far as Dubbo, and took the coach traffic off those old bush roads. A man named Brighten lived there. He was a selector; did a little farming, and as much sly-grog selling as he could. He was married—but it wasn't that: I'd thought of them, but she was a childish, worn-out, spiritless woman, and both were pretty "ratty" from hardship and loneliness—they weren't likely to be of any use to me. But it was this: I'd heard talk, among some women in Gulgong, of a sister of Brighten's wife who'd gone out to live with them lately: she'd been a hospital matron in the city, they said; and there were yarns about her. Some said she got the sack for exposing the doctors—or carrying on with them—I didn't remember which. The fact of a city woman going out to live in such a place, with such people, was enough to make talk among women in a town twenty miles away, but then there must have been something extra about her, else bushmen wouldn't have talked and carried her name so far; and I wanted a woman out of the ordinary now. I even reasoned this way, thinking like lightning, as I knelt over Jim between the big back wheels of the wagon.

I had an old racing mare that I used as a riding hack, following the team. In a minute I had her saddled and bridled; I tied the end of a half-full chaff-bag, shook the chaff into each end and dumped it on to the pommel as a cushion or buffer for Jim; I wrapped him in a blanket, and scrambled into the saddle with him.

The next minute we were stumbling down the steep bank, clattering and splashing over the crossing, and struggling up the opposite bank to the level. The mare, as I told you, was an old racer, but broken-winded—she must have run without wind after the first half-mile. She had the old racing instinct in her strong, and whenever I rode in company I'd have to pull her hard else she'd race the other horse or burst. She ran low fore and aft, and was the easiest horse I ever rode. She ran like wheels on rails, with a bit of a tremble now and then—like a railway carriage—when she settled down to it.

The chaff-bag had slipped off, in the creek I suppose, and I let the bridle-rein go and held Jim up to me like a baby the whole way. Let the strongest man, who isn't used to it, hold a baby in one position for five minutes—and Jim was fairly heavy. But I never felt the ache in my arms that night—it must have gone before I was in a fit state of mind to feel it. And at home I'd often growled about being asked to hold the baby for a few minutes. I could never brood comfortably and nurse a baby at the same time. It was a ghostly moonlight night. There's no timber in the world so ghostly as the Australian bush in moonlight—or just about daybreak. The allshaped patches of moonlight falling between ragged, twisted boughs; the ghostly blue-white bark of the "white-box" trees; a dead, naked white ring-barked tree, or dead white stump starting out here and there, and the ragged patches of shade and light on the road that made anything, from the shape of a spotted bullock to a naked corpse laid out stark. Roads and tracks through the bush made by moonlight—every one seeming straighter and clearer than the real one; you have to trust to your horse then. Sometimes the naked white trunk of a red stringy-bark tree, where a sheet of bark had been taken off, would start out like a ghost from the dark bush. And dew or frost glistening on these things according to the season. Now and again a great grey kangaroo, that had been feeding on a green patch down by the road, would start with a "thump-thump," and away up the siding.

The bush seemed full of ghosts that night—all going my way—and being left behind by the mare. Once I stopped to look at Jim: I just sat back and the mare "propped"—she'd been a stock-horse, and was used to "cutting-out." I felt Jim's hands and forehead; he was in a burning fever. I bent forward, and the old mare settled down to it again. I kept saying out loud—and Mary and me often laughed about it (afterwards): "He's limp yet!—Jim's limp yet!" (the words seemed jerked out of me by sheer fright)— "He's limp yet!" till the mare's feet took it up. Then, just when I thought she was doing her best and racing her hardest, she suddenly started forward, like a cable tram gliding along on its own and the grip put on suddenly. It was just what she'd do when I'd be riding alone and a strange horse drew up from behind—the old racing instinct. I *felt* the thing too! I felt as if a strange horse *was* there! And then—the words just jerked out of me by sheer funk—I started saying, "Death is riding to-night! . . . Death is racing to-night! . . . Death is riding to-night!" till the hoof-beats took that up. And I believe the old mare felt the black horse at her side and was going to beat him or break her heart.

I was mad with anxiety and fright: I remember I kept saying, "I'll be kinder to Mary after this! I'll take more notice of Jim!" and the rest of it.

I don't know how the old mare got up the last "pinch." She must have slackened pace, but I never noticed it: I just held Jim up to me and gripped the saddle with my knees—I remember the saddle jerked from the desperate jumps of her till I thought the girth would go. We topped the gap and were going down into a gully they called Dead Man's Hollow, and there, at the back of a ghostly clearing that opened from the road where there were some black-soil springs, was a long, low, oblong weatherboard-and-shingle building, with blind, broken windows in the gable-ends, and a wide steep veranda roof slanting down almost to the level of the window-sills—there was something sinister about it, I thought—like the hat of a jail-bird slouched over his eyes. The place looked both deserted and haunted. I saw no light, but that was because of the moonlight outside. The mare turned in at the corner of the clearing to take a short cut to the shanty, and, as she struggled across some marshy ground, my heart kept jerking out the words, "It's deserted! They've gone away! It's deserted!" The mare went round to the back and pulled up between the back door and a big bark-and-slab kitchen. Someone shouted from inside:

"Who's there?"

"It's me. Joe Wilson. I want your sister-in-law—I've got the boy—he's sick and dying!"

Brighten came out, pulling up his moleskins. "What boy?" he asked.

"Here, take him," I shouted, "and let me get down."

"What's the matter with him?" asked Brighten, and he seemed to hang back. And just as I made to get my leg over the saddle, Jim's head went back over my arm, he stiffened, and I saw his eyeballs turned up and glistening in the moonlight.

I felt cold all over then and sick in the stomach—but *clear-headed* in a way: strange, wasn't it? I don't know why I didn't get down and rush into the kitchen to get a bath ready. I only felt as if the worst had come, and I wished it were over and gone. I even thought of Mary and the funeral.

Then a woman ran out of the house—a big, hard-looking woman. She had on a wrapper of some sort, and her feet were bare. She laid her hand on Jim, looked at his face, and then snatched him from me and ran into the kitchen—and me down and after her. As great good luck would have it they had some dirty clothes on to boil in a kerosene-tin—dish-cloths or something.

Brighten's sister-in-law dragged a tub out from under the table, wrenched the bucket off the hook, and dumped in the water, dish-cloths and all, snatched a can of cold water from a corner, dashed that in, and felt the water with her hand—holding Jim up to her hip all the time—and I won't say how he looked. She stood him in the tub and started dashing water over him, tearing off his clothes between the splashes.

"Here, that tin of mustard—there on the shelf!" she shouted to me.

She knocked the lid off the tin on the edge of the tub, and went on splashing and spanking Jim.

It seemed an eternity. And I? Why, I never thought clearer in my life. I felt cold-blooded—I felt as if I'd like an excuse to go outside till it was all over. I thought of Mary and the funeral—and wished that that was past. All this in a flash, as it were. I felt that it would be a great relief, and only wished the funeral was months past. I felt—well, altogether selfish. I only thought of myself.

Brighten's sister-in-law splashed and spanked him hard—hard enough to break his back I thought, and—after about half an hour it seemed—the end came: Jim's limbs relaxed, he slipped down into the tub, and the pupils of his eyes came down. They seemed dull and expressionless, like the eyes of a new baby, but he was back for the world again.

I dropped on the stool by the table.

"It's all right," she said. "It's all over now. I wasn't going to let him die." I was only thinking, "Well it's over now, but it will come on again. I wish it was over for good. I'm tired of it."

She called to her sister, Mrs Brighten, a washed-out, helpless little fool of a woman, who'd been running in and out and whimpering all the time:

"Here, Jessie! bring the new white blanket off my bed. And you, Brighten, take some of that wood off the fire, and stuff something in that hole there to stop the draught."

Brighten—he was a nuggety little hairy man with no expression to be seen for whiskers—had been running in with sticks and back logs from the wood-heap. He took the wood out, stuffed up the crack, and went inside and brought out a black bottle—got a cup from the shelf, and put both down near my elbow.

Mrs Brighten started to get some supper or breakfast, or whatever it was, ready. She had a clean cloth, and set the table tidily. I noticed that all the tins were polished bright (old coffee and mustard-tins and the like, that they used instead of sugar-basins and tea-caddies and salt-cellars), and the kitchen was kept as clean as possible. She was all right at little things. I knew a haggard, worked-out bushwoman who put her whole soul—or all she'd got left—into polishing old tins till they dazzled your eyes.

I didn't feel inclined for corned beef and damper, and post-and-rail tea. So I sat and squinted, when I thought she wasn't looking, at Brighten's sister-in-law. She was a big woman, her hands and feet were big, but well-shaped and all in proportion—they fitted her. She was a handsome woman—about forty I should think. She had a square chin, and a straight thin-lipped mouth—straight save for a hint of a turn down at the corners, which I fancied (and I have strange fancies) had been a sign of weakness in the days before she grew hard. There was no sign of weakness now. She had hard grey eyes and blue-black hair. She hadn't spoken yet. She didn't ask me how the boy took ill or I got there, or who or what I was—at least not until the next evening at tea-time.

She sat upright with Jim wrapped in the blanket and laid across her knees, with one hand under his neck and the other laid lightly on him, and she just rocked him gently.

She sat looking hard and straight before her, just as I've seen a tired needlewoman sit with her work in her lap, and look away back into the past. And Jim might have been the work in her lap, for all she seemed to think of him. Now and then she knitted her forehead and blinked.

Suddenly she glanced round and said—in a tone as if I was her husband and she didn't think much of me:

"Why don't you eat something?"

"Beg pardon?"

"Eat something!"

I drank some tea, and sneaked another look at her. I was beginning to feel more natural, and wanted Jim again, now that the colour was coming back into his face, and he didn't look like an unnaturally stiff and staring corpse. I felt a lump rising, and wanted to thank her. I sneaked another look at her.

She was staring straight before her—I never saw a woman's face change so suddenly—I never saw a woman's eyes so haggard and hopeless. Then her great chest heaved twice, I heard her draw a long shuddering breath, like a knocked-out horse, and two great tears dropped from her wide open eyes down her cheeks like rain-drops on a face of stone. And in the firelight they seemed tinged with blood.

I looked away quick, feeling full up myself. And presently (I hadn't seen her look round) she said:

"Go to bed."

"Beg pardon?" (Her face was the same as before the tears.)

"Go to bed. There's a bed made for you inside on the sofa."

"But—the team—I must——"

"What?"

"The team. I left it at the camp. I must look to it."

"Oh! Well, Brighten will ride down and bring it up in the morning—or send the half-caste. Now you go to bed, and get a good rest. The boy will be all right. I'll see to that."

I went out—it was a relief to get out—and looked to the mare. Brighten had got her some corn and chaff in a candle-box, but she couldn't eat yet. She just stood or hung resting one hind leg and then the other, with her nose over the box—and she sobbed. I put my arms round her neck and my face down on her ragged mane, and cried for the second time since I was a boy.

As I started to go in I heard Brighten's sister-in-law say, suddenly and sharply:

"Take *that* away, Jessie."

And presently I saw Mrs Brighten go into the house with the black bottle.

The moon had gone behind the range. I stood for a minute between the house and the kitchen and peeped in through the kitchen window.

She had moved away from the fire and sat near the table. She bent over Jim and held him up close to her and rocked herself to and fro.

I went to bed and slept till the next afternoon. I woke just in time to hear the tail-end of a conversation between Jim and Brighten's sister-in-law. He was asking her out to our place, and she promising to come.

"And now," says Jim, "I want to go home to 'muffer' in 'The Same Ol' Fling.'"

"What?"

Jim repeated.

"Oh! 'The Same Old Thing,'—the wagon."

The rest of the afternoon I poked round the gullies with old Brighten, looking at some "indications" (of the existence of gold) he had found. It was no use trying to "pump" him concerning his sister-in-law; Brighten was an "old hand," and had learned in the old bushranging and cattle-stealing days to know nothing about other people's business. And, by the way, I noticed then that the more you talk and listen to a bad character, the more you lose your dislike for him.

I never saw such a change in a woman as in Brighten's sister-in-law that evening. She was bright and jolly, and seemed at least ten years younger. She bustled round and helped her sister to get tea ready. She rooted out some old china that Mrs Brighten had stowed away somewhere, and set the table as I seldom saw it set out there. She propped Jim up with pillows, and laughed and played with him like a great girl. She described Sydney and Sydney life as I'd never heard it described before; and she knew as much about the bush and old diggings days as I did. She kept old Brighten and me listening and laughing till nearly midnight. And she seemed quick to understand everything when I talked. If she wanted to explain anything that we hadn't seen, she wouldn't say that it was "like a—like a"—and hesitate (you know what I mean); she'd hit the right thing on the head at once. A squatter with a very round, flaming red face and a white cork hat had gone by in the afternoon: she said it was "like a mushroom on the rising moon." She gave me a lot of good hints about children.

But she was quiet again next morning. I harnessed up, and she dressed Jim and gave him his breakfast, and made a comfortable place for him on the load with a possum rug and a spare pillow. She got up on the wheel to do it herself. Then was the awkward time. I'd half start to speak to her, and then turn away and go fixing up round the horses, and then make another false start to say good-bye. At last she took Jim up in her arms and kissed him, and lifted him on the wheel; but he put his arms tight round her neck, and kissed her—a thing Jim seldom did with anybody, except his mother, for he wasn't what you'd call an affectionate child—he'd never more than offer his cheek to me, in his old-fashioned way. I'd got up the other side of the load to take him from her.

"Here, take him," she said.

I saw his mouth twitching as I lifted him. Jim seldom cried nowadays—no matter how much he was hurt. I gained some time fixing Jim comfortable.

"You'd better make a start," she said. "You want to get home early with that boy."

I got down and went round to where she stood. I held out my hand and tried to speak, but my voice went like an ungreased wagon-wheel, and I gave it up, and only squeezed her hand.

"That's all right," she said; then tears came into her eyes, and she suddenly put her hand on my shoulder and kissed me on the cheek. "You be off—you're only a boy yourself. Take care of that boy; be kind to your wife, and take care of yourself."

"Will you come to see us?"

"Some day," she said.

I started the horses, and looked round once more. She was looking up at Jim, who was waving his hand to her from the top of the load. And I saw that haggard, hungry, hopeless look come into her eyes in spite of the tears.

I smoothed over that story and shortened it a lot when I told it to Mary—I didn't want to upset her. But, some time after I brought Jim home from Gulgong, and while I was at home with the team for a few days, nothing would suit Mary but she must go over to Brighten's shanty and see Brighten's sister-in-law. So James drove her over one morning in the spring-cart: it was a long way, and they stayed at Brighten's overnight and didn't get back till late the next afternoon. I'd got the place in a pig-muck, as Mary said, "doing for" myself, and I was having a snooze on the sofa when they got back. The first thing I remember was someone stroking my head and kissing me, and I heard Mary saying "My poor boy! My poor old boy!"

I sat up with a jerk. I thought that Jim had gone off again. But it seems that Mary was only referring to me. Then she started to pull grey hairs out of my head and put 'em in an empty match-box—to see how many she'd got. She used to do this when she felt a bit soft. I don't know what she said to Brighten's sister-in-law or what Brighten's sister-in-law said to her, but Mary was extra gentle for the next few days.

"WATER THEM GERANIUMS"

I

A LONELY TRACK

The time Mary and I shifted out into the bush from Gulgong to "settle on the land" at Lahey's Creek.

I'd sold the two tip-drays that I used for tank-sinking and dam-making, and I took the traps out in the wagon on top of a small load of rations and horse-feed that I was taking to a sheep station out that way. Mary drove out in the spring-cart. You remember we left little Jim with his aunt in Gulgong till we got settled down. I'd sent James (Mary's brother) out the day before, on horseback, with two or three cows and some heifers and steers and calves we had, and I'd told him to clean up a bit, and make the hut as bright and cheerful as possible before Mary came.

We hadn't much in the way of furniture. There was the four-poster cedar bedstead that I bought before we were married, and Mary was rather proud of it: it had "turned" posts and joints that bolted together. There was a plain hardwood table, that Mary called her "ironing-table," upside down on top of the load, with the bedding and blankets between the legs; there were four of those common black kitchen-chairs—with apples painted on the hard board backs—that we used for the parlour; there was a cheap batten sofa with arms at the ends and turned rails between the uprights of the arms (we were a little proud of the turned rails); and there was the camp-oven, and the three-legged pot, and pans and buckets, stuck about the load and hanging under the tail-board of the wagon.

There was the little Wilcox & Gibb's sewing-machine—my present to Mary when we were married (and what a present, looking back to it!). There was a cheap little rocking-chair, and a looking-glass and some pictures that were presents from Mary's friends and sister. She had her mantelshelf ornaments and crockery and nick-nacks packed away, in the linen and old clothes, in a big tub made of half a cask, and a box that had been Jim's cradle. The live stock was a cat in one box, and in another an old rooster, and three hens that formed cliques, two against one, turn about, as three of the same sex will do all over the world. I had my old cattle-dog, and of course a pup on the load—I always had a pup that I gave away, or sold and didn't get paid for, or had "touched" (stolen) as soon as it was old enough. James had his three spidery, sneaking, thieving, cold-blooded kangaroo-dogs with him. I was taking out three months' provisions in the way of ration-sugar, tea, flour, and potatoes.

I started early, and Mary caught up to me at Ryan's Crossing on Sandy Creek, where we boiled the billy and had some dinner.

Mary bustled about the camp and admired the scenery and talked too much, for her, and was extra cheerful, and kept her face turned from me as much as possible. I soon saw what was the matter. She'd been crying to herself coming along the road. I thought it was all on account of leaving little Jim behind for the first time. She told me that she couldn't make up her mind till the last moment to leave him, and that, a mile or two along the road, she'd have turned back for him, only that she knew her sister would laugh at her. She was always terribly anxious about the children.

We cheered each other up, and Mary drove with me the rest of the way to the creek, along the lonely branch track, across native apple-tree flats. It was a dreary, hopeless track. There was no horizon, nothing but the rough ashen trunks of the gnarled and stunted trees in all directions, little or no undergrowth, and the ground, save for the coarse, brownish tufts of dead grass, as bare as the road, for it was a dry season: there had been no rain for months, and I wondered what I should do with the cattle if there wasn't more grass on the creek.

In this sort of country a stranger might travel for miles without seeming to have moved, for all the difference there is in the scenery. The new tracks were "blazed"—that is, slices of bark cut off from both sides of trees, within sight of each other, in a line, to mark the track until the horses and wheel marks made it plain. A smart bushman, with a sharp tomahawk, can blaze a track as he rides. But a bushman a little used to the country soon picks out differences amongst the trees, half unconsciously as it were, and so finds his way about.

Mary and I didn't talk much along this track—we couldn't have heard each other very well, anyway, for the "clock-clock" of the wagon and the rattle of the cart over the hard lumpy ground. And I suppose we both began to feel pretty dismal as the shadows lengthened. I'd noticed lately that Mary and I had got out of the habit of talking to each other—noticed it in a vague sort of way that irritated me (as vague things will irritate one) when I thought of it. But then I thought, "It won't last long—I'll make life brighter for her by and by."

As we went along—and the track seemed endless—I got brooding, of course, back into the past. And I feel now, when it's too late, that Mary must have been thinking that way too. I thought of my early boyhood, of the hard life of "grubbin' " and "milkin' " and "fencin' " and "ploughin' " and "ringbarkin'," and all for nothing. The few months at the little bark school, with a teacher who couldn't spell. The cursed ambition or craving that tortured my soul as a boy—ambition or craving for—I didn't know what for! For something better and brighter, anyhow. And I made the life harder by reading at night.

It all passed before me as I followed on in the wagon, behind Mary in the spring-cart. I thought of these old things more than I thought of her. She had tried to help me to better things. And I tried too—I had the energy of half a dozen men when I saw a road clear before me, but shied at the first check. Then I brooded, or dreamed of making a home—that one might call a home—for Mary—some day. Ah, well!——

And what was Mary thinking about, along the lonely, changeless miles? I never thought of that. Of her kind, careless, gentleman father, perhaps. Of her girlhood. Of her homes—not the huts and camps she lived in with me. Of our future?—she used to plan a lot, and talk a good deal of our future—but not lately. These things didn't strike me at the time—I was so deep in my own brooding. Did she think now—did she begin to feel now that she had made a great mistake and thrown away her life, but must make the best of it? This might have roused me, had I thought of it. But whenever I thought Mary was getting indifferent towards me, I'd think, "I'll soon win her back. We'll be sweethearts again—when things brighten up a bit."

It's an awful thing to me, now I look back to it, to think how far apart we had grown, what strangers we were to each other. It seems, now, as though we had been sweethearts long years before, and had parted, and had never really met since.

The sun was going down when Mary called out:

"There's our place, Joe!"

She hadn't seen it before, and somehow it came new and with a shock to me, who had been out here several times. Ahead, through the trees to the right, was a dark green clump of the oaks standing out of the creek, darker for the dead grey grass and blue-grey bush on the barren ridge in the background. Across the creek (it was only a deep, narrow gutter—a water-course with a chain of waterholes after rain), across on the other bank, stood the hut, on a narrow flat between the spur and the creek, and a little higher than this side. The land was much better than on our old selection, and there was good soil along the creek on both sides: I expected a rush of selectors out here soon. A few acres round the hut were cleared and fenced in by a light two-rail fence of timber split from logs and saplings. The man who took up this selection left it because his wife died here.

It was a small oblong hut built of split slabs, and he had roofed it with shingles which he split in spare times. There was no veranda, but I built one later on. At the end of the house was a big slab-and-bark shed, bigger than the hut itself, with a kitchen, a skillion for tools, harness, and horse-feed, and a spare bedroom partitioned off with sheets of bark and old chaff-bags. The house itself was floored roughly, with cracks between the boards; there were cracks between the slabs all round—though he'd nailed strips of tin, from old kerosene-tins, over some of them; the partitioned-off bedroom was lined with old chaff-bags with newspapers pasted over them for wall-paper. There was no ceiling, calico or otherwise, and we could see the round pine rafters and battens, and the under ends of the shingles. But ceilings make a hut hot and harbour insects and reptiles—snakes sometimes. There was one small glass window in the "dining-room" with three panes and a sheet of greased paper, and the rest were rough wooden shutters. There was a pretty good cow-yard and calf-pen, and—that was about all. There was no dam or tank (I made one later on); there was a water-cask, with the hoops falling off and the staves gaping, at the corner of the house, and spouting, made of lengths of bent tin, ran round the eaves. Water from a new shingle roof is wine-red for a year or two, and water from a stringy-bark roof is like tan-water for years. In dry weather the selector had got his house water from a cask sunk in the gravel at the bottom of the deepest waterhole in the creek, and the longer the drought lasted, the farther he had to go down the creek for his water, with a cask on a cart, and take his cows to drink, if he had any. Four, five, six, or seven miles—even ten miles to water is nothing in some places.

James hadn't found himself called upon to do more than milk old "Spot" (the grandmother cow of our mob), pen the calf at night, make a fire in the kitchen, and sweep out the house with a bough. He helped me unharness and water and feed the horses, and then started to get the furniture off the wagon and into the house. James wasn't lazy, so long as one thing didn't last too long; but he was too uncomfortably practical and matter-of-fact for me. Mary and I had some tea in the kitchen. The kitchen was permanently furnished with a table of split slabs, adzed smooth on top, and supported by four stakes driven into the ground, a three-legged stool and a block of wood, and two long stools made of half-round slabs (sapling trunks split in halves) with auger-holes bored in the round side and sticks stuck into them for legs. The floor was of clay; the chimney of slabs and tin; the fire-place was about eight feet wide, lined with clay, and with a blackened pole across, with sooty chains and wire hooks on it for the pots.

Mary didn't seem able to eat. She sat on the three-legged stool near the fire, though it was warm weather, and kept her face turned from me. Mary was still pretty, but not the little dumpling she had been: she was thinner now. She had big dark hazel eyes that shone a little too much when she was pleased or excited. I thought at times that there was something very German about her expression; also something aristocratic about the turn of her nose, which nipped in at the nostrils when she spoke. There was nothing aristocratic about me. Mary was German in figure and walk. I used sometimes to call her "Little Duchy" and "Pigeon Toes." She had a will of her own, as shown sometimes by the obstinate knit in her forehead between the eyes.

Mary sat still by the fire, and presently I saw her chin tremble.

"What is it, Mary?"

She turned her face farther from me. I felt tired, disappointed, and irritated—suffering from a reaction.

"Now, what is it, Mary?" I asked; "I'm sick of this sort of thing. Haven't you got everything you wanted? You've had your own way. What's the matter with you now?"

"You know very well, Joe."

"But I *don't* know," I said. I knew too well.

She said nothing.

"Look here, Mary," I said, putting my hand on her shoulder, "don't go on like that; tell me what's the matter."

"It's only this," she said suddenly, "I can't stand this life here; it will kill me!"

I had a pannikin of tea in my hand, and I banged it down on the table.

"This is more than a man can stand!" I shouted. "You know very well that it was you that dragged me out here. You run me on to this. Why weren't you content to stay in Gulgong?"

"And what sort of a place was Gulgong, Joe?" asked Mary quietly.

(I thought even then in a flash what sort of a place Gulgong was. A wretched remnant of a town on an abandoned goldfield. One street, each side of the dusty main road three or four one-storey square brick cottages with hip-roofs of galvanized iron that glared in the heat—four rooms and a passage—the police station, bank-manager and schoolmaster's cottages. Half a dozen tumble-down weather-board shanties—the three pubs, the two stores, and the post office. The town tailing off into weather-board boxes with tin tops, and old bark huts—relics of the digging days—propped up by many rotting poles. The men, when at home, mostly asleep or droning over their pipes or hanging about the veranda-posts of the pubs, saying " 'Ullo, Bill!" or " 'Ullo, Jim!"—or sometimes drunk. The women, mostly hags, who blackened each other's and girls' characters with their tongues, and criticized the aristocracy's washing hung out on the line: "And the colour of the clothes! Does that woman wash her clothes at all? or only soak 'em and hang 'em out?"—that was Gulgong.)

"Well, why didn't you come to Sydney, as I wanted you to?" I asked Mary.

"You know very well, Joe," said Mary quietly.

(I knew very well, but the knowledge only maddened me. I had had an idea of getting a billet in one of the big woolstores—I was a fair wool expert—but Mary was afraid of the drink. I could keep well away from it so long as I worked hard in the bush. I had gone to Sydney twice since I met Mary, once before we were married, and she forgave me when I came back; and once afterwards. I got a billet there then, and was going to send for her in a month. After eight weeks she raised the money somehow and came to Sydney and brought me home. I got pretty down that time.)

"But, Mary," I said, "it would have been different this time. You would have been with me. I can take a glass now or leave it alone."

"As long as you take a glass there is danger," she said.

"Well, what did you want to advise me to come out here for, if you can't stand it? Why didn't you stay where you were?" I asked.

"Well," she said, "why weren't you more decided?"

I'd sat down, but I jumped to my feet then.

"Good God!" I shouted, "this is more than any man can stand. I'll chuck it all up! I'm damned well sick and tired of the whole thing."

"So am I, Joe," said Mary wearily.

We quarrelled badly then—that first hour in our new home. I know now whose fault it was.

I got my hat and went out and started to walk down the creek. I didn't feel bitter against Mary—I had spoken too cruelly to her to feel that way. Looking back, I could see plainly that if I had taken her advice all through instead of now and again, things would have been all right with me. I had come away and left her crying in the hut, and James telling her, in a brotherly way, that it was all her fault. The trouble was that I never liked to "give in" or go half-way to make it up—not half-way—it was all the way or nothing with our natures.

"If I don't make a stand now," I'd say, "I'll never be master. I gave up the reins when I got married, and I'll have to get them back again."

What women some men are! But the time came, and not many years after, when I stood by the bed where Mary lay, white and still; and, amongst other things, I kept saying, "I'll give in, Mary—I'll give in," and then I'd laugh. They thought I was raving mad, and took me from the room. But that time was to come.

As I walked down the creek track in the moonlight the question rang in my ears again, as it had done when I first caught sight of the house that evening:

"Why did I bring her here?"

I was not fit to "go on the land." The place was only fit for some stolid German, or Scotsman, or even Englishman and his wife, who had no ambition but to bullock and make a farm of the place. I had only drifted here through carelessness, brooding and discontent.

I walked on and on till I was more than half-way to the only neighbours—a wretched selector's family, about four miles down the creek—and I thought I'd go on to the house and see if they had any fresh meat.

A mile or two farther I saw the loom of the bark hut they lived in, on a patchy clearing in the scrub, and heard the voice of the selector's wife—I had seen her several times: she was a gaunt, haggard bushwoman, and I supposed the reason why she hadn't gone mad through hardship and loneliness was that she hadn't either the brains or the memory to go father than she could see through the trunks of the "apple-trees."

"You, An-nay!" (Annie.)

"Ye-es" (from somewhere in the gloom).

"Didn't I tell yer to water them geraniums!"

"Well, didn't I?"

"Don't tell lies or I'll break yer young back!"

"I did, I tell yer—the water won't soak inter the ashes."

Geraniums were the only flowers I saw grow in the drought out there. I remembered this woman had a few dirty grey-green leaves behind some sticks against the bark wall near the door; and in spite of the sticks the fowls used to get in and scratch beds under the geraniums, and scratch dust over them, and ashes were thrown there—with an idea of helping the flowers, I suppose; and greasy dish-water, when fresh water was scarce—till you might as well try to water a dish of fat.

Then the woman's voice again:

"You, Tom-may!" (Tommy.)

Silence, save for an echo on the ridge.

"Y-o-u T-o-m-*may*!"

"Y-e-s!" shrill shriek from across the creek.

"Didn't I tell you to ride up to them new people and see if they want any meat or anythink!" in one long screech.

"Well—I karn't find the horse."

"Well-find-it-first-think-in-the-morning-and. And-don't-for-git-to-tell-Mrs-Wi'son-that-mother'll-be-up-as-soon-as-she-can."

I didn't feel like going to the woman's house that night. I felt—and the thought came like a whipstroke on my heart—that this was what Mary would come to if I left her here.

I turned and started to walk home, fast. I'd made up my mind. I'd take Mary straight back to Gulgong in the morning—I forgot about the load I had to take to the sheep station. I'd say, "Look here,

Girlie" (that's what I used to call her), "we'll leave this wretched life; we'll leave the bush for ever. We'll go to Sydney, and I'll be a man! and work my way up." And I'd sell wagon, horses, and all, and go.

When I got to the hut it was lighted up. Mary had the only kerosene lamp, a slush-lamp, and two tallow candles going. She had got both rooms washed out—to James's disgust, for he had to move the furniture and boxes about. She had a lot of things unpacked on the table; she had laid clean newspapers on the mantelshelf—a slab on two pegs over the fire-place—and put the little wooden clock in the centre and some of the ornaments on each side, and was tacking a strip of vandyked American oil-cloth round the rough edge of the slab.

"How does that look, Joe? We'll soon get things shipshape."

I kissed her, but she had her mouth full of tacks. I went out in the kitchen, drank a pint of cold tea, and sat down.

Somehow I didn't feel satisfied with the way things had gone.

II

"PAST CARIN'"

Next morning things looked a lot brighter. Things always look brighter in the morning—more so in the Australian bush, I should think, than in most other places. It is when the sun goes down on the dark bed of the lonely bush, and the sunset flashes like a sea of fire and then fades, and then glows out again, like a bank of coals, and then burns away to ashes—it is then that old things come home to one. And strange, new-old things too, that haunt and depress you terribly, and that you can't understand. I often think how, at sunset, the past must come home to new-chum black sheep, sent out to Australia and drifted into the bush. I used to think that they couldn't have much brains, or the loneliness would drive them mad.

I'd decided to let James take the team for a trip or two. He could drive all right; he was a better business man, and no doubt would manage better than me—as long as the novelty lasted; and I'd stay at home for a week or so, till Mary got used to the place, or I could get a girl from somewhere to come and stay with her. The first weeks or few months of loneliness are the worst, as a rule, I believe, as they say the first weeks in jail are—I was never there. I know it's so with tramping or hard graft: the first day or two are twice as hard as any of the rest. But, for my part, I could never get used to loneliness and dullness; the last days used to be the worst with me: then I'd have to make a move, or drink. When you've been too much and too long alone in a lonely place, you begin to do queer things, and think queer thoughts—provided you have any imagination at all. You'll sometimes sit of an evening and watch the lonely track, by the hour, for a horseman or a cart or someone that's never likely to come that way—someone, or a stranger, that you can't and don't really expect to see. I think that most men who have been alone in the bush for any length of time—and married couples too—are more or less mad. With married couples it is generally the husband who is painfully shy and awkward when strangers come. The woman seems to stand the loneliness better, and can hold her own with strangers, as a rule. It's only afterwards, and looking back, that you see how queer you got. Shepherds and boundary-riders, who are alone for months, *must* have their periodical spree, at the nearest shanty, else they'd go raving mad. Drink is the only break in the awful monotony, and the yearly or half-yearly spree is the only thing they've got to look forward to: it keeps their minds fixed on something definite ahead.

But Mary kept her head pretty well through the first months of loneliness. *Weeks* rather, I should say, for it wasn't as bad as it might have been farther up-country: there was generally someone came of a Sunday afternoon—a spring-cart with a couple of women, or maybe a family—or a lanky shy bush native or two on lanky shy horses. On a quiet Sunday, after I'd brought Jim home, Mary would dress him and herself—just the same as if we were in town—and make me get up on one end and put on a collar and take her and Jim for a walk along the creek. She said she wanted to keep me civilized. She tried to make a gentleman of me for years, but gave it up gradually.

Well. It was the first morning on the creek: I was greasing the wagon-wheels, and James out after the horse, and Mary hanging out clothes, in an old print dress and a big ugly white hood, when I heard her being hailed as "Hi, missus!" from the front sliprails.

It was a boy on horseback. He was a light-haired, very much freckled boy of fourteen or fifteen, with a small head, but with limbs, especially his bare sun-blotched shanks, that might have belonged to a grown man. He had a good face and frank grey eyes. An old, nearly black cabbage-tree hat rested on the butts of his ears, turning them out at right angles from his head, and rather dirty sprouts they were. He wore a dirty torn Crimean shirt; and a pair of men's moleskin trousers rolled up above the knees, with a wide waistband gathered under a greenhide belt. I noticed, later on, that even when he wore trousers short enough for him, he always rolled 'em up above the knees when on horseback, for some reason of his own: to suggest leggings, perhaps, for he had them rolled up in all weathers, and he wouldn't have bothered to save them from the sweat of the horse, even if that horse ever sweated.

He was seated astride a three-bushel bag thrown across the ridge-pole of a big grey horse, with a coffin-shaped head, and built astern something after the style of a roughly put up hiproofed box-bark humpy. His colour was like old box-bark, too, a dirty bluish-grey; and, one time, when I saw his rump looming out of the scrub, I really thought it was some old shepherd's hut that I hadn't noticed there before. When he cantered it was like the humpy starting off on its corner-posts.

"Are you Mrs Wilson?" asked the boy.

"Yes," said Mary.

"Well, mother told me to ride acrost and see if you wanted anythink. We killed lars' night, and I fetched a piece er cow."

"Piece of *what*?" asked Mary.

He grinned and handed a sugar-bag across the rail with something heavy in the bottom of it, that nearly jerked Mary's arm out when she took it. It was a piece of beef, that looked as if it had been cut off with a wood-axe, but it was fresh and clean.

"Oh, I'm so glad!" cried Mary. She was always impulsive, save to me sometimes. "I was just wondering where we were going to get any fresh meat. How kind of your mother! Tell her I'm very much obliged to her indeed." And she felt behind her for a poor little purse she had. "And now—how much did your mother say it would be?"

The boy blinked at her, and scratched his head.

"How much will it be," he repeated, puzzled. "Oh—how much does it weigh I-s'pose-yer-mean. Well, it ain't been weighed at all—we ain't got no scales. A butcher does all that sort of think. We just kills it, and cooks it, and eats it—and goes by guess. What won't keep we salts down in the cask. I reckon it weighs about a ton by the weight of it if yer wanter know. Mother thought that if she sent any more it would go bad before you could scoff it. I can't see——"

"Yes, yes," said Mary, getting confused. "But what I want to know is, how do you manage when you sell it?"

He glared at her, and scratched his head. "Sell it? Why, we only goes halves in a steer with someone, or sells steers to the butcher—or maybe some meat to a party of fencers or surveyors, or tank-sinkers, or them sorter people——"

"Yes, yes; but what I want to know is, how much am I to send your mother for this?"

"How much what?"

"Money, of course, you stupid boy," said Mary. "You seem a very stupid boy."

Then he saw what she was driving at. He began to fling his heels convulsively against the sides of his horse, jerking his body backward and forward at the same time, as if to wind up and start some clockwork machinery inside the horse, that made it go, and seemed to need repairing or oiling.

"We ain't that sorter people, missus," he said. "We don't sell meat to new people that come to settle here." Then, jerking his thumb contemptuously towards the ridges, "Go over ter Wall's if yer wanter buy meat; they sell meat ter strangers." (Wall was the big squatter over the ridges.)

"Oh!" said Mary, "I'm *so* sorry. Thank your mother for me. She *is* kind."

"Oh, that's nothink. She said to tell yer she'll be up as soon as she can. She'd have come up yesterday evening—she thought yer'd feel lonely comin' new to a place like this—but she couldn't git up."

The machinery inside the old horse showed signs of starting. You almost heard the wooden joints *creak* as he lurched forward, like an old propped-up humpy when the rotting props give way; but at the sound of Mary's voice he settled back on his foundations again. It must have been a very poor selection that couldn't afford a better spare horse than that.

"Reach me that lump er wood, will yer, missus?" said the boy, and he pointed to one of my "spreads" (for the teamchains) that lay inside the fence. "I'll fling it back agin over the fence when I git this ole cow started."

"But wait a minute—I've forgotton your mother's name," said Mary.

He grabbed at his thatch impatiently. "Me mother—oh!—the old woman's name's Mrs Spicer. (Git up, karn't yer)" He twisted himself round, and brought the stretcher down on one of the horse's "points" (and he had many) with a crack that must have jarred his wrist.

"Do you go to school?" asked Mary. There was a three-days-a-week school over the ridges at Wall's station.

"No!" he jerked out, keeping his legs going. "Me—why I'm going on fur fifteen. The last teacher at Wall's finished me. I'm going to Queensland next month drovin'." (Queensland border was over three hundred miles away.)

"Finished you? How?" asked Mary.

"Me edgercation, of course! How do yer expect me to start this horse when yer keep talkin'?"

He split the "spread" over the horse's point, threw the pieces over the fence, and was off, his elbows and legs flying wildly, and the old saw-stool lumbering along the road like an old working bullock trying a canter. That horse wasn't a trotter.

And next month he *did* start for Queensland. He was a younger son and a surplus boy on a wretched, poverty-stricken selection; and as there was "northin' doin'" in the district, his father (in a burst of fatherly kindness, I suppose) made him a present of the old horse and a new pair of blucher boots, and I gave him an old saddle and a coat, and he started for the Never-Never country.

And I'll bet he got there. But I'm doubtful if the old horse did.

Mary gave the boy five shillings, and I don't think he had anything more except a clean shirt and an extra pair of white cotton socks.

"Spicer's farm" was a big bark humpy on a patchy clearing in the native apple-tree scrub. The clearing was fenced in by a light "dog-legged" fence (a fence of sapling poles resting on forks and X-shaped uprights), and the dusty ground round the house was almost entirely covered with cattle-dung. There was no attempt at cultivation when I came to live on the creek; but there were old furrow-marks amongst the stumps of another shapeless patch in the scrub near the hut. There was a wretched sapling cow-yard and calf-pen, and a cow-bail with one sheet of bark over it for shelter. There was no dairy to be seen, and I suppose the milk was set in one of the two skillion rooms, or lean-to's behind the hut—the other was "the boys' bedroom." The Spicers kept a few cows and steers, and had thirty or forty sheep. Mrs Spicer used to drive down the creek once a week, in her rickety old spring-cart, to Cobborah, with butter and eggs. The hut was nearly as bare inside as it was out—just a frame of "round-timber" (sapling poles) covered with bark. The furniture was permanent (unless you rooted it up), like in our kitchen: a rough slab table on stakes driven into the ground, and seats made the same way. Mary told me afterwards that the beds in the bag-and-bark partitioned-off room ("mother's bedroom") were simply poles laid side by side on cross-pieces supported by stakes driven into the ground, with straw mattresses and some worn-out bed-clothes. Mrs Spicer had an old patchwork quilt, in rags, and the remains of a white one, and Mary said it was pitiful to see how these things would be spread over the beds—to hide them as much as possible—when she went down there. A packing-case, with something like an old print skirt draped round it, and a cracked looking-glass (without a frame) on top, was the dressing-table. There were a couple of gin-cases for a wardrobe. The boys' beds were three-bushel bags stretched between poles fastened to uprights. The floor was the original surface, tramped hard, worn uneven with much sweeping, and with puddles in rainy weather where the roof leaked. Mrs Spicer used to stand old tins, dishes, and buckets under as many of the leaks as she could. The saucepans, kettles and boilers were old kerosene-tins and billies. They used kerosene-tins, too, cut longways in halves, for setting the milk in. The plates and cups were of tin; there were two or three cups without saucers, and a crockery plate or two—also two mugs, cracked, and without handles, one with "For a Good Boy" and the other with "For a Good Girl" on it; but all these were kept on the mantelshelf for ornament and for company. They were the only ornaments in the house, save a little wooden clock that hadn't gone for years. Mrs Spicer had a superstition that she had "some things packed away from the children."

The pictures were cut from old copies of the *Illustrated Sydney News* and pasted on to the bark. I remember this, because I remembered, long ago, the Spencers, who were our neighbours when I was a boy, had the walls of their bedroom covered with illustrations of the American Civil War, cut from illustrated London papers, and I used to "sneak" into "mother's bedroom" with Fred Spencer whenever we got a chance, and gloat over the prints. I gave him the blade of a pocket-knife once, for taking me in there.

I saw very little of Spicer. He was a big, dark, dark-haired and whiskered man. I had an idea that he wasn't a selector at all, only a "dummy" for the squatter of the Cobborah run. You see, selectors were allowed to take up land on runs or pastoral leases. The squatters kept them off as much as possible, by all manner of dodges and paltry persecution. The squatter would get as much freehold as he could afford, "select" as much land as the law allowed one man to take up, and then employ dummies (dummy selectors) to take up bits of land that he fancied about his run, and hold them for him.

Spicer seemed gloomy and unsociable. He was seldom at home. He was generally supposed to be away shearin', or fencin', or workin' on somebody's station. It turned out that the last six months he was away it was on the evidence of a cask of beef and a hide with the brand cut out, found in his camp on a fencing contract up-country, and which he and his mates couldn't account for satisfactorily, while the squatter could. Then the family lived mostly on bread and honey, or bread and treacle, or bread and dripping, and tea. Every ounce of butter and every egg was needed for the market, to keep them in flour, tea, and sugar. Mary found that out, but couldn't help them much—except by "stuffing" the children with bread and meat or bread and jam whenever they came up to our place—for Mrs Spicer was proud with the pride that lies down in the end and turns its face to the wall and dies.

Once, when Mary asked Annie, the eldest girl at home, if she was hungry, she denied it—but she looked it. A ragged mite she had with her explained things. The little fellow said:

"Mother told Annie not to say we was hungry if yer asked; but if yer give us anythink to eat, we was to take it an' say thenk yer, Mrs Wilson."

"I wouldn't 'a' told yer a lie; but I thought Jimmy would split on me, Mrs Wilson," said Annie. "Thenk yer, Mrs Wilson."

She was not a big woman. She was gaunt and flat-chested, and her face was "burnt to a brick," as they say out there. She had brown eyes, nearly red, and a little wild-looking at times, and a sharp face—ground sharp by hardship—the cheeks drawn in. She had an expression like—well, like a woman who had been very curious and suspicious at one time, and wanted to know everybody's business and hear everything, and had lost all her curiosity, without losing the expression or the quick suspicious movements of the head. I don't suppose you understand. I can't explain it any other way. She was not more than forty.

I remember the first morning I saw her. I was going up the creek to look at the selection for the first time, and called at the hut to see if she had a bit of fresh mutton, as I had none and was sick of "corned beef."

"Yes—of—course," she said, in a sharp nasty tone, as if to say, "Is there anything more you want while the shop's open?" I'd met just the same sort of woman years before while I was carrying swag between the shearing-sheds in the awful scrubs out west of the

Darling River, so I didn't turn on my heels and walk away. I waited for her to speak again.

"Come—inside," she said, "and sit down. I· see you've got the wagon outside. I s'pose your name's Wilson, ain't it? You're thinkin' about takin' on Harry Marshfield's selection up the creek, so I heard. Wait till I fry you a chop, and boil the billy."

Her voice sounded, more than anything else, like a voice coming out of a phonograph—I heard one in Sydney the other day—and not like a voice coming out of her. But sometimes when she got outside her everyday life on this selection she spoke in a sort of—in a sort of lost groping-in-the-dark kind of voice.

She didn't talk much this time—just spoke in a mechanical way of the drought, and the hard times, "an' butter 'n' eggs bein' down, an' her husban' an' eldest son bein' away, an' that makin' it so hard for her."

I don't know how many children she had. I never got a chance to count them, for they were nearly all small, and shy as piccaninnies, and used to run and hide when anybody came. They were mostly nearly as black as piccaninnies too. She must have averaged a baby a year for years—and God only knows how she got over her confinements! Once, they said she only had a black gin with her. She had an elder boy and girl, but she seldom spoke of them. The girl, "Liza," was "in service in Sydney." I'm afraid I knew what that meant. The elder son was "away." He had been a bit of a favourite round there, it seemed.

Someone might ask her, "How's your son Jack, Mrs Spicer?" or, "Heard of Jack lately? and where is he now?"

"Oh, he's somewheres up-country," she'd say in the "groping" voice, or "He's drovin' in Queenslan'," or "Shearin' on the Darlin' the last time I heerd from him. We ain't had a line from him since—le's see—since Chris-mas 'fore last."

And she'd turn her haggard eyes in a helpless, hopeless sort of way towards the west—towards "up-country" and "out back."*

The eldest girl at home was nine or ten, with a little old face and lines across her forehead: she had an older expression than her mother. Tommy went to Queensland, as I told you. The eldest son at home, Bill (older than Tommy), was "a bit wild."

I've passed the place on smothering hot mornings in December, when the droppings about the cow-yard had crumpled to dust that

---

* "Outback" is always west of the bushman, no matter how far out he be.

rose in the warm, sickly, sunrise wind, and seen that woman at work in the cow-yard, "bailing up" and leg-roping cows, milking, or hauling at a rope round the neck of a half-grown calf that was too strong for her (and she was tough as fencing-wire), or humping great buckets of sour milk to the pigs or the "poddies" (hand-fed calves) in the pen. I'd get off the horse and give her a hand sometimes with a young steer, or a cranky old cow that wouldn't "bail-up" and threatened her with her horns. She'd say:

"Thenk yer, Mr Wilson. Do yer think we're ever goin' to have any rain?"

I've ridden past the place on bitter black rainy mornings in June or July, and seen her trudging about the yard—that was ankle-deep in black liquid filth—with an old pair of blucher boots on, and an old coat of her husband's, or maybe a three-bushel bag over her shoulders. I've seen her climbing on the roof by means of the water-cask at the corner, and trying to stop a leak by shoving a piece of tin in under the bark. And when I'd fixed the leak:

"Thenk yer, Mr Wilson. This drop of rain's a blessin'! Come in and have a dry at the fire and I'll make yer a cup of tea." And, if I was in a hurry, "Come in, man alive! Come in! and dry yerself a bit till the rain holds up. Yer can't go home like this! Yer'll git yer death o' cold."

I've even seen her, in the terrible drought, climbing sheoaks and apple-trees by a makeshift ladder, and awkwardly lopping off boughs to feed the starving cattle.

"Jist tryin' ter keep the milkers alive till the rain comes."

They said that when the pleuro-pneumonia was in the district and amongst her cattle she bled and physicked them herself, and fed those that were down with slices of half-ripe pumpkins (from a crop that had failed).

"An', one day," she told Mary, "there was a bit barren heifer (that we called Queen Elizabeth) that was down with the ploorer. She'd been down for four days and hadn't moved, when one mornin' I dumped some wheaten chaff—we had a few bags that Spicer brought home—I dumped it in front of her nose, an'—would yer b'lieve me, Mrs Wilson?—she stumbled onter her feet an' chased me all the way to the house! I had to pick up me skirts an' run! Wasn't it redic'lus?"

They had a sense of the ridiculous, most of those poor sun-dried bushwomen. I fancy that that helped save them from madness.

"We lost nearly all our milkers," she told Mary. "I remember one day Tommy came running to the house and screamed: 'Marther! [mother] there's another milker down with the ploorer!' Jist as if it was great news. Well, Mrs Wilson, I was dead-beat, an' I giv' in. I jist sat down to have a good cry, and felt for my han'kerchief—it *was* a rag of a han'kerchief, full of holes (all me others was in the wash). Without seein' what I was doin' I put my finger through the hole in the han'kerchief an' me thumb through the other, and poked me fingers into me eyes, instead of wipin' them. Then I had to laugh."

There's a story that once, when the bush, or rather grass, fires were out all along the creek on Spicer's side, Wall's station-hands were up above our place, trying to keep the fire back from the boundary, and towards the evening one of the men happened to think of the Spicers: they saw smoke down that way. Spicer was away from home, and they had a small crop of wheat, nearly ripe, on the selection.

"My God! that poor devil of a woman will be burnt out, if she ain't already!" shouted young Billy Wall. "Come along, three or four of you chaps"—it was shearing-time, and there were plenty of men on the station.

They raced down the creek to Spicer's, and were just in time to save the wheat. She had her sleeves tucked up, and was beating out the burning grass with a bough. She'd been at it for an hour, and was as black as a gin, they said. She only said when they'd turned the fire: "Thenk yer! Wait an' I'll make some tea."

After tea the first Sunday she came to see us, Mary asked:

"Don't you feel lonely, Mrs Spicer, when your husband goes away?"

"Well—no, Mrs Wilson," she said in the groping sort of voice. "I uster, once. I remember, when we lived on the Cudgegong River—we lived in a brick house then—the first time Spicer had to go away from home I nearly fretted my eyes out. And he was only goin' shearin' for a month. I muster bin a fool; but then we were only jist married a little while. He's been away drovin' in Queenslan' as long as eighteen months at a time since then. But" (her voice seemed to grope in the dark more than ever) "I don't mind—I somehow seem to have got past carin'. Besides—besides, Spicer was a very different man then to what he is now. He's got so moody and gloomy at home, he hardly ever speaks."

Mary sat silent for a minute thinking. Then Mrs Spicer roused herself:

"Oh, I don't know what I'm talkin' about! You mustn't take any notice of me, Mrs Wilson—I don't often go on like this. I do believe I'm gittin' a bit ratty at times. It must be the heat and the dullness."

But once or twice afterwards she referred to a time "when Spicer was a different man to what he was now."

I walked home with her a piece along the creek. She said nothing for a long time, and seemed to be thinking in a puzzled way. Then she said suddenly:

"What-did-you-bring-her-here-for? She's only a girl."

"I beg pardon, Mrs Spicer."

"Oh, I don't know what I'm talkin' about! I b'lieve I'm gittin' ratty. You mustn't take any notice of me, Mr Wilson."

She wasn't much company for Mary; and often, when she had a child with her, she'd start taking notice of the baby while Mary was talking, which used to exasperate Mary. But poor Mrs Spicer couldn't help it, and she seemed to hear all the same.

Her great trouble was that she "couldn't git no reg'lar schoolin' for the children."

"I learns 'em at home as much as I can. But I don't git a minute to call me own; an' I'm ginerally that dead-beat at night that I'm fit for nothink."

Mary had some of the children up now and then later on, and taught them a little. When she first offered to do so, Mrs Spicer laid hold of the handiest youngster and said:

"There—do you hear that? Mrs Wilson is goin' to teach yer, an' it's more than yer deserve!" (the youngster had been cryin' over something). "Now, go up an' say 'Thenk yer, Mrs Wilson.' And if yer ain't good, and don't do as she tells yer, I'll break every bone in yer young body!"

The poor little devil stammered something, and escaped.

The children were sent by turns over to Wall's to Sunday-school. When Tommy was at home he had a new pair of elastic-side boots, and there was no end of rows about them in the family—for the mother made him lend them to his sister Annie, to go to Sunday-school in her turn. There were only about three pairs of anyway decent boots in the family, and these were saved for great occasions. The children were always clean and tidy as possible when they came to our place.

And I think the saddest and most pathetic sight on the face of God's earth is the children of very poor people made to appear well: the broken worn-out boots polished or greased, the blackened (inked) pieces of string for laces; the clean patched pinafores over the wretched threadbare frocks. Behind the little row of children hand-in-hand—and no matter where they are—I always see the worn face of the mother.

Towards the end of the first year on the selection our little girl came. I'd sent Mary to Gulgong for four months that time, and when she came back with the baby Mrs Spicer used to come up pretty often. She came up several times when Mary was ill, to lend a hand. She wouldn't sit down and condole with Mary, or waste her time asking questions, or talking about the time when she was ill herself. She'd take off her hat—a shapeless little lump of black straw she wore for visiting—give her hair a quick brush back with the palms of her hands, roll up her sleeves, and set to work to "tidy up." She seemed to take most pleasure in sorting out our children's clothes, and dressing them. Perhaps she used to dress her own like that in the days when Spicer was a different man from what he was now. She seemed interested in the fashion-plates of some women's journals we had, and used to study them with an interest that puzzled me, for she was not likely to go in for fashion. She never talked of her early girlhood; but Mary, from some things she noticed, was inclined to think that Mrs Spicer had been fairly well brought up. For instance, Dr Balanfantie, from Cudgegong, came out to see Wall's wife, and drove up the creek to our place on his way back to see how Mary and the baby were getting on. Mary got out some crockery and some table-napkins that she had packed away for occasions like this; and she said that the way Mrs Spicer handled the things, and helped set the table (though she did it in a mechanical sort of way), convinced her that she had been used to table-napkins at one time in her life.

Sometimes, after a long pause in the conversation, Mrs Spicer would say suddenly:

"Oh, I don't think I'll come up next week, Mrs Wilson."

"Why, Mrs Spicer?"

"Because the visits doesn't do me any good. I git the dismals afterwards."

"Why, Mrs Spicer? What on earth do you mean?"

"Oh, I-don't-know-what-I'm-talkin'-about. You mustn't take any notice of me." And she'd put on her hat, kiss the children—and Mary too, sometimes, as if she mistook her for a child—and go.

Mary thought her a little mad at times. But I seemed to understand.

Once, when Mrs Spicer was sick, Mary went down to her, and down again next day. As she was coming away the second time Mrs Spicer said:

"I wish you wouldn't come down any more till I'm on my feet, Mrs Wilson. The children can do for me."

"Why, Mrs Spicer?"

"Well, the place is in such a muck, and it hurts me."

We were the aristocrats of Lahey's Creek. Whenever we drove down on Sunday afternoon to see Mrs Spicer, and as soon as we got near enough for them to hear the rattle of the cart, we'd see the children running to the house as fast as they could split, and hear them screaming:

"Oh, marther! Here comes Mr and Mrs Wilson in their spring-cart."

And we'd see her bustle round, and two or three fowls fly out the front door, and she'd lay hold of a broom (made of a bound bunch of "broom-stuff"—coarse reedy grass or bush from the ridges—with a stick stuck in it) and flick out the floor, with a flick or two round in front of the door perhaps. The floor nearly always needed at least one flick of the broom on account of the fowls. Or she'd catch a youngster and scrub his face with a wet end of a cloudy towel or twist the towel round her finger and dig out his ears—as if she was anxious to have him hear every word that was going to be said.

No matter what state the house would be in she'd always say, "I was jist expectin' yer, Mrs Wilson." And she was original in that, anyway.

She had an old patched and darned white table-cloth that she used to spread on the table when we were there, as a matter of course ("The others is in the wash, so you must excuse this, Mrs Wilson"), but I saw by the eyes of the children that the cloth was rather a wonderful thing for them. "I must really git some more knives and forks next time I'm in Cobborah," she'd say. "The children will break an' lose 'em till I'm ashamed ter ask Christians ter sit down ter the table."

She had many bush yarns, some of them very funny, some of them rather ghastly, but all interesting, and with a grim sort of humour about them. But the effect was often spoilt by her screaming at the children to "Drive out them fowls, karn't yer," or "Take yer maulies [hands] outer the sugar," or "Don't touch Mrs Wilson's baby with them dirty maulies," or "Don't stand starin' at Mrs Wilson with yer mouth an' ears in that vulgar way."

Poor woman! she seemed everlastingly nagging at the children. It was a habit, but they didn't seem to mind. Most bush-women get the nagging habit. I remember one, who had the prettiest, dearest, sweetest, most willing, and affectionate little girl I think I ever saw, and she nagged that child from daylight till dark—and after it. Taking it all round, I think that the nagging habit in a mother is often worse on ordinary children, and more deadly on sensitive youngsters, than the drinking habit in a father.

One of the yarns Mrs Spicer told us was about a squatter she knew who used to go wrong in his head every now and again, and try to commit suicide. Once, when the station-hand, who was watching him, had his eye off him for a minute, he hanged himself to a beam in the stable. The men ran in and found him hanging and kicking. "They let him hang for a while," said Mrs Spicer, "till he went black in the face and stopped kicking. Then they cut him down and threw a bucket of water over him."

"Why! what on earth did they let the man hang for?" asked Mary.

"To give him a good bellyful of it: they thought it would cure him of tryin' to hang himself again."

"Well, that's the coolest thing I ever heard of," said Mary.

"That's jist what the magistrate said, Mrs Wilson," said Mrs Spicer.

"One morning," said Mrs Spicer, "Spicer had gone off on his horse somewhere, and I was alone with the children, when a man came to the door and said:

"'For God's sake, woman, give me a drink!'

"Lord only knows where he came from! He was dressed like a new chum—his clothes was good, but he looked as if he'd been sleepin' in them in the bush for a month. He was very shaky. I had some coffee that mornin' so I gave him some in a pint-pot; he drank it, and then he stood on his head till he tumbled over, and then he stood up on his feet and said, 'Thank yer, mum.'

"I was so surprised that I didn't know what to say, so I jist said, 'Would you like some more coffee?'

"'Yes, thenk yer,' he said—'about two quarts.'

"I nearly filled the pint-pot, and he drank it and stood on his head as long as he could, and when he got right end up he said, 'Thenk yer, mum—it's a fine day,' and then he walked off. He had two saddle-straps in his hands."

"Why, what did he stand on his head for?" asked Mary.

"To wash it up and down, I suppose, to get twice as much taste of the coffee. He had no hat. I sent Tommy across to Wall's to tell them that there was a man wanderin' about the bush in the horrors of drink, and to get someone to ride for the police. But they were too late, for he hanged himself that night."

"O Lord!" cried Mary.

"Yes, right close to here, jist down the creek where the track to Wall's branches off. Tommy found him while he was out after the cows. Hangin' to the branch of a tree with the two saddle-straps."

Mary stared at her, speechless.

"Tommy came home yellin' with fright. I sent him over to Wall's at once. After breakfast, the minute my eyes was off them, the children slipped away and went down there. They came back screamin' at the tops of their voices. I did give it to them. I reckon they won't want ter see a dead body again in a hurry. Every time I'd mention it they'd huddle together, or ketch hold of me skirts and howl.

" 'Yer'll go agen when I tell yer not to,' I'd say.

" 'Oh no, mother,' they'd howl.

" 'Yer wanted ter see a man hangin',' I said.

" 'Oh, don't, mother! Don't talk about it.'

" 'Yer wouldn't be satisfied till yer see it,' I'd say; 'yer had to see it or burst. Yer satisfied now, ain't yer?'

" 'Oh, don't, mother!'

" 'Yer run all the way there, I s'pose!'

" 'Don't, mother!'

" 'But yer run faster back, didn't yer?'

" 'Oh, don't, mother.'

"But," said Mrs Spicer, in conclusion, "I'd been down to see it myself before they was up."

"And ain't you afraid to live alone here, after all these horrible things?" asked Mary.

"Well, no; I don't mind. I seem to have got past carin' for anythink now. I felt it a little when Tommy went away—the first time I felt anythink for years. But I'm over that now."

"Haven't you got any friends in the district, Mrs Spicer?"

"Oh yes. There's me married sister near Cobborah, and a married brother near Dubbo; he's got a station. They wanted to take me an' the children between them, or take some of the younger children. But I couldn't bring my mind to break up the home. I want to keep the children together as much as possible. There's enough of them gone, God knows. But it's a comfort to know that there's someone to see to them if anythink happens me."

One day—I was on my way home with the team that day—Annie Spicer came running up the creek in terrible trouble.

"Oh, Mrs Wilson! something terrible's happened at home. A trooper" (mounted policeman—they called them "mounted troopers" out there), "a trooper's come and took Billy!" Billy was the eldest son at home.

"What?"

"It's true, Mrs Wilson."

"What for? What did the policeman say?"

"He—he—he said, 'I—I'm very sorry, Mrs Spicer; but—I—I want William.'"

It turned out that William was wanted on account of a horse missed from Wall's station and sold down-country.

"An' mother took on awful," sobbed Annie; "an' now she'll only sit stock-still an' stare in front of her, and won't take no notice of any of us. Oh! it's awful, Mrs Wilson. The policeman said he'd tell Aunt Emma" (Mrs Spicer's sister at Cobborah), "and send her out. But I had to come to you, an' I've run all the way."

James put the horse to the cart and drove Mary down.

Mary told me all about it when I came home.

"I found her just as Annie said; but she broke down and cried in my arms. Oh, Joe! it was awful. She didn't cry like a woman. I heard a man at Haviland cry at his brother's funeral, and it was just like that. She came round a bit after a while. Her sister's with her now.... Oh, Joe! you must take me away from the bush."

Later on Mary said:

"How the oaks are sighing to-night, Joe!"

Next morning I rode across to Wall's station and tackled the old man; but he was a hard man, and wouldn't listen to me—in fact, he ordered me off the station. I was a selector and that was enough for him. But young Billy Wall rode after me.

"Look here, Joe!" he said, "it's a blanky shame. All for the sake of a horse! As if that poor devil of a woman hasn't got enough to put up with already! I wouldn't do it for twenty horses. *I'll* tackle the boss, and if he won't listen to me, I'll walk off the run for the last time, if I have to carry my swag."

Billy Wall managed it. The charge was withdrawn, and we got young Billy Spicer off up-country.

But poor Mrs Spicer was never the same after that. She seldom came up to our place unless Mary dragged her, so to speak; and then she would talk of nothing but her last trouble, till her visits were painful to look forward to.

"If it only could have been kep' quiet—for the sake of the other children; they are all I think of now. I tried to bring 'em all up decent, but I s'pose it was my fault, somehow. It's the disgrace that's killin' me—I can't bear it."

I was at home one Sunday with Mary, and a jolly bush-girl named Maggie Charlsworth, who rode over sometimes from Wall's station (I must tell you about her some other time; James was "shook after her"), and we got talkin' about Mrs Spicer. Maggie was very warm about old Wall.

"I expected Mrs Spicer up to-day," said Mary. "She seems better lately."

"Why!" cried Maggie Charlsworth, "if that ain't Annie coming running up along the creek. Something's the matter!"

We all jumped up and ran out.

"What is it, Annie?" cried Mary.

"Oh, Mrs Wilson! Mother's asleep, and we can't wake her!"

"What?"

"It's—it's the truth, Mrs Wilson."

"How long has she been asleep?"

"Since lars' night."

"My God!" cried Mary, "*since last night?*"

"No, Mrs Wilson, not all the time; she woke wonst, about daylight this mornin'. She called me and said she didn't feel well, and I'd have to manage the milkin'."

"Was that all she said?"

"No. She said not to go for you; and she said to feed the pigs and calves; and she said to be sure and water them geraniums."

Mary wanted to go, but I wouldn't let her. James and I saddled our horses and rode down the creek.

Mrs Spicer looked very little different from what she did when I last saw her alive. It was some time before we could believe that she was dead. But she was "past carin'" right enough.

A DOUBLE BUGGY AT LAHEY'S CREEK

I

SPUDS, AND A WOMAN'S OBSTINACY

Ever since we were married it had been Mary's great ambition to
have a buggy. The house or furniture didn't matter so much—out
there in the bush where we were—but, where there were no railways
or coaches, and the roads were long and mostly hot and dusty, a
buggy was the great thing. I had a few pounds when we were
married, and was going to get one then; but new buggies went high,
and another party got hold of a second-hand one that I'd had my eye
on, so Mary thought it over and at last she said, "Never mind the
buggy, Joe; get a sewing-machine and I'll be satisfied. I'll want the
machine more than the buggy, for a while. Wait till we're better off."

After that, whenever I took a contract—to put up a fence or
wool-shed, or sink a dam or something—Mary would say, "You
ought to knock a buggy out of this job, Joe;" but something always
turned up—bad weather or sickness. Once I cut my foot with the
adze and was laid up; and, another time, a dam I was making was
washed away by a flood before I finished it. Then Mary would say,
"Ah, well—never mind, Joe. Wait till we are better off." But she felt
it hard the time I built a wool-shed and didn't get paid for it, for
we'd as good as settled about another second-hand buggy then.

I always had a fancy for carpentering, and was handy with tools. I
made a spring-cart—body and wheels—in spare time, out of
colonial hardwood, and got Little the blacksmith to do the ironwork:
I painted the cart myself. It wasn't much lighter than one of the
tip-drays I had, but it *was* a spring-cart, and Mary pretended to be
satisfied with it: anyway, I didn't hear any more of the buggy for a
while.

I sold that cart for fourteen pounds, to a Chinese gardener who
wanted a strong cart to carry his vegetables round through the bush.
It was just before our first youngster came: I told Mary that I
wanted the money in case of extra expense—and she didn't fret
much at losing the cart. But the fact was that I was going to make
another try for a buggy, as a present for Mary when the child was
born. I thought of getting the turnout while she was laid up, keeping
it dark from her till she was on her feet again, and then showing her

the buggy standing in the shed. But she had a bad time, and I had to
have the doctor regularly, and get a proper nurse, and a lot of things
extra; so the buggy idea was knocked on the head. I was set on it,
too; I'd thought of how, when Mary was up and getting strong, I'd
say one morning, "Go round and have a look in the shed. Mary; I've
got a few fowls for you," or something like that—and follow her
round to watch her eyes when she saw the buggy. I never told Mary
about that—it wouldn't have done any good.

Later on I got some good timber—mostly scraps that were given
to me—and made a light body for a spring-cart. Galletly, the
coach-builder at Cudgegong, had got a dozen pairs of American
hickory wheels up from Sydney, for light spring-carts, and he let me
have a pair for cost price and carriage. I got him to iron the cart, and
he put it through the paint-shop for nothing. He sent it out, too, at
the tail of Tom Tarrant's big van—to increase the surprise. We were
swells then for a while; I heard no more of a buggy until after we'd
been settled at Lahey's Creek for a couple of years.

I told you how I went into the carrying line, and took up a
selection at Lahey's Creek—for a run for the horses and to grow a bit
of feed—and shifted Mary and little Jim out there from Gulgong,
with Mary's young scamp of a brother James to keep them company,
while I was on the road. The first year I did well enough carrying,
but I never cared for it—it was too slow; and, besides, I was always
anxious when I was away from home. The game was right enough
for a single man—or a married one whose wife had got the nagging
habit (as many bushwomen have—God help 'em), and who wanted
peace and quietness sometimes. Besides, other small carriers started
(seeing me getting on); Tom Tarrant, the coach-builder at
Cudgegong, had another heavy spring-van built, and put it on the
road, and he took a lot of the light stuff.

The second year I made a rise—out of "spuds," of all the things in
the world. It was Mary's idea. Down at the lower end of our
selection—Mary called it "the run"—was a shallow watercourse
called Snake's Creek, dry most of the year, except for a muddy
waterhole or two; and, just above the junction, where it ran into
Lahey's Creek, was a low piece of good black-soil flat, on our
side—about three acres. The flat was fairly clear when I came to the
selection—save for a few logs that had been washed up there in some
big "old man" flood, way back in blackfellows' times: and one day
when I had a spell at home, I got the horses and trace-chains and
dragged the logs together—those that wouldn't split for fencing

timber—and burnt them off. I had a notion to get the flat ploughed and make a lucerne-paddock of it. There was a good waterhole, under a clump of she-oak in the bend, and Mary used to take her stools and tubs and boiler down there in the spring-cart in hot weather, and wash the clothes under the shade of the trees—it was cooler, and saved carrying water to the house. And one evening after she'd done the washing she said to me:

"Look here, Joe; the farmers out here never seem to get a new idea: they don't seem to me ever to try and find out beforehand what the market is going to be like—they just go on farming the same old way, and putting in the same old crops year after year. They sow wheat, and, if it comes on anything like the thing, they reap and thresh it; if it doesn't they mow it for hay—and some of 'em don't have the brains to do that in time. Now I was looking at that bit of flat you cleared, and it struck me that it wouldn't be a half-bad idea to get a bag of seed potatoes, and have the land ploughed—old Corny George would do it cheap—and get them put in at once. Potatoes have been dear all round for the last couple of years."

I told her she was talking nonsense, that the ground was no good for potatoes, and the whole district was too dry. "Everybody I know has tried it, one time or another, and made nothing of it," I said.

"All the more reason why you should try it, Joe," said Mary. "Just try one crop. It might rain for weeks, and then you'll be sorry you didn't take my advice."

"But I tell you the ground is not potato-ground," I said.

"How do you know? You haven't sown any there yet."

"But I've turned up the surface and looked at it. It's not rich enough, and too dry, I tell you. You need swampy, boggy ground for potatoes. Do you think I don't know land when I see it?"

"But you haven't tried to grow potatoes there yet, Joe. How do you know——"

I didn't listen to any more. Mary was obstinate when she got an idea into her head. It was no use arguing with her. All the time I'd be talking she'd just knit her forehead and go on thinking straight ahead, on the track she'd started—just as if I wasn't there—and it used to make me mad. She'd keep driving at me till I took her advice or lost my temper—I did both at the same time, mostly.

I took my pipe and went out to smoke and cool down.

A couple of days after the potato breeze, I started with the team down to Cudgegong for a load of fencing-wire I had to bring out; and after I'd kissed Mary good-bye, she said:

"Look here, Joe, if you bring out a bag of seed potatoes, Jame
and I will slice them, and old Corny George down the creek woul
bring his plough up in the dray, and plough the ground for ver
little. We could put the potatoes in ourselves if the ground were onl
ploughed."

I thought she'd forgotten all about it. There was no time t
argue—I'd be sure to lose my temper, and then I'd either have t
waste an hour comforting Mary, or go off in a "huff," as the wome
call it, and be miserable for the trip. So I said I'd see about it. Sh
gave me another hug and a kiss. "Don't forget, Joe," she said as
started. "Think it over on the road." I reckon she had the best of i
that time.

About five miles along, just as I turned into the main road,
heard someone galloping after me, and I saw young James on hi
hack. I got a start, for I thought that something had gone wrong a
home. I remember the first day I left Mary on the creek, for the firs
five or six miles I was half a dozen times on the point of turnin
back—only I thought she'd laugh at me.

"What is it, James?" I shouted, before he came up—but I saw h
was grinning.

"Mary says to tell you not to forget to bring a hoe out with you."

"You clear off home!" I said, "or I'll lay the whip about you
young hide; and don't come riding after me again as if the run wa
on fire."

"Well, you needn't get shirty with me!" he said. "*I* don't want t
have anything to do with a hoe." And he rode off.

I *did* get thinking about those potatoes, though I hadn't meant to
I knew of an independent man in that district who'd made hi
money out of a crop of potatoes; but that was away back in th
roaring fifties—fifty-four—when spuds went up to twenty-eigh
shillings a hundredweight (in Sydney), on account of the gold rush
We might get good rain now, and, anyway, it wouldn't cost much t
put the potatoes in. If they came on well, it would be a few pounds i
my pocket; if the crop was a failure, I'd have a better show wit
Mary next time she was struck by an idea outside housekeeping, an
have something to grumble about when I felt grumpy.

I got a couple of bags of potatoes—we could use those that wer
left over; and I got a small iron plough and harrow that Little th
blacksmith had lying in his yard and let me have cheap—only abou
a pound more than I told Mary I gave for them. When I took advic
I generally made the mistake of taking more than was offered, o

adding notions of my own. It was vanity, I suppose. If the crop came on well I could claim the plough-and-harrow part of the idea, anyway. (It didn't strike me that if the crop failed Mary would have the plough and harrow against me, for old Corny would plough the ground for ten or fifteen shillings.) Anyway, I'd want a plough and harrow later on, and I might as well get it now; it would give James something to do.

I came out by the western road, by Guntawang, and up the creek home; and the first thing I saw was old Corny George ploughing the flat. And Mary was down on the bank superintending. She'd got James with the trace-chains and the spare horses, and had made him clear off every stick and bush where another furrow might be squeezed in. Old Corny looked pretty grumpy on it—he'd broken all his ploughshares but one, in the roots; and James didn't look much brighter. Mary had an old felt hat and a new pair of 'lastic-side boots of mine on, and the boots were covered with clay, for she'd been down hustling James to get a rotten old stump out of the way by the time old Corny came round with his next furrow.

"I thought I'd make the boots easy for you, Joe," said Mary.

"It's all right, Mary," I said, "I'm not going to growl." Those boots were a bone of contention between us; but she generally got them off before I got home.

Her face fell when she saw the plough and harrow in the wagon, but I said that would be all right—we'd want a plough anyway.

"I thought you wanted old Corny to plough the ground," she said.

"I never said so."

"But when I sent Jim after you about the hoe to put the spuds in, you didn't say you wouldn't bring it," she said.

I had a few days at home, and entered into the spirit of the thing. When Corny was done, James and I cross-ploughed the land, and got a stump or two, a big log, and some scrub out of the way at the upper end and added nearly an acre, and ploughed that. James was all right at most bushwork: he'd bullock so long as the novelty lasted; he liked ploughing or fencing, or any graft he could make a show at. He didn't care for grubbing out stumps, or splitting posts and rails. We sliced the potatoes of an evening—and there was trouble between Mary and James over cutting through the "eyes." There was no time for the hoe—and besides it wasn't a novelty to James—so I just ran furrows and they dropped the spuds in behind me, and I turned another furrow over them, and ran the harrow over the ground. I think I hilled those spuds, too, with furrows—or a crop of Indian corn I put in later on.

It rained heavens-hard for over a week: we had regular showers all through, and it was the finest crop of potatoes ever seen in the district. I believe at first Mary used to slip down at daybreak to see if the potatoes were up; and she'd write to me about them, on the road. I forget how many bags I got but the few who had grown potatoes in the district sent theirs to Sydney, and spuds went up to twelve and fifteen shillings a hundredweight in that district. I made a few quid out of mine—and saved carriage too, for I could take them out on the wagon. Then Mary began to hear (through James) of a buggy that someone had for sale cheap, or a dogcart that somebody else wanted to get rid of—and let me know about it, in an off-hand way.

II

JOE WILSON'S LUCK

There was good grass on the selection all the year. I'd picked up a small lot—about twenty head—of half-starved steers for next to nothing, and turned them on the run; they came on wonderfully, and my brother-in-law (Mary's sister's husband), who was running a butchery at Gulgong, gave me a good price for them. His carts ran out twenty or thirty miles, to little bits of gold rushes that were going on at th' Home Rule, Happy Valley, Guntawang, Tallawang, and Cooyal, and those places round there, and he was doing well.

Mary had heard of a light American wagonette, when the steers went—a tray-body arrangement, and she thought she'd do with that. "It would be better than the buggy, Joe," she said. "There'd be more room for the children, and, besides, I could take butter and eggs to Gulgong, or Cobborah, when we get a few more cows." Then James heard of a small flock of sheep that a selector—who was about starved off his selection out Talbragar way—wanted to get rid of. James reckoned he could get them for less than half a crown a head. We'd had a heavy shower of rain, that came over the ranges and didn't seem to go beyond our boundaries. Mary said, "It's a pity to see all that grass going to waste, Joe. Better get those sheep and try your luck with them. Leave some money with me, and I'll send James over for them. Never mind about the buggy—we'll get that when we're on our feet."

So James rode across to Talbragar and drove a hard bargain with that unfortunate selector, and brought the sheep home. There were about two hundred, wethers and ewes, and they were young and looked a good breed too, but so poor they could scarcely travel; they soon picked up, though. The drought was blazing all round and out back, and I think that my corner of the ridges was the only place where there was any grass to speak of. We had another shower or two, and the grass held out. Chaps began to talk of "Joe Wilson's luck."

I would have liked to shear those sheep; but I hadn't time to get a shed or anything ready—along towards Christmas there was a bit of a boom in the carrying line. Wethers in wool were going as high as thirteen to fifteen shillings at the Homebush yards at Sydney, so I arranged to truck the sheep down from the river by rail, with another small lot that was going, and I started James off with them. He took the west road, and down Guntawang way a big farmer who saw James with the sheep (and who was speculating, or adding to his stock, or took a fancy to the wool) offered James as much for them as he reckoned I'd get in Sydney, after paying the carriage and the agents and the auctioneer. James put the sheep in a paddock and rode back to me. He was all there where riding was concerned. I told him to let the sheep go. James made a Greener shot-gun, and got his saddle done up, out of that job.

I took up a couple more forty-acre blocks—one in James's name, to encourage him with the fencing. There was a good slice of land in an angle between the range and the creek, farther down, which everybody thought belonged to Wall, the squatter, but Mary got an idea, and went to the local land office, and found out that it was unoccupied Crown land, and so I took it up on pastoral lease, and got a few more sheep—I'd saved some of the best-looking ewes from the last lot.

One evening—I was going down next day for a load of fencing-wire for myself—Mary said:

"Joe! do you know that the Matthews have got a new double buggy?"

The Matthews were a big family of cockatoos, along up the main road, and I didn't think much of them. The sons were all "bad-eggs," though the old woman and girls were right enough.

"Well, what of that?" I said. "They're up to their neck in debt, and camping like blackfellows in a big bark humpy. They do well to go flashing round in a double buggy."

"But that isn't what I was going to say," said Mary. "They want to sell their old single buggy, James says. I'm sure you could get it for six or seven pounds; and you could have it done up."

"I wish James to the devil!" I said. "Can't he find anything better to do than ride round after cock-and-bull yarns about buggies?"

"Well," said Mary, "it was James who got the steers and the sheep."

Well, one word led to another, and we said things we didn't mean—but couldn't forget in a hurry. I remember I said something about Mary always dragging me back just when I was getting my head above water and struggling to make a home for her and the children; and that hurt her, and she spoke of the "homes" she'd had since she was married. And that cut me deep.

It was about the worst quarrel we had. When she began to cry I got my hat and went out and walked up and down by the creek. I hated anything that looked like injustice—I was so sensitive about it that it made me unjust sometimes. I tried to think I was right, but I couldn't—it wouldn't have made me feel any better if I could have thought so. I got thinking of Mary's first year on the selection and the life she'd had since we were married.

When I went in she'd cried herself to sleep. I bent over and, "Mary," I whispered.

She seemed to wake up.

"Joe—Joe!" she said.

"What is it, Mary?" I said.

"I'm pretty sure that old Spot's calf isn't in the pen. Make James go at once!"

Old Spot's last calf was two years old now; so Mary was talking in her sleep, and dreaming she was back in her first year.

We both laughed when I told her about it afterwards; but I didn't feel like laughing just then.

Later on in the night she called out in her sleep:

"Joe—Joe! Put that buggy in the shed, or the sun will blister the varnish!"

I wish I could say that that was the last time I ever spoke unkindly to Mary.

Next morning I got up early and fried the bacon and made the tea, and took Mary's breakfast in to her—like I used to do, sometimes, when we were first married. She didn't say anything—just pulled my head down and kissed me.

When I was ready to start, Mary said:

"You'd better take the spring-cart in behind the dray, and get the tyres cut and set. They're ready to drop off, and James has been wedging them up till he's tired of it. The last time I was out with the children I had to knock one of them back with a stone: there'll be an accident yet."

So I lashed the shafts of the cart under the tail of the wagon, and mean and ridiculous enough the cart looked, going along that way. It suggested a man stooping along handcuffed, with his arms held out and down in front of him.

It was dull weather, and the scrubs looked extra dreary and endless—and I got thinking of old things. Everything was going all right with me, but that didn't keep me from brooding sometimes— trying to hatch out stones, like an old hen we had at home. I think, taking it all round, I used to be happier when I was mostly hard up—and more generous. When I had ten pounds I was more likely to listen to a chap who said, "Lend me a pound note, Joe," than when I had fifty; *then* I fought shy of careless chaps—and lost mates that I wanted afterwards—and got the name of being mean. When I got a good cheque I'd be as miserable as a miser over the first ten pounds I spent; but when I got down to the last I'd buy things for the house. And now that I was getting on, I hated to spend a pound on anything. But then, the farther I got away from poverty the greater the fear I had of it—and, besides, there was always before us all the thought of the terrible drought, with blazing runs as bare and dusty as the road, and dead stock rotting every yard, all along the barren creeks.

I had a long yarn with Mary's sister and her husband that night in Gulgong, and it brightened me up. I had a fancy that that sort of a brother-in-law made a better mate than a nearer one; Tom Tarrant had one, and he said it was sympathy. But while we were yarning I couldn't help thinking of Mary, out there in the hut on the creek, with no one to talk to but the children, or James, who was sulky at home, or Black Mary or Black Jimmy (our black boy's father and mother), who weren't over-sentimental. Or, maybe, a selector's wife (the nearest was five miles away) who could talk only of two or three things—"lambin'" and "shearin'" and "cookin' for the men," and what she said to her old man, and what he said to her—and her own ailments over and over again.

It's a wonder it didn't drive Mary mad!—I know I could never listen to that woman more than an hour. Mary's sister said:

"Now if Mary had a comfortable buggy, she could drive in with the children oftener. Then she wouldn't feel the loneliness so much."

I said "Good night" then and turned in. There was no getting away from that buggy. Whenever Mary's sister started hinting about a buggy, I reckoned it was a put-up job between them.

III

THE GHOST OF MARY'S SACRIFICE

When I got to Cudgegong I stopped at Galletly's coach-shop to leave the cart. The Galletlys were good fellows: there were two brothers—one was a saddler and harness-maker. Big brown-bearded men—the biggest men in the district, 'twas said.

Their old man had died lately and left them some money; they had men, and only worked in their shops when they felt inclined, or there was a special work to do; they were both first-class tradesmen. I went into the painter's shop to have a look at a double buggy that Galletly had built for a man who couldn't pay cash for it when it was finished—and Galletly wouldn't trust him.

There it stood, behind a calico screen that the coach-painters used to keep out the dust when they were varnishing. It was a first-class piece of work—pole, shafts, cushions, whip, lamps, and all complete. If you only wanted to drive one horse you could take out the pole and put in the shafts, and there you were. There was a tilt over the front seat; if you only wanted the buggy to carry two, you could fold down the back seat, and there you had a handsome, roomy, single buggy. It would go near fifty pounds.

While I was looking at it, Bill Galletly came in and slapped me on the back.

"Now, there's a chance for you, Joe!" he said. "I saw you rubbing your head round that buggy the last time you were in. You wouldn't get a better one in the colonies, and you won't see another like it in the district again in a hurry—for it doesn't pay to build 'em. Now you're a full-blown squatter, and it's time you took little Mary for a fly round in her own buggy now and then, instead of having her stuck out there in the scrub, or jolting through the dust in a cart like some old Mother Flourbag."

He called her "Little Mary" because the Galletly family had
known her when she was a girl.

I rubbed my head and looked at the buggy again. It was a great
temptation.

"Look here, Joe," said Bill Galletly in a quieter tone. "I'll tell you
what I'll do. I'll let *you* have the buggy. You can take it out and send
along a bit of a cheque when you feel you can manage it, and the rest
later on—a year will do, or even two years. You've had a hard pull,
and I'm not likely to be hard up for money in a hurry."

They were good fellows the Galletlys, but they knew their men. I
happened to know that Bill Galletly wouldn't let the man he built
the buggy for take it out of the shop without cash down, though he
was a big-bug round there. But that didn't make it easier for me.

Just then Robert Galletly came into the shop. He was rather
quieter than his brother, but the two were very much alike.

"Look here, Bob," said Bill; "here's a chance for you to get rid of
our harness. Joe Wilson's going to take that buggy off my hands."

Bob Galletly put his foot up on a saw-stool, took one hand out of
his pockets, rested his elbow on his knee and his chin on the palm of
his hand, and bunched up his big beard with his fingers, as he
always did when he was thinking. Presently he took his foot down,
put his hand back in his pocket, and said to me, "Well, Joe, I've got
a double set of harness made for the man who ordered that damned
buggy, and if you like I'll let you have it. I suppose when Bill there
has squeezed all he can out of you I'll stand a show of getting
something. He's a regular Shylock, he is."

I pushed my hat forward and rubbed the back of my head and
stared at the buggy.

"Come across to the Royal, Joe," said Bob.

But I knew that a beer would settle the business, so I said I'd get
the wool up to the station first and think it over, and have a drink
when I came back.

I thought it over on the way to the station, but it didn't seem good
enough. I wanted to get some more sheep, and there was the new
run to be fenced in, and the instalments on the selections. I wanted
lots of things that I couldn't well do without. Then, again, the
further I got away from debt and hard-upedness the greater the
horror I had of it. I had two horses that would do; but I'd have to get
another later on, and altogether the buggy would run me nearer a
hundred than fifty pounds. Supposing a dry season threw me back

with that buggy on my hands. Besides, I wanted a spell. If I got tl
buggy it would only mean an extra turn of hard graft for me. No, I
take Mary for a trip to Sydney, and she'd have to be satisfied wi
that.

I'd got it settled, and was just turning in through the big whi
gates to the goods-shed when young Black, the squatter, dashed pa
to the station in his big new wagonette, with his wife and a driv
and a lot of portmanteaux and rugs and things. They were going
do the grand in Sydney over Christmas. Now it was young Bla
who was so shook after Mary when she was in service with t
Blacks before the old man died, and if I hadn't come along—and
girls never cared for vagabonds—Mary would have been mistress
Haviland homestead, with servants to wait on her; and she was
better fitted for it than the one that was there. She would have be
going to Sydney every holiday and putting up at the old Royal, wi
every comfort that a woman could ask for, and seeing a play eve
night. And I'd have been knocking around amongst the big statio
out back, or maybe drinking myself to death at the shanties.

The Blacks didn't see me as I went by, ragged and dusty, ar
with an old, nearly black, cabbage-tree hat drawn over my eyes.
didn't care a damn for them, or anyone else, at most times, but I h
moods when I felt things.

One of Black's big wool-teams was just coming away from t
shed, and the driver, a big, dark, rough fellow, with some forei
blood in him, didn't seem inclined to wheel his team an inch out
the middle of the road. I stopped my horses and waited. He look
at me and I looked at him—hard. Then he wheeled off, scowlir
and swearing at his horses. I'd given him a hiding, six or seven yea
before, and he hadn't forgotten it. And I felt then as if I would
mind trying to give someone a hiding.

The goods clerk must have thought that Joe Wilson was pre
grumpy that day. I was thinking of Mary, out there in the lonely h
on a barren creek in the bush—for it was little better—with no o
to speak to except a haggard, worn-out bushwoman or two, th
came to see her on Sunday. I thought of the hardships she we
through in the first year—that I haven't told you about yet; of t
time she was ill, and I away, and no one to understand; of the tir
she was alone with James and Jim sick; and of the loneliness s
fought through out there. I thought of Mary, outside in the blazi
heat, with an old print dress and a felt hat, and a pair of 'lastic-side
of mine on, doing the work of a station manager as well as that o

housewife and mother. And her cheeks were getting thin, and the colour was going: I thought of the gaunt, brick-brown saw-file voiced, hopeless and spiritless bushwomen I knew—and some of them not much older than Mary.

When I went back into the town, I had a drink with Bill Galletly at the Royal, and that settled the buggy; then Bob shouted, and I took the harness. Then I shouted, to wet the bargain. When I was going, Bob said, "Send in that young scamp of a brother of Mary's with the horses: if the collars don't fit I'll fix up a pair of makeshifts, and alter the others." I thought they both gripped my hand harder than usual, but that might have been the beer.

IV

THE BUGGY COMES HOME

I "whipped the cat" a bit, the first twenty miles or so, but then, I thought, what did it matter? What was the use of grinding to save money until we were too old to enjoy it. If we had to go down in the world again, we might as well fall out of a buggy as out of a dray—there'd be some talk about it, anyway, and perhaps a little sympathy. When Mary had the buggy she wouldn't be tied down so much to that wretched hole in the bush; and the Sydney trips needn't be off either. I could drive down to Wallerawang on the main line, where Mary had some people, and leave the buggy and horses there, and take the train to Sydney, or go right on, by the old coach road, over the Blue Mountains: it would be a grand drive. I thought best to tell Mary's sister at Gulgong about the buggy; I told her I'd keep it dark from Mary till the buggy came home. She entered into the spirit of the thing, and said she'd give the world to be able to go out with the buggy, if only to see Mary open her eyes when she saw it; but she couldn't go, on account of a new baby she had. I was rather glad she couldn't, for it would spoil the surprise a little, I thought. I wanted that all to myself.

I got home about sunset next day, and, after tea, when I'd finished telling Mary all the news, and a few lies as to why I didn't bring the cart back, and one or two other things, I sat with James, out on a log of the wood-heap, where we generally had our smokes and interviews, and told him all about the buggy. He whistled, then he said:

"But what do you want to make it such a bushranging business for? Why can't you tell Mary now? It will cheer her up. She's been pretty miserable since you've been away this trip."

"I want it to be a surprise," I said.

"Well, I've got nothing to say against a surprise, out in a hole like this; but it 'ud take a lot to surprise me. What am I to say to Mary about taking the two horses in? I'll only want one to bring the cart out, and she's sure to ask."

"Tell her you're going to get yours shod."

"But he had a set of slippers only the other day. She knows as much about horses as we do. I don't mind telling a lie so long as a chap has only got to tell a straight lie and be done with it. But Mary asks so many questions."

"Well, drive the other horse up the creek early, and pick him up as you go."

"Yes. And she'll want to know what I want with two bridles. But I'll fix her—*you* needn't worry."

"And, James," I said, "get a chamois leather and sponge—we'll want 'em anyway—and you might give the buggy a wash down in the creek, coming home. It's sure to be covered with dust."

"Oh!—orlright."

"And if you can, time yourself to get here in the cool of the evening, or just about sunset."

"What for?"

I'd thought it would be better to have the buggy there in the cool of the evening, when Mary would have time to get excited and get over it—better than in the blazing hot morning, when the sun rose as hot as at noon, and we'd have the long broiling day before us.

"What do you want me to come at sunset for?" asked James. "Do you want me to camp out in the scrub and turn up like a blooming sundowner?"

"Oh well," I said, "get here at midnight if you like."

We didn't say anything for a while—just sat and puffed at our pipes. Then I said:

"Well, what are you thinking about?"

"I'm thinking it's time you got a new hat, the sun seems to get in through your old one too much," and he got out of my reach and went to see about penning the calves. Before we turned in he said

"Well, what am I to get out of the job, Joe?"

He had his eye on a double-barrel gun that Franca the gun-smith in Cudgegong had—one barrel shot, and the other rifle; so I said

"How much does Franca want for that gun?"

"Five-ten; but I think he'd take my single barrel off it. Anyway, I an squeeze a couple of quid out of Phil Lambert for the single arrel." (Phil was his bosom chum.)

"All right," I said. "Make the best bargain you can."

He got his own breakfast and made an early start next morning, to et clear of any instructions or messages that Mary might have orgotten to give him overnight. He took his gun with him.

I'd always thought that a man was a fool who couldn't keep a ecret from his wife—that there was something womanish about im. I found out. Those three days waiting for the buggy were about he longest I ever spent in my life. It made me scotty with everyone nd everything; and poor Mary had to suffer for it. I put in the time atching up the harness and mending the stockyard and the roof, nd, the third morning, I rode up the ridges to look for trees for ncing timber. I remember I hurried home that afternoon because I hought the buggy might get there before me.

At tea-time I got Mary on to the buggy business.

"What's the good of a single buggy to you, Mary?" I asked. There's only room for two, and what are you going to do with the hildren when we go out together?"

"We can put them on the floor at our feet, like other people do. I an always fold up a blanket or possum rug for them to sit on."

But she didn't take half so much interest in buggy talk as she vould have taken at any other time; when I didn't want her to. Vomen are aggravating that way. But the poor girl was tired and ot very well, and both the children were cross. She did look nocked up.

"We'll give the buggy a rest, Joe," she said. (I thought I heard it oming then.) 'It seems as far off as ever. I don't know why you want harp on it to-day. Now, don't look so cross, Joe—I didn't mean to urt you. We'll wait until we can get a double buggy, since you're so et on it. There'll be plenty of time when we're better off."

After tea, when the youngsters were in bed, and she'd washed up, e sat on the edge of the veranda floor, Mary sewing, and I smoking nd watching the track up the creek.

"Why don't you talk, Joe?" asked Mary. "You scarcely ever speak me now: it's like drawing blood out of a stone to get a word from ou. What makes you so cross, Joe?"

"Well, I've got nothing to say."

"But you should find something. Think of me—it's very miserable

for me. Have you anything on your mind? Is there any new trouble?
Better tell me, no matter what it is, and not go worrying and
brooding and making both our lives miserable. If you never tell one
anything, how can you expect me to understand?"

I said there was nothing the matter.

"But there must be, to make you so unbearable. Have you been
drinking, Joe—or gambling?"

I asked her what she'd accuse me of next.

"And another thing I want to speak to you about," she went on.
"Now, don't knit up your forehead like that, Joe, and get
impatient——"

"Well, what is it?"

"I wish you wouldn't swear in the hearing of the children. Now
little Jim to-day, he was trying to fix his little go-cart, and it
wouldn't run right, and—and——"

"Well, what did he say?"

"He—he" (she seemed a little hysterical, trying not to laugh)—
"he said, 'Damn it!' "

I had to laugh. Mary tried to keep serious but it was no use.

"Never mind, old woman," I said, putting an arm round her, for
her mouth was trembling, and she was crying more than laughing.
"It won't be always like this. Just wait till we're a bit better off."

Just then a black boy we had (I must tell you about him some
other time) came sidling along by the wall, as if he were afraid
somebody was going to hit him—poor little devil! I never did.

"What is it, Harry?" said Mary.

"Buggy comin', I bin thinkit."

"Where?"

He pointed up the creek.

"Sure it's a buggy?"

"Yes, missus."

"How many horses?"

"One—two."

We knew that he could hear and see things long before we could.
Mary went and perched on the wood-heap, and shaded her
eyes—though the sun had gone—and peered through between the
eternal grey trunks of the stunted trees on the flat across the creek.
Presently she jumped down and came running in.

"There's someone coming in a buggy, Joe!" she cried, excitedly.
"And both my white table-cloths are rough dry. Harry! put two
flat-irons down to the fire, quick, and put on some more wood. It's

lucky I kept those new sheets packed away. Get up out of that, Joe! What are you sitting grinning like that for? Go and get on another shirt. Hurry——Why, it's only James—by himself."

She stared at me, and I sat there, grinning like a fool.

"Joe!" she said. "Whose buggy is that?"

"Well, I suppose it's yours," I said.

She caught her breath, and stared at the buggy, and then at me again. James drove down out of sight into the crossing, and came up close to the house.

"Oh, Joe! what have you done?" cried Mary. "Why, it's a new double buggy." Then she rushed at me and hugged my head. "Why didn't you tell me, Joe? You poor old boy!—and I've been nagging at you all day!" And she hugged me again.

James got down and started taking the horses out—as if it was an everyday occurrence. I saw the double-barrel gun sticking out from under the seat. He'd stopped to wash the buggy, and I suppose that's what made him grumpy. Mary stood on the veranda, with her eyes twice as big as usual, and breathing hard—taking the buggy in.

James skimmed the harness off, and the horses shook themselves and went down to the dam for a drink. "You'd better look under the seats," growled James, as he took his gun out with great care.

Mary dived for the buggy. There was a dozen of lemonade and ginger-beer in a candle-box from Galletly—James said that Galletly's men had a gallon of beer, and they cheered him, James (I suppose he meant they cheered the buggy), as he drove off; there was a "little bit of a ham" from Pat Murphy, the storekeeper at Home Rule, that he'd "cured himself"—it was the biggest I ever saw; there were three loaves of baker's bread, a cake, and a dozen yards of something "to make up for the children," from Aunt Gertrude at Gulgong; there was a fresh-water cod, that long Dave Regan had caught the night before in the Macquarie River, and sent out packed in salt in a box; there was a holland suit for the black boy, with red braid to trim it; and there was a jar of preserved ginger, and some lollies (sweets) ("for the lil' boy"), and a rum-looking Chinese doll and a rattle ("for lil' girl") from Sun Tong Lee, our storekeeper at Gulgong—James was chummy with Sun Tong Lee, and got his powder and shot and caps there on tick when he was short of money. And James said that the people would have loaded the buggy with "rubbish" if he'd waited. They all seemed glad to see Joe Wilson getting on—and these things did me good.

We got the things inside, and I don't think either of us knew what we were saying or doing for the next half-hour. Then James put his head in and said, in a very injured tone:

"What about my tea? I ain't had anything to speak of since I left Cudgegong. I want some grub."

Then Mary pulled herself together.

"You'll have your tea directly," she said. "Pick up that harness at once, and hang it on the pegs in the skillion; and you, Joe, back that buggy under the end of the veranda, the dew will be on it presently—and we'll put wet bags up in front of it to-morrow, to keep the sun off. And James will have to go back to Cudgegong for the cart—we can't have that buggy to knock about in."

"All right," said James—"anything! Only get me some grub."

Mary fried the fish, in case it wouldn't keep till the morning, and rubbed over the table-cloths, now the irons were hot—James growling all the time—and got out some crockery she had packed away that had belonged to her mother, and set the table in a style that made James uncomfortable.

"I want some grub—not a blooming banquet!" he said. And he growled a lot because Mary wanted him to eat his fish without a knife, "and that sort of tommy-rot." When he'd finished he took his gun, and the black boy, and the dogs, and went out possum-shooting.

When we were alone Mary climbed into the buggy to try the seat, and made me get up alongside her. We hadn't had such a comfortable seat for years; but we soon got down, in case anyone came by, for we began to feel like a pair of fools up there.

Then we sat, side by side, on the edge of the veranda, and talked more than we'd done for years—and there was a good deal of "Do you remember?" in it—and I think we got to understand each other better that night.

And at last Mary said, "Do you know, Joe, why, I feel to-night just—just like I did the day we were married."

And somehow I had that strange, shy sort of feeling too.

THE WRITER WANTS TO SAY A WORD

In writing the first sketch of the Joe Wilson series, which happened to be "Brighten's Sister-in-Law," I had an idea of making Joe Wilson a strong character. Whether he is or not, the reader must judge. It seems to me that the man's natural sentimental selfishness, good-nature, "softness," or weakness—call it which you like—developed as I wrote on.

I know Joe Wilson very well. He has been through deep trouble since the day he brought the double buggy to Lahey's Creek. I met him in Sydney the other day. Tall and straight yet—rather straighter than he had been—dressed in a comfortable, serviceable sac suit of "saddle-tweed," and wearing a new sugar-loaf, cabbage-tree hat, he looked over the hurrying street people calmly as though they were sheep of which he was not in charge, and which were not likely to get "boxed" with his. Not the worst way in which to regard the world.

He talked deliberately and quietly in all that roar and rush. He is a young man yet, comparatively speaking, but it would take little Mary a long while now to pick the grey hairs out of his head, and the process would leave him pretty bald.

In two or three short sketches in another book I hope to complete the story of his life.

JOE WILSON'S MATES

THE GOLDEN GRAVEYARD

Mother Middleton was an awful woman, an "old hand" (transported convict) some said. The prefix "mother" in Australia mostly means "old hag," and is applied in that sense. In early boyhood we understood, from old diggers, that Mother Middleton—in common with most other "old hands"—had been sent out for "knocking a donkey off a hen-roost." We had never seen a donkey. She drank like a fish and swore like a trooper when the spirit moved her; she went on periodical sprees, and swore on most occasions. There was a fearsome yarn, which impressed us greatly as boys, to the effect that once, in her best (or worst) days, she had pulled a mounted policeman off his horse, and half-killed him with a heavy pick-handle, which she used for poking down clothes in her boiler. She said that he had insulted her.

She could still knock down a tree and cut a load of firewood with any bushman; she was square and muscular, with arms like a navvy's; she had often worked shifts, below and on top, with her husband, when he'd be putting down a prospecting shaft without a mate, as he often had to do—because of her mainly. Old diggers said that it was lovely to see how she'd spin up a heavy greenhide bucket full of clay and "tailings," and land and empty it with a twist of her wrist. Most men were afraid of her, and few diggers' wives were strong-minded enough to seek a second row with Mother Middleton. Her voice could be heard right across Golden Gully and Specimen Flat, wheather raised in argument or in friendly greeting. She came to the old Pipeclay diggings with the "rough crowd" (mostly Irish), and when the old and new Pipeclays were worked out, she went with the rush to Gulgong (about the last of the great alluvial or "poor-man's" goldfields) and came back to Pipeclay when the Log Paddock goldfield "broke out," adjacent to the old fields, and so helped prove the truth of the old diggers' saying, that no matter how thoroughly ground has been worked, there is always room for a new Ballarat.

Jimmy Middleton died at Log Paddock, and was buried, about the last, in the little old cemetery—appertaining to the old farming town on the river, about four miles away—which adjoined the district racecourse, in the bush, on the far edge of Specimen Flat.

She conducted the funeral. Some said she made the coffin, and there were alleged jokes to the effect that her tongue had provided the corpse; but this, I think, was unfair and cruel, for she loved Jimmy Middleton in her awful way, and was, for all I ever heard to the contrary, a good wife to him. She then lived in a hut in Log Paddock, on a little money in the bank, and did sewing and washing for single diggers.

I remember hearing her one morning in neighbourly conversation, carried on across the gully, with a selector, Peter Olsen, who was hopelessly slaving to farm a dusty patch in the scrub.

"Why don't you chuck up that dust-hole and go up-country and settle on good land, Peter Olsen? You're only slaving your stomach out here." (She didn't say stomach.)

Peter Olsen (mild-whiskered little man, afraid of his wife): "But then you know my wife is so delicate, Mrs Middleton. I wouldn't like to take her out in the bush."

Mrs Middleton: "Delicate be damned! She's only shamming!" (at her loudest.) "Why don't you kick her off the bed and the book out of her hand, and make her go to work? She's as delicate as I am. Are you a man, Peter Olsen, or a ——?"

This for the edification of the wife and of all within half a mile.

Log Paddock was "petering." There were a few claims still being worked down at the lowest end, where big, red-and-white waste-heaps of clay and gravel, rising above the blue-grey gum-bushes, advertised deep sinking; and little, yellow, clay-stained streams, running towards the creek over the drought-parched surface, told of trouble with the water below—time lost in bailing and extra expense in timbering. And diggers came up with their flannels and moleskins yellow and heavy, and dripping with wet "mullock."

Most of the diggers had gone to other fields, but there were a few prospecting, in parties and singly, out on the flats and amongst the ridges round Pipeclay. Sinking holes in search of a new Ballarat.

Dave Regan—lanky, easygoing bush native; Jim Bently—a bit of a "Flash Jack;" and Andy Page—a character like what Kit (in the *Old Curiosity Shop*) might have been after a voyage to Australia and some Colonial experience. These three were mates from habit and not necessity, for it was all shallow sinking where they worked. They were poking down pot-holes in the scrub in the vicinity of the racecourse, where the sinking was from ten to fifteen feet.

Dave had theories—"ideers" or "notions" he called them; Jim Bently laid claim to none—he ran by sight, not scent, like a

kangaroo-dog. Andy Page—by the way, great admirer and faithful
retainer of Dave Regan—was simple and trusting, but, on critical
occasions, he was apt to be obstinately, uncomfortably, exasperatingly truthful, honest, and he had reverence for higher things.

Dave thought hard all one quiet drowsy Sunday afternoon, and
next morning he, as head of the party, started to sink a hole as close
to the cemetery fence as he dared. It was a nice quiet spot in the
thick scrub, about three panels along the fence from the farthest
corner post from the road. They bottomed here at nine feet, and
found encouraging indications. They "drove" (tunnelled) inwards
at right angles to the fence, and at a point immediately beneath it
they were "making tucker;" a few feet farther and they were making
wages. The old alluvial bottom sloped gently that way. The bottom
here, by the way, was shelving, brownish, rotten rock.

Just inside the cemetery fence, and at right angles to Dave's drive,
lay the shell containing all that was left of the late fiercely lamented
James Middleton, with older graves close at each end. A grave was
supposed to be six feet deep, and local gravediggers had been
conscientious. The old alluvial bottom sloped from nine to fifteen
feet here.

Dave worked the ground all round from the bottom of his shaft,
timbering—i.e., putting in a sapling prop—here and there where he
worked wide; but the "payable dirt" ran in under the cemetery, and
in no other direction.

Dave, Jim, and Andy held a consultation in camp over their pipes
after tea, as a result of which Andy next morning rolled up his swag,
sorrowfully but firmly shook hands with Dave and Jim, and started
to tramp out back to look for work on a sheep station.

This was Dave's theory—drawn from a little experience and
many long yarns with old diggers:—

He had bottomed on a slope to an old original watercourse,
covered with clay and gravel from the hills by centuries of rains to
the depth of from nine or ten to twenty feet; he had bottomed on a
gutter running into the bed of the old buried creek, and carrying
patches and streaks of "wash" or goldbearing dirt. If he went on he
might strike it rich at any stroke of his pick; he might strike the rich
"lead" which was supposed to exist round there. (There was always
supposed to be a rich lead round there somewhere. "There's gold in
them ridges yet—if a man can only git at it," says the toothless old
relic of the Roaring Days.)

Dave might strike a ledge, "pocket," or "pot-hole" holding wash rich with gold. He had prospected on the opposite side of the cemetery, found no gold, and the bottom sloping upwards towards the graveyard. He had prospected at the back of the cemetery, found a few "colours," and the bottom sloping downwards towards the point under the cemetery towards which all indications were now leading him. He had sunk shafts across the road opposite the cemetery frontage and found the sinking twenty feet and not a colour of gold. Probably the whole of the ground under the cemetery was rich—maybe the richest in the district. The old gravediggers had not been gold-diggers—besides, the graves, being six feet, would, none of them, have touched the alluvial bottom. There was nothing strange in the fact that none of the crowd of experienced diggers who rushed the district had thought of the cemetery and racecourse. Old brick chimneys and houses, the clay for the bricks of which had been taken from sites of subsequent goldfields, had been put through the crushing-mill in subsequent years and had yielded "payable gold." Fossicking Chinamen were said to have been the first to detect a case of this kind.

Dave reckoned to strike the "lead," or a shelf or ledge with a good streak of wash lying along it, at a point about forty feet within the cemetery. But a theory in alluvial gold-mining was much like a theory in gambling, in some respects. The theory might be right enough, but old volcanic disturbances—"the shrinkage of the earth's surface," and that sort of old thing—upset everything. You might follow good gold along a ledge, just under the grass, till it suddenly broke off and the continuation might be a hundred feet or so under your nose.

Had the "ground" in the cemetery been "open" Dave would have gone to the point under which he expected the gold to lie, sunk a shaft there, and worked the ground. It would have been the quickest and easiest way—it would have saved the labour and the time lost in dragging heavy buckets of dirt along a low lengthy drive to the shaft outside the fence. But it was very doubtful if the Government could have been moved to open the cemetery even on the strongest evidence of the existence of a rich goldfield under it, and backed by the influence of a number of diggers and their backers—which last was what Dave wished for least of all. He wanted, above all things, to keep the thing shady. Then, again, the old clannish local spirit of the old farming town, rooted in years way back of the goldfields, would have been too strong for the Government, or even a rush of wild diggers.

"We'll work this thing on the strict Q.T.," said Dave.

He and Jim had a consultation by the camp-fire outside their tent. Jim grumbled, in conclusion:

"Well, then, best go under Jimmy Middleton. It's the shortest and straightest, and Jimmy's the freshest, anyway."

Then there was another trouble. How were they to account for the size of the waste-heap of clay on the surface which would be the result of such an extraordinary length of drive or tunnel for shallow sinkings? Dave had an idea of carrying some of the dirt away by night and putting it down a deserted shaft close by; but that would double the labour, and might lead to detection sooner than anything else. There were boys possum-hunting on those flats every night. Then Dave got an idea.

There was supposed to exist—and it has since been proved—another, a second gold-bearing alluvial bottom on that field, and several had tried for it. One, the town watchmaker, had sunk all his money in "duffers," trying for the second bottom. It was supposed to exist at a depth of from eighty to a hundred feet—on solid rock, I suppose. This watchmaker, an Italian, would put men on to sink, and superintend in person, and whenever he came to a little "colour"-showing shelf, or false bottom, thirty or forty feet down—he'd go rooting round and spoil the shaft, and then start to sink another. It was extraordinary that he hadn't the sense to sink straight down, thoroughly test the second bottom, and if he found no gold there, to fill the shaft up to the other bottoms, or build platforms at the proper level and then explore them. He was living in a lunatic asylum the last time I heard of him. And the last time I heard from that field, they were boring the ground like a sieve, with the latest machinery, to find the best place to put down a deep shaft, and finding gold from the second bottom on the bore. But I'm right off the line again.

"Old Pinter," Ballarat digger—his theory on second and other bottoms ran as follows:—

"Ye see *this* here grass surface—this here surface with trees an' grass on it, that we're livin' on, has got nothin' to do with us. This here bottom in the shaller sinkin's that we're workin' on is the slope to the bed of the *new* crick that was on the surface about the time that men was missin'-links. The false bottoms, thirty or forty feet down, kin be said to have been on the surface about the time that men was monkeys. The *secon'* bottom—eighty or a hundred feet down—was on the surface about the time when men was frogs. Now——"

But it's with the missing-link surface we have to do, and had the friends of the local departed known what Dave and Jim were up to they would have regarded them as something lower than missing-links.

"We'll give out we're tryin' for the second bottom," said Dave Regan. "We'll have to rig a fan for air, anyhow, and you don't want air in shallow sinkings."

"And someone will come poking round, and look down the hole and see the bottom," said Jim Bently.

"We must keep 'em away," said Dave. "Tar the bottom, or cover it with tarred canvas, to make it black. Then they won't see it. There's not many diggers left, and the rest are going; they're chucking up the claims in Log Paddock. Besides, I could get drunk and pick rows with the rest and they wouldn't come near me. The farmers ain't in love with us diggers, so they won't bother us. No man has a right to come poking round another man's claim: it ain't ettykit—I'll root up that old ettykit and stand to it—it's rather worn out now, but that's no matter. We'll shift the tent down near the claim and see that no one comes nosing round on Sunday. They'll think we're only some more second-bottom lunatics, like Francea [the mining watchmaker]. We're going to get our fortune out from under that old graveyard, Jim. You leave it all to me till you're born again with brains."

Dave's schemes were always elaborate, and that was why they so often came to the ground. He logged up his windlass platform a little higher, bent about eighty feet of rope to the bole of the windlass, which was a new one, and thereafter, whenever a suspicious-looking party (that is to say, a digger) hove in sight, Dave would let down about forty feet of rope and then wind, with simulated exertion, until the slack was taken up and the rope lifted the bucket from the shallow bottom.

"It would look better to have a whip-pole and a horse, but we can't afford them just yet," said Dave.

But I'm a little behind. They drove straight in under the cemetery, finding good wash all the way. The edge of Jimmy Middleton's box appeared in the top corner of the "face" (the working end) of the drive. They went under the butt-end of the grave. They shoved up the end of the shell with a prop, to prevent the possibility of an accident which might disturb the mound above; they puddled—i.e. rammed—stiff clay up round the edges to keep the loose earth from dribbling down; and having given the bottom of the coffin a good coat of tar, they got over, or rather under, an unpleasant matter.

Jim Bently smoked and burnt paper during his shift below, and grumbled a good deal. "Blowed if I ever thought I'd be rooting for gold down among the blanky dead men," he said. But the dirt panned out better every dish they washed, and Dave worked the "wash" out right and left as they drove.

But, one fine morning, who should come along but the very last man whom Dave wished to see round there—"Old Pinter" (James Poynton), Californian and Victorian digger of the old school. He'd been prospecting down the creek, carried his pick over his shoulder—threaded through the eye in the heft of his big-bladed, short-handled shovel that hung behind—and his gold-dish under his arm.

" 'Ello, Dave!" said Pinter, after looking with mild surprise at the size of Dave's waste-heap. "Tryin' for the second bottom?"

"Yes," said Dave, guttural.

Pinter dropped his tools with a clatter at the foot of the waste-heap and scratched under his ear like an old cockatoo, which bird he resembled. Then he went to the windlass, and resting his hands on his knees, he peered down, while Dave stood by helpless and hopeless.

Pinter straightened himself, blinking like an owl, and looked carelessly over the graveyard.

"Tryin' for a secon' bottom," he reflected absently. "Eh, Dave?"

Dave only stood and looked black.

Pinter tilted back his head and scratched the roots of his chin-feathers, which stuck out all round like a dirty, ragged fan held horizontally.

"Kullers is safe," reflected Pinter.

"All right," snapped Dave. "I suppose we must let him into it."

"Kullers" was a big American buck nigger, and had been Pinter's mate for some time—Pinter was a man of odd mates; and what Pinter meant was that Kullers was safe to hold his tongue.

Next morning Pinter and his coloured mate appeared on the ground early, Pinter with some tools and the nigger with a windlass-bole on his shoulders. Pinter chose a spot about three panels or thirty feet along the other fence, the back fence of the cemetery, and started his hole. He lost no time for the sake of appearances; he sunk his shaft and started to drive straight for the point under the cemetery for which Dave was making; he gave out that he had bottomed on good "indications" running in the other direction, and would work the ground outside the fence. Meanwhile Dave rigged a fan—partly for the sake of appearances, but mainly because his and Jim's lively imaginations made the air in the drive worse than it really was.

Dave was working the ground on each side as he went, when one morning a thought struck him that should have struck him the day Pinter went to work. He felt mad that it hadn't struck him sooner.

Pinter and Kullers had also shifted their tent down into a nice quiet place in the bush close handy; so, early next Sunday morning, while Pinter and Kullers were asleep, Dave posted Jim Bently to watch their tent, and whistle an alarm if they stirred, and then dropped down into Pinter's hole and saw at a glance what he was up to.

After that Dave lost no time: he drove straight on, encouraged by the thuds of Pinter's and Kullers' picks drawing nearer. They would strike his tunnel at right angles. Both parties worked long hours, only knocking off to fry a bit of steak in the pan, boil the billy, and throw themselves dressed on their bunks to get a few hours' sleep. Pinter had practical experience and a line clear of graves, and he made good time. The two parties now found it more comfortable to be not on speaking terms. Individually they grew furtive, and began to feel criminal like—at least Dave and Jim did. They'd start if a horse stumbled through the bush, and expected to see a mounted policeman ride up at any moment and hear him ask questions. They had drive about thirty-five feet when, one Saturday afternoon, the strain became too great, and Dave and Jim got drunk. The spree lasted over Sunday, and on Monday morning they felt too shaky to come to work, and had more drink. On Monday afternoon, Kullers, whose shift it was below, stuck his pick through the face of his drive into the wall of Dave's, about four feet from the end of it: the clay flaked away, leaving a hole as big as a wash-hand basin. They knocked off for the day and decided to let the other party take the offensive.

Tuesday morning Dave and Jim came to work, still feeling shaky. Jim went below, crawled along the drive, lit his candle, and stuck it in the spiked iron socket and the spike in the wall of the drive, quite close to the hole, without noticing either the hole or the increased freshness of the air. He started picking away at the "face" and scraping the clay back from under his feet, and didn't hear Kullers come to work. Kullers came in softly and decided to try a bit of cheerful bluff. He stuck his great round black face through the hole, the whites of his eyes rolling horribly in the candle-light, and said, with a deep guffaw:

" 'Ullo! you dar'?"

No bandicoot ever went into his hole with the dogs after him quicker than Jim came out of his. He scrambled up the shaft by the foot-holes, and sat on the edge of the waste-heap, looking very pale.

"What's the matter?" asked Dave. "Have you seen a ghost?"

"I've seen the—the devil!" gasped Jim. "I'm—I'm done with this here ghoul business."

The parties got on speaking terms again. Dave was very warm, but Jim's language was worse. Pinter scratched his chin-feathers reflectively till the other party cooled. There was no appealing to the commissioner for goldfields; they were outside all law, whether of the goldfields or otherwise—so they did the only thing possible and sensible, they joined forces and became "Poynton, Regan & Party." They agreed to work the ground from the separate shafts, and decided to go ahead, irrespective of appearances, and get as much dirt out and cradled as possible before the inevitable exposure came along. They found plenty of "payable dirt," and soon the drive ended in a cluster of roomy chambers. They timbered up many coffins of various ages, burnt tarred canvas and brown paper, and kept the fan going. Outside they paid the storekeeper with difficulty and talked of hard times.

But one fine sunny morning, after about a week of partnership, they got a bad scare. Jim and Kullers were below, getting out dirt for all they were worth, and Pinter and Dave at their windlasses, when who should march down from the cemetery gate but Mother Middleton herself. She was a hard woman to look at. She still wore the old-fashioned crinoline and her hair in a greasy net; and on this as on most other sober occasions, she wore the expression of a rough Irish navvy who has just enough drink to make him nasty, and is looking out for an excuse for a row. She had a stride like a grenadier. A digger had once measured her step by her footprints in the mud where she had stepped across a gutter: it measured three feet from toe to heel.

She marched to the grave of Jimmy Middleton, laid a dingy bunch of flowers thereon, with the gesture of an angry man banging his fist down on the table, turned on her heel, and marched out. The diggers were dirt beneath her feet. Presently they heard her drive on in her spring-cart on her way into town, and they drew breaths of relief.

It was afternoon. Dave and Pinter were feeling tired, and were just deciding to knock off work for that day when they heard a scuffling in the direction of the different shafts, and both Jim and Kullers dropped down and bundled in in a great hurry. Jim chuckled in a silly way, as if there was something funny, and Kullers guffawed in sympathy.

"What's up now?" demanded Dave apprehensively.

"Mother Middleton," said Jim; "she's blind mad drunk, and she's got a bottle in one hand and a new pitchfork in the other, that she's bringing out for someone."

"How the hell did she drop to it?" exclaimed Pinter.

"Dunno," said Jim. "Anyway, she's coming for us. Listen to her!"

They didn't have to listen hard. The language which came down the shaft—they weren't sure which one—and along the drives was enough to scare up the dead and make them take to the bush.

"Why didn't you fools make off into the bush and give us a chance, instead of giving her a lead here?" asked Dave.

Jim and Kullers began to wish they had done so.

Mrs Middleton began to throw stones down the shaft—it was Pinter's—and they, even the oldest and most anxious, began to grin in spite of themselves, for they knew she couldn't hurt them from the surface, and that, though she had been a working digger herself, she couldn't fill both shafts before the fumes of liquor overtook her.

"I wonder which shaf' she'll come down," asked Kullers in a tone befitting the place and occasion.

"You'd better go and watch your shaft, Pinter," said Dave, "and Jim and I'll watch mine."

"I—I won't," said Pinter hurriedly. "I'm—I'm a modest man."

Then they heard a clang in the direction of Pinter's shaft.

"She's thrown her bottle down," said Dave.

Jim crawled along the drive a piece, urged by curiosity, and returned hurriedly.

"She's broke the pitchfork off short, to use in the drive, and I believe she's coming down."

"Her crinoline'll handicap her," said Pinter vacantly, "that's a comfort."

"She's took it off!" said Dave excitedly; and peering along

Pinter's drive, they saw first an elastic-sided boot, then a red-striped stocking, then a section of scarlet petticoat.

"Lemme out!" roared Pinter, lurching forward and making a swimming motion with his hands in the direction of Dave's drive. Kullers was already gone and Jim well on the way. Dave, lanky and awkward, scrambled up the shaft last. Mrs Middleton made good time, considering she had the darkness to face and didn't know the workings, and when Dave reached the top he had a tear in the leg of his moleskins, and the blood ran from a nasty scratch. But he didn't wait to argue over the price of a new pair of trousers. He made off through the bush in the direction of an encouraging whistle thrown back by Jim.

"She's too drunk to get her story listened to to-night," said Dave. "But to-morrow she'll bring the neighbourhood down on us."

"And she's enough, without the neighbourhood," reflected Pinter.

Some time after dark they returned cautiously, reconnoitred their camp, and after hiding in a hollow log such things as they couldn't carry, they rolled up their tents like the Arabs, and silently stole away.

THE CHINAMAN'S GHOST

"Simple as striking matches," said Dave Regan, bushman; "but it gave me the biggest scare I ever had—except, perhaps, the time I stumbled in the dark into a six-foot digger's hole, which might have been eighty feet deep for all I knew when I was falling. (There was an eighty-foot shaft left open close by.)

"It was the night of the day after the Queen's birthday. I was sinking a shaft with Jim Bently and Andy Page on the old Redclay goldfield, and we camped in a tent on the creek. Jim and me went to some races that was held at Peter Anderson's pub, about four miles across the ridges, on Queen's birthday. Andy was a quiet sort of chap, a teetotaller, and we'd disgusted him the last time he was out for a holiday with us, so he stayed at home and washed and mended his clothes, and read an arithmetic book. (He used to keep the accounts, and it took him most of his spare time.)

"Jim and me had a pretty high time. We all got pretty tight after the races, and I wanted to fight Jim, or Jim wanted to fight me—I don't remember which. We were old chums, and we nearly always wanted to fight each other when we got a bit on, and we'd fight if we weren't stopped. I remember once Jim got maudlin drunk and begged and prayed of me to fight him, as if he was praying for his life. Tom Tarrant, the coach-driver, used to say that Jim and me must be related, else we wouldn't hate each other so much when we were tight and truthful.

"Anyway, this day, Jim got the sulks, and caught his horse and went home early in the evening. My dog went home with him, too; I must have been carrying on pretty bad to disgust the dog.

"Next evening I got disgusted with myself, and started to walk home. I'd lost my hat, so Peter Anderson lent me an old one of his, that he'd worn on Ballarat he said: it was a hard, straw, flat, broad-brimmed affair, and fitted my headache pretty tight. Peter gave me a small flask of whisky to help me home. I had to go across some flats and up a long dark gully called Murderer's Gully, and over a gap called Dead Man's Gap, and down the ridge and gullies of Redclay Creek. The lonely flats were covered with blue-grey gum-bush, and looked ghostly enough in the moonlight, and I was pretty shaky, but I had a pull at the flask and a mouthful of water at a creek and felt right enough. I began to whistle and then to sing: I never used to sing unless I thought I was a couple of miles out of earshot of anyone.

"Murderer's Gully was deep and pretty dark most times, and of course it was haunted. Women and children wouldn't go through it after dark; and even me, when I'd grown up, I'd hold my back pretty holler, and whistle, and walk quick going along there at night-time. We're all afraid of ghosts, but we won't let on.

"Someone had skinned a dead calf during the day and left it on the track, and it gave me a jump, I promise you. It looked like two corpses laid out naked. I finished the whisky and started up over the gap. All of a sudden a great "old man" kangaroo went across the track with a thud-thud, and up the siding, and that startled me. Then the naked, white, glistening trunk of a stringy-bark tree, where someone had stripped off a sheet of bark, started out from a bend in the track in a shaft of moonlight, and that gave me a jerk. I was pretty shaky before I started. There was a Chinaman's grave close by the track on the top of the gap. An old Chow had lived in a but there for many years, and fossicked on the old diggings, and one day he was found dead in the hut, and the Government gave someone a pound to bury him. When I was a nipper we reckoned that his ghost haunted the gap, and cursed in Chinese because the bones hadn't been sent home to China. It was a lonely, ghostly place enough.

"It had been a smotheringly hot day and very close coming across the flats and up the gully—not a breath of air; but now as I got higher I saw signs of the thunderstorm we'd expected all day, and felt the breath of a warm breeze on my face. When I got into the top of the gap the first thing I saw was something white amongst the dark bushes over the spot where the Chinaman's grave was, and I stood staring at it with both eyes. It moved out of the shadow presently, and I saw that it was a white bullock, and I felt relieved. I'd hardly felt relieved when, all at once, there came a 'pat-pat-pat' of running feet close behind me! I jumped round quick, but there was nothing there, and while I stood staring all ways for Sunday, there came a 'pat-pat,' then a pause, and then 'pat-pat-pat-pat' behind me again: it was like someone dodging and running off that time. I started to walk down the track pretty fast, but hadn't gone a dozen yards when 'pat-pat-pat,' it was close behind me again. I jerked my eyes over my shoulder but kept my legs going. There was nothing behind, but I fancied I saw something slip into the bush to the right. It must have been the moonlight on the moving boughs; there was a good breeze blowing now. I got down to a more level track, and was making across a spur to the main road, when 'pat-pat, pat-pat-pat, pat-pat-pat!' it was after me again. Then I began to run—and it began to run, too! 'pat-pat-pat' after me all the time. I hadn't time to look round. Over the spur and down the siding and across the flat to the road I went as fast as I could split my legs apart. I had a scared idea that I was getting a touch of the 'jim-jams,' and that frightened me more than any outside ghost could have done. I stumbled a few times, and saved myself, but, just before I reached the road, I fell slithering on to my hands on the grass and gravel. I thought I'd broken both my wrists. I stayed for a moment on my hands and knees, quaking and listening, squinting round like a great goanna; I couldn't hear nor see anything. I picked myself up, and had hardly got on one end, when 'pat-pat!' it was after me again. I must have run a mile and a half altogether that night. It was still about three-quarters of a mile to the camp, and I ran till my heart beat in my head and my lungs choked up in my throat. I saw our tent-fire and took off my hat to run faster. The footsteps stopped, then something about the hat touched my fingers, and I stared at it—and the thing dawned on me. I hadn't noticed at Peter Anderson's—my head was too swimmy to notice anything. It was an old hat of the style that the first diggers used to wear, with a couple of loose ribbon ends, three or four inches long, from the band behind. As long as I walked quietly through the gully, and there was no wind, the tails didn't flap, but when I got up into the breeze, they flapped or were still according to how the wind lifted them or pressed them down flat on the brim. And when I ran they tapped all the time; and the hat being tight on my head, the tapping of the ribbon ends against the straw sounded loud, of course.

"I sat down on a log for a while to get some of my wind back and cool down, and then I went to the camp as quietly as I could, and had a long drink of water.

" 'You seem to be a bit winded, Dave,' said Jim Bently, 'and mighty thirsty. Did the Chinaman's ghost chase you?'

"I told him not to talk rot, and went into the tent, and lay down on my bunk, and had a good rest."

THE LOADED DOG

Dave Regan, Jim Bently, and Andy Page were sinking a shaft at Stony Creek in search of a rich gold quartz reef which was supposed to exist in the vicinity. There is always a rich reef supposed to exist in the vicinity; the only questions are whether it is ten feet or hundreds beneath the surface, and in which direction. They had struck some pretty solid rock, also water which kept them baling. They used the old-fashioned blasting-powder and time-fuse. They'd make a sausage or cartridge of blasting-powder in a skin of strong calico or canvas, the mouth sewn and bound round the end of the fuse; they'd dip the cartridge in melted tallow to make it watertight, get the drill-hole as dry as possible, drop in the cartridge with some dry dust, and wad and ram with stiff clay and broken brick. Then they'd light the fuse and get out of the hole and wait. The result was usually an ugly pot-hole in the bottom of the shaft and half a barrow-load of broken rock.

There was plenty of fish in the creek, fresh-water bream, cod, cat-fish, and tailers. The party were fond of fish, and Andy and Dave of fishing. Andy would fish for three hours at a stretch if encouraged by a "nibble" or a "bite" now and then—say once in twenty minutes. The butcher was always willing to give meat in exchange for fish when they caught more than they could eat; but now it was winter, and these fish wouldn't bite. However, the creek was low, just a chain of muddy waterholes, from the hole with a few bucketfuls in it to the sizable pool with an average depth of six or seven feet, and they could get fish by bailing out the smaller holes or muddying up the water in the larger ones till the fish rose to the surface. There was the cat-fish, with spikes growing out of the sides of its head, and if you got pricked you'd know it, as Dave said. Andy took off his boots, tucked up his trousers, and went into a hole one day to stir up the mud with his feet, and he knew it. Dave scooped one out with his hand and got pricked, and he knew it too; his arm swelled, and the pain throbbed up into his shoulder, and down into his stomach, too, he said, like a toothache he had once, and kept him awake for two nights—only the toothache pain had a "burred edge," Dave said.

Dave got an idea.

"Why not blow the fish up in the big waterhole with a cartridge?" he said. "I'll try it."

He thought the thing out and Andy Page worked it out. Andy usually put Dave's theories into practice if they were practicable, or bore the blame for the failure and the chaffing of his mates if they weren't.

He made a cartridge about three times the size of those they used in the rock. Jim Bently said it was big enough to blow the bottom out of the river. The inner skin was of stout calico; Andy stuck the end of a six-foot piece of fuse well down in the powder and bound the mouth of the bag firmly to it with whipcord. The idea was to sink the cartridge in the water with the open end of the fuse attached to a float on the surface, ready for lighting. Andy dipped the cartridge in melted bees'-wax to make it watertight. "We'll have to leave it some time before we light it," said Dave, "to give the fish time to get over their scare when we put it in, and come nosing round again; so we'll want it well watertight."

Round the cartridge Andy, at Dave's suggestion, bound a strip of sail canvas—that they used for making water-bags—to increase the force of the explosion, and round that he pasted layers of stiff brown paper—on the plan of the sort of fireworks we called "gun-crackers." He let the paper dry in the sun, then he sewed a covering of two thicknesses of canvas over it, and bound the thing from end to end with stout fishing-line. Dave's schemes were elaborate, and he often worked his inventions out to nothing. The cartridge was rigid and solid enough now—a formidable bomb; but Andy and Dave wanted to be sure. Andy sewed on another layer of canvas, dipped the cartridge in melted tallow, twisted a length of fencing-wire round it as an afterthought, dipped it in tallow again, and stood it carefully against a tent-peg, where he'd know where to find it, and wound the fuse loosely round it. Then he went to the camp-fire to try some potatoes which were boiling in their jackets in a billy, and to see about frying some chops for dinner. Dave and Jim were at work in the claim that morning.

They had a big black young retriever dog—or rather an overgrown pup, a big, foolish, four-footed mate, who was always slobbering round them and lashing their legs with his heavy tail that swung round like a stock-whip. Most of his head was usually a red, idiotic slobbering grin of appreciation of his own silliness. He seemed to take life, the world, his two-legged mates, and his own instinct as a huge joke. He'd retrieve anything; he carted back most of the camp rubbish that Andy threw away. They had a cat that died in hot weather, and Andy threw it a good distance away in the scrub; and early one morning the dog found the cat, after it had been dead a week or so, and carried it back to camp, and laid it just inside the tent-flaps, where it could best make its presence known when the mates should rise and begin to sniff suspiciously in the sickly smothering atmosphere of the summer sunrise. He used to retrieve them when they went in swimming; he'd jump in after them, and take their hands in his mouth, and try to swim out with them, and scratch their naked bodies with his paws. They loved him for his good-heartedness and his foolishness, but when they wished to enjoy a swim they had to tie him up in camp.

He watched Andy with great interest all the morning making the cartridge, and hindered him considerably, trying to help; but about noon he went off to the claim to see how Dave and Jim were getting on, and to come home to dinner with them. Andy saw them coming, and put a panful of mutton-chops on the fire. Andy was cook to-day; Dave and Jim stood with their backs to the fire, as bushmen do in all weathers, waiting till dinner should be ready. The retriever went nosing round after something he seemed to have missed.

Andy's brain still worked on the cartridge; his eye was caught by the glare of an empty kerosene-tin lying in the bushes, and it struck him that it wouldn't be a bad idea to sink the cartridge packed with clay, sand, or stones in the tin, to increase the force of the explosion. He may have been all out, from a scientific point of view, but the notion looked all right to him. Jim Bently, by the way, wasn't interested in their "damned silliness." Andy noticed an empty treacle-tin—the sort with the little tin neck or spout soldered on to the top for the convenience of pouring out the treacle—and it struck him that this would have made the best kind of cartridge-case: he would only have had to pour in the powder, stick the fuse in through the neck, and cork and seal it with bees'-wax. He was turning to suggest this to Dave, when Dave glanced over his shoulder to see how the chops were doing—and bolted. He explained afterwards that he thought he heard the pan spluttering extra, and looked to see if the chops were burning. Jim Bently looked behind and bolted after Dave. Andy stood stock-still, staring after them.

"Run, Andy! Run!" they shouted back at him. "Run! Look behind you, you fool!" Andy turned slowly and looked, and there, close behind him, was the retriever with the cartridge in his mouth—wedged into his broadest and silliest grin. And that wasn't all. The dog had come round the fire to Andy, and the loose end of the fuse had trailed and waggled over the burning sticks into the blaze; Andy had slit and nicked the firing end of the fuse well, and now it was hissing and spitting properly.

Andy's legs started with a jolt; his legs started before his brain did, and he made after Dave and Jim. And the dog followed Andy.

Dave and Jim were good runners—Jim the best—for a short distance; Andy was slow and heavy, but he had the strength and the wind and could last. The dog capered round him, delighted as a dog could be to find his mates, as he thought, on for a frolic. Dave and Jim kept shouting back, "Don't foller us! Don't foller us, you coloured fool!" But Andy kept on, no matter how they dodged. They could never explain, any more than the dog, why they followed each other, but so they ran, Dave keeping in Jim's track in all its turnings, Andy after Dave, and the dog circling round Andy—the live fuse swishing in all directions and hissing and spluttering and stinking. Jim yelling to Dave not to follow him, Dave shouting to Andy to go in another direction—to "spread out," and Andy roaring at the dog to go home. Then Andy's brain began to work, stimulated by the crisis: he tried to get a running kick at the dog, but the dog dodged; he snatched up sticks and stones and threw them at the dog and ran on again. The retriever saw that he'd made a mistake about Andy, and left him and bounded after Dave. Dave, who had the presence of mind to think that the fuse's time wasn't up yet, made a dive and a grab for the dog, caught him by the tail, and as he swung round snatched the cartridge out of his mouth and flung it as far as he could; the dog immediately bounded after it and retrieved it. Dave roared and cursed at the dog, who, seeing that Dave was offended, left him and went after Jim, who was well ahead. Jim swung to a sapling and went up it like a native bear; it was a young sapling, and Jim couldn't safely get more than ten or twelve feet from the ground. The dog laid the cartridge, as carefully as if it were a kitten, at the foot of the sapling, and capered and leaped and whooped joyously round under Jim. The big pup reckoned that this was part of the lark—he was all right now—it was Jim who was out for a spree. The fuse sounded as if it were going a mile a minute. Jim tried to climb higher and the sapling bent and cracked. Jim fell on his feet and ran. The dog swooped on the cartridge and followed. It all took but a very few moments. Jim ran to a digger's hole, about ten feet deep, and dropped down into it—landing on soft mud—and was safe. The dog grinned sardonically down on him, over the edge, for a moment, as if he thought it would be a good lark to drop the cartridge down on Jim.

"Go away, Tommy," said Jim feebly, "go away."

The dog bounded off after Dave, who was the only one in sight now; Andy had dropped behind a log, where he lay flat on his face, having suddenly remembered a picture of the Russo-Turkish war with a circle of Turks lying flat on their faces (as if they were ashamed) round a newly-arrived shell.

There was a small hotel or shanty on the creek, on the main road, not far from the claim. Dave was desperate, the time flew much faster in his stimulated imagination than it did in reality, so he made for the shanty. There were several casual bushmen on the veranda and in the bar; Dave rushed into the bar, banging the door to behind him. "My dog!" he gasped, in reply to the astonished stare of the publican, "the blanky retriever—he's got a live cartridge in his mouth——"

The retriever, finding the front door shut against him, had bounded round and in by the back way, and now stood smiling in the doorway leading from the passage, the cartridge still in his mouth and the fuse spluttering. They burst out of that bar. Tommy bounded first after one and then after another, for, being a young dog, he tried to make friends with everybody.

The bushmen ran round corners, and some shut themselves in the stable. There was a new weather-board and corrugated-iron kitchen and wash-house on piles in the backyard, with some women washing clothes inside. Dave and the publican bundled in there and shut the door—the publican cursing Dave and calling him a crimson fool, in hurried tones, and wanting to know what the hell he came here for.

The retriever went in under the kitchen, amongst the piles, but, luckily for those inside, there was a vicious yellow mongrel cattle-dog sulking and nursing his nastiness under there—a sneaking, fighting, thieving canine, whom neighbours had tried for years to shoot or poison. Tommy saw his danger—he'd had experience from this dog—and started out and across the yard, still sticking to the cartridge. Half-way across the yard the yellow dog caught him and nipped him. Tommy dropped the cartridge, gave one terrified yell, and took to the bush. The yellow dog followed him to the fence and then ran back to see what he had dropped. Nearly a dozen other dogs came from round all the corners and under the buildings— spidery, thievish, cold-blooded kangaroo dogs, mongrel sheep- and cattle-dogs, vicious black and yellow dogs—that slip after you in the dark, nip your heels, and vanish without explaining—and yapping, yelping small fry. They kept at a respectable distance round the nasty yellow dog, for it was dangerous to go near him when he thought he had found something which might be good for a dog or cat. He sniffed at the cartridge twice, and was just taking a third cautious sniff when——

It was very good blasting-powder—a new brand that Dave had recently got up from Sydney; and the cartridge had been excellently well made. Andy was very patient and painstaking in all he did, and nearly as handy as the average sailor with needles, twine, canvas and rope.

Bushmen say that that kitchen jumped off its piles and on again. When the smoke and dust cleared away, the remains of the nasty yellow dog were lying against the paling fence of the yard looking as if he had been kicked into a fire by a horse and afterwards rolled in the dust under a barrow, and finally thrown against the fence from a distance. Several saddle-horses, which had been "hanging-up" round the veranda, were galloping wildly down the road in clouds of dust, with broken bridle-reins flying; and from a circle round the outskirts, from every point of the compass in the scrub, came the yelping of dogs. Two of them went home, to the place where they were born, thirty miles away, and reached it the same night and stayed there; it was not till towards evening that the rest came back cautiously to make inquiries. One was trying to walk on two legs, and most of 'em looked more or less singed; and a little, singed, stumpy-tailed dog, who had been in the habit of hopping the back half of him along on one leg, had reason to be glad that he'd saved up the other leg all those years, for he needed it now. There was one old one-eyed cattle-dog round that shanty for years afterwards, who couldn't stand the smell of a gun being cleaned. He it was who had taken an interest, only second to that of the yellow dog, in the cartridge. Bushmen said that it was amusing to slip up on his blind side and stick a dirty ramrod under his nose: he wouldn't wait to bring his solitary eye to bear—he'd take to the bush and stay out all night.

For half an hour or so after the explosion there were several bushmen round behind the stable who crouched, doubled up, against the wall, or rolled gently on the dust, trying to laugh without shrieking. There were two white women in hysterics at the house, and a half-caste rushing aimlessly round with a dipper of cold water. The publican was holding his wife tight and begging her between her squawks, to "hold up for my sake, Mary, or I'll lam the life out of ye."

Dave decided to apologize later on, "when things had settled a bit," and went back to camp. And the dog that had done it all, Tommy, the great, idiotic mongrel retriever, came slobbering round Dave and lashing his legs with his tail, and trotted home after him, smiling his broadest, longest, and reddest smile of amiability, and apparently satisfied for one afternoon with the fun he'd had.

Andy chained the dog up securely, and cooked some more chops, while Dave went to help Jim out of the hole.

And most of this is why, for years afterwards, lanky, easygoing bushmen, riding lazily past Dave's camp, would cry, in a lazy drawl and with just a hint of the nasal twang:

" 'Ello, Da-a-ve! How's the fishin' getting on, Da-a-ve?"

POISONOUS JIMMY GETS LEFT

I

DAVE REGAN'S YARN

"When we got tired of digging about Mudgee-Budgee, and getting no gold," said Dave Regan, bushman, "me and my mate, Jim Bently, decided to take a turn at droving; so we went with Bob

Baker, the drover, overland with a big mob of cattle, way up into northern Queensland.

"We couldn't get a job on the home track, and we spent most of our money, like a pair of fools, at a pub at a town way up over the border, where they had a flash barmaid from Brisbane. We sold our packhorses and pack-saddles, and rode out of that town with our swags on our riding-horses in front of us. We had another spree at another place, and by the time we got near New South Wales we were pretty well stumped.

"Just the other side of Mulgatown, near the border, we came on a big mob of cattle in a paddock, and a party of drovers camped on the creek. They had brought the cattle down from the north and were going no farther with them; their boss had ridden on into Mulgatown to get the cheques to pay them off, and they were waiting for him.

"'And Poisonous Jimmy is waiting for us,' said one of them.

"Poisonous Jimmy kept a shanty a piece along the road from their camp towards Mulgatown. He was called 'Poisonous Jimmy' perhaps on account of his liquor, or perhaps because he had a job of poisoning dingoes on a station in the Bogan scrubs at one time. He was a sharp publican. He had a girl, and they said that whenever a shearing-shed cut out on his side and he saw the shearers coming along the road, he'd say to the girl, 'Run and get your best frock on, Mary! Here's the shearers comin'.' And if a chequeman wouldn't drink he'd try to get him into his bar and shout for him till he was too drunk to keep his hands out of his pockets.

"'But he won't get us,' said another of the drovers. 'I'm going to ride straight into Mulgatown and send my money home by the post as soon as I get it.'

"'You've always said that, Jack,' said the first drover.

"We yarned a while, and had some tea, and then me and Jim got on our horses and rode on. We were burned to bricks and ragged and dusty and parched up enough, and so were our horses. We only had a few shillings to carry us four or five hundred miles home, but it was mighty hot and dusty, and we felt that we must have a drink at the shanty. This was west of the sixpenny-line at that time—all drinks were a shilling along here.

"Just before we reached the shanty I got an idea.

"'We'll plant our swags in the scrub,' I said to Jim.

"'What for?' said Jim.

"'Never mind—you'll see,' I said.

"So we unstrapped our swags and hid them in the mulga scrub by the side of the road; then we rode on to the shanty, got down, and hung our horses to the veranda-posts.

" 'Poisonous' came out at once, with a smile on him that would have made anybody home-sick.

"He was a short nuggety man, and could use his hands, they said; he looked as if he'd be a nasty, vicious, cool customer in a fight—he wasn't the sort of man you'd care to try and swindle a second time. He had a monkey shave when he shaved, but now it was all frill and stubble—like a bush fence round a stubble-field. He had a broken nose, and a cunning, sharp, suspicious eye that squinted, and a cold stony eye that seemed fixed. If you didn't know him well you might talk to him for five minutes, looking at him in the cold stony eye, and then discover that it was the sharp cunning little eye that was watching you all the time. It was awful embarrassing. It must have made him awkward to deal with in a fight.

" 'Good day, mates,' he said.

" 'Good day,' we said.

" 'It's hot.'

" 'It's hot.'

"We went into the bar, and Poisonous got behind the counter.

" 'What are you going to have?' he asked, rubbing up his glasses with a rag.

"We had two long beers.

" 'Never mind that,' said Poisonous, seeing me put my hand in my pocket; 'it's my shout. I don't suppose your boss is back yet? I saw him go in to Mulgatown this morning.'

" 'No, he ain't back,' I said; 'I wish he was. We're getting tired of waiting for him. We'll give him another hour, and then some of us will have to ride in to see whether he's got on the booze, and get hold of him if he has.'

" 'I suppose you're waiting for your cheques?' he said, turning to fix some bottles on the shelf.

" 'Yes,' I said, 'we are;' and I winked at Jim, and Jim winked back as solemn as an owl.

"Poisonous asked us all about the trip, and how long we'd been on the track, and what sort of a boss we had, dropping the questions offhand now an' then, as for the sake of conversation. We could see that he was trying to get at the size of our supposed cheques, so we answered accordingly.

" 'Have another drink,' he said, and he filled the pewters up

again. 'It's up to me,' and he set to work boring out the glasses with
his rag, as if he was short-handed and the bar was crowded with
customers, and screwing up his face into what I suppose he
considered an innocent or unconscious expression. The girl began to
sidle in and out with a smart frock and a see-you-after-dark smirk
on.

" 'Have you had dinner?' she asked. We could have done with a
good meal, but it was too risky—the drovers' boss might come along
while we were at dinner and get into conversation with Poisonous.
So we said we'd had dinner.

"Poisonous filled our pewters again in an offhand way.

" 'I wish the boss would come,' said Jim with a yawn. 'I want to
get into Mulgatown to-night, and I want to get some shirts and
things before I go in. I ain't got a decent rag to me back. I don't
suppose there's ten bob amongst the lot of us.'

"There was a general store back on the creek, near the drovers'
camp.

" 'Oh, go to the store and get what you want,' said Poisonous,
taking a sovereign from the till and tossing it on to the counter. 'You
can fix it up with me when your boss comes. Bring your mates
along.'

" 'Thank you,' said Jim, taking up the sovereign carelessly and
dropping it into his pocket.

" 'Well, Jim,' I said, 'suppose we get back to camp and see how
the chaps are getting on?'

" 'All right,' said Jim.

" 'Tell them to come down and get a drink,' said Poisonous; 'or,
wait, you can take some beer along to them if you like,' and he gave
us half a gallon of beer in a billy-can. He knew what the first drink
meant with bushmen back from a long dry trip.

"We got on our horses, I holding the billy very carefully, and rode
back to where our swags were.

" 'I say,' said Jim, when we'd strapped the swags to the saddles,
'suppose we take the beer back to those chaps: it's meant for them,
and it's only a fair thing, anyway—we've got as much as we can hold
till we get into Mulgatown.'

" 'It might get them into a row,' I said, 'and they seem decent
chaps. Let's hang the billy on a twig, and that old swagman that's
coming along will think there's angels in the bush.'

" 'Oh! what's a row?' said Jim. 'They can take care of themselves;

they'll have the beer anyway and a lark with Poisonous when they take the can back and it comes to explanations. I'll ride back to them.'

"So Jim rode back to the drovers' camp with the beer, and when he came back to me he said that the drovers seemed surprised, but they drank good luck to him.

"We rode round through the mulga behind the shanty and came out on the road again on the Mulgatown side: we only stayed at Mulgatown to buy some tucker and tobacco, then we pushed on and camped for the night about seven miles on the safe side of the town."

II

TOLD BY ONE OF THE OTHER DROVERS

"Talkin' o' Poisonous Jimmy, I can tell you a yarn about him. We'd brought a mob of cattle down for a squatter the other side of Mulgatown. We camped about seven miles the other side of the town, waitin' for the station-hands to come and take charge of the stock, while the boss rode on into town to draw our money. Some of us was goin' back, though in the end we all went into Mulgatown and had a booze up with the boss. But while we was waitin' there come along two fellers that had been drivin' up north. They yarned a while, an' then went on to Poisonous Jimmy's place, an' in about an hour one on 'em come ridin' back with a can of beer that he said Poisonous had sent for us. We all knew Jimmy's little games—the beer was a bait to get us on the drunk at his place; but we drunk the beer, and reckoned to have a lark with him afterwards. When the boss come back, an' the station-hands to take the bullocks, we started into Mulgatown. We stopped outside Poisonous's place an' handed the can to the girl that was grinnin' on the veranda. Poisonous come out with a grin on him like a parson with a broken nose.

" 'Good day, boys!' he says.

" 'Good day, Poisonous,' we says.

" 'It's hot,' he says.

" 'It's blanky hot,' I says.

"He seemed to expect us to get down. 'Where are you off to?' he says.

" 'Mulgatown,' I says. 'It will be cooler there,' and we sung out, 'So-long, Poisonous!' and rode on.

"He stood starin' for a minute; then he started shoutin', 'Hi! hi there!' after us, but we took no notice, an' rode on. When we looked back last he was runnin' into the scrub with a bridle in his hand.

"We jogged along easily till we got within a mile of Mulgatown, when we heard somebody gallopin' after us, an' lookin' back we saw it was Poisonous.

"He was too mad and too winded to speak at first, so he rode along with us a bit gasping: then he burst out.

" 'Where's them other two carnal blanks?' he shouted.

" 'What other two?' I asked. 'We're all here. What's the matter with you, anyway?'

" 'All here!' he yelled. 'You're a lurid liar! What the flamin' sheol do you mean by swiggin' my beer an' flingin' the coloured can in me face? Without as much as thank yer! D'yer think I'm a flamin'——!'

"Oh, but Poisonous Jimmy was wild.

" 'Well, we'll pay for your dirty beer,' says one of the chaps, puttin' his hand in his pocket. 'We didn't want yer slush. It tasted as if it had been used before.'

" 'Pay for it!' yelled Jimmy. 'I'll —— well take it out of yer bleedin' hides!'

"We stopped at once, and I got down an' obliged Jimmy for a few rounds. He was a nasty customer to fight; he could use his hands, and was cool as a cucumber as soon as he took his coat off; besides, he had one squirmy little business eye, and a big wall-eye, an', even if you knowed him well, you couldn't help watchin' the stony eye—it was no good watchin' his eyes, you had to watch his hands, and he might have managed me if the boss hadn't stopped the fight. The boss was a big, quiet-voiced man, that didn't swear.

" 'Now, look here, Myles,' said the boss (Jimmy's name was Myles)—'Now, look here, Myles,' sez the boss, 'what's all this about?'

" 'What's all this about?' says Jimmy, gettin' excited agen. 'Why, two fellers that belonged to your party came along to my place an' put up half a dozen drinks and borrered a sovereign, an' got a can o' beer on the strength of their cheques. They sez they was waitin' for you—an' I want my crimson money out o' someone!'

" 'What was they like?' asks the boss.

" 'Like?' shouted Poisonous, swearin' all the time. 'One was a blanky long, sandy, sawny feller, and the other was a short, slim feller with black hair. Your blanky men knows all about them because they had the blanky billy o' beer.'

" 'Now, what's this all about, you chaps?' sez the boss to us.

"So we told him as much as we knowed about them two fellers.

"I've heard men swear that could swear in a rough shearin'-shed, but I never heard a man swear like Poisonous Jimmy when he saw how he'd been left. It was enough to split stumps. He said he wanted to see those fellers, just once, before he died.

"He rode with us into Mulgatown, got mad drunk, an' started out along the road with a tomahawk after the long sandy feller; and the slim dark feller; but two mounted police went after him and fetched him back. He said he only wanted justice; he said he only wanted to stun them two fellers till he could give 'em in charge.

"They fined him ten bob."

THE GHOSTLY DOOR

TOLD BY ONE OF DAVE'S MATES

Dave and I were tramping on a lonely bush track in New Zealand, making for a sawmill where we expected to get work, and we were caught in one of those three days' gales, with rain and hail in it and cold enough to cut off a man's legs. Camping out was not to be thought of, so we just tramped on in silence, with the stinging pain coming between our shoulder-blades—from cold, weariness, and the weight of our swags—and our boots, full of water, going splosh, splosh, splosh along the track. We were settled to it—to drag on like wet, weary, muddy working bullocks till we came to somewhere—when, just before darkness settled down, we saw the loom of a humpy of some sort on the slope of a tussock hill, back from the road, and we made for it, without holding a consultation.

It was a two-roomed hut built of waste timber from a saw-mill, and was either a deserted settler's home or a hut attached to an abandoned sawmill round there somewhere. The windows were boarded up. We dumped our swags under the little veranda and banged at the door, to make sure; then Dave pulled a couple of

oards off a window and looked in: there was light enough to see
hat the place was empty. Dave pulled off some more boards, put his
rm in through a broken pane, clicked the catch back, and then
ushed up the window and got in. I handed in the swags to him. The
oom was very draughty; the wind came in through the broken
indow and the cracks between the slabs, so we tried the
artitioned-off room—the bedroom—and that was better. It had
een lined with chaff-bags, and there were two stretchers left by
ome timber-getters or other bush contractors who'd camped there
ast; and there were a box and a couple of three-legged stools.

We carried the remnant of the wood-heap inside, made a fire, and
ut the billy on. We unrolled our swags and spread the blankets on
e stretchers; and then we stripped and hung our clothes about the
re to dry. There was plenty in our tucker-bags, so we had a good
ed. I hadn't shaved for days, and Dave had a coarse red beard with
twist in it like an ill-used fibre brush—a beard that got redder the
onger it grew; he had a hooked nose, and his hair stood straight up
I never saw a man so easygoing about the expression and so scared
bout the head), and he was very tall, with long, thin, hairy legs. We
ust have looked a weird pair as we sat there, naked, on the low
ree-legged stools, with the billy and the tucker on the box between
s, and ate our bread and meat with clasp-knives.

"I shouldn't wonder," says Dave, "but this is the whare where the
urder was that we heard about along the road. I suppose if anyone
as to come along now and look in he'd get scared." Then after a
hile he looked down at the flooring-boards close to my feet, and
cratched his ear, and said, "That looks very much like a blood-stain
nder your stool, doesn't it, Jim?"

I shifted my feet and presently moved the stool farther away from
e fire—it was too hot.

I wouldn't have liked to camp there by myself, but I don't think
ave would have minded—he'd knocked round too much in the
ustralian bush to mind anything much, or to be surprised at
nything; besides, he was more than half-murdered once by a man
ho said afterwards that he'd mistook him for someone else; he must
ave been a very short-sighted murderer.

Presently we put tobacco, matches, and bits of candle we had, on
e two stools by the heads of our bunks, turned in, and filled up and
moked comfortably, dropping in a lazy word now and again about
othing in particular. Once I happened to look across at Dave, and
w him sitting up a bit and watching the door. The door opened

very slowly, wide, and a black cat walked in, looked first at me, then at Dave, and walked out again; and the door closed behind it

Dave scratched his ear. "That's rum," he said. "I could have sworn I fastened that door. They must have left the cat behind."

"It looks like it," I said. "Neither of us has been on the booze lately."

He got out of bed and up on his long hairy spindle-shanks.

The door had the ordinary, common black oblong lock with a brass knob. Dave tried the latch and found it fast; he turned the knob, opened the door, and called, "Puss—puss—puss!" but the cat wouldn't come. He shut the door, tried the knob to see that the catch had caught, and got into bed again.

He'd scarcely settled down when the door opened slowly, the black cat walked in, stared hard at Dave, and suddenly turned and darted out as the door closed smartly.

I looked at Dave and he looked at me—hard; then he scratched the back of his head. I never saw a man look so puzzled in the face and scared about the head.

He got out of bed very cautiously, took a stick of firewood in his hand, sneaked up to the door, and snatched it open. There was no one there. Dave took the candle and went into the next room, but couldn't see the cat. He came back and sat down by the fire and meowed, and presently the cat answered him and came in from somewhere—she'd been outside the window, I suppose; he kept on meowing and she sidled up and rubbed against his hairy shin. Dave could generally bring a cat that way. He had a weakness for cats. I seen him kick a dog, and hammer a horse—brutally, I thought—but I never saw him hurt a cat or let anyone else do it. Dave was good to cats: if a cat had a family where Dave was round, he'd see her right and comfortable, and only drown a fair surplus. He said once to me, "I can understand a man kicking a dog, or hammering a horse when it plays up, but I can't understand a man hurting a cat."

He gave this cat something to eat. Then he went and held the light close to the lock of the door, but could see nothing wrong with it. He found a key on the mantelshelf and locked the door. He got into bed again, and the cat jumped up and curled down at the foot and started her old drum going, like shot in a sieve. Dave bent down and patted her, to tell her he'd meant no harm when he stretched out his legs, and then he settled down again.

We had some books of the "Deadwood Dick" school. Dave was

eading *The Grisly Ghost of the Haunted Gulch*, and I had *The
Dismembered Hand*, or *The Disembowelled Corpse*, or some such names.
They were first-class preparation for a ghost.

I was reading away, and getting drowsy, when I noticed a
movement and saw Dave's frightened head rising, with the terrified
shadow of it on the wall. He was staring at the door, over his book,
with both eyes. And that door was opening again—slowly—and
Dave had locked it! I never felt anything so creepy: the foot of my
bunk was behind the door, and I drew up my feet as it came open; it
opened wide, and stood so. We waited, for five minutes it seemed,
hearing each other breathe, watching for the door to close; then
Dave got out very gingerly, and up on one end, and went to the door
like a cat on wet bricks.

"You shot the bolt *outside* the catch," I said, as he caught hold of
the door—like one grabs a crawfish.

"I'll swear I didn't," said Dave. But he'd already turned the key a
couple of times, so he couldn't be sure. He shut and locked the door
again. "Now, get out and see for yourself," he said.

I got out, and tried the door a couple of times and found it all
right. Then we both tried, and agreed that it was locked.

I got back into bed, and Dave was about half in when a thought
struck him. He got the heaviest piece of firewood and stood it against
the door.

"What are you doing that for?" I asked.

"If there's a broken-down burglar camped round here, and trying
any of his funny business, we'll hear him if he tries to come in while
we're asleep," says Dave. Then he got back into bed. We composed
our nerves with the *Haunted Gulch* and *The Disembowelled Corpse*, and
after a while I heard Dave snore, and was just dropping off when the
stick fell from the door against my big toe and then to the ground
with tremendous clatter. I snatched up my feet and sat up with a
jerk, and so did Dave—the cat went over the partition. The door
opened, only a little way this time, paused, and shut suddenly. Dave
got out, grabbed a stick, skipped to the door, and clutched at the
knob as if it were a nettle, and the door wouldn't come!—it was fast
and locked! Then Dave's face began to look as frightened as his hair.
He lit his candle at the fire, and asked me to come with him; he
unlocked the door and we went into the other room, Dave shading
his candle very carefully and feeling his way slow with his feet. The
room was empty; we tried the outer door and found it locked.

"It muster gone by the winder," whispered Dave. I noticed tha he said "it" instead of "he." I saw that he himself was shook up, an it only needed that to scare me bad.

We went back to the bedroom, had a drink of cold tea, and lit ou pipes. Then Dave took the waterproof cover off his bunk, spread i on the floor, laid his blankets on top of it, his spare clothes, etc., o top of them, and started to roll up his swag.

"What are you going to do, Dave?" I asked.

"I'm going to take the track," says Dave, "and camp somewher farther on. You can stay here, if you like, and come on in th morning."

I started to roll up my swag at once. We dressed and fastened o the tucker-bags, took up the billies, and got outside without makin any noise. We held our backs pretty hollow till we got down on t the road.

"That comes of camping in a deserted house," said Dave, whe we were safe on the track. No Australian bushman cares to camp i an abandoned homestead, or even near it—probably because deserted home looks ghostlier in the Australian bush than anywher else in the world.

It was blowing hard, but not raining so much.

We went on along the track for a couple of miles and camped o the sheltered side of a round tussock hill, in a hole where there ha been a landslip. We used all our candle-ends to get a fire alight, bu once we got it started we knocked the wet bark off *manuka* sticks an logs and piled them on, and soon had a roaring fire. When th ground got a little drier we rigged a bit of a shelter from the shower with some sticks and the oil-cloth swag-covers; then we made som coffee and got through the night pretty comfortably. In the mornin Dave said, "I'm going back to that house."

"What for?" I said.

"I'm going to find out what's the matter with that crimson door If I don't I'll never be able to sleep easy within a mile of a door s long as I live."

So we went back. It was still blowing. The thing was simpl enough by daylight—after a little watching and experimenting. Th house was built of odds and ends and badly fitted. It "gave" in th wind in almost any direction—not much, not more than an inch o so, but just enough to throw the door-frame out of plumb and out o square in such a way as to bring the latch and bolt of the lock clear o the catch (the door-frame was of scraps joined). Then the doo swung open according to the hang of it; and when the gust was over the house gave back, and the door swung to—the frame easing just a little in another direction. I suppose it would take Edison to invent a thing like that, that came about by accident. The different strengths and directions of the gusts of wind must have accounted for the variations of the door's movements—and maybe the draught of our big fire had helped.

Dave scratched his head a good bit.

"I never lived in a house yet," he said, as we came away—"I never lived in a house yet without there was something wrong with it. Gimme a good tent."

A WILD IRISHMAN

About seven years ago I drifted from out back in Australia to Wellington, the capital of New Zealand, and up-country to a little town called Pahiatua, which meaneth the "home of the gods," and is situated in the Wairarappa (rippling or sparkling water) district. They have a pretty little legend to the effect that the name of the district was not originally suggested by its rivers, streams, and lakes, but by the tears alleged to have been noticed, by a dusky squire, in the eyes of a warrior chief who was looking his first, or last—I don't remember which—upon the scene. He was the discoverer, I suppose, now I come to think of it, else the place would have been already named. Maybe the scene reminded the old cannibal of the home of his childhood.

Pahiatua was not the home of my god; and it rained for five weeks. While waiting for a remittance, from an Australian newspaper—which, I anxiously hoped, would arrive in time for enough of it to be left (after paying board) to take me away somewhere—I spent many hours in the little shop of a shoemaker who had been a digger; and he told me yarns of the old days on the West Coast of Middle Island. And, ever and anon, he returned to one, a hard case from the West Coast, called "The Flour of Wheat," and his cousin, and his mate, Dinny Murphy, dead. And ever and again the shoemaker (he war large, humorous, and good natured) made me promise that, when I dropped across an old West Coast digger—no matter who or what he was, or whether he was drunk or sober—I'd ask him if he knew the Flour of Wheat, and hear what he had to say.

I make no attempt to give any one shade of the Irish brogue—it can't be done in writing.

"There's the little red Irishman," said the shoemaker, who was Irish himself, "who always wants to fight when he has a glass in him; and there's the big sarcastic dark Irishman who makes more trouble and fights at a spree than half a dozen little red ones put together; and there's the cheerful easygoing Irishman. Now the Flour was a combination of all three and several other sorts. He was known from the first amongst the boys at Th' Canary as the Flour o' Wheat, but no one knew exactly why. Some said that the right name was the F-l-o-w-e-r, not F-l-o-u-r, and that he was called that because there was no flower on wheat. The name might have been a compliment paid to the man's character by someone who understood and appreciated it—or appreciated it without understanding it. Or it might have come of some chance saying of the Flour himself, or his mates—or an accident with bags of flour. He might have worked in a mill. But we've had enough of that. It's the man—not the name. He was just a big, dark, blue-eyed Irish digger. He worked hard, drank hard, fought hard—and didn't swear. No man had ever heard him swear (except once); all things were "lovely" with him. He was always lucky. He got gold and threw it away.

"The Flour was sent out to Australia (by his friends) in connection with some trouble in Ireland in eighteen-something. The date doesn't matter; there was mostly trouble in Ireland in those days; and nobody, that knew the man, could have the slightest doubt that he helped the trouble—provided he was there at the time. I heard all this from a man who knew him in Australia. The relatives that he was sent out to were soon very anxious to see the end of him. He was as wild as they made them in Ireland. When he had a few drinks, he'd walk restlessly to and fro outside the shanty, swinging his right arm across in front of him with elbow bent and hand closed as if he had a head in chancery, and muttering, as though in explanation to himself:

"'Oi must be walkin' or foightin'!—Oi must be walkin' or foightin'!—Oi must be walkin' or foightin'!'

"They say that he wanted to eat his Australian relatives before he was done; and the story goes that one night, while he was on the spree, they put their belongings into a cart and took to the bush.

"There's no Floury record for several years; then the Flour turned up on the west coast of New Zealand and was never very far from a pub kept by a cousin (that he had tracked, unearthed, or discovered somehow) at a place called Th' Canary. I remember the first time I saw the Flour.

"I was on a bit of a spree myself, at Th' Canary, and one evening I was standing outside Brady's (the Flour's cousin's place) with Tom Lyons and Dinny Murphy, when I saw a bit man coming across the flat with a swag on his back.

" 'B' God, there's the Flour o' Wheat comin' this minute,' says Dinny Murphy to Tom, 'an' no one else.'

" 'B' God, ye're right! says Tom.

"There were a lot of new chums in the big room at the back, drinking and dancing and singing, and Tom says to Dinny:

" 'Dinny, I'll bet you a quid an' the Flour'll run against some of those new chums before he's an hour on the spot.'

"But Dinny wouldn't take him up. He knew the Flour.

" 'Good day, Tom! Good day, Dinny!'

" 'Good day to you, Flour!'

"I was introduced.

" 'Well, boys, come along,' says the Flour.

"And so we went inside with him. The Flour had a few drinks, and then he went into the back-room where the new chums were. One of them was dancing a jig, and so the Flour stood up in front of him and commenced to dance too. And presently the new chum made a step that didn't please the Flour, so he hit him between the eyes, and knocked him down—fair an' flat on his back.

" 'Take that,' he says. 'Take that, me lovely whipper-snapper, an' lay there! You can't dance. How dare ye stand up in front of me face to dance when ye can't dance?'

"He shouted, and drank, and gambled, and danced, and sang, and fought the new chums all night, and in the morning he said:

" 'Well, boys, we had a grand time last night. Come and have a drink with me.'

"And of course they went in and had a drink with him.

"Next morning the Flour was walking along the street, when he met a drunken disreputable old hag, known among the boys as the 'Nipper.'

" 'Good *morning*, me lovely Flour o' Wheat!' says she.

" 'Good *morning*, me lovely Nipper!' says the Flour.

"And with that she outs with a bottle she had in her dress, and
smashed him across the face with it. Broke the bottle to smithereens!

"A policeman saw her do it, and took her up; and they had the
Flour as a witness, whether he liked it or not. And a lovely sight he
looked, with his face all done up in bloody bandages, and only one
damaged eye and a corner of his mouth on duty.

"'It's nothing at all, your Honour,' he said to the S.M.; 'only a
pin-scratch—it's nothing at all. Let it pass. I had no right to speak to
the lovely woman at all.'

"But they didn't let it pass—they fined her a quid.

"And the Flour paid the fine.

"But, alas for human nature! It was pretty much the same even in
those days, and amongst those men, as it is now. A man couldn't do
a woman a good turn without the dirty-minded blackguards taking
it for granted there was something between them. It was a great joke
amongst the boys who knew the Flour, and who also knew the
Nipper; but as it was carried too far in some quarters, it got to be no
joke to the Flour—nor to those who laughed too loud or grinned too
long.

"The Flour's cousin thought he was a sharp man. The Flour got
'stiff.' He hadn't any money, and his credit had run out, so he went
and got a blank summons from one of the police he knew. He
pretended that he wanted to frighten a man who owed him some
money. Then he filled it up and took it to his cousin.

"'What d'ye think of that?' he says, handing the summons across
the bar. 'What d'ye think of me lovely Dinny Murphy now?'

"'Why, what's this all about?'

"'That's what I want to know. I borrowed a five-pound note off o'
him a fortnight ago when I was drunk, an' now he sends me that.'

"'Well, I never would have dream'd that of Dinny,' says the
cousin, scratching his head and blinking. 'What's come over him at
all?'

"'That's what I want to know.'

"'What have you been doing to the man?'

"'Divil a thing that I'm aware of.'

"The cousin rubbed his chin-tuft between his forefinger and
thumb.

"'Well, what am I to do about it?' asked the Flour impatiently.

"'Do? Pay the man, of course.'

" 'How can I pay the lovely man when I haven't got the price of a drink about me?'

"The cousin scratched his chin.

" 'Well—here, I'll lend you a five-pound note for a month or two. Go and pay the man, and get back to work.'

"And the Flour went and found Dinny Murphy, and the pair of them had a howling spree together up at Brady's, the opposition pub. And the cousin said he thought all the time he was being had.

'He was nasty sometimes, when he was about half-drunk. For instance, he'd come on the ground when the Orewell sports were in full swing and walk round, soliloquizing just loud enough for you to hear; and just when a big event was coming off he'd pass within earshot of some committee men—who had been bursting themselves for weeks to work the thing up and make it a success—saying to himself:

" 'Where's the Orewell sports that I hear so much about? I don't see them! Can any one direct me to the Orewell sports?'

"Or he'd pass a raffle, lottery, lucky-bag, or golden-barrel business of some sort——

" 'No gamblin' for the Flour. I don't believe in their little shwindles. It ought to be shtopped. Leadin' young people ashtray.'

"Or he'd pass an Englishman he didn't like—

" 'Look at Jinneral Roberts! He's a man! He's an Irishman! England has to come to Ireland for its Jinnerals! Luk at Jinneral Roberts in the marshes of Candyhar!'

'They always had sports at Orewell Creek on New Year's Day—except once—and old Duncan was always there—never missed it till the day he died. He was a digger, a humorous and good-hearted 'hard case.' They all knew 'old Duncan.'

"But one New Year's Eve he didn't turn up, and was missed at once. 'Where's old Duncan? Any one seen old Duncan?' 'Oh, he'll turn up alright.' They inquired, and argued, and waited, but Duncan didn't come.

"Duncan was working at Duffers. The boys inquired of fellows who came from Duffers, but they hadn't seen him for two days. They had fully expected to find him at the creek. He wasn't at Aliaura nor Notown. They inquired of men who came from Nelson Creek, but Duncan wasn't there.

" 'There's something happened to the lovely man,' said the Flour of Wheat at last. 'Some of us had better see about it.'

"Pretty soon this was the general opinion, and so a party started out over the hills to Duffers before daylight in the morning, headed by the Flour.

"The door of Duncan's whare was closed—*but not padlocked*. The Flour noticed this, gave his head a jerk, opened the door, and went in. The hut was tidied up and swept out—even the fire-place Duncan had 'lifted the boxes' and 'cleaned up,' and his little bag of gold stood on a shelf by his side—all ready for his spree. On the table lay a clean neckerchief folded ready to tie on. The blankets had been folded neatly and laid on the bunk, and on them was stretched old Duncan, with his arms lying crossed on his chest, and one foot—with a boot on—resting on the ground. He had his 'clean things' on, and was dressed except for one boot, the necktie, and his hat. Heart disease.

" 'Take your hats off and come in quietly, lads,' said the Flour 'Here's the lovely man lying dead in his bunk.'

"There were no sports at Orewell that New Year. Someone said that the crowd from Nelson Creek might object to the sports being postponed on old Duncan's account, but the Flour said he'd see to that.

"One or two did object, but the Flour reasoned with them and there were no sports.

"And the Flour used to say, afterwards, 'Ah, but it was a grand time we had at the funeral when Duncan died at Duffers.'

"The Flour of Wheat carried his mate, Dinny Murphy, all the way in from Th' Canary to the hospital on his back. Dinny was very bad—the man was dying of the dysentery or something. The Flour laid him down on a spare bunk in the reception-room, and hailed the staff.

" 'Inside there—come out!'

"The doctor and some of the hospital people came to see what was the matter. The doctor was a heavy swell, with a big cigar, held up in front of him between two fat, soft, yellow-white fingers, and a dandy little pair of gold-rimmed eye-glasses nipped on to his nose with a spring.

" 'There's me lovely mate lying there dying of the dysentery,' say the Flour, 'and you've got to fix him up and bring him round.'

"Then he shook his fist in the doctor's face and said:

" 'If you let that lovely man die—look out!'

"The doctor was startled. He backed off at first; then he took a puff at his cigar, stepped forward, had a careless look at Dinny, and gave some order to the attendants. The Flour went to the door, turned half round as he went out, and shook his fist at them again, and said:

" 'If you let that lovely man die—mind!'

"In about twenty minutes he came back, wheeling a case of whisky in a barrow. He carried the case inside, and dumped it down on the floor.

" 'There,' he said, 'pour that into the lovely man.'

"Then he shook his fist at such members of the staff as were visible, and said:

" 'If you let that lovely man die—look out!'

"They were used to hard cases, and didn't take much notice of him, but he had the hospital in an awful mess; he was there all hours of the day and night; he would go down town, have a few drinks and a fight maybe, and then he'd say, 'Ah, well, I'll have to go up and see how me lovely mate's getting on.'

"And every time he'd go up he'd shake his fist at the hospital in general and threaten to murder 'em all if they let Dinny Murphy die.

"Well, Dinny Murphy died one night. The next morning the Flour met the doctor in the street, and hauled off and hit hit between the eyes, and knocked him down before he had time to see who it was.

" 'Stay there, ye little whipper-snapper,' said the Flour of Wheat; 'you let that lovely man die!'

"The police happened to be out of town that day, and while they were waiting for them the Flour got a coffin and carried it up to the hospital, and stood it on end by the doorway.

" 'I've come for me lovely mate!' he said to the scared staff—or as much of it as he baled up and couldn't escape him. 'Hand him over. He's going back to be buried with his friends at Th' Canary. Now, don't be sneaking round and sidling off, you there; you needn't be frightened; I've settled with the doctor.'

"But they called in a man who had some influence with the Flour, and between them—and with the assistance of the prettiest nurse on the premises—they persuaded him to wait. Dinny wasn't ready yet;

there were papers to sign; it wouldn't be decent to the dead; he had to be prayed over; he had to be washed and shaved, and fixed up decent and comfortable. Anyway, they'd have him ready in an hour, or take the consequences.

"The Flour objected on the ground that all this could be done equally as well and better by the boys at Th' Canary. 'However,' he said, 'I'll be round in an hour, and if you haven't got me lovely mate ready—look out!' Then he shook his fist sternly at them once more and said:

" 'I know yer dirty tricks and dodges, and if there's e'er a pin-scratch on me mate's body—look out! If there's a parin' of Dinny's toe-nail missin'—look out!'

"Then he went out—taking the coffin with him.

"And when the police came to his lodgings to arrest him, they found the coffin on the floor by the side of the bed, and the Flour lying in it on his back, with his arms folded peacefully on his bosom. He was as dead drunk as any man could get to be and still be alive. They knocked air-holes in the coffin lid, screwed it on, and carried the coffin, the Flour, and all to the local lock-up. They laid their burden down on the bare, cold floor of the prison-cell, and then went out, locked the door, and departed several ways to put the 'boys' up to it. And about midnight the 'boys' gathered round with a supply of liquor, and waited, and somewhere along in the small hours there was a howl, as of a strong Irishman in Purgatory, and presently the voice of the Flour was heard to plead in changed and awful tones:

" 'Pray for me soul, boys—pray for me soul! Let bygones be bygones between us, boys, and pray for me lovely soul! The lovely Flour's in Purgatory!'

"Then silence for a while; and then a sound like a dray-wheel passing over a packing-case. . . . That was the only time on record that the Flour was heard to swear. And he swore then.

"They didn't pray for him—they gave him a month. And, when he came out, he went half-way across the road to meet the doctor, and he—to his credit, perhaps—came the other half. They had a drink together, and the Flour presented the doctor with a fine specimen of coarse gold for a pin.

" 'It was the will o' God, arter all, doctor,' said the Flour. 'It was the will o' God. Let bygones be bygones between us; gimme your hand, doctor. . . . Good-bye.'

"Then he left for Th' Canary."

THE BABIES IN THE BUSH

> Oh, tell her a tale of the fairies bright—
>   That only the Bushmen know—
> Who guide the feet of the lost aright,
> Or carry them up through the starry night,
>   Where the Bush-lost babies go.

He was one of those men who seldom smile. There are many in the
Australian bush, where drift wrecks and failures of all stations and
professions (and of none) and from all the world. Or, if they do smile
the smile is either mechanical or bitter as a rule—cynical. They
seldom talk. The sort of men who, as bosses, are set down by the
majority—and without reason or evidence—as being proud, hard,
and selfish—"too mean to live, and too big for their boots."

But when the boss did smile his expression was very, very gentle,
and very sad. I have seen· him smile down on a little child who
persisted in sitting on his knee and prattling to him, in spite of his
silence and gloom. He was tall and gaunt, with haggard grey
eyes—haunted grey eyes sometimes—and hair and beard thick and
strong; but grey. He was not above forty-five. He was of the type of
men who die in harness, with their hair thick and strong, but grey or
white when it should be brown. The opposite type, I fancy, would be
the soft, dark-haired, blue-eyed men who grow bald sooner than
they grow grey, and fat and contented, and die respectably in their
beds.

His name was Head—Walter Head. He was a boss drover on the
overland routes. I engaged with him at a place north of the
Queensland border to travel down to Bathurst, on the Great
Western Line in New South Wales, with something over a thousand
head of store bullocks for the Sydney market. I am an Australian
bushman (with city experience)—a rover, of course, and a ne'er-do-
well, I suppose. I was born with brains and a thin skin—worse luck!
It was in the days before I was married, and I went by the name of
"Jack Ellis" this trip,—not because the police were after me, but
because I used to tell yarns about a man named Jack Ellis—and so
the chaps nicknamed me.

The boss spoke little to the men: he'd sit at tucker or with his pipe
by the camp-fire nearly as silently as he rode his night-watch round
the big, restless, weird-looking mob of bullocks camped on the dusky
starlit plain. I believe that from the first he spoke oftener and more

confidentially to me than to any other of the droving party. There was a something of sympathy between us—I can't explain what it was. It seemed as though it were an understood thing between us that we understood each other. He sometimes said things to me which would have needed a deal of explanation—so I thought—had he said them to any other of the party. He'd often, after brooding a long while, start a sentence, and break off with "You know, Jack." And somehow I understood, without being able to explain why. We had never met before I engaged with him for this trip. His men respected him, but he was not a popular boss: he was too gloomy, and never drank a glass nor "shouted" on the trip: he was reckoned a "mean boss," and rather a nigger-driver.

He was full of Adam Lindsay Gordon, the English-Australian poet who shot himself, and so was I. I lost an old copy of Gordon's poems on the route, and the boss overheard me inquiring about it; later on he asked me if I liked Gordon. We got to it rather sheepishly at first, but by and by we'd quote Gordon freely in turn when we were alone in camp. "Those are grand lines about Burke and Wills, the explorers, aren't they, Jack?" he'd say, after chewing his cud, or rather the stem of his briar, for a long while without a word. (He had his pipe in his mouth as often as any of us, but somehow I fancied he didn't enjoy it: an empty pipe or a stick would have suited him just as well, it seemed to me.) "Those are great lines," he'd say:

> "In Collins Street standeth a statue tall—
> A statue tall on a pillar of stone—
> Telling its story to great and small
> Of the dust reclaimed from the sand-waste lone.

> "Weary and wasted, worn and wan,
> Feeble and faint, and languid and low,
> He lay on the desert a dying man,
> Who has gone, my friend, where we all must go.

"That's a grand thing, Jack. How does it go?—

> "With a pistol clenched in his failing hand,
> And the film of death o'er his fading eyes,
> He saw the sun go down on the sand,"—

The boss would straighten up with a sigh that might have been half a yawn—

> "And he slept and never saw it rise,"

—speaking with a sort of quiet force all the time. Then maybe he'd stand with his back to the fire roasting his dusty leggings, with his hands behind his back and looking out over the dusky plain.

> "What mattered the sand or the whit-ning chalk,
>   The blighted herbage or blackened log,
> The crooked beak of the eagle-hawk,
>   Or the hot red tongue of the native dog"

"They don't matter much, do they, Jack?"
"Damned if I think they do, boss!" I'd say.

> "The couch was rugged, those sextons rude,
> But, in spite of a leaden shroud, we know
> That the bravest and fairest are earth-worms' food
> When once they have gone where we all must go."

Once he repeated the poem containing the lines:

> "Love, when we wandered here together,
> Hand in hand through the sparkling weather—
>   God surely loved us a little then.

"Beautiful lines those, Jack.

> "Then skies were fairer and shores were firmer,
>   And the blue sea over the white sand rolled—
> Babble and prattle, and prattle and murmur—

"How does it go, Jack?" He stood up and turned his face to the light, but not before I had a glimpse of it. I think that the saddest eyes on earth are mostly women's eyes, but I've seen few so sad as the boss's were just then.

It seemed strange that he, a bushman, preferred Gordon's sea poems to his horsey and bushy rhymes; but so he did. I fancy his favourite poem was that one of Gordon's with the lines:

> I would that with sleepy soft embraces
>   The sea would fold me, would find me rest
> In the luminous depths of its secret places,
>   Where the wealth of God's marvels is manifest!

He usually spoke quietly, in a tone as though death were in camp; but after we'd been on Gordon's poetry for a while he'd end it abruptly with, "Well, it's time to turn in," or, "It's time to turn out," or he'd give me an order in connection with the cattle. He had been a well-to-do squatter on the Lachlan river-side, in New

South Wales, and had been ruined by the drought, they said. One night in camp, and after smoking in silence for nearly an hour, he asked:

"Do you know Fisher, Jack—the man that owns these bullocks?"

"I've heard of him," I said. Fisher was a big squatter, with stations both in New South Wales and in Queensland.

"Well, he came to my station on the Lachlan years ago without a penny in his pocket, or decent rag to his back, or a crust in his tucker-bag, and I gave him a job. He's my boss now. Ah, well! it's the way of Australia, you know, Jack."

The boss had one man who went on every droving trip with him; he was "bred" on the boss's station, they said, and had been with him practically all his life. His name was "Andy." I forget his other name, if he really had one. Andy had charge of the "droving-plant" (a tilted two-horse wagonette, in which we carried the rations and horse-feed), and he did the cooking and kept accounts. The boss had no head for figures. Andy might have been twenty-five or thirty-five, or anything in between. His hair stuck up like a well-made brush all round, and his big grey eyes also had an inquiring expression. His weakness was girls, or he theirs, I don't know which (half-castes not barred). He was, I think, the most innocent, good-natured, and open-hearted scamp I ever met. Towards the middle of the trip Andy spoke to me one night alone in camp about the boss.

"The boss seems to have taken to you, Jack, all right."

"Think so?" I said. I thought I smelt jealousy and detected a sneer.

"I'm sure of it. It's very seldom *he* takes to any one."

I said nothing.

Then after a while Andy said suddenly:

"Look here, Jack, I'm glad of it. I'd like to see him make a chum of someone, if only for one trip. And don't you make any mistake about the boss. He's a white man. There's precious few that know him—precious few now; but I do, and it'll do him a lot of good to have someone to yarn with." And Andy said no more on the subject for that trip.

The long, hot, dusty miles dragged by across the blazing plains—big clearings rather—and through the sweltering hot scrubs, and we reached Bathurst at last; and then the hot dusty days and weeks and months that we'd left behind us to the Great North-West seemed as nothing—as I suppose life will seem when we come to the end of it.

The bullocks were going by rail from Bathurst to Sydney. We were all one long afternoon getting them into the trucks, and when we'd finished the boss said to me:

"Look here, Jack, you're going on to Sydney, aren't you?"

"Yes; I'm going down to have a fly round."

"Well, why not wait and go down with Andy in the morning? He's going down in charge of the cattle. The cattle-train starts about daylight. It won't be so comfortable as the passenger; but you'll save your fare, and you can give Andy a hand with the cattle. You've only got to have a look at 'em every other station, and poke up any that fall down in the trucks. You and Andy are mates, aren't you?"

I said it would just suit me. Somehow I fancied that the boss seemed anxious to have my company for one more evening, and, to tell the truth, I felt really sorry to part with him. I'd had to work as hard as any of the other chaps; but I liked him, and I believed he liked me. He'd struck me as a man who'd been quietened down by some heavy trouble, and I felt sorry for him without knowing what the trouble was.

"Come and have a drink, boss," I said. The agent had paid us off during the day.

He turned into a hotel with me.

"I don't drink, Jack," he said; "but I'll take a glass with you."

"I didn't know you were a teetotaller, boss," I said. I had not been surprised at his keeping so strictly from the drink on the trip; but now that it was over it was a different thing.

"I'm not a teetotaller, Jack," he said. "I can take a glass or leave it." And he called for a long beer, and we drank "Here's luck!" to each other.

"Well," I said, "I wish I could take a glass or leave it." And I meant it.

Then the boss spoke as I'd never heard him speak before. I thought for the moment that the one drink had affected him; but I understood before the night was over. He laid his hand on my shoulder with a grip like a man who has suddenly made up his mind to lend you five pounds. "Jack!" he said, "there's worse things than drinking, and there's worse things than heavy smoking. When a man who smokes gets such a load of trouble on him that he can find no comfort in his pipe, then it's a heavy load. And when a man who drinks gets so deep into trouble that he can find no comfort in liquor, then it's deep trouble. Take my tip for it, Jack."

He broke off, and half turned away with a jerk of his head, as if impatient with himself; then presently he spoke in his usual quiet tone:

"But you're only a boy yet, Jack. Never mind me. I won't ask you to take the second drink. You don't want it; and, besides, I know the signs."

He paused, leaning with both hands on the edge of the counter, and looking down between his arms at the floor. He stood that way thinking for a while; then he suddenly straightened up, like a man who'd made up his mind to something.

"I want you to come along home with me, Jack," he said; "we'll fix you a shake-down."

I forgot to tell you that he was married and lived in Bathurst.

"But won't it put Mrs Head about?"

"Not at all. She's expecting you. Come along; there's nothing to see in Bathurst, and you'll have plenty of knocking round in Sydney. Come on, we'll just be in time for tea."

He lived in a brick cottage on the outskirts of the town—an old-fashioned cottage, with ivy and climbing roses, like you see in some of those old settled districts. There was, I remember, the stump of a tree in front, covered with ivy till it looked like a giant's club with the thick end up.

When we got to the house the boss paused a minute with his hand on the gate. He'd been home a couple of days, having ridden in ahead of the bullocks.

"Jack," he said, "I must tell you that Mrs Head had a great trouble at one time. We—we lost our two children. It does her good to talk to a stranger now and again—she's always better afterwards; but there's very few I care to bring. You—you needn't notice anything strange. And agree with her, Jack. You know, Jack."

"That's all right, boss," I said. I'd knocked about the bush too long, and run against too many strange characters and things, to be surprised at anything much.

The door opened, and he took a little woman in his arms. I saw by the light of a lamp in the room behind that the woman's hair was grey, and I reckoned that he had his mother living with him. And—we do have odd thoughts at odd times in a flash—and I wondered how Mrs Head and her mother-in-law got on together. But the next minute I was in the room, and introduced to "My wife, Mrs Head," and staring at her with both eyes.

It was his wife. I don't think I can describe her. For the first minute or two, coming in out of the dark and before my eyes got used to the lamp-light, I had an impression as of a little old

woman—one of those fresh-faced, well-preserved, little old ladies—
who dressed young, wore false teeth, and aped the giddy girl. But
this was because of Mrs Head's impulsive welcome of me, and her
grey hair. The hair was not so grey as I thought at first, seeing it
with the lamp-light behind it: it was like dull-brown hair lightly
dusted with flour. She wore it short, and it became her that way.
There was something aristocratic about her face—her nose and
chin—I fancied, and something that you couldn't describe. She had
big dark eyes—dark-brown, I thought, though they might have been
hazel: they were a bit too big and bright for me, and now and again,
when she got excited, the white showed all round the pupils—just a
little, but a little was enough.

She seemed extra glad to see me. I thought at first that she was a
bit of a gusher.

"Oh, I'm so glad you've come, Mr Ellis," she said, giving my
hand a grip. "Walter—Mr Head—has been speaking to me about
you. I've been expecting you. Sit down by the fire, Mr Ellis; tea will
be ready presently. Don't you find it a bit chilly?" She shivered. It
was a bit chilly now at night on the Bathurst plains. The table was
set for tea, and set rather in swell style. The cottage was too well
furnished even for a lucky boss drover's home; the furniture looked
as if it had belonged to a toney homestead at one time. I felt a bit
strange at first, sitting down to tea, and almost wished that I was
having a comfortable tuck-in at a restaurant or in a pub
dining-room. But she knew a lot about the bush, and chatted away,
and asked questions about the trip, and soon put me at my ease. You
see, for the last year or two I'd taken my tucker in my hands—hunk
of damper and meat and a clasp-knife mostly—sitting on my heel in
the dust, or on a log or a tucker-box.

There was a hard, brown, wrinkled old woman that the Heads
called "Auntie." She waited at the table; but Mrs Head kept
bustling round herself most of the time, helping us. Andy came in
to tea.

Mrs Head bustled round like a girl of twenty instead of a woman
of thirty-seven, as Andy afterwards told me she was. She had the
figure and movements of a girl, and the impulsiveness and
expression too—a womanly girl; but sometimes I fancied there was
something very childish about her face and talk. After tea she and
the boss sat on one side of the fire and Andy and I on the
other—Andy a little behind me at the corner of the table.

"Walter—Mr Head—tells me you've been out on the Lachlan
River, Mr Ellis?" she said as soon as she'd settled down, and she

leaned forward, as if eager to hear that I'd been there.

"Yes, Mrs Head. I've knocked round all about out there."

She sat up straight, and put the tips of her fingers to the side of her forehead and knitted her brows. This was a trick she had—she often did it during the evening. And when she did that she seemed to forget what she'd said last.

She smoothed her forehead, and clasped her hands in her lap.

"Oh, I'm so glad to meet somebody from the back country, Mr Ellis," she said. "Walter so seldom brings a stranger here, and I get tired of talking to the same people about the same things, and seeing the same faces. You don't know that a relief it is, Mr Ellis, to see a new face and talk to a stranger."

"I can quite understand that, Mrs Head," I said. And so I could. I never stayed more than three months in one place if I could help it.

She looked into the fire and seemed to try to think. The boss straightened up and stroked her head with his big sun-browned hand, and then put his arm round her shoulders. This brought her back.

"You know we had a station out on the Lachlan, Mr Ellis. Did Walter ever tell you about the time we lived there?"

"No," I said, glancing at the boss. "I know you had a station there; but, you know, the boss doesn't talk much."

"Tell Jack, Maggie," said the boss; "I don't mind."

She smiled. "You know Walter, Mr Ellis," she said. "You won't mind him. He doesn't like me to talk about the children; he thinks it upsets me, but that's foolish: it always relieves me to talk to a stranger." She leaned forward, eagerly it seemed, and went on quickly: "I've been wanting to tell you about the children ever since Walter spoke to me about you. I knew you would understand directly I saw your face. These town people don't understand. I like to talk to a bushman. You know we lost our children out on the station. The fairies took them. Did Walter ever tell you about the fairies taking the children away?"

This was a facer. "I—I beg pardon," I commenced, when Andy gave me a dig in the back. Then I saw it all.

"No, Mrs Head. The boss didn't tell me about that."

"You surely know about the Bush Fairies, Mr Ellis," she said, her big eyes fixed on my face—"the Bush Fairies that look after the little ones that are lost in the bush, and take them away from the bush if they are not found? You've surely heard of them, Mr Ellis? Most bushmen have that I've spoken to. Maybe you've seen them? Andy there has?" Andy gave me another dig.

"Of course I've heard of them, Mrs Head," I said; "but I can't swear that I've seen one."

"Andy has. Haven't you, Andy?"

"Of course I have, Mrs Head. Didn't I tell you all about it the last time we were home?"

"And didn't you ever tell Mr Ellis, Andy?"

"Of course he did!" I said, coming to Andy's rescue; "I remember it now. You told me that night we camped on the Bogan River, Andy."

"Of course!" said Andy.

"Did he tell you about finding a lost child and the fairy with it?"

"Yes," said Andy; "I told him all about that."

"And the fairy was just going to take the child away when Andy found it, and when the fairy saw Andy she flew away."

"Yes," I said; "that's what Andy told me."

"And what did you say the fairy was like, Andy?" asked Mrs Head, fixing her eyes on his face.

"Like? It was like one of them angels you see in Bible pictures, Mrs Head," said Andy promptly, sitting bolt upright, and keeping his big innocent grey eyes fixed on hers lest she might think he was telling lies. "It was just like the angel in that Christ-in-the-stable picture we had at home on the station—the right-hand one in blue."

She smiled. You couldn't call it an idiotic smile, nor the foolish smile you see sometimes in melancholy mad people. It was more of a happy childish smile.

"I was so foolish at first, and gave poor Walter and the doctors a lot of trouble," she said. "Of course it never struck me, until afterwards, that the fairies had taken the children."

She pressed the tips of the fingers of both hands to her forehead, and sat so for a while; then she roused herself again—

"But what am I thinking about? I haven't started to tell you about the children at all yet. Auntie! bring the children's portraits, will you, please? You'll find them on my dressing-table."

The old woman seemed to hesitate.

"Go on, Auntie, and do what I ask you," said Mrs Head. "Don't be foolish. You know I'm all right now."

"You mustn't take any notice of Auntie, Mr Ellis," she said with a smile, while the old woman's back was turned. "Poor old body, she's a bit crotchety at times, as old women are. She doesn't like me to get talking about the children. She's got an idea that if I do I'll start talking nonsense, as I used to do the first year after the children were lost. I was very foolish then, wasn't I, Walter?"

"You were, Maggie," said the boss. "But that's all past. You mustn't think of that time any more."

"You see," said Mrs Head, in explanation to me, "at first nothing would drive it out of my head that the children had wandered about until they perished of hunger and thirst in the bush. As if the Bush Fairies would let them do that."

"You were very foolish, Maggie," said the boss; "but don't think about that."

The old woman brought the portraits, a little boy and a little girl: they must have been very pretty children.

"You see," said Mrs Head, taking the portraits eagerly, and giving them to me one by one, "we had these taken in Sydney some years before the children were lost; they were much younger then. Wally's is not a good portrait; he was teething then, and very thin. That's him standing on the chair. Isn't the pose good? See, he's got one hand and one little foot forward, and an eager look in his eyes. The portrait is very dark, and you've got to look close to see the foot. He wants a toy rabbit that the photographer is tossing up to make him laugh. In the next portrait he's sitting on the chair—he's just settled himself to enjoy the fun. But see how happy little Maggie looks! You can see my arm where I was holding her in the chair. She was six months old then, and little Wally had just turned two."

She put the portraits up on the mantelshelf.

"Let me see; Wally (that's little Walter, you know)—Wally was five and little Maggie three and a half when we lost them. Weren't they, Walter?"

"Yes, Maggie," said the boss.

"You were away, Walter, when it happened."

"Yes, Maggie," said the boss—cheerfully, it seemed to me—"I was away."

"And we couldn't find you, Walter. You see," she said to me, "Walter—Mr Head—was away in Sydney on business, and we couldn't find his address. It was a beautiful morning, though rather warm, and just after the break-up of the drought. The grass was knee-high all over the run. It was a lonely place; there wasn't much bush cleared round the homestead, just a hundred yards or so, and the great awful scrubs ran back from the edges of the clearing all round for miles and miles—fifty or a hundred miles in some directions without a break; didn't they, Walter?"

"Yes, Maggie."

"I was alone at the house except for Mary, a half-caste girl we had, who used to help me with the housework and the children.

Andy was out on the run with the men, mustering sheep; weren't you, Andy?"

"Yes, Mrs Head."

"I used to watch the children close as they got to run about, because if they once got into the edge of the scrub they'd be lost; but this morning little Wally begged hard to be let take his little sister down under a clump of blue-gums in a corner of the home paddock to gather buttercups. You remember that clump of gums, Walter?"

"I remember, Maggie."

" 'I won't go through the fence a step, mumma,' little Wally said. I could see Old Peter—an old shepherd and station-hand we had—I could see him working on a dam we were making across a creek that ran down there. You remember Old Peter, Walter?"

"Of course I do, Maggie."

"I knew that Old Peter would keep an eye to the children; so I told little Wally to keep tight hold of his sister's hand and go straight down to Old Peter and tell him I sent them."

She was leaning forward with her hands clasping her knee, and telling me all this with a strange sort of eagerness.

"The little ones toddled off hand in hand, with their other hands holding fast their straw hats. 'In case a bad wind blowed,' as little Maggie said. I saw them stoop under the first fence, and that was the last that any one saw of them."

"Except the fairies, Maggie," said the boss quickly.

"Of course, Walter, except the fairies."

She pressed her fingers to her temples again for a minute.

"It seems that Old Peter was going to ride out to the musterers' camp that morning with bread for the men, and he left his work at the dam and started into the bush after his horse just as I turned back into the house, and before the children got near him. They either followed him for some distance or wandered into the bush after flowers and butterflies——" She broke off, and then suddenly asked me, "Do you think the Bush Fairies would entice children away, Mr Ellis?"

The boss caught my eye, and frowned and shook his head slightly.

"No. I'm sure they wouldn't, Mrs Head," I said—"at least not from what I know of them."

She thought, or tried to think, again for a while, in her helpless puzzled way. Then she went on, speaking rapidly, and rather mechanically, it seemed to me—

"The first I knew of it was when Peter came to the house about an hour afterwards, leading his horse, and without the children. I said—I said, 'O my God! where's the children?' " Her fingers fluttered up to her temples.

"Don't mind about that, Maggie," said the boss, hurriedly, stroking her head. "Tell Jack about the fairies."

"You were away at the time, Walter?"

"Yes, Maggie."

"And we couldn't find you, Walter?"

"No, Maggie," very gently. He rested his elbow on his knee and his chin on his hand, and looked into the fire.

"It wasn't your fault, Walter; but if you had been at home do you think the fairies would have taken the children?"

"Of course they would, Maggie. They had to: the children were lost."

"And they're bringing the children home next year?"

"Yes, Maggie—next year."

She lifted her hands to her head in a startled way, and it was some time before she went on again. There was no need to tell me about the lost children. I could see it all. She and the half-caste rushing towards where the children were seen last, with Old Peter after them. The hurried search in the nearer scrub. The mother calling all the time for Maggie and Wally, and growing wilder as the minutes flew past. Old Peter's ride to the musterers' camp. Horsemen seeming to turn up in no time and from nowhere, as they do in a case like this, and no matter how lonely the district. Bushmen galloping through the scrub in all directions. The hurried search the first day, and the mother mad with anxiety as night came on. Her long, hopeless, wild-eyed watch through the night; starting up at every sound of a horse's hoof, and reading the worst in one glance at the rider's face. The systematic work of the search-parties next day and the days following. How those days do fly past. The women from the next run or selection, and some from the town, driving from ten or twenty miles, perhaps, to stay with and try to comfort the mother. ("Put the horse to the cart, Jim: I must go to that poor woman!") Comforting her with improbable stories of children who had been lost for days, and were none the worse for it when they were found. The mounted policemen out with the black trackers. Search-parties cooeeing to each other about the bush, and lighting signal-fires. The reckless breakneck rides for news or more help. And the boss himself, wild-eyed and haggard, riding about the bush with Andy and one or two others perhaps, and searching hopelessly, days after the rest had given up all hope of finding the children alive. All this passed before me as Mrs Head talked, her voice sounding the while

as if she were in another room; and when I roused myself to listen,
she was on to the fairies again.

"It was very foolish of me, Mr Ellis. Weeks after—months after, I
think—I'd insist on going out on the veranda at dusk and calling for
the children. I'd stand there and call 'Maggie!' and 'Wally!' until
Walter took me inside; sometimes he had to force me inside. Poor
Walter! But of course I didn't know about the fairies then, Mr Ellis.
I was really out of my mind for a time."

"No wonder you were, Mrs Head," I said. "It was terrible
trouble."

"Yes, and I made it worse. I was so selfish in my trouble. But it's
all right now, Walter," she said, rumpling the boss's hair. "I'll never
be so foolish again."

"Of course you won't, Maggie."

"We're very happy now, aren't we, Walter?"

"Of course we are, Maggie."

"And the children are coming back next year."

"Next year, Maggie."

He leaned over the fire and stirred it up.

"You mustn't take any notice of us, Mr Ellis," she went on. "Poor
Walter is away so much that I'm afraid I make a little too much of
him when he does come home."

She paused and pressed her fingers to her temples again. Then she
said quickly:

"They used to tell me that it was all nonsense about the fairies,
but they were no friends of mine. I shouldn't have listened to them,
Walter. You told me not to. But then I was really not in my right
mind."

"Who used to tell you that, Mrs Head?" I asked.

"The Voices," she said; "you know about the Voices, Walter?"

"Yes, Maggie. But you don't hear the Voices now, Maggie?" he
asked anxiously. "You haven't heard them since I've been away this
time, have you, Maggie?"

"No, Walter. They've gone away a long time. I hear voices now
sometimes, but they're the Bush Fairies' voices. I hear them calling
Maggie and Wally to come with them." She paused again. "And
sometimes I think I hear them call me. But of course I couldn't go
away without you, Walter. But I'm foolish again. I was going to ask
you about the other voices, Mr Ellis. They used to say that it was
madness about the fairies; but then, if the fairies hadn't taken the
children, Black Jimmy, or the black trackers with the police, could
have tracked and found them at once."

"Of course they could, Mrs Head," I said.

"They said that the trackers couldn't track them because there was rain a few hours after the children were lost. But that was ridiculous. It was only a thunderstorm."

"Why!" I said, "I've known the blacks to track a man after a week's heavy rain."

She had her head between her fingers again, and when she looked up it was in a scared way.

"Oh, Walter!" she said, clutching the boss's arm; "whatever have I been talking about? What must Mr Ellis think of me? Oh! why did you let me talk like that?"

He put his arm round her. Andy nudged me and got up.

"Where are you going, Mr Ellis?" she asked hurriedly. "You're not going to-night. Auntie's made a bed for you in Andy's room. You mustn't mind me."

"Jack and Andy are going out for a little while," said the boss. "They'll be in to supper. We'll have a yarn, Maggie."

"Be sure you come back to supper, Mr Ellis," she said. "I really don't know what you must think of me—I've been talking all the time."

"Oh, I've enjoyed myself, Mrs Head," I said; and Andy hooked me out.

"She'll have a good cry and be better now," said Andy when we got away from the house. "She might be better for months. She has been fairly reasonable for over a year, but the boss found her pretty bad when he came back this time. It upset him a lot, I can tell you. She has turns now and again, and always ends up like she did just now. She gets a longing to talk about it to a bushman and a stranger; it seems to do her good. The doctor's against it, but doctors don't know everything."

"It's all true about the children, then?" I asked.

"It's cruel true," said Andy.

"And were the bodies never found?"

"Yes;" then, after a long pause, "I found them."

"You did!"

"Yes; in the scrub, and not so very far from home either—and in a fairly clear space. It's a wonder the search-parties missed it; but it often happens that way. Perhaps the little ones wandered a long way and came round in a circle. I found them about two months after they were lost. They had to be found, if only for the boss's sake. You see, in a case like this, and when the bodies aren't found, the parents never quite lose the idea that the little ones are wandering about the bush tonight (it might be years after) and perishing from hunger, thirst, or cold. That mad idea haunts 'em all their lives. It's the same, I believe, with friends drowned at sea. Friends ashore are haunted for a long while with the idea of the white sodden corpse tossing about and drifting round in the water."

"And you never told Mrs Head about the children being found?"

"Not for a long time. It wouldn't have done any good. She was raving mad for months. He took her to Sydney and then to Melbourne—to the best doctors he could find in Australia. They could do no good, so he sold the station—sacrificed everything, and took her to England."

"To England?"

"Yes; and then to Germany to a big German doctor there. He'd offer a thousand pounds where they only wanted fifty. It was no good. She got worse in England, and raved to go back to Australia and find the children. The doctors advised him to take her back, and he did. He spent all his money, travelling saloon, and with reserved cabins, and a nurse, and trying to get her cured; that's why he's droving now. She was restless in Sydney. She wanted to go back to the station and wait there till the fairies brought the children home. She'd been getting the fairy idea into her head slowly all the time. The boss encouraged it. But the station was sold, and he couldn't have lived there anyway without going mad himself. He'd married her from Bathurst. Both of them have got friends and relations here, so he thought best to bring her here. He persuaded her that the fairies were going to bring the children here. Everybody's very kind to them. I think it's a mistake to run away from a town where you're known, in a case like this, though most people do it. It was years before he gave up hope. I think he has hopes yet—after she's been fairly well for a longish time."

"And you never tried telling her that the children were found?"

"Yes; the boss did. The little ones were buried on the Lachlan River at first; but the boss got a horror of having them buried in the bush, so he had them brought to Sydney and buried in the Waverley Cemetery near the sea. He bought the ground, and room for himself and Maggie when they go out. It's all the ground he owns in wide Australia, and once he had thousands of acres. He took her to the grave one day. The doctors were against it; but he couldn't rest till he tried it. He took her out, and explained it all to her. She scarcely seemed interested. She read the names on the stone, and said it was a nice stone, and asked questions about how the children were found and brought here. She seemed quite sensible, and very cool about it.

But when he got her home she was back on the fairy idea again. He tried another day, but it was no use; so then he let it be. I think it's better as it is. Now and again, at her best, she seems to understand that the children were found dead, and buried, and she'll talk sensibly about it, and ask questions in a quiet way, and make him promise to take her to Sydney to see the grave next time he's down. But it doesn't last long, and she's always worse afterwards."

We turned into a bar and had a beer. It was a very quiet drink. Andy "shouted" in his turn, and while I was drinking the second beer a thought struck me.

"The boss was away when the children were lost?"

"Yes," said Andy.

"Strange you couldn't find him."

"Yes, it was strange; but *he'll* have to tell you about that. Very likely he will; it's either all or nothing with him."

"I feel damned sorry for the boss," I said.

"You'd be sorrier if you knew all," said Andy. "It's the worst trouble than can happen to a man. It's like living with the dead. It's—it's like a man living with his dead wife."

When we went home supper was ready. We found Mrs Head, bright and cheerful, bustling round. You'd have thought her one of the happiest and brightest little women in Australia. Not a word about children or the fairies. She knew the bush and asked me all about my trips. She told some good bush stories too. It was the pleasantest hour I'd spent for a long time.

"Good night, Mr Ellis," she said brightly, shaking hands with me when Andy and I were going to turn in. "And don't forget your pipe. Here it is! I know that bushmen like to have a whiff or two when they turn in. Walter smokes in bed. I don't mind. You can smoke all night if you like."

"She seems all right," I said to Andy when we were in our room.

He shook his head mournfully. We'd left the door ajar, and we could hear the boss talking to her quietly. Then we heard her speak; she had a very clear voice.

"Yes, I'll tell you the truth, Walter. I've been deceiving you, Walter, all the time, but I did it for the best. Don't be angry with me, Walter! The Voices did come back while you were away. Oh, how I longed for you to come back! They haven't come since you've been home, Walter. You must stay with me a while now. Those awful Voices kept calling me, and telling me lies about the children, Walter! They told me to kill myself; they told me it was all my own fault—that I killed the children. They said I was a drag on you, and they'd laugh—Ha! ha! ha!—like that. They'd say, 'Come on, Maggie; come on, Maggie.' They told me to come to the river, Walter."

Andy closed the door. His face was very miserable.

We turned in, and I can tell you I enjoyed a soft white bed after months and months of sleeping out at night, between watches, on the hard ground or the sand, or at best on a few boughs when I wasn't too tired to pull them down, and my saddle for a pillow.

But the story of the children haunted me for an hour or two. I've never since quite made up my mind as to why the boss took me home. Probably he really did think it would do his wife good to talk to a stranger; perhaps he wanted me to understand—maybe he was weakening as he grew older, and craved for a new word or hand-grip of sympathy now and then.

When I did get to sleep I could have slept for three or four days, but Andy roused me out about four o'clock. The old woman that they called Auntie was up and had a good breakfast of eggs and bacon and coffee ready in the detached kitchen at the back. We moved about on tiptoe and had our breakfast quietly.

"The wife made me promise to wake her to see to our breakfast and say good-bye to you; but I want her to sleep this morning, Jack," said the boss. "I'm going to walk down as far as the station with you. She made up a parcel of fruit and sandwiches for you and Andy. Don't forget it."

Andy went on ahead. The boss and I walked down the wide silent street, which was also the main road; and we walked two or three hundred yards without speaking. He didn't seem sociable this morning, or any way sentimental; when he did speak it was something about the cattle.

But I had to speak; I felt a swelling and rising up in my chest, and at last I made a swallow and blurted out:

"Look here, boss, old chap? I'm damned sorry!"

Our hands came together and gripped. The ghostly Australian daybreak was over the Bathurst plains.

We went on another hundred yards or so, and then the boss said quietly:

"I was away when the children were lost, Jack. I used to go on a howling spree every six or nine months. Maggie never knew. I'd tell her I had to go to Sydney on business, or out back to look after some stock. When the children were lost, and for nearly a fortnight after, I was beastly drunk in an out-of-the-way shanty in the bush—a sly-grog shop. The old brute that kept it was too true to me. He thought that the story of the lost children was a trick to get me home, and he swore that he hadn't seen me. He never told me. I could have found those children, Jack. They were mostly new chums and fools about the run, and not one of the three policemen was a bushman. I knew those scrubs better than any man in the country."

I reached for his hand again, and gave it a grip. That was all I could do for him.

"Good-bye, Jack!" he said at the door of the brake-van. "Good-bye, Andy!—keep those bullocks on their feet."

The cattle-train went on towards the Blue Mountains. Andy and I sat silent for a while, watching the guard fry three eggs on a plate over a coal-stove in the centre of the van.

"Does the boss never go to Sydney?" I asked.

"Very seldom," said Andy, "and then only when he has to, on business. When he finishes his business with the stock agents, he takes a run out to Waverley Cemetery perhaps, and comes home by the next train."

After a while I said, "He told me about the drink, Andy—about his being on the spree when the children were lost."

"Well, Jack," said Andy, "that's the thing that's been killing him ever since, and it happened over ten years ago."

A BUSH DANCE

"Tap, tap, tap, tap."

The little school-house and residence in the scrub was lighted brightly in the midst of the "close," solid blackness of that moonless December night, when the sky and stars were smothered and suffocated by drought haze.

It was the evening of the school children's "feast." That is to say that the children had been sent, and "let go," and the younger ones "fetched" through the blazing heat to the school, one day early in the holidays, and raced—sometimes in couples tied together by the legs, and caked, and bunned, and finally improved upon by the local Chadband, and got rid of. The schoolroom had been cleared for dancing, the maps rolled and tied, the desks and blackboards stacked against the wall outside. Tea was over, and the trestles and boards, whereon had been spread better things than had been provided for the unfortunate youngsters, had been taken outside to keep the desks and blackboards company.

On stools running end to end along one side of the room sat about twenty more or less blooming country girls of from fifteen to twenty odd.

On the rest of the stools, running end to end along the other wall, sat about twenty more or less blooming chaps.

It was evident that something was seriously wrong. None of the girls spoke above a hushed whisper. None of the men spoke above a hushed oath. Now and again two or three sidled out, and if you had followed them you would have found that they went outside to listen hard into the darkness and to swear.

"Tap, tap, tap."

The rows moved uneasily, and some of the girls turned pale faces nervously towards the side door, in the direction of the sound.

"Tap—tap."

The tapping came from the kitchen at the rear of the teacher's residence, and was uncomfortably suggestive of a coffin being made: it was also accompanied by a sickly, indescribable odour—more like that of warm cheap glue than anything else.

In the schoolroom was a painful scene of strained listening. Whenever one of the men returned from outside, or put his head in at the door, all eyes were fastened on him in the flash of a single eye, and then withdrawn hopelessly. At the sound of a horse's step all eyes and ears were on the door, till someone muttered, "It's only the horses in the paddock."

Some of the girls' eyes began to glisten suspiciously, and at last the belle of the party—a great, dark-haired, pink-and-white Blue Mountain girl, who had been sitting for a full minute staring before her, with blue eyes unnaturally bright, suddenly covered her face with her hands, rose, and started blindly from the room, from which she was steered in hurry by two sympathetic and rather "upset" girl friends, and as she passed out she was heard sobbing hysterically:

"Oh, I can't help it! I did want to dance! It's a sh-shame! I can't help it! I—I want to dance! I rode twenty miles to dance—and—and I want to dance!"

A tall, strapping young bushman rose, without disguise, and followed the girl out. The rest began to talk loudly of stock, dogs, and horses, and other bush things; but above their voices rang out that of the girl from the outside—being man comforted:

"I can't help it, Jack! I did want to dance! I—I had such—such—
a job—to get mother—and—and father to let me come—and—and
now!"

The two girl friends came back. "He sez to leave her to him," they
whispered, in reply to an interrogatory glance from the schoolmistress.

"It's—it's no use, Jack!" came the voice of grief. "You don't know
what—what father and mother—is. I—I won't—be able to ge-get
away—again—for—for—not till I'm married, perhaps."

The schoolmistress glanced uneasily along the row of girls. "I'll
take her into my room and make her lie down," she whispered to her
sister, who was staying with her. "She'll start some of the other girls
presently—it's just the weather for it," and she passed out quietly.
That schoolmistress was a woman of penetration.

A final "tap-tap" from the kitchen; then a sound like the squawk
of a hurt or frightened child, and the faces in the room turned
quickly in that direction and brightened. But there came a bang and
a sound like "damn!" and hopelessness settled down.

A shout from the outer darkness, and most of the men and some
of the girls rose and hurried out. Fragments of conversation heard
in the darkness:

"It's two horses, I tell you!"

"It's three, you——!"

"Lay you ——!"

"Put the stuff up!"

A clack of gate thrown open.

"Who is it, Tom?"

Voices from gatewards, yelling, "Johnny Mears! They've got
Johnny Mears!"

Then rose yells, and a cheer such as is seldom heard in
scrublands.

Out in the kitchen long Dave Regan grabbed, from the far side of
the table, where he had thrown it, a burst and battered concertina,
which he had been for the last hour vainly trying to patch and make
air-tight; and, holding it out towards the back door, between his
palms, as a football is held, he let it drop, and fetched it neatly on the
toe of his riding-boot. It was a beautiful kick, the concertina shot out
into the blackness, from which was projected, in return, first a short,
sudden howl, then a face with one eye glaring and the other covered
by an enormous brick-coloured hand, and a voice that wanted to
know who shot "that lurid loaf of bread?"

But from the schoolroom was heard the loud, free voice of Joe Matthews, M.C.:

"Take yer partners! Hurry up! Take yer partners! They've got Johnny Mears with his fiddle!"

THE BUCK-JUMPER

Saturday afternoon.

There were about a dozen bush natives, from anywhere, most of them lanky and easygoing, hanging about the little slab-and-bark hotel on the edge of the scrub at Capertee Camp (a teamster's camp) when Cobb & Co.'s mail-coach, and six came dashing down the siding from round Crown Ridge, in all its glory, to the end of the twelve-mile stage. Some dusty, wiry, ill-used hacks were hanging to the fence and to saplings about the place. The fresh coach-horses stood ready in a stockyard close to the shanty. As the coach climbed the nearer bank of the creek at the foot of the ridge, six of the bushmen detached themselves from veranda-posts, from their heels, from the clay floor of the veranda and the rough slab wall against which they'd been resting, and joined a group of four or five who stood round one. He stood with his back to the corner post of the stockyard, his feet well braced out in front of him, and contemplated the toes of his tight new 'lastic-side boots and whistled softly. He was a clean-limbed, handsome fellow, with riding-cords, leggings, and a blue sash; he was Graeco-Roman-nosed, blue-eyed, and his glossy, curly black hair bunched up in front of the brim of a new cabbage-tree hat, set well back on his head.

"Do it for a quid, Jack?" asked one.

"Damned if I will, Jim!" said the young man at the post. "I'll do it for a fiver—not a blanky sprat less."

Jim took off his hat and "shoved" it round, and "bobs" were "chucked" into it. The result was about thirty shillings.

Jack glanced contemptuously into the crown of the hat.

"Not me!" he said, showing some emotion for the first time. "D'yer think I'm going to risk me blanky neck for your blanky amusement for thirty blanky bob? I'll ride the blanky horse for a fiver, and I'll feel the blanky quids in my pocket before I get on."

Meanwhile the coach had dashed up to the door of the shanty. There were about twenty passengers aboard—inside, on the box-seat, on the tail-board, and hanging on to the roof—most of them Sydney men going up to the Mudgee races. They got down and went inside with the driver for a drink, while the stablemen changed horses. The bushmen raised their voices a little and argued.

One of the passengers was a big, stout, hearty man—a good-hearted, sporting man and a racehorse-owner, according to his brands. He had a round red face and a white cork hat. "What's those chaps got on ouside?" he asked the publican.

"Oh, it's a bet they've got on about riding a horse," replied the publican. "The flash-looking chap with the sash is Flash Jack, the horse-breaker; and they reckon they've got the champion outlaw in the district out there—that chestnut horse in the yard."

The sporting man was interested at once, and went out and joined the bushmen.

"Well, chaps! what have you got on here?" he asked cheerily.

"Oh," said Jim carelessly, "it's only a bit of a bet about ridin' that blanky chestnut in the corner of the yard there." He indicated an ungroomed chestnut horse, fenced off by a couple of long sapling poles in a corner of the stockyard. "Flash Jack there—he reckons he's the champion horse-breaker round here—Flash Jack reckons he can take it out of that horse first try."

"What's up with the horse?" inquired the big, red-faced man. "It looks quiet enough. Why, I'd ride it myself."

"Would yer?" said Jim, who had hair that stood straight up, and an innocent, inquiring expression. "Looks quiet, does he? *You* ought to know more about horses than to go by the looks of 'em. He's quiet enough just now, when there's no one near him; but you should have been here an hour ago. That horse has killed two men and put another chap's shoulder out—besides breaking a cove's leg. It took six of us all the morning to run him in and get the saddle on him; and now Flash Jack wants to back out of it."

"Euraliar!" remarked Flash Jack cheerfully. "I said I'd ride that blanky horse out of the yard for a fiver. I ain't goin' to risk my blanky neck for nothing and only to amuse you blanks."

"He said he'd ride the horse inside the yard for a quid," said Jim.

"And get smashed against the rails!" said Flash Jack. "I would be a fool. I'd rather take my chance outside in the scrub—and it's rough country round here."

"Well, how much do you want?" asked the man in the mushroom hat.

"A fiver, I said," replied Jack indifferently. "And the blanky stuff in my pocket before I get on the blanky horse."

"Are you frightened of us running away without paying you?" inquired one of the passengers who had gathered round.

"I'm frightened of the horse bolting with me without me being paid," said Flash Jack. "I know that horse; he's got a mouth like iron. I might be at the bottom of the cliff on Crown Ridge road in twenty minutes with my head caved in, and then what chance for the quids?"

"You wouldn't want 'em then," suggested a passenger. "Or, say!—we'd leave the fiver with the publican to bury you."

Flash Jack ignored that passenger. He eyed his boots and softly whistled a tune.

"All right!" said the man in the cork hat, putting his hand in his pocket. "I'll start with a quid; stump up, you chaps."

The five pounds were got together.

"I'll lay a quid to half a quid he don't stick on ten minutes!" shouted Jim to his mates as soon as he saw that the event was to come off. The passengers also betted amongst themselves. Flash Jack, after putting the money in his breeches-pocket, let down the rails and led the horse into the middle of the yard.

"Quiet as an old cow!" snorted a passenger in disgust. "I believe it's a sell!"

"Wait a bit," said Jim to the passenger, "wait a bit and you'll see."

They waited and saw.

Flash Jack leisurely mounted the horse, rode slowly out of the yard, and trotted briskly round the corner of the shanty and into the scrub, which swallowed him more completely than the sea might have done.

Most of the other bushmen mounted their horses and followed Flash Jack to a clearing in the scrub, at a safe distance from the shanty; then they dismounted and hung on to saplings, or leaned against their horses, while they laughed.

At the hotel there was just time for another drink. The driver climbed to his seat and shouted, "All aboard!" in his usual tone. The passengers climbed to their places, thinking hard. A mile or so along the road the man with the cork hat remarked, with much truth:

"Those blanky bushmen have got too much time to think." The bushmen returned to the shanty as soon as the coach was out of sight, and proceeded to "knock down" the fiver.

JIMMY GRIMSHAW'S WOOING

The Half-way House at Tinned Dog (out back in Australia) kept Daniel Myers—licensed to retail spirituous and fermented liquors—in drink and the horrors for upward of five years, at the end of which time he lay hidden for weeks in a back skillion, an object which no decent man would care to see—or hear when it gave forth sound. "Good accommodation for man and beast;" but few shanties save his own might, for a consideration, have accommodated the sort of beast which the man Myers had become towards the end of his career. But at last the eccentric bush doctor, "Doc. Wild" (who perhaps could drink as much as Myers without its having any further effect upon his temperament than to keep him awake and cynical), pronounced the publican dead enough to be buried legally; so the widow buried him, had the skillion cleaned out, and the sign altered to read, "Margaret Myers, licensed, etc.," and continued to conduct the pub just as she had run it for over five years, with the joyful and blessed exception that there was no longer a human pig and pigsty attached, and that the atmosphere was calm. Most of the regular patrons of the Half-way House could have their horrors decently, and, comparatively, quietly—or otherwise have them privately—in the Big Scrub adjacent; but Myers had not been one of that sort.

Mrs Myers settled herself to enjoy life comfortably and happily, at the fixed age of thirty-nine, for the next seven years or so. She was a pleasant-faced dumpling, who had been baked solid in the droughts of Out Back without losing her good looks, and had put up with a hard life, and Myers, all those years without losing her good humour and nature. Probably, had her husband been the opposite kind of man, she would have been different—haggard, bad-tempered, and altogether impossible—for of such is woman. But then it might be taken into consideration that she had been practically a widow during at least the last five years of her husband's alleged life.

Mrs Myers was reckoned a good catch in the district, but it soon seemed that she was not to be caught.

"It would be a grand thing," one of the periodical boozers of Tinned Dog would say to his mates, "for one of us to have his name up on a pub; it would save a lot of money."

"It wouldn't save you anything, Bill, if I got it," was the retort. "You needn't come round chewing my lug then. I'd give you one drink and no more."

The publican at Dead Camel, station managers, professional shearers, even one or two solvent squatters and promising cockatoos, tried their luck in vain. In answer to the suggestion that she ought to have a man to knock round and look after things, she retorted that she had had one, and was perfectly satisfied. Few travellers on those tracks but tried "a bit of bear-up" in that direction, but all to no purpose. Chequemen knocked down their cheques manfully at the Half-way House—to get courage and good will and "put it off" till, at the last moment, they offered themselves abjectly to the landlady; which was worse than bad judgment on their part—it was very silly, and she told them so.

One or two swore off, and swore to keep straight; but she had no faith in them, and when they found that out, it hurt their feelings so much that they "broke out" and went on record-breaking sprees.

About the end of each shearing the sign was touched up, with an extra coat of paint on the "Margaret," whereat suitors looked hopeless.

One or two of the rejected died of love in the horrors in the Big Scrub—anyway, the verdict was that they died of love aggravated by the horrors. But the climax was reached when a Queensland shearer, seizing the opportunity when the mate, whose turn it was to watch him, fell asleep, went down to the yard and hanged himself on the butcher's gallows—having first removed his clothes, with some drink-lurid idea of leaving the world as naked as he came into it. He climbed the pole, sat astride on top, fixed the rope to neck and bar, but gave a yell—a yell of drunken triumph—before he dropped, and woke his mates.

They cut him down and brought him to. Next day he apologized to Mrs Myers, said, "Ah, well! So-long!" to the rest, and departed—cured of drink and love apparently. The verdict was that the blanky fool should have dropped before he yelled; but she was upset and annoyed, and it began to look as though, if she wished to continue to live on happily and comfortably for a few years longer at the fixed age of thirty-nine, she would either have to give up the pub or get married.

Her fame was carried far and wide, and she became a woman whose name was mentioned with respect in rough shearing-sheds and huts, and round the camp-fire.

About thirty miles south of Tinned Dog one James Grimshaw, widower—otherwise known as "Old Jimmy," though he was little past middle age—had a small selection which he had worked, let, given up, and tackled afresh (witth sinews of war drawn from fencing contracts) ever since the death of his young wife some fifteen years agone. He was a practical, square-faced, clean-shaven, clean, and tidy man, with a certain "cleanness" about the shape of his limbs which suggested the old jockey or hostler. There were two strong theories in connection with Jimmy—one was that he had had a university education, and the other that he couldn't write his own name. Not nearly such a ridiculous nor simple case out back as it might seem.

Jimmy smoked and listened without comment to the "heard tells" in connection with Mrs Myers, till at last one night, at the end of his contract and over a last pipe, he said quietly, "I'll go up to Tinned Dog next week and try my luck."

His mates and the casual Jims and Bills were taken too suddenly to laugh, and the laugh having been lost, as Bland Holt, the Australian actor would put it in a professional sense, the audience had time to think, with the result that the joker swung his hand down through an imaginary table and exclaimed:

"By God! Jimmy'll do it." (Applause.)

So one drowsy afternoon at the time of the year when the breathless day runs on past 7 p.m., Mrs Myers sat sewing in the bar-parlour, when a clean-shaved, clean-shirted, clean-neckerchiefed, clean-moleskinned, greased-bluchered—altogether a model or stage swagman came up, was served in the bar by the half-caste female cook, and took his way to the river-bank, where he rigged a small tent and made a model camp.

A couple of hours later he sat on a stool on the veranda, smoking a clean clay pipe. Just before the sunset meal Mrs Myers asked, "Is that trav'ler there yet, Mary?"

"Yes, missus. Clean pfellar that."

The landlady knitted her forehead over her sewing, as women do when limited for "stuff" or wondering whether a section has been cut wrong—or perhaps she thought of that other who hadn't been a "clean pfellar." She put her work aside, and stood in the doorway, looking out across the clearing.

"Good day, mister," she said, seeming to become aware of him for the first time.

"Good day, missus!"

"Hot!"

"Hot!"

Pause.

"Trav'lin'?"

"No, not particular!"

She waited for him to explain. Myers was always explaining when he wasn't raving. But the swagman smoked on.

"Have a drink?" she suggested, to keep her end up.

"No, thank you, missus. I had one an hour or so ago. I never take more than two a day—one before breakfast, if I can get it, and a night-cap."

What a contrast to Myers! she thought.

"Come and have some tea; it's ready."

"Thank you. I don't mind if I do."

They got on very slowly, but comfortably. She got little out of him except the facts that he had a selection, had finished a contract, and was "just having a look at the country." He politely declined a "shake-down," saying he had a comfortable camp, and preferred being out this weather. She got his name with a "by the way" as he rose to leave, and he went back to camp.

He caught a cod, and they had it for breakfast next morning, and got along so comfortable over breakfast that he put in the forenoon pottering about the gates and stable with a hammer, a saw, and a box of nails.

And, well—to make it short—when the big Tinned Dog Shed had cut out, and the shearers struck the Half-way House, they were greatly impressed by a brand-new sign whereon glistened the words:

HALF-WAY HOUSE HOTEL
By
JAMES GRIMSHAW
GOOD STABLING

The last time I saw Mrs Grimshaw she looked about thirty-five.

AT DEAD DINGO

It was blazing hot outside and smothering hot inside the weather-board and iron shanty at Dead Dingo, a place on the Cleared Road, where there was a pub and a police station, and which was sometimes called "Roasted," and other times "Potted Dingo"—nicknames suggested by the everlasting drought and the vicinity of the one-pub township of Tinned Dog.

From the front veranda the scene was straight-cleared road, running right and left to Out Back, and to Bourke (and ankle-deep in the red sand dust for perhaps a hundred miles); the rest blue-grey bush, dust, and the heat-wave blazing across every object.

There were only four in the bar-room, though it was New Year's Day. There weren't many more in the county. The girl sat behind the bar—the coolest place in the shanty—reading "Deadwood Dick." On a worn and torn and battered horsehair sofa, which had seen cooler places and better days, lay an awful and healthy example, a bearded swagman, with his arms twisted over his head and his face to the wall, sleeping off the death of the dead drunk. Bill and Jim—shearer and rouseabout—sat at a table playing cards. It was about three o'clock in the afternoon, and they had been gambling since nine—and the greater part of the night before—so they were, probably, in a worse condition morally (and perhaps physically) than the drunken swagman on the sofa.

Close under the bar, in a dangerous place for his legs and tail, lay a sheep-dog with a chain attached to his collar and wound round his neck.

Presently a thump on the table, and Bill, unlucky gambler, rose with an oath that would have been savage if it hadn't been drawled.

"Stumped?" inquired Jim.

"Not a blanky, lurid deener!" drawled Bill.

Jim drew his reluctant hands from the cards, his eyes went slowly and hopelessly round the room and out the door. There was something in the eyes of both, except when on the card-table, of the look of a man waking in a strange place.

"Got anything?" asked Jim, fingering the cards again.

Bill sucked in his cheeks, collecting the saliva with difficulty, and spat out on to the veranda floor.

"That's all I got," he drawled. "It's gone now."

Jim leaned back in his chair, twisted, yawned, and caught sight of the dog.

"That there dog yours?" he asked, brightening.

They had evidently been strangers the day before, or as strange to each other as bushmen can be.

Bill scratched behind his ear, and blinked at the dog. The dog woke suddenly to a flea fact.

"Yes," drawled Bill, "he's mine."

"Well, I'm going out back, and I want a dog," said Jim, gathering the cards briskly. "Half a quid agin the dog?"

"Half a quid be ——!" drawled Bill. "Call it a quid?"

"Half a blanky quid!"

"A gory, lurid quid!" drawled Bill desperately, and he stooped over his swag.

But Jim's hands were itching in a ghastly way over the cards.

"All right. Call it a —— quid."

The drunkard on the sofa stirred, showed signs of waking, but died again. Remember this, it might come in useful.

Bill sat down to the table once more.

Jim rose first, winner of the dog. He stretched, yawned "Ah, well!" and shouted drinks. Then he shouldered his swag, stirred the dog up with his foot, unwound the chain, said "Ah, well—so-long!" and drifted out and along the road toward Out Back, the dog following with head and tail down.

Bill scored another drink on account of girl-pity for bad luck, shouldered his swag, said "So-long, Mary!" and drifted out and along the road towards Tinned Dog, on the Bourke side. A long, drowsy, half-hour passed—the sort of half-hour that is as long as an hour in the places where days are as long as years, and years hold about as much as days do in other places.

The man on the sofa woke with a start, and looked scared and wild for a moment; then he brought his dusty broken boots to the floor, rested his elbows on his knees, took his unfortunate head between his hands, and came back to life gradually.

He lifted his head, looked at the girl across the top of the bar, and formed with his lips, rather than spoke, the words:

"Put up a drink?"*

She shook her head tightly and went on reading.

He staggered up, and, leaning on the bar, made desperate distress signals with hand, eyes, and mouth.

"No!" she snapped. "I means no when I says no! You've had too many last drinks already, and the boss says you ain't to have another. If you swear again, or bother me, I'll call him."

---

* "Put up a drink"—i.e., "Give me a drink on credit," or "Chalk it up."

He hung sullenly on the counter for a while, then lurched to his swag, and shouldered it hopelessly and wearily. Then he blinked round, whistled, waited a moment, went on to the front veranda, peered round, through the heat, with bloodshot eyes, and whistled again. He turned and started through to the back door.

"What the devil do you want now?" demanded the girl, interrupted in her reading for the third time by him. "Stampin' all over the house. You can't go through there! It's privit! I do wish to goodness you'd git!"

"Where the blazes is that there dog o' mine get to?" he muttered. "Did you see a dog?"

"No! What do I want with your dog?"

He whistled out in front again, and round each corner. Then he came back with a decided step and tone.

"Look here! that there dog was lyin' there agin the wall when I went to sleep. He wouldn't stir from me, or my swag, in a year, if he wasn't dragged. He's been blanky well touched [stolen], and I wouldn'ter lost him for a fiver. Are you sure you ain't seen a dog?" Then suddenly, as the thought struck him: "Where's them two chaps that was playin' cards when I wenter sleep?"

"Why!" exclaimed the girl, without thinking, "there was a dog, now I come to think of it, but I thought it belonged to one of them chaps. Anyway, they played for it, and the other chap won it and took it away."

He stared at her blankly, with thunder gathering in the blankness.

"What sort of a dog was it?"

Dog described; the chain round the neck settled it.

He scowled at her darkly.

"Now, look here," he said, "you've allowed gamblin' in this bar—your boss has. You've got no right to let spielers gamble away a man's dog. Is a customer to lose his dog every time he has a doze to suit your boss? I'll go straight across to the police camp and put you away, and I don't care if you lose your licence. I ain't goin' to lose my dog. I wouldn'ter taken a ten-pound note for that blanky dog! I——"

She was filling a pewter hastily.

"Here! for God's sake have a drink an' stop yer row."

He drank with satisfaction. Then he hung on the bar with one elbow and scowled out the door.

"Which blanky way did them chaps go?" he growled.

"The one that took the dog went towards Tinned Dog."

"And I'll haveter go all the blanky way back after him, and most likely lose me shed! Here!" jerking the empty pewter across the bar, "fill that up again; I'm narked properly, I am, and I'll take twenty-four blanky hours to cool down now. I wouldn'ter lost that dog for twenty quid."

He drank again with deeper satisfaction, then he shuffled out, muttering, swearing, and threatening louder every step, and took the track to Tinned Dog.

Now the man, girl, or woman, who told me this yarn has never quite settled it in his or her mind as to who really owned the dog. I leave it to you.

TELLING MRS BAKER

Most bushmen who hadn't "known Bob Baker to speak to," had "heard tell of him." He'd been a squatter, not many years before, on the Macquarie River in New South Wales, and had made money in the good seasons, and had gone in for horse-racing and racehorse-breeding, and long trips to Sydney, where he put up at swell hotels and went the pace. So after a pretty severe drought, when the sheep died by thousands on his runs, Bob Baker went under, and the bank took over his station and put a manager in charge.

He'd been a jolly, open-handed, popular man, which means that he'd been a selfish man as far as his wife and children were concerned, for they had to suffer for it in the end. Such generosity is often born of vanity, or moral cowardice, or both mixed. It's very nice to hear the chaps sing "For he's a jolly good fellow," but you've mostly got to pay for it twice—first in company, and afterwards alone. I once heard the chaps singing that I was a jolly good fellow, when I was leaving a place and they were giving me a send-off. It thrilled me, and brought a warm gush to my eyes; but, all the same, I wished I had half the money I'd lent them, and spent on 'em, and I wished I'd used the time I'd wasted to be a jolly good fellow.

When I first met Bob Baker he was a boss drover on the great north-western route, and his wife lived at the township of Solong on the Sydney side. He was going north to new country round by the

Gulf of Carpentaria with a big mob of cattle, on a two years' trip; and I and my mate, Andy M'Culloch, engaged to go with him. We wanted to have a look at the Gulf Country.

After we had crossed the Queensland border it seemed to me that the boss was too fond of going into wayside shanties and town pubs. Andy had been with him on another trip, and he told me that the boss was only going this way lately. Andy knew Mrs Baker well, and seemed to think a deal of her. "She's a good little woman," said Andy. "One of the right stuff. I worked on their station for a while when I was a nipper, and I know. She was always a damned sight too good for the boss, but she believed in him. When I was coming away this time she says to me, 'Look here, Andy, I am afraid Robert is drinking again. Now I want you to look after him for me, as much as you can—you seem to have as much influencce with him as anyone. I want you to promise me that you'll never have a drink with him.'

"And I promised," said Andy, "and I'll keep my word." Andy was a chap who could keep his word, and nothing else. And, no matter how the boss persuaded, or sneered, or swore at him, Andy would never drink with him.

It got worse and worse: the boss would ride on ahead and get drunk at a shanty, and sometimes he'd be days behind us; and when he'd catch up to us his temper would be just about as much as we could stand. At last he went on a howling spree at Mulgatown, about a hundred and fifty miles north of the border, and, what was worse, he got in tow with a flash barmaid there—one of those girls who are engaged, by the publicans up-country, as baits for chequemen.

He went mad over that girl. He drew an advance cheque from the stock-owner's agent there, and knocked that down; then he raised some more money somehow, and spent that—mostly on the girl.

We did all we could. Andy got him along the track for a couple of stages, and just when we thought he was all right, he slipped us in the night and went back.

We had two other men with us, but had the devil's own bother on account of the cattle. It was a mixed-up job all round. You see it was all big runs round there, and we had to keep the bullocks moving along the route all the time, or else get into trouble for trespass. The agent wasn't going to go to the expense of putting the cattle in a paddock until the boss sobered up; there was very little grass on the route or the travelling-stock reserves or camps, so we had to keep travelling for grass.

The world might wobble and all the banks go bung, but the cattle have to go through—that's the law of the stock-routes. So the agent wired to the owners, and, when he got their reply, he sacked the boss and sent the cattle on in charge of another man. The new boss was a drover coming south after a trip; he had his two brothers with him, so he didn't want me and Andy; but, anyway, we were full up of this trip, so we arranged, between the agent and the new boss, to get most of the wages due to us—the boss had drawn some of our stuff and spent it.

We could have started on the back track at once, but, drunk or sober, mad or sane, good or bad, it isn't bush religion to desert a mate in a hole; and the boss was a mate of ours: so we stuck to him. We camped on the creek outside the town, and kept him in the camp with us as much as possible, and did all we could for him.

"How could I face his wife if I went home without him?" asked Andy, "or any of his old mates?"

The boss got himself turned out of the pub where the barmaid was, and then he'd hang round the other pubs, and get drink somehow, and fight, and get knocked about. He was an awful object by this time, wild-eyed and gaunt, and he hadn't washed or shaved for days.

Andy got the constable in charge of the police station to lock him up for a night, but it only made him worse: we took him back to the camp next morning, and while our eyes were off him for a few minutes he slipped away into the scrub, stripped himself naked, and started to hang himself to a leaning tree with a piece of clothes-line rope. We got to him just in time.

Then Andy wired to the boss's brother Ned, who was fighting the drought, the rabbit pest, and the banks, on a small station back on the border. Andy reckoned it was about time to do something.

Perhaps the boss hadn't been quite right in his head before he started drinking—he had acted queer sometimes, now we came to think of it; maybe he'd got a touch of sunstroke or got brooding over his troubles—anyway he died in the horrors within the week.

His brother Ned turned up on the last day, and Bob thought he was the devil, and grappled with him. It took the three of us to hold the boss down sometimes.

Sometimes, towards the end, he'd be sensible for a few minutes and talk about his "poor wife and children;" and immediately afterwards he'd fall a-cursing me, and Andy, and Ned, and calling us devils. He cursed everything; he cursed his wife and children, and yelled that they were dragging him down to hell. He died raving mad. It was the worst case of death in the horrors of drink that I ever saw or heard of in the bush.

Ned saw to the funeral: it was very hot weather, and men have to be buried quick who die out there in the hot weather—especially men who die in the state the boss was in. Then Ned went to the public-house where the barmaid was and called the landlord out. It was a desperate fight: the publican was a big man, and a bit of a fighting man; but Ned was one of those quiet, simple-minded chaps who will carry a thing through to death when they make up their minds. He gave that publican nearly as good a thrashing as he deserved. The constable in charge of the station backed Ned, while another policeman picked up the publican. Sounds queer to you city people, doesn't it?

Next morning we three started south. We stayed a couple of days at Ned Baker's station on the border, and then started on our three-hundred-mile ride down-country. The weather was still very hot, so we decided to travel at night for a while, and left Ned's place at dusk. He parted from us at the homestead gate. He gave Andy a small packet, done up in canvas, for Mrs Baker, which Andy told me contained Bob's pocket-book, letters, and papers. We looked back, after we'd gone a piece along the dusty road, and saw Ned still standing by the gate; and a very lonely figure he looked. Ned was a bachelor. "Poor old Ned," said Andy to me. "He was in love with Mrs Bob Baker before she got married, but she picked the wrong man—girls mostly do. Ned and Bob were together on the Macquarie, but Ned left when his brother married, and he's been up in these God-forsaken scrubs ever since. Look, I want to tell you something, Jack: Ned has written to Mrs Bob to tell her that Bob died of fever, and everything was done for him that could be done, and that he died easy—and all that sort of thing. Ned sent her some money, and she is to think that it was the money due to Bob when he died. Now I'll have to go and see her when we get to Solong; there's no getting out of it, I'll have to face her—and you'll have to come with me."

"Damned if I will!" I said.

"But you'll have to," said Andy. "You'll have to stick to me; you're surely not crawler enough to desert a mate in a case like this? I'll have to lie like hell—I'll have to lie as I never lied to a woman before; and you'll have to back me and corroborate every lie."

I'd never seen Andy show so much emotion.

"There's plenty of time to fix up a good yarn," said Andy. He said no more about Mrs Baker, and we only mentioned the boss's name casually, until we were within about a day's ride of Solong; then Andy told me the yarn he'd made up about the boss's death.

"And I want you to listen, Jack," he said, "and remember every word—and if you can fix up a better yarn you can tell me afterwards. Now it was like this: the boss wasn't too well when he crossed the border. He complained of pains in his back and head and a stinging pain in the back of his neck, and he had dysentery bad—but that doesn't matter; it's lucky I ain't supposed to tell a woman all the symptoms. The boss stuck to the job as long as he could, but we managed the cattle and made it as easy as we could for him. He'd just take it easy, and ride on from camp to camp, and rest. One night I rode to a town off the route (or you did, if you like) and got some medicine for him; that made him better for a while, but at last, a day or two this side of Mulgatown, he had to give up. A squatter there drove him into town in his buggy and put him up at the best hotel. The publican knew the boss and did all he could for him—put him in the best room and wired for another doctor. We wired for Ned as soon as we saw how bad the boss was, and Ned rode night and day and got there three days before the boss died. The boss was a bit off his head some of the time with the fever, but was calm and quiet towards the end and died easy. He talked a lot about his wife and children, and told us to tell the wife not to fret but to cheer up for the children's sake. How does that sound?"

I'd been thinking while I listened, and an idea struck me.

"Why not let her know the truth?" I asked. "She's sure to hear of it sooner or later; and if she knew he was only a selfish, drunken blackguard she might get over it all the sooner."

"You don't know women, Jack," said Andy quietly. "And, anyway, even if she is a sensible woman, we've got a dead mate to consider as well as a living woman."

"But she's sure to hear the truth sooner or later," I said. "The boss was so well known."

"And that's just the reason why the truth might be kept from her," said Andy. "If he wasn't well known—and nobody could help liking him, after all, when he was straight—if he wasn't so well known the truth might leak out unawares. She won't know if I can help it, or at least not yet a while. If I see any chaps that come from the north I'll put them up to it. I'll tell M'Grath, the publican at Solong, too: he's a straight man—he'll keep his ears open and warn chaps. One of Mrs Baker's sisters is staying with her, and I'll give her a hint so that she can warn off any women that might get hold of a yarn. Besides, Mrs Baker is sure to go and live in Sydney, where all her people are—she was a Sydney girl; and she's not likely to meet anyone there that will tell her the truth. I can tell her that it was the last wish of the boss that she should shift to Sydney."

We smoked and thought a while, and by and by Andy had what he called a "happy thought." He went to his saddle-bags and got out the small canvas packet that Ned had given him: it was sewn up with packing-thread, and Andy ripped it open with his pocket-knife.

"What are you doing, Andy?" I asked.

"Ned's an innocent old fool, as far as sin is concerned," said Andy. "I guess she hasn't looked through the boss's letters, and I'm just going to see that there's nothing here that will make liars of us."

He looked through the letters and papers by the light of the fire. There were some letters from Mrs Baker to her husband, also a portrait of her and the children; these Andy put aside. But there were other letters from barmaids and women who were not fit to be seen in the same street with the boss's wife; and there were portraits—one or two flash ones. There were two letters from other men's wives too.

"And one of those men, at least, was an old mate of his!" said Andy, in a tone of disgust.

He threw the lot into the fire; then he went through the boss's pocket-book and tore out some leaves that had notes and addresses on them, and burnt them too. Then he sewed up the packet again and put it away in his saddle-bag.

"Such is life!" said Andy, with a yawn that might have been half a sigh.

We rode into Solong early in the day, turned our horses out in a paddock, and put up at M'Grath's pub until such time as we made up our minds as to what we'd do or where we'd go. We had an idea of waiting until the shearing season started and then making out back to the big sheds.

Neither of us was in a hurry to go and face Mrs Baker. "We'll go after dinner," said Andy at first; then after dinner we had a drink, and felt sleepy—we weren't used to big dinners of roast-beef and vegetables and pudding, and, besides, it was drowsy weather—so we decided to have a snooze and then go. When we woke up it was late in the afternoon, so we thought we'd put it off until after tea. "It wouldn't be manners to walk in while they're at tea," said Andy—"it would look as if we only came for some grub."

But while we were at tea a little girl came with a message that Mrs

Baker wanted to see us, and would be very much obliged if we'd call
up as soon as possible. You see, in those small towns you can't move
without the thing getting round inside of half an hour.

"We'll have to face the music now!" said Andy, "and no get out of
it." He seemed to hang back more than I did. There was another
pub opposite where Mrs Baker lived, and when we got up the street
a bit I said to Andy:

"Suppose we go and have another drink first, Andy? We might be
kept in there an hour or two."

"You don't want another drink," said Andy, rather short. "Why,
you seem to be going the same way as the boss!" But it was Andy
who edged off towards the pub when we got near Mrs Baker's place.
"All right!" he said. "Come on! We'll have this other drink, since
you want it so bad."

We had the drink, then we buttoned up our coats and started
across the road—we'd bought new shirts and collars, and spruced
up a bit. Half-way across Andy grabbed my arm and asked:

"How do you feel now, Jack?"

"Oh, *I'm* all right," I said.

"For God's sake," said Andy, "don't put your foot in it and make
a mess of it."

"I won't, if you don't."

Mrs Baker's cottage was a little weather-board box affair back in
a garden. When we went in through the gate Andy gripped my arm
again and whispered:

"For God's sake, stick to me now, Jack!"

"I'll stick all right," I said—"you've been having too much beer,
Andy."

I had seen Mrs Baker before, and remembered her as a cheerful,
contented sort of woman, bustling about the house and getting the
boss's shirts and things ready when we started north. Just the sort of
woman that is contented with housework and the children, and with
nothing particular about her in the way of brains. But now she sat
by the fire looking like the ghost of herself. I wouldn't have
recognized her at first. I never saw such a change in a woman, and it
came like a shock to me.

Her sister let us in, and after a first glance at Mrs Baker I had eyes
for the sister and no one else. She was a Sydney girl, about
twenty-four or twenty-five, and fresh and fair—not like the
sun-browned women we were used to see. She was a pretty,
bright-eyed girl, and seemed quick to understand, and very

sympathetic. She had been educated, Andy had told me, and wrote stories for the Sydney *Bulletin* and other Sydney papers. She had her hair done and was dressed in the city style, and that took us back a bit at first.

"It's very good of you to come," said Mrs Baker in a weak, weary voice, when we first went in. "I heard you were in town."

"We were just coming when we got your message," said Andy. "We'd have come before, only we had to see to the horses."

"It's very kind of you, I'm sure," said Mrs Baker.

They wanted us to have tea, but we said we'd just had it. Then Miss Standish (the sister) wanted us to have tea and cake; but we didn't feel as if we could handle cups and saucers and pieces of cake successfully just then.

There was something the matter with one of the children in a back room, and the sister went to see to it. Mrs Baker cried a little quietly.

"You mustn't mind me," she said. "I'll be all right presently, and then I want you to tell me all about poor Bob. It's seeing you, that saw the last of him, that set me off."

Andy and I sat stiff and straight, on two chairs against the wall, and held our hats tight, and stared at a picture of Wellington meeting Blücher on the opposite wall. I thought it was lucky that that picture was there.

The child was calling "mumma," and Mrs Baker went in to it, and her sister came out. "Best tell her all about it and get it over," she whispered to Andy. "She'll never be content until she hears all about poor Bob from someone who was with him when he died. Let me take your hats. Make yourselves comfortable."

She took the hats and put them on the sewing-machine. I wished she'd let us keep them, for now we had nothing to hold on to, and nothing to do with our hands; and as for being comfortable, we were just about as comfortable as two cats on wet bricks.

When Mrs Baker came into the room she brought little Bobby Baker, about four years old; he wanted to see Andy. He ran to Andy at once, and Andy took him up on his knee. He was a pretty child, but he reminded me too much of his father.

"I'm so glad you've come, Andy!" said Bobby.

"Are you, Bobby?"

"Yes. I wants to ask you about daddy. You saw him go away, didn't you?" and he fixed his great wondering eyes on Andy's face.

"Yes," said Andy.

"He went up among the stars, didn't he?"

"Yes," said Andy.

"And he isn't coming back to Bobby any more?"

"No," said Andy. "But Bobby's going to him by and by."

Mrs Baker had been leaning back in her chair, resting her head on her hand, tears glistening in her eyes; now she began to sob, and her sister took her out of the room.

Andy looked miserable. "I wish to God I was off this job!" he whispered to me.

"Is that the girl that writes the stories?" I asked.

"Yes," he said, staring at me in a hopeless sort of way, "and poems too."

"Is Bobby going up among the stars?" asked Bobby.

"Yes," said Andy—"if Bobby's good."

"And auntie?"

"Yes."

"And mumma?"

"Yes."

"Are you going, Andy?"

"Yes," said Andy, hopelessly.

"Did you see daddy go up among the stars, Andy?"

"Yes," said Andy, "I saw him go up."

"And he isn't coming down again any more?"

"No," said Andy.

"Why isn't he?"

"Because he's going to wait up there for you and mumma, Bobby."

There was a long pause, and then Bobby asked:

"Are you going to give me a shilling, Andy?" with the same expression of innocent wonder in his eyes.

Andy slipped half a crown into his hand. "Auntie" came in and told him he'd see Andy in the morning and took him away to bed, after he'd kissed us both solemnly; and presently she and Mrs Baker settled down to hear Andy's story.

"Brace up now, Jack, and keep your wits about you," whispered Andy to me just before they came in.

"Poor Bob's brother Ned wrote to me," said Mrs Baker, "but he scarcely told me anything. Ned's a good fellow, but he's very simple, and never thinks of anything."

Andy told her about the boss not being well after he crossed the border.

"I knew he was not well," said Mrs Baker, "before he left. I didn't want him to go. I tried hard to persuade him not to go this trip. I had a feeling that I oughtn't to let him go. But he'd never

think of anything but me and the children. He promised he'd give up
droving after this trip, and get something to do near home. The life
was too much for him—riding in all weathers and camping out in
the rain, and living like a dog. But he was never content at home. It
was all for the sake of me and the children. He wanted to make
money and start on a station again. I shouldn't have let him go. He
only thought of me and the children! Oh! my poor, dear, kind, dead
husband!" She broke down again and sobbed, and her sister
comforted her, while Andy and I stared at Wellington meeting
Blücher on the field at Waterloo. I thought the artist had heaped up
the dead a bit extra, and I thought that I wouldn't like to be trod on
by horses, even if I was dead.

"Don't you mind," said Miss Standish, "she'll be all right
presently," and she handed us the *Illustrated Sydney Journal*. This was
a great relief—we bumped our heads over the pictures.

Mrs Baker made Andy go on again, and he told her how the boss
broke down near Mulgatown. Mrs Baker was opposite him and
Miss Standish opposite me. Both of them kept their eyes on Andy's
face: he sat, with his hair straight up like a brush as usual, and kept
his big innocent grey eyes fixed on Mrs Baker's face all the time he
was speaking. I watched Miss Standish. I thought she was the
prettiest girl I'd ever seen; it was a bad case of love at first sight; but
she was far and away above me, and the case was hopeless. I began
to feel pretty miserable, and to think back into the past; I just heard
Andy droning away by my side.

"So we fixed him up comfortable in the wagonette with the
blankets and coats and things," Andy was saying, "and the squatter
started into Mulgatown. . . . It was about thirty miles, Jack, wasn't
it?" he asked, turning suddenly to me. He always looked so innocent
that there were times when I itched to knock him down.

"More like thirty-five," I said, waking up.

Miss Standish fixed her eyes on me, and I had another look at
Wellington and Blücher.

"They were all very good and kind to the boss," said Andy.
"They thought a lot of him up there. Everybody was fond of him."

"I know it," said Mrs Baker. "Nobody could help liking him. He
was one of the kindest men that ever lived."

"Tanner, the publican, couldn't have been kinder to his own
brother," said Andy. "The local doctor was a decent chap, but he
was only a young fellow, and Tanner hadn't much faith in him, so he

wired for an older doctor at Mackintyre, and he even sent out fresh horses to meet the doctor's buggy. Everything was done that could be done, I assure you, Mrs Baker."

"I believe it," said Mrs Baker. "And you don't know how it relieves me to hear it. And did the publican do all this at his own expense?"

"He wouldn't take a penny, Mrs Baker."

"He must have been a good true man. I wish I could thank him."

"Oh, Ned thanked him for you," said Andy, though without meaning more than he said.

"I wouldn't have fancied that Ned would have thought of that," said Mrs Baker. "When I first heard of my poor husband's death, I thought perhaps he'd been drinking again—that worried me a bit."

"He never touched a drop after he left Solong, I can assure you, Mrs Baker," said Andy quickly.

Now I noticed that Miss Standish seemed surprised or puzzled, once or twice, while Andy was speaking, and leaned forward to listen to him; then she leaned back in her chair and clasped her hands behind her head and looked at him, with half-shut eyes, in a way I didn't like. Once or twice she looked at me as if she was going to ask me a question, but I always looked away quick and stared at Blücher and Wellington, or into the empty fire-place, till I felt her eyes were off me. Then she asked Andy a question or two, in all innocence I believe now, but it scared him, and at last he watched his chance and winked at her sharp. Then she gave a little gasp and shut up like a steel trap.

The sick child in the bedroom coughed and cried again. Mrs Baker went to it. We three sat like a deaf-and-dumb institution, Andy and I staring all over the place: presently Miss Standish excused herself, and went out of the room after her sister. She looked hard at Andy as she left the room, but he kept his eyes away.

"Brace up now, Jack," whispered Andy to me, "the worst is coming."

When they came in again Mrs Baker made Andy go on with his story.

"He—he died very quietly," said Andy, hitching round, and resting his elbows on his knees, and looking into the fire-place so as to have his face away from the light. Miss Standish put her arm round her sister. "He died very easy," said Andy. "He was a bit off his head at times, but that was while the fever was on him. He didn't

suffer much towards the end—I don't think he suffered at all. . . .
He talked a lot about you and the children." (Andy was speaking
very softly now.) "He said that you were not to fret, but to cheer up
for the children's sake. . . . It was the biggest funeral ever seen
round there."

Mrs Baker was crying softly. Andy got the packet half-out of his
pocket, but shoved it back again.

"The only thing that hurts me now," said Mrs Baker presently,
"is to think of my poor husband buried out there in the lonely bush,
so far from home. It's—cruel!" and she was sobbing again.

"Oh, that's all right, Mrs Baker," said Andy, losing his head a
little. "Ned will see to that. Ned is going to arrange to have him
brought down and buried in Sydney." Which was about the first
thing Andy had told her that evening that wasn't a lie. Ned had said
he would do it as soon as he sold his wool.

"It's very kind indeed of Ned," sobbed Mrs Baker. "I'd never
have dreamed he was so kind-hearted and thoughtful. I misjudged
him all along. And that is all you have to tell me about poor
Robert?"

"Yes," said Andy—then one of his "happy thoughts" struck him.
"Except that he hoped you'd shift to Sydney, Mrs Baker, where
you've got friends and relations. He thought it would be better for
you and the children. He told me to tell you that."

"He was thoughtful up to the end," said Mrs Baker. "It was just
like poor Robert—always thinking of me and the children. We are
going to Sydney next week."

Andy looked relieved. We talked a little more, and Miss Standish
wanted to make coffee for us, but we had to go and see to our horses.
We got up and bumped against each other, and got each other's
hats, and promised Mrs Baker we'd come again.

"Thank you very much for coming," she said, shaking hands with
us. "I feel much better now. You don't know how much you have
relieved me. Now, mind, you have promised to come and see me
again for the last time."

Andy caught her sister's eye and jerked his head towards the door
to let her know he wanted to speak to her outside.

"Good-bye, Mrs Baker," he said, holding on to her hand. "And
don't you fret. You've—you've got the children yet. It's—it's all for
the best; and, besides, the boss said you wasn't to fret." And he
blundered out after me and Miss Standish.

She came out to the gate with us, and Andy gave her the packet.

"I want you to give that to her," he said: "it's his letters and
papers. I hadn't the heart to give it to her, somehow."

"Tell me, Mr M'Culloch," she said. "You've kept something

back—you haven't told her the truth. It would be better and safer for me to know. Was it an accident—or the drink?"

"It was the drink," said Andy. "I was going to tell you—I thought it would be best to tell you. I had made up my mind to do it, but, somehow, I couldn't have done it if you hadn't asked me."

"Tell me all," she said. "It would be better for me to know."

"Come a little farther away from the house," said Andy. She came along the fence a piece with us, and Andy told her as much of the truth as he could.

"I'll hurry her off to Sydney," she said. "We can get away this week as well as next." Then she stood for a minute before us, breathing quickly, her hands behind her back and her eyes shining in the moonlight. She looked splendid.

"I want to thank you for her sake," she said quickly. "You are good men! I like the bushmen! They are grand men—they are noble. I'll probably never see either of you again, so it doesn't matter," and she put her white hand on Andy's shoulder and kissed him fair and square on the mouth. "And you, too!" she said to me. I was taller than Andy, and had to stoop. "Good-bye!" she said, and ran to the gate and in, waving her hand to us. We lifted our hats again and turned down the road.

I don't think it did either of us any harm.

A HERO IN DINGO-SCRUBS

This is a story—about the only one—of Job Falconer, boss of the Talbragar sheep station up-country in New South Wales in the early eighties—when there were still runs in the dingo-scrubs out of the hands of the banks, and yet squatters who lived on their stations.

Job would never tell the story himself, at least not complete, and as his family grew up he would become as angry as it was in his easygoing nature to become if reference were made to the incident in his presence. But his wife—little, plump, bright-eyed Gerty Falconer—often told the story (in the mysterious voice which women use in speaking of private matters amongst themselves—but with brightening eyes) to women friends over tea; and always to a new woman friend. And on such occasions she would be particularly tender towards the unconscious Job, and ruffle his thin, sandy hair in a way that embarrassed him in company—made him look as sheepish as an old big-horned ram that has just been shorn and turned amongst the ewes. And the woman friend on parting would give Job's hand a squeeze which would surprise him mildly, and look at him as if she could love him.

According to a theory of mine, Job, to fit the story, should have been tall, and dark, and stern, or gloomy and quick-tempered. But he wasn't. He was fairly tall, but he was fresh-complexioned and sandy (his skin was pink to scarlet in some weathers, with blotches of umber), and his eyes were pale-grey; his big forehead loomed babyishly, his arms were short, and his legs bowed to the saddle. Altogether he was an awkward, unlovely bush bird—on foot; in the saddle it was different. He hadn't even a "temper."

The impression on Job's mind which many years afterwards brought about the incident was strong enough. When Job was a boy of fourteen he saw his father's horse come home riderless—circling and snorting up by the stockyard, head jerked down whenever the hoof trod on one of the snapped ends of the bridle-reins, and saddle twisted over the side with bruised pommel and knee-pad broken off.

Job's father wasn't hurt much, but Job's mother, an emotional woman, and then in a delicate state of health, survived the shock for three months only. "She wasn't quite right in her head," they said, "from the day the horse came home till the last hour before she died." And, strange to say, Job's father (from whom Job inherited his seemingly placid nature) died three months later. The doctor from the town was of the opinion that he must have "sustained internal injuries" when the horse threw him. "Doc. Wild" reckoned that Job's father was hurt inside when his wife died, and hurt so badly that he couldn't pull round. But doctors differ all over the world.

Well, the story of Job himself came about in this way. He had been married a year, and had lately started wool-raising on a pastoral lease he had taken up at Talbragar: it was a new run, with new slab-and-bark huts on the creek for a homestead, new shearing-shed, yards—wife and everything new, and he was expecting a baby. Job felt brand-new himself at the time, so he said. It was a lonely place for a young woman; but Gerty was a settler's daughter. The newness took away some of the loneliness, she said, and there was truth in that: a bush home in the scrubs looks lonelier the older it gets, and ghostlier in the twilight, as the bark and slabs whiten, or rather grow grey, in fierce summers. And there's nothing under God's sky so weird, so aggressively lonely, as a deserted old home in the bush.

Job's wife had a half-caste gin for company when Job was away on the run, and the nearest white woman (a hard but honest

Lancashire woman from within the kicking radius in Lancashire—
wife of a selector) was only seven miles away. She promised to be on
hand, and came over two or three times a week; but Job grew
restless as Gerty's time drew near, and wished that he had insisted
on sending her to the nearest town (thirty miles away), as originally
proposed. Gerty's mother, who lived in town, was coming to see her
over her trouble; Job had made arrangements with the town doctor,
but prompt attendance could hardly be expected of a doctor who
was very busy, who was too fat to ride, and who lived thirty miles
away.

Job, in common with most bushmen and their families round
there, had more faith in Doc. Wild, a weird Yankee who made
medicine in a saucepan, and worked more cures on bushmen than
did the other three doctors of the district together—maybe because
the bushmen had faith in him, or he knew the bush and bush
constitutions—or, perhaps, because he'd do things which no
"respectable practitioner" dared do. I've described him in another
story. Some said he was a quack, and some said he wasn't. There are
scores of wrecks and mysteries like him in the bush. He drank
fearfully, and "on his own," but was seldom incapable of performing
an operation. Experienced bushmen preferred him three-quarters
drunk: when perfectly sober he was apt to be a bit shaky. He was
tall, gaunt, had a pointed black moustache, bushy eyebrows, and
piercing black eyes. His movements were eccentric. He lived where
he happened to be—in a town hotel, in the best room of a
homestead, in the skillion of a sly-grog shanty, in a shearer's,
digger's, shepherd's, or boundary-rider's hut; in a surveyor's camp
or a black-fellow's camp—or, when the horrors were on him, by a
log in the lonely bush. It seemed all one to him. He lost all his things
sometimes—even his clothes; but he never lost a pigskin bag which
contained his surgical instruments and papers. Except once; then he
gave the blacks £5 to find it for him.

His patients included all, from the big squatter to Black Jimmy;
and he rode as far and fast to a squatter's home as to a swagman's
camp. When nothing was to be expected from a poor selector or a
station-hand, and the doctor was hard up, he went to the squatter
for a few pounds. He had on occasions been offered cheques of £50
and £100 by squatters for "pulling round" their wives or children;
but such offers always angered him. When he asked for £5 he
resented being offered a £10 cheque. He once sued a doctor for
alleging that he held no diploma; but the magistrate, on reading
certain papers, suggested a settlement out of court, which both

doctors agreed to—the other doctor apologizing briefly in the local paper. It was noticed thereafter that the magistrate and town doctors treated Doc. Wild with great respect—even at his worst. The thing was never explained, and the case deepened the mystery which surrounded Doc. Wild.

As Job Falconer's crisis approached Doc. Wild was located at a shanty on the main road, about half-way between Job's station and the town. (Township of Come-by-Chance—expressive name; and the shanty was the "Dead Dingo Hotel," kept by James Myles—known as "Poisonous Jimmy," perhaps as a compliment to, or a libel on, the liquor he sold.) Job's brother Mac was stationed at the Dead Dingo Hotel with instructions to hang round on some pretence, see that the doctor didn't either drink himself into the d.t.'s or get sober enough to become restless; to prevent his going away, or to follow him if he did; and to bring him to the station in about a week's time. Mac (rather more careless, brighter, and more energetic than his brother) was carrying out these instructions while pretending, with rather great success, to be himself on the spree at the shanty.

But one morning, early in the specified week, Job's uneasiness was suddenly greatly increased by certain symptoms, so he sent the black boy for the neighbour's wife and decided to ride to Come-by-Chance to hurry out Gerty's mother, and see, by the way, how Doc. Wild and Mac were getting on. On the arrival of the neighbour's wife, who drove over in a spring-cart, Job mounted his horse (a freshly-broken filly) and started.

"Don't be anxious, Job," said Gerty, as he bent down to kiss her. "We'll be all right. Wait! You'd better take the gun—you might see those dingoes again. I'll get it for you."

The dingoes (native dogs) were very bad amongst the sheep; and Job and Gerty had started three together close to the track the last time they were out in company—without the gun, of course. Gerty took the loaded gun carefully down from its straps on the bedroom wall, carried it out, and handed it up to Job, who bent and kissed her again and then rode off.

It was a hot day—the beginning of a long drought, as Job found to his bitter cost. He followed the track for five or six miles through the thick, monotonous scrub, and then turned off to make a short cut to the main road across a big ring-barked flat. The tall gum-trees had been ring-barked (a ring of bark taken out round the butts), or rather "sapped"—that is, a ring cut in through the sap—in order to kill them, so that the little strength in the "poor" soil should not be drawn out by the living roots, and the natural grass (on which Australian stock depends) should have a better show. The hard, dead trees raised their barkless and whitened trunks and leafless branches for three or four miles, and the grey and brown grass stood tall between, dying in the first breaths of the coming drought. All was becoming grey and ashen here, the heat blazing and dancing across objects, and the pale brassy dome of the sky cloudless over all, the sun a glaring white disk with its edges almost melting into the sky. Job held his gun carelessly ready (it was a double-barrelled muzzle-loader, one barrel choke-bore for shot, and the other rifled), and he kept an eye out for dingoes. He was saving his horse for a long ride, jogging along in the careless bush fashion, hitched a little to one side—and I'm not sure that he didn't have a leg thrown up and across in front of the pommel of the saddle—he was riding along in the careless bush fashion and thinking fatherly thoughts in advance, perhaps, when suddenly a great black, greasy-looking goanna scuttled off from the side of the track amongst the dry tufts of grass and shreds of dead bark, and started up a sapling. "It was a whopper," Job said afterwards; "must have been over six feet, and a foot across the body. It scared me nearly as much as the filly."

The filly shied off like a rocket. Job kept his seat instinctively, as was natural to him; but before he could more than grab at the rein—lying loosely on the pommel—the filly "fetched up" against a dead box-tree, hard as cast-iron, and Job's left leg was jammed from stirrup to pocket. "I felt the blood flare up," he said, "and I knowed that that"—(Job swore now and then in an easygoing way)—"I knowed that that blanky leg was broken all right. I threw the gun from me and freed my left foot from the stirrup with my hand, and managed to fall to the right, as the filly started off again."

What follows comes from the statements of Doc. Wild and Mac Falconer, and Job's own "wanderings in his mind," as he called them. "They took a blanky mean advantage of me," he said, "when they had me down and I couldn't talk sense."

The filly circled off a bit, and then stood staring—as a mob of brumbies, when fired at, will sometimes stand watching the smoke. Job's leg was smashed badly, and the pain must have been terrible. But he thought then with a flash, as men do in a fix. No doubt the scene at the lonely bush home of his boyhood started up before him: his father's horse appeared riderless, and he saw the look in his mother's eyes.

Now a bushman's first, best, and quickest chance in a fix like this is that his horse go home riderless, the home be alarmed, and the

horse's tracks followed back to him; otherwise he might lie there fo
days, for weeks—till the growing grass buries his mouldering bones
Job was on an old sheep-track across a flat where few might hav
occasion to come for months, but he did not consider this. H
crawled to his gun, then to a log, dragging gun and smashed leg afte
him. How he did it he doesn't know. Half-lying on one side, h
rested the barrel on the log, took aim at the filly, pulled bot
triggers, and then fell over and lay with his head against the log; an
the gun-barrel, sliding down, rested on his neck. He had fainted
The crows were interested, and the ants would come by and by

Now Doc. Wild had inspirations; anyway, he did things whic
seemed, after they were done, to have been suggested by inspiratio
and in no other possible way. He often turned up where and when h
was wanted above all men, and at no other time. He had gips
blood, they said; but, anyway, being the mystery he was, and havin
the face he had, and living the life he lived—and doing the things h
did—it was quite probable that he was more nearly in touch than w
with that awful invisible world all round and between us, of whic
we only see distorted faces and hear disjointed utterances when w
are "suffering a recovery"—or going mad.

On the morning of Job's accident, and after a long broodin
silence, Doc. Wild suddenly said to Mac Falconer:

"Git the hosses, Mac. We'll go to the station."

Mac, used to the doctor's eccentricities, went to see about th
horses.

And then who should drive up but Mrs Spencer—Job's mother
in-law—on her way from the town to the station. She stayed to hav
a cup of tea and give her horses a feed. She was square-faced, an
considered a rather hard and practical woman, but she had plenty o
solid flesh, good sympathetic commonsense, and deep-set humorou
blue eyes. She lived in the town comfortably on the interest of som
money which her husband left in the bank. She drove an America
wagonette with a good width and length of "tray" behind, and o
this occasion she had a pole and two horses. In the trap were a ne
flock mattress and pillows, a generous pair of new white blankets
and boxes containing necessaries, delicacies, and luxuries. All roun
she was an excellent mother-in-law for a man to have on hand at
critical time.

And, speaking of mother-in-law, I would like to put in a word fo
her right here. She is universally considered a nuisance in times c
peace and comfort; but when illness or serious trouble comes hom

Then it's "Write to mother! Wire for mother!" Send someone to
fetch mother! I'll go and bring mother! And if she is not near: "Oh, I
wish mother were here! If mother were only near!" And when she is
on the spot, the anxious son-in-law: "Don't *you* go, mother! You'll
stay, won't you, mother?—till we're all right? I'll get someone to
look after your house, mother, while you're here." But Job Falconer
was fond of his mother-in-law, all times.

Mac had some trouble in finding and catching one of the horses.
Mrs Spencer drove on, and Mac and the doctor caught up to her
about a mile before she reached the homestead track, which turned
in through the scrubs at the corner of the big ring-barked flat.

Doc. Wild and Mac followed the cart-road, and as they jogged
along in the edge of the scrub the doctor glanced once or twice across
the flat through the dead, naked branches. Mac looked that way.
The crows were hopping about the branches of a tree way out in the
middle of the flat, flopping down from branch to branch to the grass,
then rising hurriedly and circling.

"Dead beast there!" said Mac out of his bushcraft.

"No—dying," said Doc. Wild, with less bush experience but more
intellect.

"There's some steers of Job's out there somewhere," muttered
Mac. Then suddenly, "It ain't drought—it's the ploorer at last! or
I'm blanked!"

Mac feared the advent of that cattle-plague, pleuro-pneumonia,
which was raging on some other stations, and had hitherto kept clear
of Job's run.

"We'll go and see, if you like," suggested Doc. Wild.

They turned out across the flat, the horses picking their way
amongst the dried tufts and fallen branches.

"Theer ain't no sign o' cattle theer," said the doctor; "more likely
a ewe in trouble about her lamb."

"Oh, the blanky dingoes at the sheep," said Mac. "I wish we had
a gun—might get a shot at them."

Doc. Wild hitched the skirt of a long China silk coat he wore, free
of a hip-pocket. He always carried a revolver. "In case I feel obliged
to shoot a first person singular one of these hot days," he explained
once, whereat bushmen scratched the backs of their heads and
thought feebly, without result.

"We'd never git near enough for a shot," said the doctor; then he
commenced to hum fragments from a bush song about the finding of
a lost bushman in the last stages of death by thirst:

> "The crows kept flyin' up, boys!
>   The crows kept flyin' up!
> The dog, he seen and whimpered, boys,
>   Though he was but a pup."

"It must be something or other," muttered Mac. "Look at them blanky crows!"

> "The lost was found, we brought him round,
>   And took him from the place,
> While the ants was swarmin' on the ground,
>   And the crows was sayin' grace."

"My God! what's that?" cried Mac, who was a little in advance and rode a tall horse.

It was Job's filly, lying saddled and bridled, with a rifle-bullet (as they found on subsequent examination) through shoulders and chest, and her head full of kangaroo-shot. She was feebly rocking her head against the ground, and marking the dust with her hoof, as if trying to write the reason of it there.

The doctor drew his revolver, took a cartridge from his waist-coat pocket, and put the filly out of her misery in a very scientific manner; then something—professional instinct or the something supernatural about the doctor—led him straight to the log, hidden in the grass, where Job lay as we left him, and about fifty yards from the dead filly, which must have staggered off some little way after being shot. Mac followed the doctor, shaking violently.

"Oh, my God!" he cried, with the woman in his voice—and his face so pale that his freckles stood out like buttons, as Doc. Wild said—"Oh, my God! he's shot himself!"

"No, he hasn't," said the doctor, deftly turning Job into a healthier position with his head from under the log and his mouth to the air: then he ran his eyes and hands over him, and Job moaned. "He's got a broken leg," said the doctor. Even then he couldn't resist making a characteristic remark, half to himself: "A man doesn't shoot himself when he's going to be made a lawful father for the first time, unless he can see a long way into the future." Then he took out his whisky-flask and said briskly to Mac, "Leave me your water-bag" (Mac carried a canvas water-bag slung under his horse's neck), "ride back to the track, stop Mrs Spencer, and bring the wagonette here. Tell her it's only a broken leg."

Mac mounted and rode off at breakneck pace.

As he worked the doctor muttered: "He shot his horse. That's what gits me. The fool might have lain there for a week. I'd never have suspected spite in that carcass, and I ought to know men."

But as Job came round a little Doc. Wild was enlightened.

"Where's the filly?" cried Job suddenly between groans.

"She's all right," said the doctor.

"Stop her!" cried Job, struggling to rise—"stop her!—Oh God! my leg."

"Keep quiet, you fool!"

"Stop her!" yelled Job.

"Why stop her?" asked the doctor. "She won't go fur," he added.

"She'll go home to Gerty," shouted Job. "For God's sake stop her!"

"O—h!" drawled the doctor to himself. "I might have guessed that. And I ought to know men."

"Don't take me home!" demanded Job in a semi-sensible interval. "Take me to Poisonous Jimmy's and tell Gerty I'm on the spree."

When Mac and Mrs Spencer arrived with the wagonette Doc. Wild was in his shirt-sleeves, his China silk coat having gone for bandages. The lower half of Job's trouser-leg and his 'lastic-side boot lay on the ground, neatly cut off, and his bandaged leg was sandwiched between two strips of bark, with grass stuffed in the hollows, and bound by saddle-straps.

"That's all I kin do for him for the present."

Mrs Spencer was a strong woman mentally, but she arrived rather pale and a little shaky: nevertheless she called out, as soon as she got within earshot of the doctor:

"What's Job been doing now?" (Job, by the way, had never been remarkable for doing anything.)

"He's got his leg broke and shot his horse," replied the doctor. "But," he added, "whether he's been a hero or a fool I dunno. Anyway, it's a mess all round."

They unrolled the bed, blankets, and pillows in the bottom of the trap, backed it against the log, to have a step, and got Job in. It was a ticklish job, but they had to manage it: Job, maddened by pain and heat, only kept from fainting by whisky, groaning and raving and yelling to them to stop his horse.

"Luckily we got him before the ants did," muttered the doctor. Then he had an inspiration—

"You bring him on to the shepherd's hut this side the station. We must leave him there. Drive carefully, and pour brandy into him

now and then; when the brandy's done pour whisky, then gin—keep
the rum till the last" (the doctor had put a supply of spirits in the
wagonette at Poisonous Jimmy's). "I'll take Mac's horse and ride on
and send Peter" (the station-hand) "back to the hut to meet you. I'll
be back myself if I can. *This business will hurry up things at the station.*"

Which last was one of those apparently insane remarks of the
doctor's which no sane nor sober man could fathom or see a reason
for—except in Doc. Wild's madness.

He rode off at a gallop. The burden of Job's raving, all the way,
rested on the dead filly—

"Stop her! She must not go home to Gerty! ... God help me
shoot! ... Whoa!—whoa, there! ... Cope—cope—cope—Steady,
Jessie, old girl. ... Aim straight—aim straight! Aim for me,
God!—I've missed! ... Stop her!"

"I never met a character like that," commented the doctor
afterwards, "inside a man that looked like Job on the outside. I've
met men behind revolvers and big mustarshes in Califo'nia; but I've
met a derned sight more men behind nothing but a good-natured
grin, here in Australia. These lanky sawney bushmen will do things
in an easygoing way some day that'll make the old world sit up and
think hard."

He reached the station in time, and twenty minutes or half an
hour later he left the case in the hands of the Lancashire
woman—whom he saw reason to admire—and rode back to the hut
to help Job, whom they soon fixed up as comfortably as possible.

They humbugged Mrs Falconer first with a yarn of Job's alleged
phenomenal shyness, and gradually, as she grew stronger and the
truth less important, they told it to her. And so, instead of Job being
pushed, scarlet-faced, into the bedroom to see his first-born, Gerty
Falconer herself took the child down to the hut, and so presented
Uncle Job with my first and favourite cousin and bush chum.

Doc. Wild stayed round until he saw Job comfortably moved to
the homestead, then he prepared to depart.

"I'm sorry," said Job, who was still weak—"I'm sorry for that
there filly. I was breaking her in to side-saddle for Gerty when she
should get about. I wouldn't have lost her for twenty quid."

"Never mind, Job," said the doctor. "I, too once shot an animal I
was fond of—and for the sake of a woman—but that animal walked
on two legs and wore trousers. Good-bye, Job."

And he left for Poisonous Jimmy's.

THE LITTLE WORLD LEFT BEHIND

I lately revisited a western agricultural district in Australia after many years. The railway had reached it, but otherwise things were drearily, hopelessly, depressingly unchanged. There was the same old grant, comprising several thousands of acres of the richest land in the district, lying idle still, except for a few horses allowed to run there for a shilling a head per week.

There were the same old selections—about as far off as ever from becoming freeholds—shoved back among the barren ridges; dusty little patches in the scrub, full of stones and stumps, and called farms, deserted every few years, and tackled again by some little dried-up family, or some old hatter, and then given best once more. There was the cluster of farms on the flat, and in the foot of the gully, owned by Australians of Irish or English descent, with the same number of stumps in the wheat-paddock, the same broken fences and tumble-down huts and yards, and the same weak, sleepy attempt made every season to scratch up the ground and raise a crop. And along the creek the German farmers—the only people there worthy of the name—toiling (men, women, and children) from daylight till dark, like slaves, just as they always had done; the elder sons stoop-shouldered old men at thirty.

The row about the boundary fence between the Sweeneys and the Joneses was unfinished still, and the old feud between the Dunderblitzens and the Blitzendunders was more deadly than ever—it started three generations ago over a stray bull. The O'Dunn was still fighting for his great object in life, which was not to be "onneighborly," as he put it. "I *don't* want to be onneighborly," he said, "but I'll be aven wid some of 'em yit. It's almost impossible for a dacent man to live in sich a neighborhood and not be onneighborly, thry how he will. But I'll be aven wid some of 'em yit, marruk my wurrud."

Jones's red steer—it couldn't have been the same red steer—was continually breaking into Rooney's "whate an' bringin' ivery head av the other cattle afther him, and ruinin' him intirely." The Rooneys and M'Kenzies were at daggers drawn, even to the youngest child, over the impounding of a horse belonging to Pat Rooney's brother-in-law, by a distant relation of the M'Kenzies, which had happened nine years ago.

The same sunburned, masculine women went past to market

twice a week in the same old carts and driving much the same quality of carrion. The string of overloaded spring-carts, buggies, and sweating horses went whirling into town, to "service," through clouds of dust and broiling heat, on Sunday morning, and came driving cruelly out again at noon. The neighbours' sons rode over in the afternoon, as of old, and hung up their poor, ill-used little horses to bake in the sun, and sat on their heels about the veranda, and drawled drearily concerning crops, fruit, trees, and vines, and horses and cattle; the drought and "smut" and "rust" in wheat, and the "plaorer" (pleuro-pneumonia) in cattle, and other cheerful things: that there colt or filly, or that there cattle-dog (pup or bitch) o' mine (or "Jim's"). They always talked most of farming there, where no farming worthy of the name was possible—except by Germans and Chinamen. Towards evening the old local relic of the golden days dropped in and announced that he intended to "put down a shaft" next week, in a spot where he'd been going to put it down twenty years ago—and every week since. It was nearly time that somebody sunk a hole and buried him there.

An old local body named Mrs Witherly still went into town twice a week with her "bit av prodjuce," as O'Dunn called it. She still drove a long, bony, blind horse in a long rickety dray, with a stout sapling for a whip, and about twenty yards of clothes-line reins. The floor of the dray covered part of an acre, and one wheel was always ahead of the other—or behind, according to which shaft was pulled. She wore, to all appearances, the same short frock, faded shawl, men's 'lastic sides, and white hood that she had on when the world was made. She still stopped just twenty minutes at old Mrs Leatherly's on the way in for a yarn and a cup of tea—as she had always done, on the same days and at the same time within the memory of the hoariest local liar. However, she had a new clothes-line bent on to the old horse's front end—and we fancy that was the reason she didn't recognize us at first. She had never looked younger than a hard hundred within the memory of man. Her shrivelled face was the colour of leather, and crossed and recrossed with lines till there wasn't room for any more. But her eyes were bright yet, and twinkled with humour at times.

She had been in the bush for fifty years, and had fought fires, droughts, hunger and thirst, floods, cattle and crop diseases, and all the things that God curses Australian settlers with. She had had two husbands, and it could be said of neither that he had ever done an honest day's work, or any good for himself or any one else. She had reared something under fifteen children, her own and others; and there was scarcely one of them that had not given her trouble. Her sons had brought disgrace on her old head over and over again, but she held up that same old head through it all, and looked her narrow, ignorant world in the face—and "lived it down." She had worked like a slave for fifty years; yet she had more energy and endurance than many modern city women in her shrivelled old body. She was a daughter of English aristocrats.

And we who live our weak lives of fifty years or so in the cities—we grow maudlin over our sorrows (and beer), and ask whether life is worth living or not.

I sought in the farming town relief from the general and particular sameness of things, but there was none. The railway station was about the only new building in town. The old signs even were as badly in need of retouching as of old. I picked up a copy of the local *Advertiser*, which newspaper had been started in the early days by a brilliant drunkard, who drank himself to death just as the fathers of our nation were beginning to get educated up to his style. He might have made Australian journalism very different from what it is. There was nothing new in the *Advertiser*—there had been nothing new since the last time the drunkard had been sober enough to hold a pen. There was the same old "enjoyable trip" to Drybone (whereof the editor was the hero), and something about an on-the-whole very enjoyable evening in some place that was tastefully decorated, and where the visitors did justice to the good things provided, and the small hours, and dancing, and our host and hostess, and respected fellow-townsmen; also divers young ladies sang very nicely, and a young Mr Somebody favoured the company with a comic song.

There was the same trespassing on the valuable space by the old subscriber, who said that "he had said before and would say again," and he proceeded to say the same things which he said in the same paper when we first heard our father reading it to our mother. Farther on the old subscriber proceeded to "maintain," and recalled attention to the fact that it was just exactly as he had said. After which he made a few abstract, incoherent remarks about the "surrounding district," and concluded by stating that he "must now conclude," and thanking the editor for trespassing on the aforesaid valuable space.

There was the usual leader on the Government; and an agitation was still carried on, by means of horribly-constructed correspondence to both papers, for a bridge over Dry-Hole Creek at Dustbin—a place where no sane man ever had occasion to go.

I took up the "unreliable contemporary," but found nothing there

except a letter from "Parent," another from "Ratepayer," a leader
on the Government, and "A Trip to Limeburn," which latter I
suppose was made in opposition to the trip to Drybone.

There was nothing new in the town. Even the almost inevitable
gang of city spoilers hadn't arrived with the railway. They would
have been a relief. There was the monotonous aldermanic row, and
the worse than hopeless little herd of aldermen, the weird
agricultural portion of whom came in on council days in white
starched and ironed coats, as we had always remembered them.
They were aggressively barren of ideas; but on this occasion they
had risen above themselves, for one of them had remembered
something his grandfather (old time English alderman) had told
him, and they were stirring up all the old local quarrels and family
spite of the district over a motion, or an amendment on a motion,
that a letter—from another enlightened body and bearing on an
equally important matter (which letter had been sent through the
post sufficiently stamped, delivered to the secretary, handed to the
chairman, read aloud in council, and passed round several times for
private perusal)—over a motion that such letter be received.

There was a maintenance case coming on—to the usual well-
ventilated disgust of the local religious crank, who was on the jury;
but the case differed in no essential point from other cases which
were always coming on and going off in my time. It was not at all
romantic. The local youth was not even brilliant in adultery.

After I had been a week in that town the Governor decided to visit
it, and preparations were made to welcome him and present him
with an address. Then I thought that it was time to go, and slipped
away unnoticed in the general lunacy.

THE ROMANCE OF THE SWAG

THE ROMANCE OF THE SWAG

The Australian swag fashion is the easiest way in the world of carrying a load. I ought to know something about carrying loads: I've carried babies, which are the heaviest and most awkward and heartbreaking loads in this world for a boy or man to carry, I fancy. God remember mothers who slave about the housework (and do sometimes a man's work in addition in the bush) with a heavy, squalling kid on one arm! I've humped logs on the selection, "burning-off," with loads of fencing-posts and rails and palings out of steep, rugged gullies (and was happier then, perhaps); I've carried a shovel, crowbar, heavy "rammer," a dozen insulators on an average (strung round my shoulders with raw flax)—to say nothing of soldiering kit, tucker-bag, billy and climbing spurs—all day on a telegraph line in rough country in New Zealand, and in places where a man had to manage his load with one hand and help himself climb with the other; and I've helped hump and drag telegraph-poles up cliffs and sidings where the horses couldn't go. I've carried a portmanteau on the hot dusty roads in green old jackeroo days. Ask any actor who's been stranded and had to count railway sleepers from one town to another! he'll tell you what sort of an awkward load a portmanteau is, especially if there's broken-hearted man underneath it. I've tried knapsack fashion—one of the least healthy and most likely to give a man sores; I've carried my belongings in a three-bushel sack slung over my shoulder—blankets, tucker, spare boots and poetry all lumped together. I tried carrying a load on my head, and got a crick in my neck and spine for days. I've carried a load on my mind that should have been shared by editors and publishers. I've helped hump luggage and furniture up to, and down from, a top flat in London. And I've carried swag for months out back in Australia—and it was life, in spite of its "squalidness" and meanness and wretchedness and hardship, and in spite of the fact that the world would have regarded us as "tramps"—and a free life amongst *men* from all the world!

The Australian swag was born of Australia and no other land—of the Great Lone Land of magnificent distances and bright heat; the land of self-reliance, and never-give-in, and help-your-mate. The grave of many of the world's tragedies and comedies—royal and otherwise. The land where a man out of employment might shoulder his swag in Adelaide and take the track, and years later walk into a hut on the Gulf, or never be heard of any more, or a body be found in the bush and buried by the mounted police, or never found and never buried—what does it matter?

The land I love above all others—not because it was kind to me, but because I was born on Australian soil, and because of the foreign father who died at his work in the ranks of Australian pioneers, and because of many things. Australia! My country! Her very name is music to me. God bless Australia! for the sake of the great hearts of the heart of her! God keep her clear of the old-world shams and social lies and mockery, and callous commercialism, and sordid shame! And heaven send that, if ever in my time her sons are called upon to fight for her young life and honour, I die with the first rank of them and be buried in Australian ground.

But this will probably be called false, forced or "maudlin sentiment" here in England, where the mawkish sentiment of the music-halls, and the popular applause it receives, is enough to make a healthy man sick, and is only equalled by music-hall vulgarity. So I'll get on.

In the old digging days the knapsack, or straps-across-the chest fashion, was tried, but the load pressed on a man's chest and impeded his breathing, and a man needs to have his bellows free on long tracks in hot, stirless weather. Then the "horse-collar," or rolled military overcoat style—swag over one shoulder and under the other arm—was tried, but it was found to be too hot for the Australian climate, and was discarded along with Wellington boots and leggings. Until recently, Australian city artists and editors—who knew as much about the bush as Downing Street knows about the British colonies in general—seemed to think the horse-collar swag was still in existence; and some artists gave the swagman a stick, as if he were a tramp of civilization with an eye on the back-yard and a fear of the dog. English artists, by the way, seem firmly convinced that the Australian bushman is born in Wellington boots with a polish on 'em you could shave yourself by.

The swag is usually composed of a tent "fly" or strip of calico (a cover for the swag and a shelter in bad weather—in New Zealand it is oilcloth or waterproof twill), a couple of blankets, blue by custom and preference, as that colour shows the dirt less than any other (hence the name "bluey" for swag), and the core is composed of spare clothing and small personal effects. To make or "roll up" your swag: lay the fly or strip of calico on the ground, blueys on top of it; across one end, with eighteen inches or so to spare, lay your spare trousers and shirt, folded, light boots tied together by the laces toe to heel, books, bundle of old letters, portraits, or whatever little knick-knacks you have or care to carry, bag of needles, thread, pen and ink, spare patches for your pants, and bootlaces. Lay or arrange the pile so that it will roll evenly with the swag (some pack the lot in an old pillowslip or canvas bag), take a fold over of blanket and calico the whole length on each side, so as to reduce the width of the swag to, say, three feet, throw the spare end, with an inward fold, over the little pile of belongings, and then roll the whole to the other end, using your knees and judgment to make the swag tight, compact and artistic; when within eighteen inches of the loose end take an inward fold in that, and bring it up against the body of the swag. There is a strong suggestion of a roley-poley in a rag about the business, only the ends of the swag are folded in, in rings, and not tied. Fasten the swag with three or four straps, according to judgment and the supply of straps. To the top strap, for the swag is carried (and eased down in shanty bars and against walls or veranda-posts when not on the track) in a more or less vertical position—to the top strap, and lowest, or lowest but one, fasten the ends of the shoulder strap (usually a towel is preferred as being softer to the shoulder), your coat being carried outside the swag at the back, under the straps. To the top strap fasten the string of the nose-bag, a calico bag about the size of a pillowslip, containing the tea, sugar and flour bags, bread, meat, baking-powder and salt, and brought, when the swag is carried from the left shoulder, over the right on to the chest, and so balancing the swag behind. But a swagman can throw a heavy swag in a nearly vertical position against his spine, slung from one shoulder only and without any balance, and carry it as easily as you might wear your overcoat. Some bushmen arrange their belongings so neatly and conveniently, with swag straps in a sort of harness, that they can roll up the swag in about a minute, and unbuckle it and throw it out as easily as a roll of wall-paper, and there's the bed ready on the ground with the wardrobe for a pillow wardrobe for a pillow. The swag is always used for a seat on the track; it is a soft seat, so trousers last a long time. And, the dust being mostly soft and silky on the long tracks out back, boots last marvellously. Fifteen miles a day is the average with the swag, but you must travel according to the water: if the next bore or tank is five miles on, and the next twenty beyond, you camp at the five-mile water to-night and do the twenty next day. But if it's thirty miles you have to do it. Travelling with the swag in Australia is variously and picturesquely described as "humping bluey," "walking Matilda," "humping Matilda," "humping your drum," "being on the wallaby," "jabbing trotters," and "tea and sugar burglaring," but most travelling shearers now call themselves trav'lers, and say simply "on the track," or "carrying swag."

And there you have the Australian swag. Men from all the world have carried it—lords and low-class Chinamen, saints and world martyrs, and felons, thieves, and murderers, educated gentlemen and boors who couldn't sign their mark, gentlemen who fought for Poland and convicts who fought the world, women, and more than one woman disguised as a man. The Australian swag has held in its core letters and papers in all languages, the honour of great houses, and more than one national secret, papers that would send well-known and highly-respected men to jail, and proofs of the innocence of men going mad in prisons, life tragedies and comedies, fortunes and papers that secured titles and fortunes, and the last pence of lost fortunes, life secrets, portraits of mothers and dead loves, pictures of fair women, heart-breaking old letters written long ago by vanished hands, and the pencilled manuscript of more than one book which will be famous yet.

The weight of the swag varies from the light rouseabout's swag, containing one blanket and a clean shirt, to the "royal Alfred," with tent and all complete, and weighing part of a ton. Some old sundowners have a mania for gathering, from selectors' and shearers' huts, and dust-heaps, heart-breaking loads of rubbish which can never be of any possible use to them or anyone else. Here is an inventory of the contents of the swag of an old tramp who was found dead on the track, lying on his face on the sand, with his swag on top of him, and his arms stretched straight out as if he were embracing the mother earth, or had made, with his last movement, the sign of the cross to the blazing heavens:

Rotten old tent in rags. Filthy blue blanket, patched with squares of red and calico. Half of "white blanket" nearly black now, patched with pieces of various material and sewn to half of red blanket. Three-bushel sack slit open. Pieces of sacking. Part of a woman's skirt. Two rotten old pairs of mole-skin trousers. One leg of a pair of trousers. Back of a shirt. Half a waistcoat. Two tweed coats, green, old and rotting, and patched with calico. Blanket, etc. Large bundle of assorted rags for patches, all rotten. Leaky billy-can, containing fishing-line, papers, suet, needles and cotton, etc. Jam-tin, medicine bottles, corks on strings, to hang to his hat to keep the flies off (a sign of madness in the bush, for the corks would madden a sane man sooner than the flies could). Three boots of different sizes, all belonging to the right foot, and a left slipper. Coffee-pot, without handle or spout, and quart-pot full of rubbish—broken knives and forks, with the handles burnt off, spoons, etc., picked up on rubbish-heaps; and many rusty nails, to be used as buttons, I suppose.

Broken saw blade, hammer, broken crockery, old pannikins, small rusty frying-pan without a handle, children's old shoes, many bits of old bootleather and greenhide, part of yellow-back novel, mutilated English dictionary, grammar and arithmetic book, a ready reckoner, a cookery book, a bulgy anglo-foreign dictionary, part of a Shakespeare, book in French and book in German, and a book on etiquette and courtship. A heavy pair of blucher boots, with uppers parched and cracked, and soles so patched (patch over patch) with leather, boot protectors, hoop-iron and hobnails that they were about two inches thick, and the boots weighed over five pounds. (If you don't believe me go into the Melbourne Museum, where, in a glass case in a place of honour, you will see a similar, perhaps the same, pair of bluchers labelled "An example of colonial industry.") And in the core of the swag was a sugar-bag tied tightly with a whip-lash, and containing another old skirt, rolled very tight and fastened with many turns of a length of clothes-line, which last, I suppose, he carried to hang himself with if he felt that way. The skirt was rolled round a small packet of old portraits and almost indecipherable letters—one from a woman who had evidently been a sensible woman and a widow, and who stated in the letter that she did not intend to get married again as she had enough to do already, slavin' her finger-nails off to keep a family, without having a second husband to keep. And her answer was "final for good and all," and it wasn't no use comin' "bungfoodlin'" round her again. If he did she'd set Satan on to him. "Satan" was a dog, I suppose.

The letter was addressed to "Dear Bill," as were others. There were no envelopes. The letters were addressed from no place in particular, so there weren't any means of identifying the dead man. The police buried him under a gum, and a young trooper cut on the tree the words:

SACRED TO THE MEMORY OF

BILL
WHO DIED.

"BUCKOLTS' GATE"

PROLOGUE

Old Abel Albury had a genius for getting the bull by the tail with a tight grip, and holding on with both hands and an obstinacy born of ignorance—and not necessarily for the sake of self-preservation or selfishness—while all the time the bull might be, so to speak, rooting up life-long friendships and neighbourly relations, and upsetting domestic customs and traditions with his horns.

Yes, Uncle Abel was always grasping the wrong end of things, and sticking to it with that human mulishness which is often stronger, and more often wearies and breaks down the opposition than an intelligent man's arguments. He was—or professed to be, the family said—unable for a long time to distinguish between his two grand-nephews, one of whom was short and fat, while the other was tall and thin, the only points of resemblance between them being that each possessed the old family nose and eyes. When they were boys he used to lay the strap about one in mistake for the other. They had a saying that Uncle Abel saw with ten squinting eyes.

Also, he could never—or would not, as the family said—remember names. He referred to Mrs Porter, a thin, haggard selector's wife, as "Mrs Stout" and he balanced matters by calling Mrs Southwick "Mrs Porterwicket"—when he didn't address her as "Mrs What's-the-woman's name"—and he succeeded in deeply offending both ladies.

Uncle Abel was Mrs Carey's uncle. Down at the lower end of Carey's selection at Rocky Rises, in the extreme corner of the lower or outer paddock, were sliprails opening into the main road, which ran down along the siding, round the foot of a spur from ridge, and out west. These sliprails were called "The Lower Sliprails" by the family, and it occurred to Uncle Abel to refer to them as "Buckolts' Gate," for no other reason apparently than that Buckolts' farm lay in that direction. The farm was about a mile further on, on the other side of the creek, and the gate leading to it from the main road was round the spur, out of sight of Carey's selection. It is quite possible that Uncle Abel reasoned the thing out for days, for of such material are some human brains. Sliprails, or a slip-panel, is a panel of fencing of which the rails are made to be slipped out of the mortise holes in the posts so as to give passage to horses, vehicles and cattle. I suppose Abel called it a gate, because he was always going to hang a proper gate there some day. The family were unaware of his new name for the Lower Sliprails, and after he had, on one or two occasions, informed the boys that they would find a missing cow or horse at the Buckolts' Gate, and they had found it calmly camped at the Lower Sliprails, and after he had made several appointments to meet parties at Buckolts' Gate, and had been found leaning obstinately on the fence by the Lower Sliprails with no explanation to offer other than that he *was* waiting at Buckolts' Gate, they began to fear that he was becoming weak in his mind.

ACT I

It was New Year's Eve at Rocky Rises. There was no need for fireworks nor bonfires, for the bush-fires were out all along the ranges to the east, and, as night came on, lines and curves of lights—clear lights, white lights, and, in the nearer distance, red lights and smoky lights—marked the sidings and ridges of a western spur of the Blue Mountain Range, and seemed suspended against a dark sky, for the stars and the loom of the hills were hidden by smoke and drought haze.

There was a dance at Careys'. Old Carey was a cheerful, broad-minded bushman, haunted at times by the memories of old days, when he was the beau of the bush balls, and so when he built his new slab-and-bark barn he had it properly floored with hard-wood, and the floor well-faced "to give the young people a show when they wanted a dance," he said. The floor had a spring in it, and bush boys and girls often rode twenty miles and more to dance on that floor. The girls said it was a lovely floor.

On this occasion Carey had stacked his wheat outside until after the New Year. Spring-carts, and men and girls on horse-back came in from miles round. "Sperm" candles had been cut up and thrown on the floor during the afternoon, and rubbed over by feet cased tightly in 'lastic-sides; and hoops were hung horizontally from the tie-beams, with candles stuck round them. There were fresh-faced girls, and sweet, freckled-faced girls, and jolly girls, and shy girls—all sorts of girls except sulky, "toney" girls—and lanky chaps, most of them sawney, and weird, whiskered agriculturists, who watched the dancers with old, old time-worn smiles, or stood, or sat on their heels yarning, with their pipes, outside, where two boilers were slung over a log-fire to boil water for tea; and there were leathery women, with complexions like dried apples, who gossiped—for the first time in months perhaps—and watched the young people, and thought at times, no doubt, of other days—of other days when they were girls. (And not so far distant either, in some cases, for women dry quickly in the bush.)

And there were one or two old soldiers and their wives, whose eyes glistened when Jim Bullock played "The Girl I Left Behind Me."

Jim Bullock was there with his concertina. He sat on a stool in front of a bench, on which was a beer-keg, piles of teacups and saucers, several big tin teapots, and plates of sandwiches, sponge-cakes, and tarts. Jim sat in his shirt-sleeves, with his flat-brimmed, wire-bound, "hard-hitter" hat on, slanting over his weaker eye. He held one leg loosely and the other rigid, with the concertina on his knee, and swanked away at the instrument by the hour, staring straight in front of him with the expression of a cod-fish, and never moving a muscle except the muscles of his great hairy arms and big chapped and sun-blotched hands; while chaps in tight "larstins" (elastic-side boots), slop suits of black, bound with braid, and with coats too short in the neck and arms, and trousers bell-mouthed at the bottoms, and some with paper collars, narrow red ribbon ties, or scarfs through walnut shells, held their partners rigidly, and went round the room with their eyes—most of them—cocked at the rafters in semi-idiotic ecstasy.

But there was tall, graceful, pink-and-white Bertha Buckolt, blue-eyed and blue-black-haired, and little Mary Carey with the kind, grey eyes and red-gold hair; there was Mary's wild brother Jim, with curly black hair and blue eyes and dimples of innocence; and there was Harry Dale, the drover, Jim's shearing and droving mate, a tall, good-looking, brown-eyed and brown-haired young fellow, a "better-class" bushman and the best dancer in the district. Uncle Abel usurped the position of M.C., and roared "Now then! take yer partners!" and bawled instructions and interrupted and tangled up the dancers, until they got used to taking no notice of his bull voice. Mary Carey was too shy—because she loved him, and secretly and fondly hoped and doubted that he cared for her—to be

seen dancing more than once with Harry Dale, so he shared Bertha
Buckolt, the best girl dancer there, with Jim Carey, who danced
with his sister when Harry was dancing with Bertha Buckolt, and
who seemed, for some reason best known to himself, to be perfectly
satisfied with the arrangement. Poor little Mary began to fret
presently, and feel a little jealous of Bertha, her old schoolmate. She
was little and couldn't dance like Bertha, and she couldn't help
noticing how well Bertha looked to-night, and what a well-matched
pair she and Harry made; and so, when twelve o'clock came and
they all went outside to watch the Old Year out and the New Year
in—with a big bonfire on the distant ridge where the grass fires had
reached a stretch of dry scrub—and to join hands all round and sing
"Auld Lang Syne," little Mary was not to be found, for she was
sitting on a log round behind the cow-yard, crying softly to herself.

And when about three o'clock they all started home, Mary gave
Bertha her cheek to kiss instead of her mouth, and that hurt Bertha,
who had *her* cry riding home, to the astonishment and irritation of
her brother Jack, who rode home with her.

But when they were all gone Mary was missing again and when
her mother called her, and, after a pause, the voice of Harry Dale
said, respectfully, in the darkness, "She's here, Mrs Carey, she's all
right," the two were discovered sitting on a convenient log of the
wood-heap, with an awkward and over-acted interval of log between
them.

Old Carey liked Harry Dale, and seemed very well satisfied with
the way things appeared to be going. He pressed Harry to stay at the
selection overnight. "The missus will make you a shake-down on the
floor," he said. Harry had no appointments, and stayed cheerfully,
and old Carey, having had a whisky or two, insisted on Mary
making the shake-down, and the old folks winked at each other
behind the young folks' backs to see how poor little Mary spread a
spare mattress, with red-hot, averted face, and found an extra pillow
and a spare pair of ironed sheets for the shake-down.

At sunrise she stole out to milk the cows, which was her regular
duty; there was no other way out from her room than through the
dining-room, where Harry lay on his back, with his arms folded,
resting peacefully. He seemed sound asleep and safe for a good two
hours, so she ventured. As she passed out she paused a moment
looking down on him with all the love-light in her eyes, and, obeying
a sudden impulse, she stooped softly and touched his forehead with

her lips, then she slipped out. Harry stretched, opened his eyes, winked solemnly at the ceiling, and then, after a decent interval, he got up, dressed, and went out to help her to milk.

Harry Dale and Jim Carey were going out to take charge of a mob of bullocks going north-west, away up in Queensland, and as they had lost a day and night to be at the dance, they decided to start in the cool of the evening and travel all night. Mary walked from the homestead to the Lower Sliprails between her brother, who rode—because he was her brother—and led a packhorse on the other side, and Harry, who walked and led his horse—because he was her sweetheart, avowed only since last night.

There were thunderstorms about, and Mary had repented sufficiently with regard to Bertha Buckolt to wear on her shoulders a cape which Bertha had left behind her last night.

When they reached the Lower Sliprails Jim said he'd go on and that Harry needn't hurry: he stooped over his horse's neck, kissed his sister, promised to keep away from the drink, not to touch a card, and to leave off fighting, and rode on. And when he rounded the Spur he saw a tall, graceful figure slipping through the trees from the creek towards Buckolts' Gate.

Then came the critical time at the Lower Sliprails. The shadows from the setting sun lengthened quickly on the siding, and then the sun slipped out of sight over a "saddle" in the ridges, and all was soon dusk save the sunlit peaks of the Blue Mountains away to the east over the sweeps of blue-grey bush.

"Ah, well! Mary," said Harry, "I must make a start now."

"You'll—you'll look after Jim, won't you, Harry?" said Mary.

"I will, Mary, for your sake."

Her mouth began to twitch, her chin to tremble, and her eyes brimmed suddenly.

"You must cheer up, Mary," he said with her in his arms. "I'll be back before you know where you are, and then we'll be married right off at once and settle down for life."

She smiled bravely.

"Good-bye, Mary!"

"Good-bye, Harry!"

He led his horse through the rails and lifted them, with trembling hands, and shot them home. Another kiss across the top rail and he got on his horse. She mounted the lower rail, and he brought his horse close alongside the fence and stooped to kiss her again.

"Cheer up, Mary!" he said. "I'll tell you what I'll do—when I come back I'll whistle when I reach the Spur and you be here to let the sliprails down for me. I'll time myself to get here about sundown. I'll whistle 'Willie Riley,' so you'll know it's me. Good-bye, little girl! I must go now. Don't fret—the time will soon go by."

He turned, swung his horse, and rode slowly down the track, turning now and again to wave his hand to her, with a farewell flourish of his hat as he rounded the Spur. His track, five hundred miles, or perhaps a thousand, into the great north-west; his time, six months, or perhaps a year. Hers a hundred yards or so back to the dusty, dreary drudgery of selection life.

The daylight faded into starlight, the sidings grew very dim, and a faint white figure blurred against the bars of the slip-panel.

ACT II

It was the last day of the threshing—shortly after New Year—at Rocky Rises. The green boughs, which had been lashed to the veranda-posts on Christmas Eve, had withered and been used for firewood. The travelling steamer had gone with its gang of men, and the family sat down to tea, the men tired with hard work and heat, and with prickly heat and irritating wheaten chaff and dust under their clothes—and with smut (for the crop had been a smutty one) "up their brains" as Uncle Abel said—the women worn out with cooking for a big gang of shearers.

Good-humoured Aunt Emma—who was Uncle Abel's niece—recovered first, and started the conversation. There were one or two neighbours' wives who had lent crockery and had come over to help with the cooking in their turns. Jim Carey's name came up incidentally, but was quickly dropped, for ill reports of Jim had come home. Then Aunt Emma mentioned Harry Dale, and glanced meaningly at Mary, whose face flamed as she bent over her plate.

"Never mind, Mary," said Aunt Emma, "it's nothing to be ashamed of. We were all girls once. There's many a girl would jump at Harry."

"Who says I'm ashamed?" said Mary, straightening up indignantly.

"Don't tease her, Emma," said Mrs Carey, mildly.

"I'll tell yer what," said young Tom Carey, frankly, "Mary got a letter from him to-day. I seen her reading it behind the house."

Mary's face flamed again and went down over her plate.

"Mary," said her mother, with sudden interest, "did Harry say anything of Jim?"

"No, mother," said Mary. "And that's why I didn't tell you about the letter."

There was a pause. Then Tommy said, with that delightful tact which usually characterizes young Tommies:

"Well, Mary needn't be so cocky about Harry Dale, anyhow. I seen him New Year's Eve when we had the dance. I seen him after the dance liftin' Bertha Buckolt onter her horse in the dark—as if she couldn't get on herself—she's big enough. I seen him lift her on, an' he took her right up an' lifted her right inter the saddle, 'stead of holdin' his hand for her to tread on like that new-chum jackeroo we had. An', what's more, I seen him hug her an' give her a kiss before he lifted her on. He told her he was as good as her brother."

"What did he mean by that, Tommy?" asked Mrs Porter, to break an awkward pause.

"How'm I ter know what he means?" said Tommy, politely.

"And, Tommy, I seen Harry Dale give young Tommy Carey a lick with a strap the day before New Year's Eve for throwing his sister's cat into the dam," said Aunt Emma, coming to poor Mary's rescue. "Never mind, Mary, my dear, he said good-bye to you last."

"No, *he didn't!*" roared Uncle Abel.

They were used to Uncle Abel's sudden bellowing, but it startled them this time.

"Why, Uncle Abel," cried both Aunt Emma and Mrs Carey, "whatever do you mean?"

"What I means is that I ain't a-goin' to have the feelin's of a niece of mine trifled with. What I means is that I seen Harry Dale with Bertha Buckolt on New Year's night after he left here. That's what I means——"

"Don't speak so loud, Abel, we're not deaf," interrupted Carey, as Mary started up white-faced. "What do you want to always shout for?"

"I speak loud because I want people to hear me!" roared Uncle Abel, turning on him.

"Go on, Uncle Abel," said Mary, "tell me what you mean."

"I mean," said Uncle Abel, lowering his voice a little, "that I seen Harry Dale and Bertha Buckolt at Buckolts' Gate that night—I seen it all——"

"*At Buckolts'* Gate!" cried Mary.

"*Yes!* at Buckolts' Gate! Ain't I speakin' loud enough?"

"And where were you?"

"Never mind wheers I was. I was comin' home along the ridges, and I seen them. I seen them say good-bye; I seen them hug an' kiss——"

"Uncle Abel!" exclaimed Aunt Emma.

"It's no use Uncle Abelin' me. What I sez I sez. I ain't a-goin' to have a niece of mine bungfoodled——"

"Uncle Abel," cried Mary, staring at him wild-eyed. "do be careful what you say. You must have made a mistake. Are you sure it was Bertha and Harry?"

"Am I sure my head's on me neck?" roared Uncle Abel. "Would I see 'em if I didn't see 'em? I tell you——"

"Now wait a moment, Uncle Abel," interrupted Mary, with dangerous calmness. "Listen to me. Harry Dale and I are engaged to be married, and——"

"Have you got the writin's!" shouted Uncle Abel.

"The what?" said Mary.

"The writin's."

"No, of course not."

"Then that's where you are," said Uncle Abel, triumphantly. "If you had the writin's you could sue him for breach of contract."

Uncle Abel, who couldn't read, had no faith whatever in verbal agreements (he wouldn't sign one, he said), all others he referred to as "writings."

"Now, listen to me, Uncle Abel," said Mary, trembling now. "Are you sure you saw Harry Dale and Bertha Buckolt at Buckolts' Gate after he left here that night?"

"Yes. An' what's more, I seen young Tommy there ridin' on his pony along by the Spur a little while after, an' he muster seen them too, if he's got a tongue."

Mary turned quickly to her brother.

"Well, all I can say," said Tommy, quietened now, "is that I seen *her* at Buckolts' Gate that night. I was comin' home from Two-Mile Flat, and I met Jim with his packhorse about a mile the other side of Buckolts', and while we was talkin' Harry Dale caught up, so I jist said 'So-long' an' left 'em. And when I got to Buckolt's Gate I seen Bertha Buckolt. She was standin' under a tree, and she looked as if she was cryin'——"

But Mary got her bonnet and started out.

"Where are you going to, Mary?" asked her mother, starting up nervously.

"I'm going across to Buckolts' to find out the truth," said Mary, and she went out.

"Better let her go, Lizzie," said Aunt Emma, detaining her sister. "You've done it now, Uncle Abel."

"Well, why didn't she get the writin's?" retorted Uncle Abel.

Half-way to Buckolts' Mary met Bertha Buckolt herself, coming over to the selection for the first time since the night of the party. Bertha started forward to kiss Mary, but stopped short as Mary stood stock-still and faced her, with her hands behind her back.

"Why! whatever is the matter, Mary?" exclaimed Bertha.

"You know very well, Bertha."

"Why! Whatever do you mean? What have I done?"

"What haven't you done? You've—you've broken my heart."

"Good gracious me! Whatever are you talking about? Tell me what it is, Mary?"

"You met him at your gate that night?"

"I know I did."

"Oh, Bertha! How could you be so mean and deceitful?"

"Mean and deceitful! What do you mean by that? Whatever are you talking about? I suppose I've got as good a right to meet him as anyone else."

"No, you haven't," retorted Mary, "you're only stringing him on. You only did it to spite me. You helped him to deceive me. You ought to be ashamed to look me in the face."

"Good gracious! Whatever are you talking about? Ain't I good enough for him? I ought to be, God knows! I suppose he can marry who he likes, and if I'm poor fool enough to love him and marry him, what then? Mary, you ought to be the last to speak—speak to—to me like that."

"Yes. He can marry all the girls in the country for all I care. I never want to see either him or you any more. You're a cruel, deceitful, brazen-faced hussy, and he's a heartless, deceiving blackguard."

"Mary! I believe you're mad," said Bertha, firmly. "How dare you speak to me like that! And as for him being a blackguard. Why, you ought to be the last in the world to say such a thing; you ought to be the last to say a word against him. Why, I don't believe you ever cared a rap for him in spite of all your pretence. He could go to the devil for all you cared."

"That's enough, Bertha Buckolt!" cried Mary. "*You*—you! Why, you're a barefaced girl, that's what you are! I don't want to see your brazen face again." With that she turned and stumbled blindly in the direction of home.

"Send back my cape," cried Bertha as she too turned away.

Mary walked wildly home and fled to her room and locked the door. Bertha did likewise.

Mary let Aunt Emma in after a while, ceased sobbing and allowed herself to be comforted a little. Next morning she was out milking at the usual time, but there were dark hollows under her eyes, and her little face was white and set. After breakfast she rolled the cape up very tight in a brown-paper parcel, addressed it severely to—

MISS BERTHA BUCKOLT,

Eurunderee Creek,

and sent it home by one of the school-children.

She wrote to Harry Dale and told him that she knew all about it (not stating what), but she forgave him and hoped he'd be happy. She never wanted to see his face again, and enclosed his portrait.

Harry, who was as true and straight as a bushman could be, puzzled it out and decided that some one of his old love affairs must have come to Mary's ears, and wrote demanding an explanation.

She never answered that letter.

ACT III

It was Christmas Day at Rocky Rises. The plum puddings had been made, as usual, weeks beforehand, and hung in rags to the tie-beams and taken down and boiled again. Poultry had been killed and plucked and cooked, and all the toil had been gone through, and every preparation made for a red-hot dinner on a blazing hot day—and for no other reason than that our great-grandmothers used to do it in a cold climate at Christmas-times that came in mid-winter. Merry men hadn't gone forth to the wood to gather in the mistletoe (if they ever did in England, in the olden days, instead of sending shivering, wretched vassals in rags to do it); but Uncle Abel had gone gloomily up the ridge on Christmas Eve, with an axe on his shoulder (and Tommy unwillingly in tow, scowling and making faces behind his back), and had cut young pines and dragged them home and lashed them firmly to the veranda-posts, which was the custom out there.

There was little goodwill or peace between the three or four farms round Rocky Rises that Christmas Day, and Uncle Abel had been the cause of most of the ill-feeling, though they didn't know, and he was least aware of it of any.

It all came about in this way.

Shortly after last New Year Ryan's bull had broken loose and gone astray for two days and nights, breaking into neighbours' paddocks and filling himself with hay and damaging other bulls, and making love by night and hiding in the scrub all day. On the second night he broke through and jumped over Reid's fences, and destroyed about an acre of grape-vines and adulterated Reid's stock, besides interfering with certain heifers which were not of a marriageable age. There was a £5 penalty on a stray bull. Reid impounded the bull and claimed heavy damages. Ryan, a small selector of little account, was always pulling some neighbour to court when he wasn't being "pulled" himself, so he went to court over this case.

Now, it appears that the bull, on his holiday, had spent a part of the first night in Carey's lower paddock, and Uncle Abel (who was out mooching about the bush at all hours, "havin' a look at some timber" or some "indercations" [of gold], or on some mysterious business or fad, the mystery of which was of his own making)— Uncle Abel saw the bull in the paddock at daylight and turned it out the sliprails, and talked about it afterwards, referring to the sliprails as "Buckolts' Gate," of course, and spoke mysteriously of the case, and put on an appearance of great importance, and allowed people to get an idea that he knew a lot if he only liked to speak; and finally he got himself "brought up" as a witness for Ryan.

He had a lot of beer in town before he went to the courthouse. All he knew would have been of no use to either party, but he swore that he had seen Ryan's bull inside Buckolts' Gate at daylight (on the day which wasn't in question) and had turned him out. Uncle Abel mixed up the court a good deal, and roared like the bull, and became more obstinate the more he was cross-examined, and narrowly escaped being committed for contempt of court.

Ryan, who had a high opinion of the breed of his bull, got an idea that the Buckolts had enticed or driven the bull into their paddock for stock-raising purposes, instead of borrowing it honestly or offering to pay for the use of it. Then Ryan wanted to know why Abel had driven his bull out of Buckolts' Gate, and the Buckolts wanted to know what business Abel Albury had to drive Ryan's bull out of their paddock, if the bull had really ever been there. And so it went on till Rocky Rises was ripe for a tragedy.

The breach between the Careys and the Buckolts was widened, the quarrel between Ryan and Reid intensified. Ryan got a down on the Careys because he reckoned that Uncle Abel had deliberately spoilt his case with his evidence; and the Reids and Careys were no longer on speaking terms, because nothing would convince old Reid that Abel hadn't tried to prove that Ryan's bull had never been in Reid's paddock at all.

Well, it was Christmas Day, and the Carey family and Aunt Emma sat down to dinner. Jim was present, having arrived overnight, with no money, as usual, and suffering a recovery. The elder brother, Bob (who had a selection up-country), and his wife were there. Mrs Carey moved round with watchful eyes and jealous ears, lest there should be a word or a look which might hurt the feelings of her wild son—for of such are mothers.

Dinner went on very moodily, in spite of Aunt Emma, until at last Jim spoke—almost for the first time, save for a long-whispered and, on his part, repentant conversation with his mother.

"Look here, Mary!" said Jim. "What did you throw Harry Dale over for?"

"Don't ask me, Jim."

"Rot! What did he do to you? I'm your brother" (with a glance at Bob), "and I ought to know."

"Well, then, ask Bertha Buckolt. She saw him last."

"What!" cried Jim.

"Hold your tongue, Jim! You'll make her cry," said Aunt Emma.

"Well, what's it all about, anyway?" demanded Jim. "All I know is that Mary wrote to Harry and threw him over, and he ain't been the same man since. He swears he'll never come near the district again."

"Tell Jim, Aunt Emma," said Mary. And Aunt Emma started to tell the story as far as she knew.

"Saw her at Buckolt's sliprails!" cried Jim, starting up. "Well, he couldn't have had time to more than say good-bye to her, for I was with her there myself, and Harry caught up to me within a mile of the gate—and I rode pretty fast."

"He had a jolly long good-bye with her," shouted Uncle Abel. "Look here, Jim! I ain't goin' to stand by and see a nephew of mine bungfoodled by no girl; an', I tell you I seen 'em huggin' and kissin' and canoodlin' for half an hour at Buckolts' Gate!"

"It's a—a—— Look here, Uncle Abel, be careful what you say. You've got the bull by the tail again, that's what it is!" Jim's face grew whiter—and it had been white enough on account of the drink. "How did you know it was them? You're always mistaking people. It might have been someone else."

"I know Harry Dale on horseback two miles off!" roared Uncle Abel. "And I knowed her by her cape."

It was Mary's turn to gasp and stare at Uncle Abel.

"Uncle Abel," she managed to say, "Uncle Abel! Wasn't it at our Lower Sliprails you saw them and not Buckolts' Gate?"

"Well!" bellowed Uncle Abel. "You might call 'em the 'Lower Sliprails,' but I calls 'em Buckolts' Gate! They lead to'r'ds Buckolts', don't they? Hey? Them other sliprails"—jerking his arms in the direction of the upper paddock—"them theer other sliprails that leads outer Reid's lane I calls Reid's Sliprails. I don't know nothing about no upper or lower, or easter or wester, or any other la-di-dah names you like to call 'em."

"Oh, uncle," cried Mary, trembling like a leaf, "why didn't you explain this before? Why didn't you tell us?"

"What cause have I got to tell any of you everything I sez or does or thinks? It 'ud take me all me time. Ain't you got any more brains than Ryan's bull, any of you? Hey!—You've got heads, but so has cabbages. Explain! Why, if the world wasn't stuffed so full of jumped-up fools there'd be never no need for explainin'."

Mary left the table.

"What is it, Mary?" cried Aunt Emma.

"I'm going across to Bertha," said Mary, putting on her hat with trembling hands. "It was me Uncle Abel saw. I had Bertha's cape on that night."

"Oh, Uncle Abel," cried Aunt Emma, "whatever have you done?"

"Well," said Uncle Abel, "why didn't she get the writin's as I told her? It's to be hoped she won't make such a fool of herself next time."

Half an hour later, or thereabouts, Mary sat on Bertha Buckolt's bed, with Bertha beside her and Bertha's arm round her, and they were crying and laughing by turns.

"But—but—why didn't you *tell* me it was Jim?" said Mary.

"Why didn't you tell me it was Harry, Mary?" asked Bertha. "It would have saved all this year of misery.

"I didn't see Harry Dale at all that night," said Bertha. "I was—I was crying when Jim left me, and when Harry came along I slipped behind a tree until he was past. And now, look here, Mary, I can't marry Jim until he steadies down, but I'll give him another chance. But, Mary, I'd sooner lose him than you."

Bertha walked home with Mary, and during the afternoon she took Jim aside and said:

"Look here, Jim, I'll give you another chance—for a year. Now I want you to ride into town and send a telegram to Harry Dale. How long would it take him to get here?"

"He couldn't get here before New Year," said Jim.

"That will do," said Bertha, and Jim went to catch his horse. Next day Harry's reply came: "Coming."

ACT IV

New Year's Eve. The dance was at Buckolts' this year, but Bertha didn't dance much; she was down by the gate most of the time with little Mary Carey, waiting, and watching the long, white road, and listening for horses' feet, and disappointed often as other horsemen rode by or turned up to the farm.

And in the hot sunrise that morning, within a hundred miles of Rocky Rises, a tired, dusty drover camped in the edge of a scrub, boiled his quart-pot, broiled a piece of mutton on the coals, and lay down on the sand to rest an hour or so before pushing on to a cattle station he knew to try and borrow fresh horses. He had ridden all night.

Old Buckolt and Carey and Reid smoked socially under the grape-vines, with bottles of whisky and glasses, and nudged each other and coughed when they wanted to laugh at Old Abel Albury, who was, for about the first time in his life, condescending to explain. He was explaining to them what thund'rin' fools they had been.

Later on they sent a boy on horseback with a bottle of whisky and a message to Ryan, who turned up in time to see the New Year in with them and contradict certain slanders concerning the breed of his bull.

Meanwhile Bertha comforted Mary, and at last persuaded her to go home. "He's sure to be here to-morrow, Mary," she said, "and you need to look fresh and happy."

But Mary didn't sleep that night; she was up before day-light, had the kettle on and some chops ready to fry, and at daybreak she was down by the sliprails again. She was turning away for the second time when she heard a clear whistle round the Spur—then the tune of "Willie Riley," and the hobble-chains and camp-ware on the packhorse jingling to the tune.

She pulled out the rails with eager, trembling hands and leaned against the tree.

An hour later a tired drover lay on his back, in his ragged, track-worn clothes and dusty leggings, on Mary's own little bed in the skillion off the living-room, and rested. Mary bustled round getting breakfast ready, and singing softly to herself; once she slipped in, bent over Harry and kissed him gently on the lips, and ran out as he stirred.

"Why, who's that?" exclaimed Uncle Abel, poking round early and catching a glimpse of Harry through the open door.

"It's only Harry, Uncle Abel," said Mary.

Uncle Abel peered in again to make sure.

"Well, be sure you git the writin's this time," he said.

THE BUSH-FIRE

I

SQUATTER AND SELECTOR

Wall was a squatter and a hard man. There had been long years of drought and loss, and then came the rabbit pest—the rabbits swarmed like flies over his run, and cropped the ground bare where even the poor grass might have saved thousands of sheep—and the rabbits cost the squatter hundreds of pounds in "rabbit-proof" fences, trappers' wages, etc., just to keep them down. Then came arrangements with the bank. And then Wall's wife died. Wall started to brood over other days, and the days that had gone between, and developed a temper which drove his children from home one by one, till only Mary was left. She managed the lonely home with the help of a half-caste. Then in good seasons came the selectors.

Men remembered Wall as a grand boss and a good fellow, but that was in the days before rabbits and banks, and syndicates and "pastoralists," or pastoral companies instead of good squatters.

Runs were mostly pastoral leases for which the squatter paid the Government so much per square mile (almost a nominal rent). Selections were small holdings taken up by farmers under residential and other conditions and paid for by instalments. If you were not ruined by the drought, and paid up long enough, the land became freehold. The writer is heir to a dusty patch of three hundred acres or so in the scrub which was taken up thirty years ago and isn't freehold yet.

Selectors were allowed to take up land on runs or pastoral leases as well as on unoccupied Crown lands, and as they secured the best bits of land, and on water frontages if they could, and as, of course, selections reduced the area of the run, the squatters loved selectors like elder brothers. One man is allowed to select only a certain amount of land, and required by law to live on it, so the squatters bought as much freehold about the homestead as they could afford, selected as much as they are allowed to by law, and sometimes employed "dummy" selectors to take up choice bits about the runs and hold them for them. They fought selectors in many various ways, and, in some cases, annoyed and persecuted them with devilish ingenuity.

Ross was a selector, and a very hard man physically. He was a short, nuggety man with black hair and frill beard (a little dusty), bushy black eyebrows, piercing black eyes, horny knotted hands, and the obstinacy or pluck of a dozen men to fight drought and the squatter. Ross selected on Wall's run, in a bend of Sandy Creek, a nice bit of land with a black soil, flat and red soil sidings from the ridges, which no one had noticed before, and with the help of his boys he got the land cleared and fenced in a year or two—taking bush contracts about the district between whiles to make "tucker" for the family until he got his first crop off.

Wall was never accused of employing dummies, or underhanded

methods in dealings with selectors, but he had been through so much and had brooded so long that he had grown very hard and bitter and suspicious, and the reverse of generous—as many men do who start out in life too soft and goodhearted and with too much faith in human nature. He was a tall, dark man. He ordered Ross's boys off the run, impounded Ross's stock—before Ross and got his fencing finished, summoned Ross for trespass, and Ross retaliated as well as he could, until at last it mightn't have been safe for one of those men to have met the other with a gun. The impounding of the selector's cattle led to the last bad quarrel between Wall and his son Billy, who was a tall, good-natured Cornstalk, and who reckoned that Australia was big enough for all of us. One day in the drought, and in an extra bitter mood, Wall heard that some of his sheep had been dogged in the vicinity of Ross's selection, and he ordered Billy to take a station-hand and watch Ross's place all night, and, if Ross's cattle put their noses over the boundary, to drive them to the pound, fifteen miles away; also to lay poisoned baits for the dogs all round the selection. And Billy flatly refused.

"I know Ross and the boys," he said, "and I don't believe they dogged the sheep. Why, they've only got a Newfoundland pup and an old lame, one-eyed sheep-dog that couldn't hurt a flea. Now, father, this sort of thing has been going on long enough. What difference does a few paltry acres make to us? The country is big enough, God knows! Ross is a straight man and—for God's sake, give the man a chance to get his ground fenced in; he's doing it as fast as he can, and he can't watch his cattle day and night."

"Are you going to do as I tell you, or are you not?" shouted Wall.

"Well, if it comes to that, I'm not," said Billy. "I'm not going to sneak round a place all night and watch for a chance to pound a poor man's cows."

It was an awful row, down behind the wool-shed, and things looked so bad that old Peter, the station-hand, who was a witness, took off his coat and rolled up his sleeves, ready, as he said afterwards, "to roll into" either the father or the son if one raised a hand against the other.

"Father!" said Billy, though rather sobered by the sight of his father's trembling, choking passion, "do you call yourself an Englishman?"

"Yes!" yelled Wall, furiously. "What the hell do you call yourself?"

"If it comes to that I'm an Australian," said Billy, and he turned away and went to catch his horse. He went up-country and knocked about in the north-west for a year or two.

II

ROMEO AND JULIET

Mary Wall was twenty-five. She was an Australian bush girl every inch of her five-foot-nine; she had a pink-and-white complexion, dark blue eyes, blue-black hair, and "the finest figure in the district," on horseback or afoot. She was the best girl-rider too (saddle or bare-back), and they say that when she was a tomboy she used to tuck her petticoats under her and gallop man-fashion through the scrub after horses or cattle. She said she was going to be an old maid.

There came a jackeroo on a visit to the station. He was related to the bank with which Wall had relations. He was a dude, with an expensive education and no brains. He was very vain of his education and prospects. He regarded Mary with undisguised admiration, and her father had secret hopes. One evening the jackeroo was down by the homestead-gate when Mary came cantering home on her tall chestnut. The gate was six feet or more, and the jackeroo raised his hat and hastened to open it, but Mary reined her horse back a few yards and the "dood" had barely time to jump aside when there was a scuffle of hoofs on the road, a "Ha-ha-ha!" in mid-air, a landing thud, and the girl was away up the home-track in a cloud of dust.

A few days later the jackeroo happened to be at Kelly's, a wayside shanty, watching a fight between two bushmen, when Mary rode up. She knew the men. She whipped her horse in between them and struck at first one and then the other with her riding-whip.

"You ought to be ashamed of yourselves!" she said; "and both married men, too!"

It evidently struck them that way, for after a bit they shook hands and went home.

"And I wouldn't have married that girl for a thousand pounds," said the jackeroo, relating the incidents to some friends in Sydney.

Mary said she wanted a man, if she could get one.

There was no life at home nowadays, so Mary went to all the bush dances in the district. She thought nothing of riding twenty or thirty miles to a dance, dancing all night, and riding home again next morning. At one of these dances she met young Robert Ross, a clean-limbed, good-looking young fellow about her own age. She danced with him and liked him, and danced with him again, and he rode part of the way home with her. The subject of the quarrel between the two homes came up gradually.

"The boss," said Robert, meaning his father, "the boss is always ready to let bygones be bygones. It's a pity it couldn't be fixed up."

"Yes," said Mary, looking at him (Bob looked very well on horseback), "it is a pity."

They met several times, and next Prince of Wales's birthday they rode home from the races together. Both had good horses, and they happened to be far ahead of the others on the wide, straight clear road that ran between the walls of the scrub. Along, about dusk, they became very confidential indeed—Mary had remarked what a sad and beautiful sunset it was. The horses got confidential, too, and shouldered together, and touched noses, and, after a long interval in the conversation, during which Robert, for one, began to breathe quickly, he suddenly leaned over, put his arm round her waist and made to kiss her. She jerked her body away, threw up her whiphand, and Robert ducked instinctively; but she brought her whip down on her horse's flank instead, and raced ahead. Robert followed—or, rather, his horse did: he thought it was a race, and took the bit in his teeth. Robert kept calling, appealing:

"Wait a while, Mary! I want to explain! I want to appologize! For God's sake listen to me, Mary!"

But Mary didn't hear him. Perhaps she misunderstood the reason of the chase and gave him credit for a spice of the devil in his nature. But Robert grew really desperate; he felt that the thing must be fixed up now or never, and gave his horse a free rein. Her horse was the fastest, and Robert galloped in the dust from his heels for about a mile and a half; then at the foot of a rise Mary's horse stumbled and nearly threw her over his head, and then he stopped like the good horse he was.

Robert got down feeling instinctively that he might best make his peace on foot, and approached Mary with a face of misery—she had dropped her whip.

"Oh, Bob!" she said, "I'm knocked out;" and she slipped down into his arms and stayed there a while.

They sat on a log and rested, while their horses made inquiries of each other's noses, and compared notes.

And after a good while Mary said:

"No, Bob, it's no use talking of marrying just yet. I like you, Bob, but I could never marry you while things are as they are between your father and mine. Now, that'll do. Let me get on my horse, Bob. I'll be safer there."

"Why?" asked Bob.

"Come on, Bob, and don't be stupid."

She met him often and "liked" him.

III

A TRAMP'S MATCH AND WHAT IT DID

It was Christmas Eve at Wall's, but there was no score or so of buggies and horses and dozens of strange dogs round the place as of old. The glasses and decanters were dusty on the heavy old-fashioned sideboard in the dining-room; and there was only a sullen, brooding man leaning over the hurdles and looking at his rams in the yard, and a sullen, brooding half-caste at work in the kitchen. Mary had ridden away that morning to visit a girl chum.

It was towards the end of a long drought, and the country was like tinder for hundreds of miles round—the ground for miles and miles in the broiling scrubs "as bare as your hand," or covered with coarse, dry tufts. There was feed grass in places, but you had to look close to see it.

Shearing had finished the day before, but there was a black boy and a station-hand or two about the yards and six or eight shearers and rouseabouts, and a teamster camped in the men's huts—they were staying over the holidays to shear stragglers and clean up generally. Old Peter and a jackeroo were out on the run watching a bush-fire across Sandy Creek.

A swagman had happened to call at the station that morning; he asked for work and then for tucker. He irritated Wall, who told him to clear out. It was the first time that a swagman had been turned away from the station without tucker.

Swaggy went along the track some miles, brooding over his wrongs, and crossed Sandy Creek. He struck a match and dropped it into a convenient tuft of grass in a likely patch of tufts, with dead grass running from it up into the scrubby ridges—then he hurried on.

Did you ever see a bush-fire? Not sheets of flame sweeping and roaring from tree-top to tree-top, but the snaky, hissing grass-fire of hardwood country.

The whole country covered with thin blue smoke so that you never know in what direction the fire is travelling. At night you see it like the lighted streets of cities, in the distant ranges. It roars up the hollows of dead trees and gives them the appearance of factory chimneys in the dusk. It climbs, by shreds of bark, the trunks of old dead white-box and blue-gums—solid and hard as cast-iron—and cuts off the limbs. And where there's a piece of recently ringbarked country, with the dead leaves still on the trees, the fire will roar from bough to bough—a fair imitation of a softwood forest fire. The bush-fire travels through the scrubs for hundreds of miles, taking the grass to the roots, scorching the living bush but leaving it alive—for gumbush is hardest of any to kill. Where there is no undergrowth, and the country seems bare as a road for miles, the fire will cross, licking up invisible straws of grass, dusty leaves, twigs and shreds of bark on the hard ground already baking in the drought. You hear of a fire miles away, and next day, riding across the head of a gully, you hear a hissing and crackling and there is the fire running over the ground in lines and curves of thin blue smoke, snakelike, with old logs blazing on the blackened ground behind. Did you ever *hear* a fire where a fire should not be? There is something hellish in the sound of it. When the breeze is, say, from the east the fire runs round western spurs, up sheltered gullies—helped by an "eddy" in the wind perhaps—and appears along the top of the ridge, ready, with a change in the wind, to come down on farms and fields of ripe wheat, with a "front" miles long.

A selector might be protected by a wide sandy creek in front and wide cleared roads behind, and, any hour in the day or night, a shout from the farther end of the wheat paddock, and—"Oh, my God! the wheat!"

Wall didn't mind this fire much; most of his sheep were on their way out back, to a back run where there was young grass; and the dry ridges along the creek would be better for a burning-off—only he had to watch his fences.

But, about dusk, Mary came galloping home in her usual breakneck fashion.

"Father," she cried, "turn out the men and send them at once. The fire is all down by Ross's farm, and he has ten acres of wheat standing, and no one at home but him and Bob."

"How do you know?" growled Wall. Then suddenly and suspiciously, "Have you been there?"

"I came home that way."

"Well—let Ross look after his own," snarled the father.

"But he can't, father. They're fighting the fire now, and they'll be burnt out before the morning if they don't get help—for God's sake, father, act like a Christian and send the men. Remember it is Christmas-time, father. You're surely not going to see a neighbour burnt out."

"Yes, I am," shouted Wall. "I'd like to see every selector in the country burnt out, hut and all! Get off that horse and go inside. If a man leaves the station to-night he needn't come back." (This last for the benefit of the men's hut.)

"But, father——"

"Get off that horse and go inside," roared Wall.

"I—I won't."

"What!" He darted forward as though to drag her from the saddle, but she swung her horse away.

"Stop! Where are you going?"

"To help Ross," said Mary. "He had no one to send for help."

"Then go the same way as your brother!" roared her father; "and if you show your nose back again I'll horse-whip you off the run!"

"I'll go, father," said Mary, and she was away.

IV

THE FIRE AT ROSS'S FARM

Ross's farm was in a corner between the ridges and the creek. The fire had come down from the creek, but the siding on that side was fairly clear, and they had stopped the fire there. It went behind the ridge and ran up and over. The ridge was covered thickly with scrub and dead grass; the wheat-field went well up the siding, and along the top was a bush face with only a narrow bridle-track between it and the long dead grass. Everything depended on the wind. Mary saw Ross and Mrs Ross and the daughter Jenny, well up the siding above the fence, working desperately, running to and fro, and beating out the fire with green boughs. Mary left her horse, ran into

the hut, and looked hurriedly round for something to wear in place
of her riding-skirt. She only saw a couple of light print dresses. She
stepped into a skillion room, which happened to be Bob's room, and
there caught sight of a pair of trousers and a coat hanging on the
wall.

Bob Ross, beating desperately along a line of fire that curved
down-hill to his right, and half-chocked and blinded with the smoke,
almost stumbled against a figure which was too tall to be his father.

"Why! who's that?" he gasped.

"It's only me, Bob," said Mary, and she lifted her bough again.

Bob stared. He was so astonished that he almost forgot the fire
and the wheat. Bob was not thin—but——

"Don't look at me, Bob!" said Mary, hurriedly. "We're going to
be married, so it doesn't matter. Let us save the wheat."

There was no time to waste; there was a breeze now from over the
ridges, light, but enough to bear the fire down on them. Once, when
they had breathing space, Mary ran to the creek for a billy of water.
They beat out the fire all along the siding to where a rib of granite
came down over the ridge to the fence, and then they thought the
wheat was safe. They came together here, and Ross had time to look
and see who the strange man was; then he stared at Mary from
under his black, bushy eye-brows. Mary, choking and getting her
breath after her exertions, suddenly became aware, said "Oh!" and
fled round the track beyond the point of granite. She felt a gust of
wind and looked up the ridge. The bush fence ended here in a
corner, where it was met by a new wire fence running up from the
creek. It was a blind gully full of tall dead grass, and, glancing up,
Mary, saw the flames coming down fast. She ran back.

"Come on!" she cried, "come on! The fire's the other side of the
rocks!"

Back at the station, Wall walked up and down till he cooled. He
went inside and sat down, but it was no use. He lifted his head and
saw his dead wife's portrait on the wall. Perhaps his whole life ran
before him in detail—but this is not a psychological study.

There were only two tracks open to him now: either to give in, or
go on as he was going—to shut himself out from human nature and
become known as "Mean Wall," "Hungry Wall," or "Mad Wall,
the Squatter." He was a tall, dark man of strong imagination and
more than ordinary intelligence. And it was the great crisis of his
ruined life. He walked to the top of a knoll near the homestead and

saw the fire on the ridges above Ross's farm. As he turned back he saw a horseman ride up and dismount by the yard.

"Is that you, Peter?"

"Yes, boss. The fences is all right."

"Been near Ross's?"

"No. He's burnt out by this time."

Wall walked to and fro for a few minutes longer. Then he suddenly stopped and called, "Peter!"

"Ay, ay!" from the direction of the huts.

"Turn out the men!" and Wall went into a shed and came out with his saddle on his arm.

The fire rushed down the blind gully. Showers of sparks fell on the bush fence, it caught twice, and they put it out, but the third time it blazed and roared and a fire-engine could not have stopped it.

"The wheat must go," said Ross. "We've done our best," and he threw down the blackened bough and leaned against a tree, and covered his eyes with a grimy hand.

The wheat was patchy in that corner—there were many old stumps of trees, and there were bare strips where the plough had gone on each side of them. Mary saw a chance, and climbed the fence.

"Come on, Bob," she cried, "we might save it yet. Mr Ross, pull out the fence along there," and she indicated a point beyond the fire. They tramped down and tore up the wheat where it ran between the stumps—the fire was hissing and crackling round and through it, and just as it ran past them in one place there was a shout, a clatter of horses' hoofs on the stones, and Mary saw her father riding up the track with a dozen men behind him. She gave a shriek and ran straight down, through the middle of the wheat, towards the hut.

Wall and his men jumped to the ground, wrenched green boughs from the saplings, and, after twenty minutes' hard flighting, the crop was saved—save for a patchy acre or so.

When it was all over Ross sat down on a log and rested his head on his hands, and his shoulders shook.

Presently he felt a hand on his shoulder, looked up, and saw Wall.

"Shake hands, Ross," he said.

And it was Christmas Day.

But in after years they used to nearly chaff the life out of Mary. "You were in a great hurry to put on the breeches, weren't you, Mary?" "Bob's best Sunday-go-meetin's, too, wasn't they, Mary?" "Rather tight fit, wasn't they, Mary?" "Couldn't get 'em on now, could you, Mary?"

"But," reflected old Peter apart to some cronies, "it ain't every young chap as gits an idea of the shape of his wife afore he marries her—is it? An' that's sayin' somethin'."

And old Peter was set down as being an innercent sort of ole cove.

THE HOUSE THAT WAS NEVER BUILT

There had been heavy rain and landslips all along the branch railway which left the Great Western Line from Sydney just beyond the Blue Mountains, and ran through thick bush and scrubby ridgy country and along great alluvial sidings—where the hills on the opposite side of the wide valleys (misty in depths) faded from deep blue into the pale azure of the sky—and over the ends of western spurs to the little farming, mining and pastoral town of Solong, situated in a circle of blue hills on the banks of the willow-fringed Cudgegong River.

The line was hopelessly blocked, and some publicans at Solong had put on the old coach-road a couple of buggies, a wagonette, and an old mail coach—relic of the days of Cobb & Co., which had been resurrected from some backyard and tinkered up—to bring the train passengers on from the first break in the line over the remaining distance of forty miles or so. Capertee Station (old time, "Capertee Camp"—a teamster's camp) was the last station before the first washout, and there the railway line and the old road parted company for the last time before reaching Solong—the one to run round by the ends of the western spurs that spread fanlike, and the other to go through and over the rough country.

The train reached Capertee about midnight in broad moonlight that was misty in the valleys and round the blue of Crown Ridge. I got a "box-seat" beside the driver on the old coach. It was a grand old road—one of the old main coach-roads of New South Wales— broad and white, metalled nearly all the way, and in nearly as good condition as on the day when the first passenger train ran into Solong and the last-used section of the old road was abandoned. It dated back to the bushranging days—right back to convict times: it ran through tall dark bush, up over gaps or "saddles" in high ridges

down across deep dark gullies, and here and there across grey,
marshy, curlew-haunted flats. Cobb & Co.'s coach-and-six, with
"Royal Mail" gilded on the panels, had dashed over it in ten- and
twelve-mile stages in the old days, the three head-lamps flashing on
the wild dark bush at night, and maybe twenty-four passengers on
board. The biggest rushes to richest goldfields in the west had gone
over this old road on coaches, on carts, on drays, on horse and
bullock wagons, on horseback, and on foot; new chums from all the
world and from all stations in life.

> When many a step was on the mountains,
> Marching west to the land of gold.

And a few came back rich—red, round-faced and jolly—on the
box-seat of Cobb & Co.'s, treating the driver and all hands, "going
home" to sweethearts or families. (Home people will never feel the
meaning of those two words, "going home," as it is felt in a new
land.) And many came back broken men, tramping in rags, and
carrying their swags through the dusty heat of the drought in
December or the bitter, pelting rain in the mountains in June. Some
came back grey who went as boys; and there were many who never
came back.

I remembered the old mile-trees, with a section of bark cut away
and the distances cut in Roman letters in the hardened sap—the
distance from Bowenfels, the railway terminus then. It was a ghostly
old road, and if it wasn't haunted it should have been. There was an
old decaying and nearly deserted coaching town or two; there were
abandoned farms and halfway inns, built of stone, with the roofs
gone and nettles growing high between the walls; the remains of an
orchard here and there—a few gnarled quince-trees—and the bush
reclaiming its own again. It was a haunted ride for me, because I
had last ridden over this old road long ago when I was young—
going to see the city for the first time—and because I was now on my
way to attend the funeral of one of my father's blood from whom I
had parted in anger.

We slowly climbed, and almost as slowly descended, the steep
siding of a great hill called Aaron's Pass, and about a mile beyond
the foot of the hill I saw a spot I remembered passing on the last
journey down, long ago. Rising back from the road, and walled by
heavy bush, was a square clearing, and in the background I saw
plainly, by the broad moonlight, the stone foundations for a large
house; from the front an avenue of grown pines came down to the
road.

"Why!" I exclaimed, turning to the driver, "was that house burnt down?"

"No," he said slowly. "That house was never built."

I stared at the place again and caught sight of a ghostly-looking light between the lines of the foundations, which I presently made out to be a light in a tent.

"There's someone camping there," I said.

"Yes," said the driver, "some old swaggy or 'hatter.' I seen him comin' down. I don't know nothing about that there place." (I hadn't "shouted" for him yet.)

I thought and remembered. I remembered myself, as a boy, being sent a coach journey along this road to visit some relatives in Sydney. We passed this place, and the women in the coach began to talk of the fine house that was going to be built there. The ground was being levelled for the foundations, and young pines had been planted, with stakes round them to protect them from the cattle. I remembered being mightily interested in the place, for the women said that the house was to be a two-storied one. I thought it would be a wonderful thing to see a two-storied house there in the bush. The height of my ambition was to live in a house with stairs in it. The women said that this house was being built for young Brassington, the son of the biggest squatter then in the district, who was going to marry the daughter of the next biggest squatter. That was all I remember hearing the women say.

Three or four miles along the road was a public-house, with a post office, general store, and blacksmith shop attached, as is usual in such places—all that was left of the old pastoral and coaching town of Ilford. I "shouted" for the driver at the shanty, but got nothing further out of him concerning the fate of the house that was never built. I wanted that house for a story.

However, while yarning with some old residents at Solong, I mentioned the Brassingtons, and picked up a few first links in the story. The young couple were married and went to Sydney for their honeymoon. The story went that they intended to take a trip to the old country and Paris, to be away a twelve-month, and the house was to be finished and ready for them on their return. Young Brassington himself had a big sheep-run round there. The railway wasn't thought of in those days, or if it was, no Brassington could have dreamed that the line could have been brought to Solong in any other direction than through the property of the "Big Brassingtons," as they were called. Well, the young couple went to Sydney, but whether they went farther the old residents did not know. All they knew was that within a few weeks, and before the stone foundations for the brick walls of the house were completed, the building contract was cancelled, the workmen were dismissed, and the place was left as I last saw it; only the ornamental pines had now grown to trees. The Brassingtons and the bride's people were English families and reserved. They kept the story, if there was a story, to themselves. The girl's people left the district and squatted on new stations up-country. The Big Brassingtons came down in the world and drifted to the city, as many smaller people do, more and more every year. Neither young Brassington nor his wife was ever again seen or heard of in the district.

I attended my relative's funeral, and next day started back for Sydney.

Just as we reached Ilford, as it happened, the pin of the fore under-carriage of the coach broke, and it took the blacksmith several hours to set it right. The place was dull, the publican was not communicative—or else he harped on the old local grievance of the railway not having come that way—so about half an hour before I thought the coach would be ready, I walked on along the road to stretch my legs. I walked on and on until I came, almost unaware, to the site of the house that was never built. The tent was still there, in fact, it was a permanent camp, and I was rather surprised to see the man working with a trowel on a corner of the unfinished foundations of the house. At first I thought he was going to build a stone hut in the corner, but when I got close to him I saw that he was working carefully on the original plan of the building: he was building the unfinished parts of the foundation walls up to the required height. He had bricklayer's tools, a bag of lime, and a heap of sand, and had worked up a considerable quantity of mortar. It was a rubble foundation: he was knocking off the thin end of a piece of stone to make it fit, and the clanging of the trowel prevented his hearing my footsteps.

"Good day, mate," I said, close beside him.

I half expected he'd start when I spoke, but he didn't: he looked round slowly, but with a haunted look in his eyes as if I might have been one of his ghosts. He was a tall man, gaunt and haggard-eyed, as many men are in the bush; he may have been but little past middle age, and grey before his time.

"Good day," he said, and he set the stone in its place, carefully flush with the outer edge of the wall, before he spoke again. Then he looked at the sun, which was low, laid down his trowel, and asked me to come to the tent-fire. "It's turning chilly," he said. It was a model camp, everything clean and neat both inside the tent and out; he had made a stone fire-place with a bark shelter over it, and a table and bench under another little shed, with shelves for his tin cups and plates and cooking utensils. He put a box in front of the fire and folded a flour-bag on top of it for a seat for me, and hung the billy over the fire. He sat on his heels and poked the burning sticks, abstractedly I thought, or to keep his hands and thoughts steady.

"I see you're doing a bit of building," I said.

"Yes," he said, keeping his eyes on the fire; "I'm getting on with it slowly."

I don't suppose he looked at me half a dozen times the whole while I was in his camp. When he spoke he talked just as if he were sitting yarning in a row of half a dozen of us. Presently he said suddenly, and giving the fire a vicious dig with his poker:

"That house must be finished by Christmas."

"Why?" I asked, taken by surprise. "What's the hurry?"

"Because," he said, "I'm going to be married in the New Year—to the best and dearest girl in the bush."

There was an awkward pause on my part, but presently I pulled myself together.

"You'll never finish it by yourself," I said. "Why don't you put on some men?"

"Because," he said, "I can't trust them. Besides, how am I to get bricklayers and carpenters in a place like this?"

I noticed all through that his madness or the past in his mind was mixed up with the real and the present.

"Couldn't you postpone the marriage?" I asked.

"No!" he exclaimed, starting to his feet. "No!" and he looked round wildly on the darkening bush. There was madness in his tone that time, the last "No!" sounding as if from a man who was begging for his life.

"Couldn't you run up a shanty then, to live in until the house is ready?" I suggested, to soothe him.

He gave his arm an impatient swing. "Do you think I'd ask that girl to live in a hut?" he said. "She ought to live in a palace!"

There seemed no way out of it, so I said nothing: he turned his back and stood looking away over the dark, low-lying sweep of bush towards sunset. He folded his arms tight, and seemed to me to be holding himself. After a while he let fall his arms and turned and blinked at me and the fire like a man just woke from a doze or rousing himself out of a deep reverie.

"Oh, I almost forgot the billy!" he said. "I'll make some tea—you must be hungry."

He made the tea and fried a couple of slices of ham; he laid the biggest slice on a thick slice of white baker's bread on a tin plate, and put it and a pint-pot full of tea on a box by my side. "Have it here, by the fire," he said; "it's warmer and more comfortable."

I took the plate on my knee, and I must say I thoroughly enjoyed that meal. The bracing mountain air and the walk had made me hungry. The hatter had his meal standing up, cutting his ham on a slice of bread with a clasp-knife. It was bush fashion, and set me thinking of some old times. He ate very little, and, as far as I saw, he didn't smoke. Non-smokers are very scarce in the bush.

I saw by the way his tent was pitched and his camp arranged generally, and by the way he managed the cooking, that he must have knocked about the bush for some years.

He put the plates and things away and came and sat down on the other empty gin-case by my side, and fell to poking the fire again. He never showed the least curiosity as to who I was, or where I came from, or what I was doing on this deserted track: he seemed to take me as a matter of course—but all this was in keeping with bush life in general.

Presently he got up and stood looking upwards over the place where the house should have been.

"I think now," he said slowly, "I made a mistake in not having the verandas carried all round the house."

"I—I beg pardon!"

"I should have had the balcony all round instead of on two sides only, as the man who made the plan suggested; it would have looked better and made the house cooler in summer."

I thought as I listened, and presently I saw that it was a case of madness within madness, so to speak: he was mad on the idea that he could build the house himself, and then he had moods when he imagined that the house had been built and he had been married and had reared a family.

"You could easily get the balcony carried round," I said; "it wouldn't cost much—you can get good carpenters at Solong."

"Yes," he said. "I'll have it done after Christmas." Then he turned from the house and blinked down at me.

"I am sorry," he said, "that there's no one at home. I sent the wife and family to Sydney for a change. I've got the two boys at the Sydney Grammar School. I think I'll send the eldest to King's

School at Parramatta. The girls will have to get along with a governess at home and learn to help their mother——"

And so he went on talking away just as a man who has made money in the bush, and is married and settled down, might yarn to an old bachelor bush mate.

"I suppose I'll have to get a good piano," he went on. "The girls must have some amusement: there'll be no end of balls and parties. I suppose the boys will soon be talking of getting 'fivers' and 'tenners' out of the 'guvner' or 'old man.' It's the way of the world. And they'll marry and leave us. It's the way of the world——"

It was awful to hear him go on like this, the more so because he never smiled—just talked on as if he had said the same thing over and over again. Presently he stopped, and his eyes and hands began to wander: he sat down on his heel to the fire again and started poking it. I began to feel uneasy; I didn't know what other sides there might be to his madness, and wished the coach would come along.

"You've knocked about the bush a good deal?" I asked. I couldn't think of anything else to say, and I thought he might break loose if I let him brood too long.

"Yes," he said, "I have."

"Been in Queensland and the Gulf country, I suppose?"

"I have."

His tone and manner seemed a bit more natural. He had knocked about pretty well all over Australia, and had been in many places where I had been. I had got him on the right track, and after a bit he started telling bush yarns and experiences, some of them awful, some of them very funny, and all of them short and good; and now and then, looking at the side of his face, which was all he turned to me, I thought I detected the ghost of a smile.

One thing I noticed about him; when he spoke as a madman, he talked like a man who had been fairly well educated (or sometimes, I fancied, like a young fellow who was studying to be a school-teacher); his speech was deliberate and his grammar painfully correct—far more so than I have made it; but when he spoke as an old bushman, he dropped his g's and often turned his grammar back to front. But that reminds me that I have met English college men who did the same thing after being a few years in the bush; either they dropped their particular way of speaking because it was mimicked, because they were laughed and chaffed out of it, or they fell gradually into the habit of talking as rough bushmen do (they learnt Australian), as clean-mounted men fall, in spite of themselves, into the habit of swearing in the heat and hurry and rough life of a shearing-shed. And, coming back into civilized life, these men, who had been well brought up, drop into their old manner and style of speaking as readily as the foulest-mouthed man in a shed or camp—who, amongst his fellows, cannot say three words without an oath—can, when he finds himself in a decent home in the woman-and-girl world, yarn by the hour without letting slip a solitary little damn.

The hatter warmed up the tea-billy again, got out some currant buns, which he had baked himself in the camp-oven, and we were yarning comfortably like two old bushmen, and I had almost forgotten that he was "ratty," when we heard the coach coming. I jumped up to hurry down to the road. This seemed to shake him up. He gripped my hand hard and glanced round in his frightened, haunted way. I never saw the eyes of a man look so hopeless and helpless as his did just then.

"I'm sorry you're going," he said, in a hurried way. "I'm sorry you're going. But—but they all go. Come again, come again—we'll all be glad to see you."

I had to hurry off and leave him. "We all," I suppose, meant himself and his ghosts.

I ran down between the two rows of pines and reached the road just as the coach came up. I found the publican from Ilford aboard—he was taking a trip to Sydney. As the coach went on I looked up the clearing and saw the hatter standing straight behind the fire, with his arms folded and his face turned in our direction. He looked ghastly in the firelight, and at that distance his face seemed to have an expression of listening blindness. I looked round on the dark bush, with, away to the left, the last glow of sunset fading from the bed of it, like a bed of reddening coals, and I looked up at the black loom of Aaron's Pass, and thought that never a man, sane or mad, was left in such a depth of gloomy loneliness.

"I see you've been yarning with him yonder," said the publican, who seemed to have relaxed wonderfully.

"Yes."

"You know these parts, don't you?"

"Yes. I was about here as a boy."

He asked me what my name might be. I told him it was Smith. He blinked a while.

"I never heard of anyone by the name of Smith in the district," he said.

Neither had I. I told him that we lived at Solong, and didn't stay long. It saved time.

"Ever heard of the Big Brassingtons?"

"Yes."

"Ever heard the yarn of the house that wasn't built?"

I told him how much I had heard of it.

"And that's about all any on 'em knows. Have you any idea who that man back yonder is?"

"Yes, I have."

"Well, who do you think it is?"

"He is, or rather he was, young Brassington."

"You've hit it!" said the publican. "I know—and a few others."

"And do you know what became of his wife?" I asked.

"I do," said the shanty-keeper, who had a generous supply of whisky with him, and seemed to have begun to fill himself up for the trip.

He said no more for a while, and when I had remained silent long enough, he went on, very deliberately and impressively:

"One yarn is that the girl wasn't any good; that when she was married to Brassington, and as soon as they got to Sydney, she met a chap she'd been carrying on with before she married Brassington (or that she'd been married to in secret), an' she cleared off with him, leaving her fortnight-old husband. That was one yarn."

"Was it?" I said.

"Yes," said the publican. "That yarn was a lie." He opened a flask of whisky and passed it round.

"There was madness in the family," he said, after a nip.

"Whose?" I asked. "Brassington's?"

"No," said the publican, in a tone that implied contempt at my ignorance, in spite of its innocence, "the girl's. Her mother had been in a 'sylum, and so had her grandmother. It was—it was heridited. Some madnesses is heridited, an' some comes through worry and hard graft (that's mine), an' some comes through drink, and some through worse, and, but as far as I've heard, all madnesses is pretty much the same. My old man was a warder in a 'sylum. They have their madnesses a bit different, the same as boozers has their d.t.'s different; but, takin' it by the lump, it's pretty much all the same. The difference is accordin' to their natures when they're sane. All men are——"

"But about young Mrs Brassington," I interrupted.

"Young Mrs Brassington? Rosy Webb she was, daughter of Webb the squatter. Rosy was the brightest, best, good-heartedest, an' most ladylike little girl in the district, an' the heriditry business come on her in Sydney, about a week after she was married to young Brassington. She was only twenty. Here—" He passed the flask round.

"And what happened?" I asked.

"What happened?" he repeated. Then he pulled himself together, as if conscious that he had shown signs of whisky. "Everything was done, but it was no use. She died in a year in a 'sylum."

"How do you know that?"

"How do I know that?" he repeated in a tone of contempt. "How do I know that? Well, I'll tell you how. *My old wife* was in service at Brassington's station at the time—the oldest servant—an' young Brassington wired to her from Sydney to come and help him in his trouble. Old Mrs Brassington was bedridden, an' they kep' it from her."

"And about young Brassington?"

"About young Brassington? He took a swag an' wandered through the bush. We've had him at our place several times all these years, but he always wandered off again. My old woman tried everything with him, but it was all no use. Years ago she used to get him to talk of things as they was, in hopes of bringin' his mind back, but he was always worse after. She does all she can for him even now, but he's mighty independent. The last five or six years he's been taken with the idea of buildin' that cursed house. He'll stay there till he gets short of money, an' then he'll go out back, shearin', stock-ridin', drovin', cookin', fencin'—anything till he gets a few pounds. Then he'll settle down and build away at that bloody house. He's knocked about so much that he's a regular old bushman. While he's an old bushman he's all right an' amusin' an' good company; but when he's Brassington he's mad—Don't you ever let on to my old woman that I told you. I allers let my tongue run a bit when I get out of that hole we're living in. We've kept the secret all these years, but what does it matter now?—I ask you."

"It doesn't matter much," I said.

"Nothing matters much, it seems to me, nothing matters a damn. The Big Brassingtons came down years ago; the old people's gone, and the young scattered God knows where or how. The Webbs (the girl's people) are away up in new country, an' the girls (they was mostly all girls) are married an' settled down by this time. We kept the secret, an' the Webbs kept the secret—even when the dirty yarns was goin' round—so's not to spoil the chances of the other girls. What about the chances of their husbands? Some on 'em might be in the same hell as Brassington for all I know. The Brassingtons kept the secret because I suppose they reckoned it didn't matter much. Nothing matters much in this world—"

But I was thinking of another young couple who had married long ago, whose married life was twenty long years of shameful quarrels, of useless brutal recrimination—not because either was bad, but because their natures were too much alike; of the house that was built, of the family that was reared, of the sons and daughters who "went wrong," of the father and mother separated after twenty years, of the mother dead of a broken heart, of the father (in a lunatic asylum), whose mania was not to build houses, but to obtain and secrete matches for the purpose of burning houses down.

"BARNEY, TAKE ME HOME AGAIN"

This is a sketch of one of the many ways in which a young married woman, who is naturally thick-skinned and selfish—as most women are—and who thinks she loves her husband, can spoil his life because he happens to be good-natured, generous, sensitive, weak or soft, whichever you like to call it.

Johnson went out to Australia a good many years ago with his young wife and two children, as assisted emigrants. He should have left his wife and children with her mother, in a street off City Road, N., and gone out by himself and got settled down comfortably and strengthened in the glorious climate and democratic atmosphere of Australia, and in the knowledge that he could worry along a while without his wife, before sending for her. That bit of knowledge would have done her good also, and it would have been better for both of them. But no man knows the future, and few can prescribe for their own wives. If we saw our married lives as others see them, half of us would get divorced. But Johnson was sentimental, he could not bear to part from his wife for a little while. Moreover, man is instinctively against leaving his wife behind; it may be either a natural or a cowardly instinct—but we won't argue that. I don't believe that Johnson was a coward in that direction; I believe that he trusted his wife implicitly, or rather that he never dreamed of such a thing—as is the way with most married men. Sentiment is selfishness, perhaps, but we won't argue that, such arguments come to nothing.

I heard from a fellow-passenger of Johnson's that he had "a hell of a voyage" because of his young wife's ignorant selfishness and his own sensitiveness; he bribed stewards for better food and accommodation for his wife and children, paid the stewardess to help with the children, got neither rest, nor peace, nor thanks for himself, and landed in Sydney a nervous wreck, with five pounds out of the ten he started with.

Johnson was a carpenter. He got work from a firm of contractors in Sydney, who, after giving him a fortnight's trial, sent him up-country to work on the railway station buildings, at the little pastoral mining and farming town of Solong. The railway having come to Solong, things were busy in the building line, and Johnson settled there.

Johnson was thin when he came to Solong; he had landed a living skeleton, he said, but he filled out later on. The democratic atmosphere soothed his mind and he soon loved the place for its unconventional hospitality. He worked hard and seemed to have plenty of energy—he said he got it in Australia. He said that another year of the struggle in London would have driven him mad. He bathed in the river on Saturday afternoons and Sundays, and, perhaps for the first month or so, he thought that he had found peace. Johnson's wife was a rather stout, unsympathetic-looking young woman, with the knit of obstinacy in her forehead; she had that stamp of "hardness" on her face which is the rule amongst English and the exception amongst Australian women. We of Solong thought her hard, selfish and narrow-minded, and paltry; later on we thought she was a "bit touched;" but local people often think that of strangers.

By her voice and her habit of whining she should have been a thin, sharp-faced, untidy, draggled-tailed woman in a back street in London, or a worn-out selector's wife in the bush. She whined about the climate. "It will kill the children! It will kill the children! We'll never rear them here!" She whined about the "wretched hole in the bush" that her husband had brought her to; and to the women whom she condescended to visit—because a woman must have a woman to talk to—she exaggerated the miseries of the voyage until the thing became a sing-song from repetition. Later on she settled down to endless accounts of her home in London, of her mother and sisters, of the way they lived. "And I'll never see it any more. I'll never see them any more."

The Solong climate was reckoned the best in Australia; the "wretched hole" was a pretty little town on the banks of a clear,

willow-bordered river, with vineyards on the slopes, and surrounded
by a circle of blue hills and peaks. We knew nothing of London, so
she had her own way there.

"She'll feel a bit lonely at first, but she'll soon get used to
Australia," said Johnson. He seemed to me to go out of his way to
excuse his wife.

Johnson had had a few contracts in England at one time; they had
been in "better circumstances"—that was the time she looked back
to in England; the last two years of bitter, black struggle at "home"
seemed a blank in her mind—but that's how women jump over facts
when they have a selfish fad.

Johnson rented a cottage and garden on the bank of the sunny
river. He said he took the place because there was ivy growing on the
cottage, and it might cheer his wife; but he had lost sight of the fact
that, while he had been born in an English village, his wife had been
born and bred in London, and had probably never noticed ivy. She
said it was worse than living in a slum.

Johnson was clever at his trade, and at many other things, but his
wife didn't seem aware of it. He was well liked, he grew to be
popular, but she didn't seem proud of the fact; she never seemed
interested in him or his prospects. She only wanted him to take her
home again. We mustn't forget that while he had a rush of work to
occupy his mind she had not.

But Johnson grew stouter and prospered in spite of his wife—for a
year or so. New schools were being built in the district and the town
was practically re-built. Johnson took contracts for brickwork,
plumbing and house-painting, as well as carpentering, and had at
one time as many as ten men in his employ. He was making money.

I was working at my trade then, house-painting, and worked for
Johnson. I lodged at his cottage for a while, but soon got tired of
hearing about London, and Mrs Johnson's mother and sisters, and
the house they lived in, and the street it was in, and the parks where
they used to take their babies, and the shopping on Saturday
afternoon. That woman was terrible. She was at Johnson all the time
about taking her home. "We'll surely be able to go home this year,
Will." "You promised to take me home by the end of the year."
"Mother says in her last letter that Jack says there's more building
going on about London than ever." "You'll do just as well in
London as you'll do here." "What chance have the children got in a
hole like this?" And the rest of it—every night. When he took a new
contract, it would be, "What did you want to take that new contract
for, Will, when we're going home? You know you promised me you

wouldn't take any more contracts." First he'd try to cheer her, then he'd argue; but she'd only sit with the knit in her forehead deep, looking as obstinate as a mule. Then she'd sit down to a little harmonium he'd bought her and play and sing "Barney, take me Home again," and "The Old Folks at Home," and "Swannie Ribber," till I felt like hanging myself—and *I* wasn't an exile. Sometimes Johnson would flare up and there'd be a row and he'd go to the pub. Gentle persuasion, argument, or swearing, it was all the same with her.

Bosses and men were different towards each other in Solong to what they are in London; besides, when I wasn't Johnson's sub-contractor I was his foreman—so we often had a few drinks together; and one night over a beer (and after a breeze at home, I think) he said to me:

"I can't make it out, Harry; there was nothing but struggle and worry and misery for us in England, and London was smothering me, my chest was bad and the wife was always in ill-health; but I suppose I'll have to take her home in the end or else she'll go melancholy mad!" And he drew a breath that was more like a gasp than a sigh.

"Why not send her home for a trip, or a year or so, boss?" I asked. "As likely as not she'll be just as eager to get back; and that will be the end of it."

"I couldn't do that, Harry," said Johnson. "I couldn't stay here and work alone. It would be like beginning life again; I've started twice and couldn't start the third time. You'll understand when you're married, Harry."

Well, in the end, she wore Johnson out—or wore into him rather. He drank more, and once or twice I saw him drinking alone. Sometimes he'd "round on us" at work for nothing at all, and at other times he'd take no interest in the jobs—he'd let the work go on anyhow. Some thought that Johnson was getting too big for his boots, that's how men are misjudged. He grew moody and melancholy and thin again. Johnson was homesick himself. No doubt it was the misery of his domestic life in Australia that made him so.

Towards the end of the third or fourth year Johnson threw up a couple of contracts he had on hand, sacrificed a piece of land which he had bought and on which he had built a cottage in the short time he had been in Solong, and, one lovely day in June, when the skies were their fairest, the hills their bluest, the river its widest and clearest, and the grass was waving waist high after rain—one blue and green and golden day the Johnsons left Solong, with the trunks they had brought out with them, for Sydney, *en route* for smoky London.

Mrs Johnson was a woman transformed—she was happy and looked it. The last few weeks she had seemed in every way the opposite of the woman we had known: cheerful, kind to neighbours in sickness and trouble, even generous; she made many small presents in the way of mantelshelf ornaments, pictures, and house-linen. But then it was Johnson who had to pay for that in the end.

He looked worn and worried at the railway station—more like himself as he was when he first came to Solong—and as the train moved off I thought he looked—well, frightened.

That must have been nearly twenty years ago.

London last winter. It was one of those days when London's lurid sun shows up for a little while like a smoky danger signal. The snow had melted from the house-tops and the streets were as London streets are after the first fall of snow of the season. But I could stand the flat no longer, I had to go out and walk. I was sun-sick—I was heart-sick for the sun, for the sunny South—for grassy plains, blue mountains, sweeps of mountain bush and sunny ocean beaches. I walked hard; I walked till I was mud-splashed to the shoulders; I walked through the squalid, maddening sameness of miles of dingy, grimy-walled blocks and rows of four-storied houses till I felt smothered—jailed, hopelessly. "Best get home and in, and draw the blinds on it," I said, "or my brain will turn."

I was about to ask a policeman where I was when I saw, by the name on a corner of the buildings, that I was in City Road, North.

All the willow-fringed rivers and the sunny hills of Solong flashed before me at the sight of the name of that street. I had not been able to recall the name of the street off City Road in which the Johnsons lived, though I had heard it often enough in the old days from the tongue of Mrs Johnson.

I felt it would be a relief to see anyone who had been in Australia. "Now," I thought, "if I walk along City Road and see the name of that street I'll remember it"—and I did. It was a blind street, like the long, narrow yard of a jail, walled by dark houses, all alike. The next door but one to that at which I knocked to inquire was where the Johnsons lived; they lived in a four-storied house, or rather a narrow section of a four-storied terrace. I found later on that they paid the landlord, or nearly paid him, by letting lodgings. They lived in one room with the use of the parlour and the kitchen when the lodgers weren't using them, and the son shared a room with a lodger. The back windows looked out on the dead wall of a poorhouse of some kind, the front on rows of similar windows opposite—rows of the same sort of windows that run for miles and miles in London. In one a man sat smoking in his shirt-sleeves, from another a slavey leaned out watching a four-wheeler that had stopped next door, in a third a woman sat sewing, and in a fourth a woman was ironing, with a glimpse of a bedstead behind her. And all outside was gloom and soot and slush.

I would never have recognized the Johnsons. I have visited them several times since and their faces are familiar to me now, but I don't know whether any traces of the old likenesses worked up in my memory. I found Johnson an old man—old and grey before his time. He had a grizzly stubble round his chin and cheeks towards the end of the week, because he could only afford a shave on Saturday afternoon. He was working at some branch of his trade "in the shop" I understood, but he said he felt the work come heavier on him every winter. "I've felt very poorly this last winter or two," he said, "very poorly indeed." He was very sad and gentle.

Mrs Johnson was old and thin-looking, but seemed cheerful and energetic. Some chest trouble kept her within doors most of the winter.

"I don't mind so long as I can manage," she said, "but Johnson gets so depressed."

They seemed very kind towards each other; they spoke little of Australia, and then only as an incident in their lives which was not of any importance—had long been past and done with. It was all "before we went to Australia" or "after we came back from Australia," with Mrs Johnson.

The son, whom I remembered as a bright, robust little fellow, was now a tall, white-faced, clean-shaven young man, a clerk on thirty shillings a week. He wore, on Saturday afternoons and Sundays, a tall hat and a frock coat and overcoat made cheaply in the latest fashion, so he couldn't afford to help the old folk much.

"David is very extravagant," said the old man, gently. "He won't wear anything when once the gloss is off it. But," with a sad smile, "I get the left-off overcoats."

He took me across to see his daughter. She had married a tradesman and they were having a hard struggle in three rooms in a workman's dwelling. She was twenty-five, thin, yellow, and looking ten years older.

There were other children who had died. "I think we might have
done better for the children in Australia," said the old man to me,
sadly, when we got outside, "but we did our best."

We went into a hotel and had a drink. Johnson had treated last
time—twenty years before. We call treating "shouting" in Australia.
Presently Johnson let fall a word or two of Australian slang, and
brightened up wonderfully; we got back out into Australia at once
and stayed there an hour or so. Being an old man, Johnson's
memory for the long ago was better than mine, and I picked up
links; and, in return, I told him what Solong was like now, and how
some men he knew, who were going up, had gone down, and others,
who were going to the dogs in his time, had gone up—and we
philosophized. About one he'd say, "Ah, well! who'd have thought
it! I never thought that boy would come to any good;" about
another, "Ah, well! and he might have been an independent man."
How familiar that expression sounded!—I think it is used more often
in Australia than in any other country: "He might have been an
independent man."

When I left Johnson I felt less lonely in London, and rather
humbled in spirit. He seemed so resigned—I had never seen such
gentle sadness in a man's eyes, nor heard it in a man's voice. I could
get back to Australia somehow and start life again, but Johnson's
day had been dead for many years. "Besides, assisted emigration's
done away with now," he said, with his sad, sad smile.

I saw the Johnsons again later on. "Things have been going very
sadly with us, very sadly indeed," said the old man, when we'd
settled down. He had broken down at the beginning of the winter, he
had dragged himself out of bed and to work and back again until he
could do so no longer; he had been laid up most of the winter.
Mrs Johnson had not been outside the door for months.

"It comes very hard on us," she said, "and I'm so poorly, and
David out of work, too. I wouldn't mind if I could get about. But,"
she went on in her energetic manner, "we've had the house full all
the winter; we've had very good luck with the lodgers, all
respectable people, and one of them answers the door and that keeps
me away from the draught—so it might be worse, mightn't it? But
Johnson doesn't seem to mend at all, and he gets so terribly
depressed. But the warm weather coming on, etc."

They and the Lord only knew how they managed to live, for they
are honest people and the lodgers scarcely pay the rent of the house.
There was only David between them and the poor-house, as far as I
could see.

Johnson came out with me a piece and we had a drink or two together—his was gin hot. He talked a good deal about Australia, but sadly and regretfully on this occasion.

"We could have done well in Australia," he said, "very well indeed. I might have been independent and the children well started in life. But we did things for the best. Mrs Johnson didn't like Australia, you know. It was a pity we didn't stay there, a great pity. We would have done far better than in England. I'd go out again now if I had the money, but I'm getting too old."

"Would Mrs Johnson go out?" I asked.

"Oh, yes. But I'm afraid she wouldn't stand the voyage.... Things have been very sad with us ever since we came back to England, very sad indeed." And after a while he suddenly caught his breath.

"It takes me that way sometimes," he said. "I catch my breath just as if I was going to lose it."

A DROVING YARN

Andy Maculloch had heard that old Bill Barker, the well-known overland drover, had died over on the Westralian side, and Dave Regan told a yarn about Bill.

"Bill Barker," said Dave, talking round his pipe stem, "was the *quintessence* of a drover—"

"The whatter, Dave?" came the voice of Jim Bentley, in startled tones, from the gloom on the far end of the veranda.

"The quintessence," said Dave, taking his pipe out of his mouth. "You shut up, Jim. As I said, Bill Barker was the quintessence of a drover. He'd been at the game ever since he was a nipper. He run away from home when he was fourteen and went up into Queensland. He's been all over Queensland and New South Wales and most of South Australia, and a good deal of the Western, too: over the great stock routes from one end to the other, Lord knows how many times. No man could keep up with him riding out, and no one could bring a mob of cattle or a flock of sheep through like him. He knew every trick of the game; if there was grass to be had Bill'd get it, no matter whose run it was on. One of his games in a dry season was to let his mob get boxed with the station stock on a run where there was grass, and before Bill's men and the station-hands could cut 'em out, the travelling stock would have a good bellyful to carry them on the track. Billy was the daddy of the drovers. Some said that he could ride in his sleep, and that he had one old horse that could jog along in his sleep too, and that—travelling out from home to take charge of a mob of bullocks or a flock of sheep—Bill and his horse would often wake up at daylight and blink round to see where they were and how far they'd got. Then Bill would make a fire and boil his quart-pot, and roast a bit of mutton, while his horse had a mouthful of grass and a spell.

"You remember Bill, Andy? Big dark man, and a joker of the loud sort. Never slept with a blanket over him—always folded under him on the sand or grass. Seldom wore a coat on the route—though he always carried one with him, in case he came across a bush ball or a funeral. Moleskins, flannel waist-coat, cabbage-tree hat and 'lastic-side boots. When it was roasting hot on the plains and the men swore at the heat, Jim would yell, 'Call this hot? Why, you blanks, I'm freezin'! Where's me overcoat?' When it was raining and hailing and freezing on Bell's Line in the Blue Mountains in winter, and someone shivered and asked, 'Is it cold enough for yer now, Bill?' 'Cold!' Bill would bellow, 'I'm sweatin'!'

"I remember it well. I was little more than a youngster then—Bill Barker came past our place with about a thousand fat sheep for the Homebush sale-yards at Sydney, and he gave me a job to help him down with them on Bell's Line over the mountains, and mighty proud I was to go with him, I can tell you. One night we camped on the Cudgegong River. The country was dry and pretty close cropped and we'd been "sweating" the paddocks all along there for our horses. You see, where there weren't sliprails handy we'd just take the tomahawk and nick the top of a straight-grained fence-post, just above the mortise, knock out the wood there, lift the top rail out and down, and jump the horses in over the lower one—it was all two-rail fences around there with sheep wires under the lower rail. And about daylight we'd have the horses out, lift back the rail, and fit in the chock that we'd knocked out. Simple as striking matches, wasn't it?

"Well, the horses were getting a good bellyful in the police horse paddock at night, and Bill took the first watch with the sheep. It was very cold and frosty on the flat and he thought the sheep might make back for the ridges, it's always warmer up in the ridges in winter out of the frost. Bill roused me out about midnight. 'There's the sheep,' he says, pointing to a white blur. 'They've settled down. I think hey'll be quiet till daylight. Don't go round them; there's no occasion to go near 'em. You can stop by the fire and keep an eye on em.'

"The night seemed very long. I watched and smoked and toasted my shins, and warmed the billy now and then, and thought up pretty much the same sort of old things that fellers on night watch think over all over the world. Bill lay on his blanket, with his back to he fire and his arm under his head—freezing on one side and roasting on the other. He never moved. I itched once or twice to turn him over and bake the front of him—I reckoned he was about done behind.

"At last daylight showed. I took the billy and started down to the iver to get some water to make coffee; but half-way down, near the sheep camp, I stopped and stared, I was never so surprised in my life. The white blur of sheep had developed into a couple of acres of long dead silver grass!

"I woke Bill, and he swore as I never heard a man swear before—nor since. He swore at the sheep, and the grass, and at me; but it would have wasted time, and besides I was too sleepy and tired to fight. But we found those sheep scattered over a scrubby ridge about seven miles back, so they must have slipped away back of the grass and started early in Bill's watch, and Bill must have watched that blessed grass for the first half of the night and then set me to watch it. He couldn't get away from that.

"I wondered what the chaps would say if it got round that Bill Barker, the boss overland drover, had lost a thousand sheep in clear country with fences all round; and I suppose he thought that way too, for he kept me with him right down to Homebush, and when he paid me off he threw in an extra quid, and he said:

"'Now, listen here, Dave! If I ever hear a word from anyone about watching that gory grass, I'll find you, Dave, and murder you, if you're in wide Australia. I'll screw your neck, so look out.'

"But he's dead now, so it doesn't matter."

There was silence for some time after Dave had finished. The chaps made no comment on the yarn, either one way or the other, but sat smoking thoughtfully, and in a vague atmosphere as of sadness—as if they'd just heard of their mother's death and had not been listening to an allegedly humorous yarn.

Then the voice of old Peter, the station-hand, was heard to growl from the darkness at the end of the hut, where he sat on a three-bushel bag on the ground with his back to the slabs.

"What's old Peter growlin' about?" someone asked.

"He wants to know where Dave got that word," someone els[e]
replied.

"What word?"

"*Quint-essents.*"

There was a chuckle.

"He got it out back, Peter," said Mitchell, the shearer. "He got i[t]
from a new chum."

"How much did yer give for it, Dave?" growled Peter.

"Five shillings, Peter," said Dave, round his pipe stem. "An[d]
stick of tobacco thrown in."

Peter seemed satisfied, for he was heard no more that evening[.]

GETTIN' BACK ON DAVE REGAN

A RATHER FISHY YARN FROM THE BUSH

(As told by James Nowlett, Bullock-driver)

You might work this yarn up. I've often thought of doin' it mesel[f]
but I ain't got the words. I knowed a lot of funny an' rum yarn[s]
about the bush, an' I often wished I had the gift o' writin'. I coul[d]
tell a lot better yarns than the rot they put in books sometimes, but [I]
never had no eddication. But you might be able to work this yar[n]
up—as yer call it.

There useter be a teamster's camp six or seven miles out [of]
Mudgee, at a place called th' Old Pipeclay, in the days before th[e]
railroad went round to Dubbo, an' most of us bullickies useter cam[e]
there for the night. There was always good water in the crick, a[n]
sometimes we'd turn the bullicks up in the ridges an' gullies behin[d]
for grass, an' camp there for a few days, and do our washin' a[n]
mendin', and make new yokes perhaps, an' tinker up the wagons[.]

There was a woman livin' on a farm there named M[rs]
Hardwick—an' she *was* a hard wick. Her husban', Jimmy Har[d]
wick, was throwed from his horse a[g]enst a stump one day when h[e]
was sober, an' he was killed—an' she was a widder. She had a ti[dy]
bit o' land, an' a nice bit of a orchard an' vineyard, an' some cattl[e]
an' they say she had a tidy bit o' money in the bank. She had th[e]
worst tongue in the district, no one's character was safe with her; b[ut]

she wasn't old, an' she wasn't bad-lookin'—only hard—so there was some fellers hangin' round arter her. An' Dave Regan's horse was hangin' up outside her place as often as anybody else's. Dave was a native an' a bushy, an' a drover an' a digger, an' he was a bit soft in them days—he got hard enough arterwards.

Mrs Hardwick hated bullick-drivers—she had a awful down on bullickies—I dunno why. We never interfered with her fowls, an' as for swearin'! why, she could swear herself. Jimmy Hardwick was a bullick-driver when she married him, an' p'r'aps that helped to account for it. She wouldn't let us boil our billies at her kitchen fire, same as any other bushwoman, an' if one of our bullicks put his nose under her fence for a mouthful of grass, she'd set her dogs onter him. An' one of her dogs got something what disagreed with him one day, an' she accused us of layin' poisoned baits. An', arter that, she 'pounded some of our bullicks that got into her lucerne paddick one night when we was on the spree in Mudgee, an' put heavy damages on 'em. She'd left the sliprails down on purpose, I believe. She talked of puttin' the police onter us, jest as if we was a sly-grog shop. (If *she'd* kept a sly-grog shop she'd have had a different opinion about bullick-drivers.) An' all the bullick-drivers hated her because she hated bullickies.

Well, one wet season half a dozen of us chaps was camped there for a fortnight, because the roads was too boggy to travel, an' one night they got up a darnce at Peter Anderson's shanty acrost the ridges, an' a lot of gals an' fellers turned up from all round about in spite of the pourin' rain. Someone had kidded Dave Regan that Mother Hardwick was comin', an' he turned up, of course, in spite of a ragin' toothache he had. He was always ridin' the high horse over us bullickies. It was a very cold night, enough to cut the face an' hands off yer, so we had a roarin' fire in the big bark-an'-slab kitchen where the darncin' was. It was one of them big, old-fashioned, clay-lined fire-places that goes right acrost the end of the room, with a twenty-five foot slab-an'-tin chimbly outside.

Dave Regan was pretty wild about being had, an' we copped all the gals for darncin'; he couldn't get one that night, an' when he wasn't proddin' out his tooth with a red-hot wire someone was chaffin' him about Mrs Hardwick. So at last he got disgusted an' left; but before he went he got a wet three-bushel flour-bag an' climbed up very quietly onter the roof by the battens an' log weights an' riders, an' laid the wet bag very carefully acrost the top of the chimbly flue.

An' we was a mortal hour tryin's to find out what was the matter with that infernal chimbly, and tackin' bits o' tin an' baggin' acrost the top of the fire-place under the mantelshelf to try an' stop it from smokin', an' all the while the gals set there with the water runnin' out of their eyes. We took the green back log out an' fetched in a dry one, but that chimbly smoked worse than ever, an' we had to put the fire out altogther, an' the gals set there shiverin' till the rain held up a bit an' the sky cleared, an' then someone goes out an' looks up an' sings out, "Why, there's somethin' acrost the top of the blazin' chimbly!" an' someone else climbs up an' fetches down the bag. But the darnce was spoilt, an' the gals was so disgusted that they went off with their fellers while the weather held up. They reckoned some of us bullickies did it for a lark.

An' arter that Dave'd come ridin' past, an' sing out to know if we knew of a good cure for a smokin' chimbly, an' them sorter things. But he always got away before we could pull him off of his horse. Three of us chased him on horseback one day, but we didn't ketch him.

So we made up our minds to git back on Dave some way or other, an' it come about this way.

About six months arter the smoked-out darnce, four or five of us same fellers was campin' on th' Pipeclay agen, an' it was a dry season. It was dryer an' hotter than it was cold 'n' wet the larst time. Dave was still hangin' round Mrs Hardwick's an' doin' odd jobs for her. Well, one very hot day we seen Dave ridin' past into Mudgee, an' we knowed he'd have a spree in town that night, an' call at Mrs Hardwick's for sympathy comin' out next day; an' arter he'd been gone an hour or two, Tom Tarrant comes drivin' past on his mail-coach, an' drops some letters an' papers an' a bag o' groceries at our camp.

Tom was a hard case. I remember wonst I was drivin' along a lonely bit o' track, an' it was a grand mornin', an' I felt great, an' I got singin' an' practisin' a recitation that I allers meant to give at a bush darnce some night. (I never sung or spouted poetry unless I was sure I was miles away from anyone.) An' I got worked up, an' was wavin' me arms about an' throwin' it off of me chest, when Tom's coach comes up behind, round a bend in the road, an' took me by surprise. An' Tom looked at me very hard an' he says, "What are yer shoutin' an' swearin' an' darncin' an' goin' on at the bullicks like that for, Jimmy? They seem to be workin' all right." It took me back, I can tell yer. The coach was full of grinnin' passengers, an' the worst of it was that I didn't know how long Tom had been drivin' slow behind me an' takin' me out of windin'. There's nothin' upsets a cove as can't sing so much as to be caught singin' or poutin' poetry when he thinks he's privit'.

An' another time I remember Tom's coach broke down on the track, an' he had to ride inter town with the mails on horse-back; an' he left a couple of greenhides, for Skinner the tanner at Mudgee, for me to take on in the wagon, an' a bag of potatoes for Murphy the storekeeper at Home Rule, an' a note that said: "Render unto Murphy the things which is murphies, and unto Skinner them things which is skins." Tom was a hard case.

Well, this day, when Tom handed down the tucker an' letters, he got down to stretch his legs and give the horses a breathe. The coach was full of passengers, an' I noticed they all looked extra glum and sulky, but I reckoned it was the heat an' dust. Tom looked extra solemn, too, an' no one was talkin'. Then I suddenly began to notice something in the atmosphere, as if there was a dead beast not far away, an' my mates started sniffin' too. An' that reminds me, it's funny why some people allers sniff hard instead of keepin' their noses shut when there's a stink; the more it stinks the more they sniff. Tom spit in the dust an' thought a while; then he took a parcel out of the boot an' put it on the corner post of the fence. "There," he said, "There's some fresh fish that come up from Sydney by train an' Cobb & Co.'s coach larst night. They're meant for White the publican at Gulgong, but they won't keep this weather till I git out there. Pity to waste them! you chaps might as well have a feed of 'em. I'll tell White they went bad an' I had to throw them out," says Tom. Then he got on to the coach agen an' drove off in a cloud of dust. We undone the brown paper, an' the fish was in a small deal box, with a lid fastened by a catch. We nicked back the catch an' the lid flew open, an' then we knowed where the smell comed from all right. There wasn't any doubt about that! We didn't have to put our noses in the box to see if the fish was bad. They was packed in salt, but that made no difference.

You know how a smell will start sudden in the bush on a hot, still day, an' then seem to take a spell, an' then get to work agen stronger than ever. You might be clost alongside of a horse that has been dead a fortnight an' smell nothin' particular till you start to walk away, an' the further you go the worse it stinks. It seems to smell most round in a circle of a hundred yards or so. But these fish smelt from the centre right out. Tom Tarrant told us arterwards that them fish started to smell as soon as he left Mudgee. At first they reckoned it was a dead horse by the road; but arter a while the passengers commenced squintin' at each other suspicious like, an' the conversation petered out, an' Tom thought he felt all their eyes on his back, an' it was very uncomfortable; an' he sat tight an' tried to make out where the smell come from; an' it got worse every hundred yards—like as if the track was lined with dead horses, an' every one dead longer than the last—till it was like drivin' a funeral. An' Tom never thought of the fish till he got down to stretch his legs an' fetched his nose on a level with the boot.

Well, we shut down the lid of that box quick an' took it an' throwed it in the bushes a good way away from the camp, but nex mornin', while we was havin' breakfast, Billy Grimshaw got an idea an' arter breakfast he wetted a canvas bag he had an' lit up his pipe an' went an' got that there box o' fish, an' put it in the wet bag, an wrapped it tight round it an' tied it up tight with string. Billy had a nipper of a nephew with him, about fourteen, named Tommy, an' he was a sharp kid if ever there was one. So Billy says, "Look here Tommy, you take this fish up to Mrs Hardwick's an' tell her that Dave Regan sent 'em with his compliments, an' he hopes she'll enjoy 'em. Tell her that Dave fetched 'em from Mudgee, but he's gone back to look for a pound note that he dropped out of a hole in his pocket somewheers along the road, an' he asked you to take the fish up." So Tommy takes the fish an' goes up to the house with 'em. When he come back he says that Mrs Hardwick smiled like a parson an' give him a shillin'—an' he didn't wait. We watched the house an' about half an hour arterwards we seen her run out of the kitchen with the open box in her hand, an' run a good way away from the house an' throw the fish inter the bushes, an' then go back quick holdin' her nose.

An' jest then, as luck would have it, we seen Dave Regan ridin' up from the creek towards the house. He got down an' went into the kitchen, an' then come backin' out agen in a hurry with her in front of him. We could hear her voice from where we was, but we couldn't hear what she said. But we could see her arms wavin' as if she was drivin' fowls, an' Dave backed all the way to his horse an' gets on an' comes ridin' away quick, she screamin' arter him all the time. When he got down opposite the camp we sung out to know what was the matter. "What have you been doin' to Mrs Hardwick, Dave? we says. "We heerd her goin' for yer proper jest now." "Damned if I know," says Dave. "I ain't done nothin' to her that I knows of. She called me everything she can lay her tongue to, an' she's ravin about my stinkin' fish, or somethin'. I can't make it out at all. I believe she's gone ratty."

"But you *must* have been doin' somethin' to the woman," we says, "or else she wouldn't have gone on at yer like that."

But Dave swore he hadn't, an' we talked it over for a while an' couldn't make head nor tail of it, an' we come to the conclusion that it was only a touch o' the sun.

"Never mind, Dave," we says. "Go up agen in a day or two, when she's cooled down, an' find out what the matter is. Or write to her. It might only have been someone makin' mischief. That's what it is."

But Dave only sat an' rubbed his head, an' presently he started home to wherever he was hangin' out. He wanted a quiet week to think.

"Her chimbly might have been smokin', Dave," we shouted arter him, but he was too dazed like to ketch on.

Well, in a month or two we was campin' there agen, an' we found she'd fenced in a lane to the crick she had no right to, an' we had to take the bullicks a couple o' miles round to grass an' water. Well, the first mornin' we seen her down in the corner of her paddick near the camp drivin' some heifers, an' Billy Grimshaw went up to the fence an' spoke to her. Billy was the only one of us that dared face her and he was the only one she was ever civil to—p'r'aps because Billy had a squint an' a wall eye and that put her out of countenance.

Billy took off his hat very respectful an' sings out, "Mrs Hardwick." (It was Billy's bullicks she'd "pounded," by the way.)

"What is it?" she says.

"I want to speak to you, Mrs Hardwick," says Billy.

"Well, speak," she says. "I've got no time to waste talkin' to bullick-drivers."

"Well, the fact is, Mrs Hardwick," says Billy, "that I want to explain somethin', an' apologize for that young scamp of a nephew o' mine, young Tommy. He ain't here or I'd make him beg your pardon hisself, or I'd cut him to pieces with the bullick-whip. I heard all about Dave Regan sendin' you that stinkin' fish, an' I think it was a damned mean, dirty thing to do—to send stinkin' fish to a woman, an' especially to a widder an' an unprotected woman like you, Mrs Hardwick. I've had mothers an' sisters of me own. An' I want to tell you that I'm sorry a relation o' mine ever had anythin' to do with it. As soon as I heerd of it I give young Tommy a lambastin' he won't forgit in a hurry."

"Did Tommy know the fish was bad?" she says.

"It doesn't matter a rap," says Billy; "he had no right to go takin' messages from nobody to nobody."

Mrs Hardwick thought a while. Then she says: "P'r'aps arter all Dave Regan didn't know the fish was bad. I've often thought I might have been in too much of a hurry. Things goes bad so quick out here in this weather. An' Dave was always very friendly. I can't understand why he'd do a dirty thing on me like that. I never done anything to Dave."

Now I forgot to tell you that Billy had a notion that Dave helped drive his bullicks to pound that time, though I didn't believe it. So Billy says:

"Don't you believe that for a minute, Mrs Hardwick. Dave knew what he was a-doin' of all right; an' if I ketch him *I'll* give him a beltin' for it if no one else is man enough to stand up for a woman!" says Billy.

"How d'yer know Dave knew?" says Mrs Hardwick.

"Know!" says Billy. "Why, he talked about it all over the district."

"What!" she screamed out, an' I moved away from that there fence, for she had a stick to drive them heifers with. But Billy stood his ground. "Is that the truth, Billy Grimshaw?" she screams.

"Yes," he says. "I'll take me oath on it. He blowed about it all over the district, as if it was very funny, an' he says——" An' Billy stopped.

"What did he say?" she shouted.

"Well, the fact is," says Billy, "that I hardly like to tell it to a lady. I wouldn't like to tell yer, Mrs Hardwick."

"But you'll have to tell me, Billy Grimshaw," she screams. "I have a right to know. If you don't tell me I'll pull him next week an' have it dragged out of you in the witness-box!" she says. "An' I'll have satisfaction out of him in the felon's dock of a court of law!" she says. "What did the villain say?" she screams.

"Well," says Billy, "if yer must have it—an', anyway, I'm hanged if I'm goin' to stand by an' see a woman scandalized behind her back—if yer must have it I'll tell yer. Dave said that the fish didn't smell no worse than your place anyway."

We got away from there then. She cut up too rough altogether. I can't tell you what she said—I ain't got the words. She went up to the house, an' we seen the farm-hand harnessin' up the horse, an' we reckoned she was goin' to drive into town straight away an' take out a summons agenst Dave Regan. An' jest then Dave hisself comes ridin' past—jest when he was most wanted, as usual. He always rode fast past Mrs Hardwick's nowadays, an' never stopped there but Billy shouted after him:

"Hullo, Dave! I want to speak to yer," shouts Billy. An' Dave yanks his horse round.

"What is it, Billy?" he says.

"Look here, Dave," says Billy. "You had your little joke about the chimbly, an' we had our little joke about the fish an' Mrs Hardwick, so now we'll call it quits. A joke's a joke, but it can go too far, an' this one's gettin' too red-hot altogether. So we've fixed it up with Mrs Hardwick."

"What fish an' what joke?" says Dave, rubbin' his head. "An' what have yer fixed up with Mrs Hardwick? Whatever are yer talkin' about, Billy?"

So Billy told him all about us sendin' the stinkin' fish to Mrs Hardwick by Tommy, an' sayin' Dave sent 'em—Dave rubbin' the back of his neck an' starin' at Billy all the time. "An' now," says Billy, "I won't say anything about them bullicks; but I went up and seen Mrs Hardwick this mornin', an' told her the whole truth about them fish, an' how you knowed nothin' about it, an' I apologized an' told her we was very sorry; an' she says she was very sorry too on your account, an' wanted to see yer. I promised to tell yer as soon as I seen yer. It ought to be fixed up. You ought to go right up to the house an' see her now. She's awfully cut up about it."

"All right," says Dave, brightenin' up. "It was a dirty, mean trick anyway to play on a cove; but I'll go up an' see her." An' he went there 'n' then.

An' about fifteen minutes arterwards he comes boltin' back from the house one way an' his horse the other. The horse acted as if it had a big scare, an' so did Dave. Billy went an' ketched Dave's horse for him, an' I got Dave a towel to wipe the dirty dish-water off of his face an' out of his hair an' collar, an' I give him a piece of soap to rub on the places where he'd been scalded.

"Why, the woman must be ravin' mad," I says. "Whatever did yer say to her this time, Dave? Yer allers gettin' inter hot water with her."

"I didn't say nothin'," says Dave. "I jest went up laughin' like, an' says, 'How are yer, Mrs Hardwick?' an' she ups an' lets me have a dish of dirty wash-up water, an' then on top of that she let fly with a dipper of scaldin'-hot, greasy water outer the boiler. She's gone clean ravin' mad, I think."

"She's as mad as a hatter, right enough, Dave," says Billy Grimshaw. "Don't you go there no more, Dave, it ain't safe." An' we lent Dave a hat an' a clean shirt, an' he went on inter town. "You ought to have humoured her," says Billy, as Dave rode away. "You ought to have told her to put a wet bag over her chimbly an' hang the fish inside to smoke." But Dave was too stunned to ketch on. He went on inter the town an' got on a howlin' spree. An' while he was soberin' up the thing began to dawn on him. An' the nex' time he met Billy they had a fight. An' Dave got another woman to speak to Mrs Hardwick, an' Mrs Hardwick ketched young Tommy goin' past her place one day an' bailed him up an' scared the truth out of him.

"Look here!" she says to him, "I want the truth, the whole truth, an' nothin' but the truth about them fish, an' if I don't get it outer you I'll wring her young neck for tryin' to poison me, an' save yer from the gallust!" she says to Tommy.

So he told her the whole truth, swelp him, an' got away; an' he respected Mrs Hardwick arter that.

An' next time we come past with the teams we seen Dave's horse hangin' up outside Mrs Hardwick's, an' we went some miles further along the road an' camped in a new place where we'd be more comfortable. An' ever arter that we used to always whip up an' drive past her place as if we didn't know her.

"SHALL WE GATHER AT THE RIVER?"

> God's preacher, of churches unheeded,
> God's vineyard, though barren the sod,
> Plain spokesman where spokesman is needed,
> Rough link 'twixt the Bushman and God.
>
> *The Christ of the Never.*

TOLD BY JOE WILSON

I never told you about Peter M'Laughlan. He was a sort of bush missionary up-country and out back in Australia, and before he died he was known from Riverina down south in New South Wales to away up through the Never-Never country in western Queensland.

His past was a mystery, so, of course, there were all sorts of yarns about him. He was supposed to be a Scotchman from London, and some said that he had got into trouble in his young days and had had to clear out of the old country; or, at least, that he had been a ne'e-er-do-well and had been sent out to Australia on the remittance system. Some said he'd studied for the law, some said he'd studied

or a doctor, while others believed that he was, or had been, an
ordained minister. I remember one man who swore (when he was
drinking) that he had known Peter M'Laughlan as a medical
student in a big London hospital, and that he had started in practice
or himself somewhere near Gray's Inn Road in London. Anyway,
as I got to know him he struck me as being a man who had looked
into the eyes of so much misery in his life that some of it had got into
his own.

He was a tall man, straight and well built, and about forty or
orty-five, when I first saw him. He had wavy dark hair, and a close,
curly beard. I once heard a woman say that he had a beard like you
see in some Bible pictures of Christ. Peter M'Laughlan seldom
smiled; there was something in his big dark brown eyes that was
scarcely misery, nor yet sadness—a sort of haunted sympathy.

He must have had money, or else he got remittances from home,
for he paid his way and helped many a poor devil. They said that he
gave away most of his money. Sometimes he worked for a while
himself as bookkeeper at a shearing-shed, wool-sorter, shearer, even
rouseabout; he'd work at anything a bushman could get to do. Then
he'd go out back to God-forgotten districts and preach to bushmen
in one place, and get a few children together in another and teach
them to read. He could take his drink, and swear a little when he
thought it necessary. On one occasion, at a rough shearing-shed, he
called his beloved brethren "damned fools" for drinking their
cheques.

Towards the end of his life if he went into a "rough" shed or
shanty west of the Darling River—and some of them *were*
rough—there would be a rest in the language and drinking, even a
fight would be interrupted, and there would be more than one who
would lift their hats to Peter M'Laughlan. A bushman very rarely
lifts his hat to a man, yet the worst characters of the West have
listened bareheaded to Peter when he preached.

It was said in our district that Peter only needed to hint to the
squatter that he wanted fifty or a hundred pounds to help someone
or something, and the squatter would give it to him without question
or hesitation.

He'd nurse sick boundary-riders, shearers, and station-hands,
often sitting in the desolate hut by the bedside of a sick man night
after night. And, if he had time, he'd look up the local blacks and see
how they were getting on. Once, on a far out back sheep station, he
sat for three nights running, by the bedside of a young Englishman,
a B.A. they said he was, who'd been employed as tutor at the

homestead and who died a wreck, the result of five years of life in London and Paris. The poor fellow was only thirty. And the last few hours of his life he talked to Peter in French, nothing but French. Peter understood French and one or two other languages, besides English and Australian; but whether the young wreck was raving or telling the story of a love, or his life, none of us ever knew, for Peter never spoke of it. But they said that at the funeral Peter's eyes seemed haunted more than usual.

There's the yarn about Peter and the dying cattle at Piora Station one terrible drought, when the surface was as bare as your hand for hundreds of miles, and the heat like the breath of a furnace, and the sheep and cattle were perishing by thousands. Peter M'Laughlan was out on the run helping the station-hands to pull out cattle they had got bogged in the muddy waterholes and were too weak to drag themselves out, when, about dusk, a gentlemanly "piano-fingered" parson, who had come to the station from the next town, drove out in his buggy to see the men. He spoke to Peter M'Laughlan.

"Brother," he said, "do you not think we should offer up a prayer?"

"What for?" asked Peter, standing in his shirt sleeves, a rope in his hands and mud from head to foot.

"For? Why, for rain, brother," replied the parson, a bit surprised.

Peter held up his finger and said "Listen!"

Now, with a big mob of travelling stock camped on the plain at night, there is always a lowing, soughing or moaning sound, a sound like that of the sea on the shore at a little distance; and, altogether, it might be called the sigh or yawn of a big mob in camp. But the long low moaning of cattle dying of hunger and thirst on the hot barren plain in a drought is altogether different, and, at night, there is something awful about it—you couldn't describe it. This is what Peter M'Laughlan heard.

"Do you hear that?" he asked the other preacher.

The little parson said he did. Perhaps *he* only heard the weak lowing of cattle.

"Do you think that God will hear us when He does not hear *that?*" asked Peter.

The parson stared at him for a moment and then got into his buggy and drove away, greatly shocked and deeply offended. But later on, over tea at the homestead, he said that he felt sure that that "unfortunate man," Peter M'Laughlan, was not in his right mind; that his wandering, irregular life, or the heat, must have affected him.

I well remember the day when I first heard Peter M'Laughlan preach. I was about seventeen then. We used sometimes to attend service held on Sunday afternoon, about once a month, in a little slab-and-bark school-house in the scrub off the main road, three miles or so from our selection, in a barren hole amongst the western ridges of the Great Dividing Range. School was held in this hut for a few weeks or a few months now and again, when a teacher could be got to stay there and teach, and cook for himself, for a pound a week, more or less contributed by the parents. A parson from the farming town to the east, or the pastoral town over the ridges to the west, used to come in his buggy when it didn't rain and wasn't too hot to hold the service.

I remember this Sunday. It was a blazing hot day towards the end of a long and fearful drought which ruined many round there. The parson was expected, and a good few had come to "chapel" in spring-carts, on horseback, and on foot; farmers and their wives and sons and daughters. The children had been brought here to Sunday-school, taught by some of the girls, in the morning. I can see it all now quite plain: The one-roomed hut, for it was no more, with the stunted blue-grey gum scrub all round. The white, dusty road, so hot that you could cook eggs in the dust. The horses tied up, across the road, in the supposed shade under clumps of scraggy saplings along by the fence of a cattle-run. The little crowd ouside the hut: selectors in washed and mended tweeds, some with paper collars, some wearing starched and ironed white coats, and in blucher boots, greased or blackened, or the young men wearing "larstins" (elastic-side boots). The women and girls in prints and cottons (or cheap "alpaca," etc.), and a bright bit of ribbon here and there amongst the girls. The white heat blazed everywhere, and "dazzled" across light-coloured surfaces—dead white trees, fence-posts, and sand-heaps, like an endless swarm of bees passing in the sun's glare. And over above the dry box-scrub-covered ridges, the great Granite Peak, glaring like a molten mass.

The people didn't like to go inside out of the heat and sit down before the minister came. The wretched hut was a rough school, sometimes with a clay fire-place where the teacher cooked, and a corner screened off with sacking where he had his bunk; it was a camp for tramps at other times, or lizards and possums, but to-day it was a house of God, and as such the people respected it.

The town parson didn't turn up. Perhaps he was unwell, or maybe the hot, dusty ten-mile drive was too much for him to face. One of the farmers, who had tried to conduct service on a previous occasion on which the ordained minister had failed us, had broken down in the middle of it, so he was out of the question. We waited for about an hour, and then who should happened to ride along but Peter M'Laughlan, and one or two of the elder men asked him to hold service. He was on his way to see a sick friend at a sheep station over the ridges, but he said that he could spare an hour or two. (Nearly every man who was sick, either in stomach or pocket, was a friend of Peter M'Laughlan.) Peter tied up his horse under a bush shed at the back of the hut, and we followed him in.

The "school" had been furnished with a rough deal table and a wooden chair for "the teacher," and with a few rickety desks and stools cadged from an old "provisional" school in town when the new public school was built; and the desks and stools had been fastened to the floor to strengthen them; they had been made for "infant" classes, and youth out our way ran to length. But when grown men over six feet high squeezed in behind the desks and sat down on the stools the effect struck me as being ridiculous. In fact, I am afraid that on the first occasion it rather took my attention from the sermon, and I remember being made very uncomfortable by a school chum, Jack Barnes, who took a delight in catching my eye and winking or grinning. He could wink without changing a solemn line in his face and grin without exploding, and I couldn't. The boys usually sat on seats, slabs on blocks of wood, along the wall at the far end of the room, which was comfortable, for they had a rest for their backs. One or two of the boys were nearing six feet high, so they could almost rest their chins on their knees as they sat. But I squatted with some of my tribe on a stool along the wall by the teacher's table, and so could see most of the congregation.

Above us bare tie-beams and the round sapling rafters (with the bark still on), and the inner sides of the sheets of stringy-bark that formed the roof. The slabs had been lined with sacking at one time, but most of it had fallen or dry-rotted away; there were wide cracks between the slabs and we could see the white glare of sunlight outside, with a strip of dark shade, like a deep trench in the white ground, by the back wall. Someone had brought a canvas water-bag and hung it to the beam on the other side of the minister's table, with a pint-pot over the tap, and the drip, drip from the bag made the whole place seem cooler.

I studied Peter M'Laughlan first. He was dressed in washed and mended tweed vest and trousers, and had on a long, light-coloured coat of a material which we called "Chinese silk." He wore a "soft" cotton shirt with collar attached, and blucher boots.

He gave out a hymn in his quiet, natural way, said a prayer, gave out another hymn, read a chapter from the Bible, and then gave out another hymn. They like to sing, out in those places. The Southwicks used to bring a cranky little harmonium in the back of their old dog-cart, and Clara Southwick used to accompany the hymns. She was a very pretty girl, fair, and could play and sing well. I used to think she had the sweetest voice I ever heard. But—ah, well——

Peter didn't sing himself, at first. I got an idea that he couldn't. While they were singing he stood loosely, with one hand in his trouser-pocket, scratching his beard with his hymn-book, and looking as if he were thinking things over, and only rousing himself to give another verse. He forgot to give it once or twice, but we got through all right. I noticed the wife of one of the men who had asked Peter to preach looking rather black at her husband, and I reckoned that he'd get it hotter than the weather on the way home.

Then Peter stood up and commenced to preach. He stood with both hands in his pockets, at first, his coat ruffled back, and there was the stem of a clay pipe sticking out of his waistcoat-pocket. The pipe fascinated me for a while, but after that I forgot the pipe and was fascinated by the man. Peter's face was one that didn't strike you at first with its full strength, it grew on you; it grew on me, and before he had done preaching I thought it was the noblest face I had ever seen.

He didn't preach much of hope in this world. How could he? The drought had been blazing over these districts for nearly a year, with only a shower now and again, which was a mockery—scarcely darkening the baked ground. Wheat crops came up a few inches and were parched by the sun or mown for hay, or the cattle turned on them; and last year there had been rust and smut in the wheat. And, on top of it all, the dreadful cattle plague, pleuro-pneumonia, had somehow been introduced into the district. One big farmer had lost fifty milkers in a week.

Peter M'Laughlan didn't preach much of hope in his world; how could he? There were men there who had slaved for twenty, thirty, forty years; worked as farmers have to work in few other lands—first to clear the stubborn bush from the barren soil, then to fence the ground, and manure it, and force crops from it—and for what? There was Cox, the farmer, starved off his selection after thirty years and going out back with his drays to work at tank-sinking for a squatter. There was his eldest son going shearing or droving—anything he could get to do—a stoop-shouldered, young-old man of thirty. And behind them, in the end, would be a dusty patch in the scrub, a fence-post here and there, and a pile of chimney-stones and a hardwood slab or two where the hut was—for thirty hard years of the father's life and twenty of the son's.

I forget Peter's text, if he had a text; but the gist of his sermon was that there was a God—there was a heaven! And there were men there listening who needed to believe these things. There was old Ross from across the creek, old, but not sixty, a hard man. Only last week he had broken down and fallen on his knees on the baked sods in the middle of his ploughed ground and prayed for rain. His frightened boys had taken him home, and later on, the same afternoon, when they brought news of four more cows down with "the pleuro" in an outer paddock, he had stood up outside his own door and shaken his fist at the brassy sky and cursed high heaven to the terror of his family, till his brave, sun-browned wife dragged him inside and soothed him. And Peter M'Laughlan knew all about this.

Ross's family had the doctor out to him, and persuaded him to come to church this Sunday. The old man sat on the front seat, stooping forward, with his elbow resting on the desk and his chin on his hand, bunching up his beard over his mouth with his fingers and staring gloomily at Peter with dark, piercing eyes from under bushy eyebrows, just as I've since seen a Scotchman stare at Max O'Rell all through a humorous lecture called "A nicht wi' Sandy."

Ross's right hand resting on the desk was very eloquent: horny, scarred and knotted at every joint, with broken, twisted nails, and nearly closed, as though fitted to the handle of an axe or a spade. Ross was an educated man (he had a regular library of books at home), and perhaps that's why he suffered so much.

Peter preached as if he were speaking quietly to one person only, but every word was plain and every sentence went straight to someone. I believe he looked every soul in the eyes before he had done. Once he said something and caught my eye, and I felt a sudden lump in my throat. There was a boy there, a pale, thin, sensitive boy who was eating his heart out because of things he didn't understand. He was ambitious and longed for something different from this life; he'd written a story or two and some rhymes for the local paper; his companions considered him a "bit ratty" and the grown-up people thought him a "bit wrong in his head," idiotic, or at least "queer." And during his sermon Peter spoke of "unsatisfied longings," of the hope of something better, and said that one had to suffer much and for long years before he could preach or write; and then he looked at that boy. I knew the boy very well; he has risen in the world since then.

Peter spoke of the life we lived, of the things we knew, and used names and terms that we used. "I don't know whether it was a blanky sermon or a blanky lecture," said long swanky Jim Bullock afterwards, "but it was straight and hit some of us hard. It hit me once or twice, I can tell yer." Peter spoke of our lives: "And there is beauty—even in this life and in this place," he said, "Nothing is wasted—nothing is without reason. There is beauty even in this place——"

I noticed something like a hint of a hard smile on Ross's face; he moved the hand on the desk and tightened it.

"Yes," said Peter, as if an answer to Ross's expression and the movement of his hand, "there is beauty in this life here. After a good season, and when the bush is tall and dry, when the bush-fires threaten a man's crop of ripened wheat, there are tired men who run and ride from miles round to help the man, and who fight the fire all night to save his wheat—and some of them may have been wrangling with him for years. And in the morning, when the wheat is saved and the danger is past, when the fire is beaten out or turned, there are blackened, grimy hands that come together and grip—hands that have not joined for many a long day."

Old Palmer, Ross's neighbour, moved uneasily. He had once helped Ross to put to fire out, but they had quarrelled again since. Ross still sat in the same position, looking the hard man he was. Peter glanced at Ross, looked down and thought a while, and then went on again:

"There is beauty even in this life and in this place. When a man loses his farm, or his stock, or his crop, through no fault of his own, there are poor men who put their hands into their pockets to help him."

Old Kurtz, over the ridge, had had his stacked crop of wheat in sheaf burned—some scoundrel had put a match to it at night—and the farmers round had collected nearly fifty pounds for him.

"There is beauty even in this life and in this place. In the blazing drought, when the cattle lie down and cannot rise from weakness, neighbours help neighbours to lift them. When one man has hay or chaff and no stock, he gives it or sells it cheaply to the poor man who has starving cattle and no fodder."

I only knew one or two instances of this kind; but Peter was preaching of what man should do as well as what they did.

"When a man meets with an accident, or dies, there are young men who go with their ploughs and horses and plough the ground for him or his widow and put in the crop."

Jim Bullock and one or two other young men squirmed. They had

ploughed old Leonard's land for him when he met with an accident
in the shape of a broken leg got by a kick from a horse. They had also
ploughed the ground for Mrs Phipps when her husband died,
working, by the way, all Saturday afternoon and Sunday, for they
were very busy at home at that time.

"There is beauty even in this life and in this place. There are
women who were friends in girlhood and who quarrelled bitterly
over a careless word, an idle tale, or some paltry thing, who live
within a mile of each other and have not spoken for years; yet let one
fall ill, or lose husband or child, and the other will hurry across to
her place and take off her bonnet and tuck up her sleeves, and set to
work to help straighten things, and they will kiss, and cry in each
other's arms, and be sisters again."

I saw tears in the eyes of two hard and hard-faced women I knew;
but they were smiling to each other through their tears.

"And now," said Peter, "I want to talk to you about some other
things. I am not preaching as a man who has been taught to preach
comfortably, but as a man who has learned in the world's school. I
know what trouble is. Men," he said, still speaking quietly, "and
women too! I have been through trouble as deep as any of
yours—perhaps deeper. I know how you toil and suffer, I know what
battles you fight, *I* know. I too fought a battle, perhaps as hard as
any you fight. I carry a load and am fighting a battle still." His eyes
were very haggard just them. "But this is not what I wanted to talk
to you about. I have nothing to say against a young man going away
from this place to better himself, but there are young men who go
out back shearing or droving, young men who are good-hearted but
careless, who make cheques, and spend their money gambling or
drinking and never think of the old folk at home until it is too late.
They never think of the old people, alone, perhaps, in a desolate hut
on a worked-out farm in the scrub."

Jim Bullock squirmed again. He had gone out back last season
and made a cheque, and lost most of it on horse-racing and cards.

"They never think—they cannot think how, perhaps, long years
agone in the old days, the old father, as a young man, and his brave
young wife, came out here and buried themselves in the lonely bush
and toiled for many years, trying—it does not matter whether they
failed or not—trying to make homes for their children; toiled till the
young man was bowed and grey, and the young wife brown and
wrinkled and worn out. Exiles they were in the early days—boy-
husbands and girl-wives some of them, who left their native lands,
who left all that was dear, that seemed beautiful, that seemed to
make life worth living, and sacrificed their young lives in drought

and utter loneliness to make homes for their children. I want you young men to think of this. Some of them came from England, Ireland, Bonnie Scotland." Ross straightened up and let his hands fall loosely on his knees. "Some from Europe—your foreign fathers—some from across the Rhine in Germany." We looked at old Kurtz. He seemed affected.

Then Peter paused for a moment and blinked thoughtfully at Ross, then he took a drink of water. I can see now that the whole thing was a battle between Peter M'Laughlan and Robert Ross—Scot met Scot. "It seemed to me," Jim Bullock said afterwards, "that Peter was only tryin' to make some of us blanky well blubber."

"And there are men," Peter went on, "who have struggled and suffered and failed, and who have fought and failed again till their tempers are spoiled, until they grow bitter. They go in for self-pity, and self-pity leads to moping and brooding and madness; self-pity is the most selfish and useless thing on the face of God's earth. It is cruel, it is deadly, both to the man and to those who love him, and whom he ought to love. His load grows heavier daily in his imagination, and he sinks down until it is in him to curse God and die. He ceases to care for or to think of his children who are working to help him." (Ross's sons were good, steady, hard-working boys.) "Or the brave wife who has been so true to him for many hard years, who left home and friends and country for his sake. Who bears up in the blackest of times, and persists in looking at the bright side of things for his sake; who has suffered more than he if he only knew it, and suffers now, through him and because of him, but who is patient and bright and cheerful while her heart is breaking. He thinks she does not suffer, that she cannot suffer as a man does. My God! he doesn't know. He has forgotten in her the bright, fresh-faced, loving lassie he loved and won long years agone—long years agone——"

There was a sob, like the sob of an over-ridden horse as it sinks down broken-hearted, and Ross's arms went out on the desk in front of him, and his head went down on them. He was beaten.

He was steered out gently with his wife on one side of him and his eldest son on the other.

"Don't be alarmed, my friends," said Peter, standing by the water-bag with one hand on the tap and the pannikin in the other. "Mr Ross has not been well lately, and the heat has been too much for him." And he went out after Ross. They took him round under the bush shed behind the hut, where it was cooler.

When Peter came back to his place he seemed to have changed his whole manner and tone. "Our friend, Mr Ross, is much better," he said. "We will now sing"—he glanced at Clara Southwick at the

harmonium—"we will now sing 'Shall We Gather at the River?' "
We all knew that hymn; it was an old favourite round there, and
Clara Southwick played it well in spite of the harmonium.

And Peter sang—the first and last time I ever heard him sing.
never had an ear for music; but I never before nor since heard a
man's voice that stirred me as Peter M'Laughlan's. We stood like
emus, listening to him all through one verse, then we pulled
ourselves together.

> Shall we gather at the River,
>   Where bright angels' feet have trod—

The only rivers round there were barren creeks, the best of them
only strings of muddy waterholes, and across the ridge, on the
sheep-runs, the creeks were dry gutters, with baked banks and beds
and perhaps a mudhole every mile or so, and dead beasts rotting
and stinking every few yards.

> Gather with the saints at the River,
>   That flows by the throne of God.

Peter's voice trembled and broke. He caught his breath, and his
eyes filled. But he smiled then—he stood smiling at us through his
tears.

> The beautiful, the beautiful River,
>   That flows by the throne of God.

Outside I saw women kiss each other who had been at daggers
drawn ever since I could remember, and men shake hands silently
who had hated each other for years. Every family wanted Peter to
come home to tea, but he went across to Ross's, and afterwards
down to Kurtz's place, and bled and inoculated six cows or so in a
new way, and after tea he rode off over the gap to see his friend

HIS BROTHER'S KEEPER

> By his paths through the parched desolation,
>   Hot rides and the terrible tramps;
> By the hunger, the thirst, the privation
>   Of his work in the furthermost camps;

By his worth in the light that shall search men
    And prove—ay! and justify each—
I place him in front of all Churchmen
    Who feel not, who *know* not—but preach!
                    —*The Christ of the Never.*

told you about Peter M'Laughlan, the bush missionary, and how
e preached in the little slab-and-bark school-house in the scrub on
Ross's Creek that blazing hot Sunday afternoon long ago, when the
rought was ruining the brave farmers all round there and breaking
heir hearts. And how hard old Ross, the selector, broke down at the
nd of the sermon, and blubbered, and had to be taken out of
hurch.

I left home and drifted to Sydney, and "back into the Great
North-West where all the rovers go," and knocked about the
ountry for six or seven years before I met Peter M'Laughlan again.
was young yet, but felt old at times, and there were times, in the
ot, rough, greasy shearing-shed on blazing days, or in the bare
men's hut" by the flicker of the stinking slushlamp at night, or the
vretched wayside shanty with its drink-madness and blasphemy, or
ramping along the dusty, endless track—there were times when I
vished I could fall back with all the experience I'd got, and sit once
nore in the little slab-and-bark "chapel" on Ross's Creek and hear
Peter M'Laughlan and the poor, struggling selectors sing "Shall We
Gather at the River?" and then go out and start life afresh.

My old school chum and bush mate, Jack Barnes, had married
oretty little Clara Southwick, who used to play the portable
narmonium in chapel. I nearly broke my heart when they were
narried, but then I was a young fool. Clara was a year or so older
han I, and I could never get away from a boyish feeling of reverence
or her, as if she were something above and out of my world. And so,
vhile I was worshipping her in chapel once a month, and at picnics
nd parties in between, and always at a distance, Jack used to ride
ıp to Southwick's place on Saturday and Sunday afternoons, and on
other days, and hang his horse up outside, or turn it in the paddock,
nd argue with old Southwick, and agree with the old woman, and
ourt Clara on the sly. And he got her.

It was at their wedding that I first got the worse for drink.

Jack was a blue-eyed, curly black-haired, careless, popular young
camp; as good-hearted as he was careless. He could ride like a
ircus monkey, do all kinds of bush work, add two columns of figures
ıt once, and write like copper-plate.

Jack was given to drinking, gambling and roving. He steadied u[..] when he got married and started on a small selection of his own; bu[..] within the year Clara was living in a back skillion of her father['..] house and Jack was up-country shearing. He was "ringer" of th[..] shed at Piora Station one season and made a decent cheque; an[..] within a fortnight after the shed "cut out" he turned up at home in [..] very bad state from drink and with about thirty shillings in hi[..] pockets. He had fallen from his horse in the creek near Southwick'[..] and altogether he was a nice sort of young husband to go home t[..] poor, heart-broken Clara.

I remember that time well. She stopped me one day as I wa[..] riding past to ask me if I'd seen Jack, and I got off my horse. He[..] chin and mouth began to twitch and tremble and I saw her eye[..] filling with tears. She laid her hand on my arm and asked me t[..] promise not to drink with Jack if I met him, but to try and persuad[..] him to come home. And—well, have you, as a man, ever, with th[..] one woman that you can't have, and no matter at what time o[..] place, felt a sudden mad longing to take her in your arms and kis[..] her—and damn the world? I got on my horse again. She must hav[..] thought me an ignorant brute, but I felt safer there. And when [..] thought how I had nearly made a fool of myself, and been [..] cowardly brute, and a rotten mate to my mate, I rode ten miles t[..] find Jack and get him home.

He straightened up again after a bit and went out and got anothe[..] shed, and they say that Peter M'Laughlan got hold of him there. [..] don't know what Peter did to him then—Jack never spoke of it, eve[..] to me, his old mate; but, anyway, at the end of the shearing seaso[..] Jack's cheque came home to Clara in a registered envelope[..] addressed in Peter's hand-writing, and about a week later Jac[..] turned up a changed man.

He got work as a temporary clerk in the branch government lan[..] office at Solong, a pretty little farming town in a circle of blue hill[..] on the banks of a clear, willow-fringed river, where there were rich[..] black-soil, river-flat farms, and vineyards on the red soil slopes, an[..] blue peaks in the distance. It was a great contrast to Ross's Creek[..] Jack paid a deposit on an allotment of land, a bit out of town, on th[..] river bank, and built a little weather-board box of a cottage in spar[..] times, and planted roses and grape-vines to hide its ugliness by an[..] by. It wasn't much of a place, but Clara was mighty proud of i[..] because it was "our house." They were very happy, and she wa[..] beginning to feel sure of Jack. She seemed to believe that th[..] miserable old time was all past and gone.

When the work at the land's office gave out, Jack did all sorts o[..]

bs about town, and at last, one shearing season, when there was a
eavy clip of wool, and shearers were getting £1 a hundred, he
ecided to go out back. I know that Clara was against it, but he
rgued that it was the only chance for him, and she persuaded
erself that she could trust him. I was knocking about Solong at the
me, and Jack and I decided to go out together and share his
ackhorse between us. He wrote to Beenaway Shed, about three
undred miles north-west in the Great Scrubs, and got pens for both
f us.

It was a fine fresh morning when we started; it was in a good
eason and the country looked grand. When I rode up to Jack's
lace I saw his horse and packhorse tied up outside the gate. He had
anted me to come up the evening before and have tea with them
nd camp at his place for the night. "Come up! man alive!" he said.
We'll make you a shake-down!" But I wouldn't; I said I had to
neet a chap. Jack wouldn't have understood. I had been up before,
ut when I saw him and Clara so happy and comfortable, and
nought of the past and my secret, and thought of myself, a useless,
urposeless, restless, homeless sort of fellow, hanging out at a
oarding-house, it nearly broke me up, and I had to have a drink or
wo afterwards. I often wonder if Clara guessed and understood.
ou never know how much a woman knows; but—ah, well!

Jack had taken my things home with him and he and Clara had
acked them. I found afterwards that she had washed, dried and
oned some collars and handkerchiefs of mine during the night.
lara and Jack came out to the gate, and as I wouldn't go in to have
cup of tea there was nothing for it but to say good-bye. She was
ressed in a fresh-looking print blouse and dark skirt, and wore a
hite hood that feel back from her head; she was a little girl, with
weet, small, freckled features, and red-gold hair, and kind,
ympathetic grey eyes. I thought her the freshest, and fairest, and
aintiest little woman in the district.

I was Jack's mate, so she always treated me as a sort of
rother-in-law, and called me by my Christian name. Mates are
loser than brothers in the bush.

I turned my back and pretended to tighten the straps and girths
n the packhorse while she said good-bye to Jack. I heard her
peaking earnestly to him, and once I heard her mention Peter
1'Laughlan's name. I thought Jack answered rather impatiently.
Oh, that's all right, Clara," he said, "that's all over—past and
one. I wish you would believe it. You promised never to speak of
nat any more."

I know how it was. Jack never cared to hear about Peter; he was too ashamed of the past, perhaps; besides, deep down, we feel a sort of resentment towards any reference to a man who has helped or saved us in the past. It's human nature.

Then they spoke in low tones for a while, and then Jack laughed and kissed her, and said, "Oh, I'll be back before the time's up." Then he ran into the house to say good-bye to Mary's sister, who was staying with her, and who was laid up with a sprained ankle.

Then Clara stepped up to me and laid her fingers on my shoulder. I trembled from head to foot and hoped she didn't notice it.

"Joe," she said, looking at me with her big, searching grey eyes, "I believe I can trust you. I want you to look after Jack. You know why. Never let him have one drink if you can help it. One drink—the first drink will do it. I want you to promise me that you will never have a drink with Jack, no matter what happens or what he says."

"I never will," I said, and I meant it.

"It's the first time he's been away from me since he gave up drinking, and if he comes back all right this time I will be sure of him and contented. But, Joe, if he comes back wrong it will kill me; it will break my heart. I want you to promise that if anything happens you will ride or wire for Peter M'Laughlan. I hear he's wool-sorting this year at Beenaway Station. Promise me that if anything happens you will ride for Peter M'Laughlan and tell him, no matter what Jack says."

"I promise," I said.

She half-held out her hand to me, but I kept both mine behind my back. I suppose she thought I didn't notice that she wanted to shake hands on the bargain; but the truth was that my hands shook so, and I didn't want her to notice *that*.

I got on my horse and felt steadier. Then, "Good-bye, Clara"— "Good-bye, Jack." She bore up bravely, but I saw her eyes brimming. Jack got on his horse, and I bent over and shook hands with her. Jack bent down and kissed her while she stood on tiptoe. "Good-bye, little woman," he said. "Cheer up, and I'll be back before you know where you are! You mustn't fret—you know why."

"Good-bye, Jack!"—she was breaking down.

"Come on, Jack!" I said, and we rode off, turning and waving our hats to her as she stood by the gate, looking a desolate little thing, I thought, till we turned down a bend of the road into the river.

As we jogged along with the packhorse trotting behind us, and the quart-pots and hobble-chains jingling on the pack-saddle, I pictured Clara running inside, to cry a while in her sister's arms, and then to bustle round and cheer up, for Jack's sake—and for the sake of something else.

"I'll christen him after you, Joe," said Jack, later on, when we'd got confidential over our pipes after tea in our first camp. It never seemed to enter his head that there was the ghost of a chance that it might be a girl. "I'm glad he didn't come along when I was drinking," he said.

And as we lay rolled in our blankets under the stars I swore a big oath to myself.

We got along comfortably and reached Beenaway Station in about a week, the day before the shearers' roll-call. Jack never showed the slightest inclination to go into a shanty; and several times we talked about old times and what damned fools we'd been throwing away our money over shanty bars shouting for loafers and cadgers. "Isn't this ever so much better, Joe?" said Jack, as we lay on our blankets smoking one moonlight night. "There's nothing in boozing, Joe, you can take it from me. Just you sling it for a year and then look back; you won't want to touch it again. You've been straight for a couple of months. Sling it for good, Joe, before it gets a hold on you, like it did on me."

It was the morning after cut-out at Beenaway Shed, and we were glad. We were tired of the rush and roar and rattle and heat and grease and blasphemy of the big, hot, iron machine shed in that dusty patch in the barren scrubs. Swags were rolled up, saddle-bags packed, horses had been rounded up and driven in, the shearers' cook and his mate had had their fight, and about a hundred men—shearers, rouseabouts, and wool-washers—were waiting round the little iron office to get their cheques.

We were about half through when one bushman said to another: "Stop your damned swearin', Jim. Here's Peter M'Laughlan!" Peter walked up and the men made way for him and he went into the office. There was always considerably less swearing for a few feet round about where Peter M'Laughlan happened to be working in a shearing-shed. It seemed to be an understood thing with the men. He took no advantages, never volunteered to preach at a shed where he was working, and only spoke on union subjects when the men asked him to. He was "rep." (Shearers' Union representative) at this shed, but squatters and station managers respected him as much as the men did.

He seemed much greyer now, but still stood square and straight. And his eyes still looked one through.

When Peter came out and the crowd had cleared away he took Jack aside and spoke to him in a low voice for a few minutes. I heard Jack say, "Oh, that's all right, Peter! You have my word for it," and he got on his horse. I heard Peter say the one word, "Remember!" "Oh, that's all right," said Jack, and he shook hands with Peter, shouted, "Come on, Joe!" and started off with the packhorse after him.

"I wish I were going down with you, Joe." said Peter to me, "but I can't get away till to-morrow. I've got that sick rouseabout on my hands, and I'll have to see him fixed up somehow and started off to the hospital" (the nearest was a hundred miles away). "And, by the way, I've taken up a collection for him; I want a few shillings from you, Joe. I nearly forgot you. The poor fellow only got in about a fortnight's work, and there's a wife and youngsters in Sydney. I'll be down after you to-morrow. I promised to go to Comesomehow* and get the people together and start an agitation for a half-time school there. Anyway, I'll be there by the end of the week. Good-bye, Joe. I must get some more money for the rouser from some of those chaps before they start."

Comesomehow was a wretched cockatoo settlement, a bit off the track, about one hundred and fifty miles on our road home, where the settlers lived like savages and the children ran wild. I reckoned that Peter would have his work cut out to start a craving for education in that place.

By saying he'd be there I think he intended to give me a hint, in case anything happened. I believe now that Jack's wife had got anxious and had written to him.

We jogged along comfortably and happily for three or four days, and as we passed shanty after shanty, and town after town, without Jack showing the slightest inclination to pull up at any of them, I began to feel safe about him.

Then it happened, in the simplest way, as most things of this sort happen if you don't watch close.

The third night it rained, rained heavens-hard, and rainy nights can be mighty cold out on those plains, even in mid-summer. Jack and I rigged up a strip of waterproof stuff we had to cover the swags on the packhorse, but the rain drove in, almost horizontally, and we got wet through, blankets, clothes and all. Jack got a bad cold and coughed fit to break himself; so about daylight, when the rain held up a bit, we packed up and rode on to the next pub, a wretched little weatherboard place in the scrub.

Jack reckoned he'd get some stuff for his cold there. I didn't like to speak, but before we reached the place I said, "You won't touch a drink, Jack."

---

* There is a postal town in New South Wales called "Come-by-Chance."

"Do you think I'm a blanky fool?" said Jack, and I shut up.

The shanty was kept by a man who went by the name of Thomas, a notorious lamber-down,* as I found out afterwards. He was a big, awkward bullock of a man, a selfish, ignorant brute, as anyone might have seen by his face; but he had a loud voice, and adopted a careless, rollicking, hail-fellow-well-met! come-in-and-sit-down-man-alive! clap-you-on-the-back style, which deceived a good many, or which a good many pretended to believe in. His "missus" was an animal of his own species, but she was duller and didn't bellow.

He had a rather good-looking girl there—I don't know whether she was his daughter or not. They said that when he saw the shearers coming he'd say, "Run and titivate yourself, Mary; here comes the shearers!"

But what surprised me was that Jack Barnes didn't seem able to see through Thomas; he thought that he was all right, "a bit of a rough diamond." There are any amount of scoundrels and swindlers knocking about the world disguised as rough diamonds.

Jack had a fit of coughing when we came in.

"Why, Jack!" bellowed Thomas, "that's a regular churchyarder you've got. Go in to the kitchen fire and I'll mix you a stiff toddy."

"No, thank you, Thomas," said Jack, glancing at me rather sheepishly, I thought. "I'll have a hot cup of coffee presently, that'll do me more good."

"Why, man alive, one drink won't hurt you!" said Thomas. "I know you're on the straight, and you know I'm the last man that 'ud try to get you off it. But you want something for that cold. You don't want to die on the track, do you? What would your missus say? That cough of yours is enough to bust a bullock."

"Jack isn't drinking, Thomas," I said rather shortly, "and neither am I."

"I'll have a cup of coffee at breakfast," said Jack; "thank you all the same, Thomas."

"Right you are, Jack!" said Thomas. "Mary!" he roared at the girl, "chuck yerself about and get breakfast, and make a strong cup of coffee; and I say, missus" (to his wife), "git some honey and vinegar in a cup, will yer? or see if there's any of that cough stuff left in the bottle. Go into the kitchen, you chaps, and dry yourselves at the fire, you're wringing wet." Jack went through into the kitchen.

I stepped out to see if the horses were all right, and as I came in again through the bar, Thomas, who had slipped behind the counter, crooked his finger at me and poured out a stiff whisky. "I

* "Lamber-down," a shanty-keeper who entices cheque-men to drink.

thought you might like to have it on the quiet," he whispered, with a wink.

Now, there was this difference between Jack and me. When I was on the track, and healthy and contented, I could take a drink, or two drinks, and then leave it; or at other times I could drink all day, or all night, and be as happy as a lord, and be mighty sick and repentant all next day, and then not touch drink for a week; but if Jack once started, he was a lost man for days, for weeks, for months—as long as his cash or credit lasted. I felt a cold coming on me this morning, and wanted a whisky, so I had a drink with Thomas. Then, of course, I shouted in my turn, keeping an eye out in case Jack should come in. I went into the kitchen and steamed with Jack for a while in front of a big log fire, taking care to keep my breath away from him. Then we went in to breakfast. Those two drinks were all I meant to have, and we were going right on after breakfast.

It was a good breakfast, ham and eggs, and we enjoyed it. The two whiskies had got to work. I hadn't touched drink for a long time. I shouldn't like to say that Thomas put anything in the drink he gave me. Before we started breakfast he put a glass down in front of me and said:

"There's a good ginger-ale, it will warm you up."

I tasted it; it was rum, hot. I said nothing. What could I say?

There was some joke about Jack being married and settled and steadied down, and me, his old mate, still on the wallaby; and Mrs Thomas said that I ought to follow Jack's example. And just then I felt a touch of that loneliness that some men feel when an old drinking mate turns teetotaller.

Jack started coughing again, like an old cow with the pleuro.

"That cough will kill you, Jack," said Thomas. "Let's put a drop of brandy in your coffee, *that* won't start you, anyhow; it's real 'Three Star.'" And he reached a bottle from the side-table.

I should have stood up then, for my manhood, for my mate, and for little Clara, but I half rose from my chair, and Jack laughed and said, "Sit down, Joe, you old fool, you're tanked. I know all about your seeing about the horses and your ginger-ales. It's all right, old man. Do you think I'm going on the booze? Why, I'll have to hold you on the horse all day." I sat down and took up my glass.

"Here's luck, Joe!" said Jack, laughing, and lifting up his cup of coffee with the brandy in it. "Here's luck, Joe."

Then suddenly, and as clearly as I ever heard it, came Clara's voice to my ear: "Promise me, whatever you do, that you will never have a drink with Jack." And I felt cold and sick to the stomach.

I got up and went out. They thought that the drink had made me sick, but if I'd stayed there another minute I would have tackled Thomas; and I knew that I needed a clear head to tackle a bullock like him. I walked about a bit, and when I came in again Jack and Thomas were in the bar, and Jack had a glass before him.

"Come on, Joe, you old bounder," said Jack, "come and have a whisky-and-soda; it will straighten you up."

"What's that you're drinking, Jack?" I asked.

"Oh, don't be a fool!" said Jack. "One drink won't hurt me. Do you think I'm going on the booze? Have a soda and straighten up; we must make a start directly."

I remember we had two or three whiskies, and then suddenly I tackled Thomas, and Jack was holding me back, and laughing and swearing at me at the same time, and I had a tussle with him; and then I was suddenly calmer and sensible, and we were shaking hands all round, and Jack was talking about just one more spree for the sake of old times.

"A bit of a booze won't hurt me, Joe, you old fool," he said. "We'll have one more night of it, for the sake of Auld Lang Syne, and start at daylight in the morning. You go and see to the horses, it will straighten you up. Take the saddle off and hobble 'em out."

But I insisted on starting at once, and Jack promised he would. We were gloriously happy for an hour or so, and then I went to sleep.

When I woke it was late in the afternoon. I was very giddy and shaky; the girl brought me a whisky-and-soda, and that steadied me. Some more shearers had arrived, and Jack was playing cards with two of them on top of a cask in the bar. Thomas was dead drunk on the floor, or pretending to be so, and his wife was behind the bar. I went out to see to the horses; I found them in a bush yard at the back. The pack-horse was rolling in the mud with the pack-saddle and saddle-bags on. One of the chaps helped me take off the saddles and put them in the harness-room behind the kitchen.

I'll pass over that night. It wouldn't be very edifying to the great, steady-living, sober majority, and the others, the ne'er-do-wells, the rovers, wrecks and failures, will understand only too well without being told—only too well, God help them!

When I woke in the morning I couldn't have touched a drink to save my life. I was fearfully shaky, and swimming about the head, but I put my head over a tub under the pump and got the girl to pump for a while, and then I drank a pint of tea and managed to keep it down, and felt better.

All through the last half of the night I'd kept saying, in a sort of drink nightmare, "I'll go for Peter M'Laughlan in the morning. I'll go for Peter as soon as I can stand!" and repeating Clara Barnes's words, "Ride for Peter if anything happens. Ride for Peter M'Laughlan."

There were drunken shearers, horsemen and swagmen sleeping all over the place, and in all sorts of odd positions; some on the veranda with their heads on their swags, one sitting back against the wall, and one on the broad of his back with his head on the bare boards and his mouth open. There was another horse rolling in its saddle, and I took the saddle off. The horse belonged to an English University man.

I went in to see how Jack was. He was lying in the parlour on a little, worn-out, horse-hair sofa, that might have seen better days in some clean home in the woman-and-girl world. He had been drinking and playing cards till early that morning, and he looked awful—he looked as if he'd been boozing for a month.

"See what you've done!" he said, sitting up and glaring at me; then he said, "Bring me a whisky-and-soda, Joe, for God's sake!"

I got a whisky-and-soda from the girl and took it to him.

I talked to him for a while, and at last he said, "Well, go and get the horses and we'll start."

I got the horses ready and brought them round to the front, but by that time he'd had more drink, and he said he wanted to sleep before he started. Next he was playing cards with one of the chaps, and asked me to wait till he'd finished that game. I knew he'd keep promising and humbugging me till there was a row, so at last I got him aside and said:

"Look here, Jack, I'm going for Peter M'Laughlan——"

"Go to hell!" said Jack.

I put the other horses back in the yard, the saddles in the skillion, got on my horse and rode off. Thomas and the others asked me no questions, they took no notice. In a place like that a man could almost do anything, short of hanging himself, without anyone interfering or being surprised. And probably, if he did hang himself, they'd let him swing for a while to get a taste of it.

Comesomehow was about fifteen miles back on a track off the main road. I reckoned that I could find Peter and bring him on by the afternoon, and I rode hard, sick as I was. I was too sick to smoke.

As it happened, Peter had started early from his last camp and I caught him just as he was turning off into Comesomehow track.

"What's up, Joe?" he asked as I rode up to him—but he could see.

"Jack Barnes is on the booze at Thomas's," I said.

Peter just looked right through me. Then he turned his horse's head without a word, and rode back with me. And, after a while, he said, as if to himself:

"Poor Clara! Poor little lassie!"

By the time we reached the shanty it was well on in the afternoon. A fight was stopped in the first round and voices lowered when the chaps caught sight of us. As Peter walked into the bar one or two drunks straightened themselves and took off their hats with drunken sentiment.

"Where is Jack Barnes, Thomas?" asked Peter, quietly.

"He's in there if you want to see him," said Thomas, jerking his head towards the parlour.

We went in, and when Peter saw Jack lying there I noticed that swift, haunted look came into his eyes, as if he'd seen a ghost of the past.

He sat down by the sofa to wait until Jack woke. I thought as he sat there that his eyes were like a woman's for sympathy and like a dog's for faithfulness. I was very shaky.

Presently Thomas looked in. "Is there anything I can do for you, M'Laughlan?" he asked in as civil a tone as he could get to.

"Yes," said Peter, "bring me a flask of your best whisky—your own, mind—and a glass.

"We shall need the whisky for him on the track, Joe," said Peter, when the flask came. "Get another glass and a bottle of soda; you want a nip." He poured out a drink for himself.

"The first thing we've got to do is to get him away; then I'll soon put him on his feet. But we'll let him sleep a while longer. I find I've got business near Solong, and I'm going down with you."

By and by Jack woke up and glared round, and when he caught sight of Peter he just reached for his hands and said, "Peter! Thank God you've come!" Then he said, "But I must have a drink first, Peter."

"All right, Jack, you shall have a drink," said Peter; and he gave him a stiff nobbler. It steadied Jack a bit.

"Now listen to me, Jack," said Peter. "How much money have you got left?"

"I—I can't think," said Jack. "I've got a cheque for twenty pounds here, sewn inside my shirt."

"Yes; but you drew thirty-six in three cheques. Where's the rest?"

"Thomas has ten," said Jack, "and the six—well, the six is gone. I was playing cards last night."

Peter stepped out into the bar.

"Look here, Thomas," he said quietly, "you've got a ten-pound cheque from Barnes."

"I know I have."

"Well, how much of it does he owe you?"

"The whole, and more."

"Do you mean to tell me that? He has only been here since yesterday morning."

"Yes; but he's been shoutin' all round. Look at all these chaps here."

"They only came yesterday afternoon," said Peter. "Here, you had best take this and give me the cheque;" and Peter laid a five-pound note on the bar. Thomas bucked at first, but in the end he handed over the cheque—he had had several warnings from the police. Then he suddenly lost all control over himself; he came round from behind the bar and faced Peter.

"Now, look here, you mongrel parson!" he said. "What the —— do you mean by coming into my bar and interfering with me. Who the —— are you anyway? A ——!" He used the worst oaths that were used in the bush. "Take off your —— coat!" he roared at last, shaping up to Peter.

Peter stepped back a pace and buttoned his coat and threw back his head.

"No need to take off my coat, Thomas," he said, "I am ready." He said it very quietly, but there was a danger-signal—a red light in his eyes. He was quiet-voiced but hard-knuckled, as some had reason to know.

Thomas balked like a bull at a spread umbella. Jack lurched past me as I stood in the parlour door, but I caught him and held him back; and almost at the same moment a wretched old boozer that we called "Awful Example," who had been sitting huddled, a dirty bundle of rags and beard and hair, in the corner of the bar, struggled to his feet, staggered forward and faced Thomas, looking once again like something that might have been a man. He snatched a thick glass bottle from the counter and held it by the neck in his right hand.

"Stand back, Thomas!" he shouted. "Lay a hand—lay a finger on Peter M'Laughlan, and I'll smash your head, as sure as there's a God above us and I'm a ruined man!"

Peter took "Awful" gently by the shoulders and sat him down. "You keep quiet, old man," he said; "nothing is going to happen." Thomas went round behind the bar muttering something about it not being worth his while to, etc.

"You go and get the horses ready, Joe," said Peter to me; "and you sit down, Jack, and keep quiet."

"He can get the horses," growled Thomas, from behind the bar, "but I'm damned if he gets the saddles. I've got them locked up, and I'll something well keep them till Barnes is sober enough to pay me what he owes me."

Just then a tall, good-looking chap, with dark-blue eyes and a long, light-coloured moustache, stepped into the bar from the crowd on the veranda.

"What's all this, Thomas?" he asked.

"What's that got to do with you, Gentleman Once?" shouted Thomas.

"I think it's got something to do with me," said Gentleman Once. "Now, look here, Thomas; you can do pretty well what you like with us poor devils, and you know it, but we draw the line at Peter M'Laughlan. If you really itch for the thrashing you deserve you must tempt someone else to give it to you."

"What the —— are you talking about?" snorted Thomas. "You're drunk or ratty!"

"What's the trouble, M'Laughlan?" asked Gentleman Once, turning to Peter.

"No trouble at all, Gentleman Once," said Peter; "thank you all the same. I've managed worse men than our friend Thomas. Now, Thomas, don't you think it would pay you best to hand over the key of the harness-room and have done with this nonsense? I'm a patient man—a very patient man—but I've not always been so, and the old blood comes up sometimes, you know."

Thomas couldn't stand this sort of language, because he couldn't understand it. He threw the key on the bar and told us to clear out.

We were all three very quiet riding along the track that evening. Peter gave Jack a nip now and again from the flask, and before we turned in in camp he gave him what he called a soothing draught from a little medicine chest that he carried in his saddle-bag. Jack seemed to have got rid of his cough; he slept all night, and in the morning, after he'd drunk a pint of mutton-broth that Peter had made in one of the billies, he was all right—except that he was quiet and ashamed. I had never known him to be so quiet, and for such a length of time, since we were boys together. He had learned his own weakness; he'd lost all his cocksureness. I know now just exactly how he felt. He felt as if his sober year had been lost and he would have to live it all over again.

Peter didn't preach. He just jogged along and camped with us as if he were an ordinary, every-day mate. He yarned about all sorts of things. He could tell good yarns, and when he was fairly on you could listen to him all night. He seemed to have been nearly all over the world. Peter never preached except when he was asked to hold service in some bush pub, station-homestead or bush church. But in a case like ours he had a way of telling a little life story, with something in it that hit the young man he wanted to reform, and hit him hard. He'd generally begin quietly, when we were comfortable with our pipes in camp after tea, with "I once knew a young man—" or "That reminds me of a young fellow I knew—" and so on. You never knew when he was going to begin, or when he was going to hit you. In our last camp, before we reached Solong, he told two of his time-fuse yarns. I haven't time to tell them now, but one stuffed up my pipe for a while, and made Jack's hand tremble when he tried to light his. I'm glad it was too dark to see our faces. We lay a good while afterwards, rolled in our blankets, and couldn't get to sleep for thinking; but Peter seemed to fall asleep as soon as he turned in.

Next day he told Jack not to tell Clara that he'd come down with us. He said he wouldn't go right into Solong with us; he was going back along another road to stay a day or two with an old friend of his.

When we reached Solong we stopped on the river-bank just out of sight of Jack's house. Peter took the ten-pound cheque from his pocket and gave it to Jack. Jack hadn't seen Peter give the shanty-keeper the five-pound note.

"But I owed Thomas something," said Jack, staring. "However did you manage to get the cheque out of him?"

"Never mind, Jack, I managed," said Peter.

Jack sat silent for a while, then he began to breathe hard.

"I don't know what to say, Peter."

"Say nothing, Jack. Only promise me that you will give Clara the cheque as soon as you go home, and let her take care of the cash for a while."

"I will," said Jack.

Jack looked down at the ground for a while, then he lifted his head and looked Peter in the eyes.

"Peter," he said, "I can't speak. I'm ashamed to make a promise; I've broken so many. I'll try to thank you in a year's time from now."

"I ask for no promises," said Peter, and he held out his hand. Jack gripped it.

"Aren't you coming home with me, Joe?" he asked.

"No," I said; "I'll go into town. See you in the morning."

Jack rode on. When he got along a piece Peter left his horse and moved up to the head of the lane to watch Jack, and I followed. As Jack neared the cottage we saw a little figure in a cloak run out to the front gate. She had heard the horses and the jingle of the camp-ware on the pack-saddle. We saw Jack jump down and take her in his arms. I looked at Peter, and as he watched them, something, that might have been a strange look of the old days, came into his eyes.

He shook hands with me. "Good-bye, Joe."

He rode across the river again. He took the track that ran along the foot of the spurs by the river, and up over a gap in the curve of blue hills, and down and out west towards the Big Scrubs. And as he rounded the last spur, with his packhorse trotting after him, I thought he must have felt very lonely. And I felt lonely too.

THE STORY OF "GENTLEMAN ONCE"

> They learn the world from black-sheep,
> Who know it all too well.
>
> —*Out Back*.

Peter M'Laughlan, bush missionary, Joe Wilson and his mate, Jack Barnes, shearers for the present, and a casual swagman named Jack Mitchell, were camped at Cox's Crossing in a bend of Eurunderee Creek.

It was a grassy little flat with gum-trees standing clear and clean like a park. At the back was the steep grassy siding of a ridge, and far away across the creek to the south a spur from the Blue Mountain range ran west, with a tall, blue granite peak showing clear in the broad moonlight, yet dream-like and distant over the sweeps of dark green bush.

There was the jingle of hobble-chains and a crunching at the grass where the horses moved in the soft shadows amongst the trees. Up the creek on the other side was a surveyors' camp, and from there now and again came the sound of a good voice singing verses of old songs; and later on the sound of a violin and a cornet being played, sometimes together and sometimes each on its own.

Wilson and Barnes were on their way home from shearing out back in the great scrubs at Beenaway Shed. They had been rescued by Peter M'Laughlan from a wayside shanty where they had fallen, in spite of mutual oaths and past promises, sacred and profane, because they had got wringing wet in a storm on the track and caught colds, and had been tempted to take just one drink.

They were in a bad way, and were knocking down their cheques beautifully when Peter M'Laughlan came along. He rescued them and some of their cash from the soulless shanty-keeper, and was riding home with them, on some pretence, because he had known them as boys, because Joe Wilson had a vein of poetry in him—a something in sympathy with something in Peter; because Jack Barnes had a dear little girl-wife who was much too good for him, and who was now anxiously waiting for him in the pretty little farming town of Solong amongst the western spurs. Because, perhaps, of something in Peter's early past which was a mystery. Simply and plainly because Peter M'Laughlan was the kindest, straightest and truest man in the West—a "white man."

They all knew Mitchell and welcomed him heartily when he turned up in their camp, because he was a pathetic humorist and a kindly cynic—a "joker" or "hard case" as the bushmen say.

Peter was about fifty and the other three were young men.

There was another man in camp who didn't count and was supposed to be dead. Old Danny Quinn, champion "beer-chewer" of the district, was on his way out, after a spree, to one of Rouse's stations, where, for the sake of past services—long past—and because of old times, he was supposed to be working. He had spent his last penny a week before and had clung to his last-hope hotel until the landlord had taken him in one hand and his swag in the other and lifted them clear of the veranda. Danny had blundered on, this far, somehow; he was the last in the world who could have told how, and had managed to light a fire; then he lay with his head on his swag and enjoyed nips of whisky in judicious doses and at reasonable intervals, and later on a tot of mutton-broth, which he made in one of the billies.

It was after tea. Peter sat on a log by the fire with Joe and Jack Mitchell on one side and Jack Barnes on the other. Jack Mitchell sat on the grass with his back to the log, his knees drawn up, and his arms abroad on them: his most comfortable position and one which seemed to favour the flow of his philosophy. They talked of bush things or reflected, sometimes all three together, sometimes by turns.

From the surveyors' camp:

> I remember, I remember,
> The house where I was born,
> The little window where the sun
> Came peeping in at morn——

The breeze from the west strengthened and the voice was blown away.

"That chap seems a bit sentimental but he's got a good voice," said Mitchell. Then presently he remarked, round his pipe:

"I wonder if old Danny remembers?"

And presently Peter said quietly, as if the thought had just occurred to him:

"By the way, Mitchell, I forgot to ask after your old folk. I knew your father, you know."

"Oh, they're all right, Peter, thank you."

"Heard from them lately?" asked Peter, presently, in a lazy tone.

Mitchell straightened himself up. "N—no. To tell the truth, Peter, I haven't written for—I don't know how long."

Peter smoked reflectively.

"I remember your father well, Jack," he said. "He was a big-hearted man."

Old Danny was heard remonstrating loudly with spirits from a warmer clime than Australia, and Peter stepped over to soothe him.

"I thought I'd get it, directly after I opened my mouth," said Mitchell. "I suppose it will be your turn next, Joe."

"I suppose so," said Joe, resignedly.

The wind fell.

> I remember, I remember,
> And it gives me little joy,
> To think I'm further off from heaven,
> Than when I was a boy!

When Peter came back another thought seemed to have occurred to him.

"How's your mother getting on, Joe?" he asked. "She shifted to Sydney after your father died, didn't she?"

"Oh, she's getting on all right!" said Joe, without elaboration.

"Keeping a boarding-house, isn't she?"

"Yes," said Joe.

"Hard to make ends meet, I suppose?" said Peter. "It's almost a harder life than it could have been on the old selection, and there's none of the old independence about it. A woman like your mother must feel it, Joe."

"Oh, she's all right," said Joe. "She's used to it by this time. I manage to send her a few pounds now and again. I send her all I can," he added resentfully.

Peter sat corrected for a few moments. Then he seemed to change the subject.

"It's some time since you were in Sydney last, isn't it, Joe?"

"Yes, Peter," said Joe. "I haven't been there for two years. I never did any good there. I'm far better knocking about out back."

There was a pause.

"Some men seem to get on better in one place, some in another," reflected Mitchell, lazily. "For my part, I seem to get on better in another."

Peter blinked, relit his pipe with a stick from the fire and reflected. The surveyor's song had been encored:

> I remember, I remember——

Perhaps Peter remembered. Joe did, but there were no vines round the house where he was born, only drought and dust, and raspy voices raised in recrimination, and hardship most times.

"I remember," said Peter, quietly, "I remember a young fellow at home in the old country. He had every advantage. He had a first-class education, a great deal more money than he needed—almost as much as he asked for, and nearly as much freedom as he wanted. His father was an English gentleman and his mother an English lady. They were titled people, if I remember rightly. The old man was proud, but fond of his son; he only asked him to pay a little duty or respect now and again. We don't understand these things in Australia—they seem formal and cold to us. The son paid his respects to his father occasionally—a week or so before he'd be wanting money, as a rule. The mother was a dear lady. She idolized her son. She only asked for a little show of affection from him, a few days or a week of his society at home now and then—say once in three months. But he couldn't spare her even that—his time was taken up so much in fashionable London and Paris and other places. He would give the world to be able to take his proud, soft old father's hand now and look into his eyes as one man who understands another. He would be glad and eager to give his mother twelve months out of the year if he thought it would make her happier. It has been too late for more than twenty years."

Old Danny called for Peter.

Mitchell jerked his head approvingly and gave a sound like a sigh and chuckle conjoined, the one qualifying the other.

"I told you you'd get it, Joe," he said.

"I don't see how it hits me," said Joe.

"But it hit all the same, Joe."

"Well, I suppose it did," said Joe, after a short pause.

"He wouldn't have hit you so hard if you hadn't tried to parry," reflected Mitchell. "It's your turn now, Jack."

Jack Barnes said nothing.

"Now I know that Peter would do anything for a woman or child, or an honest, straight, hard-up chap," said Mitchell, straightening out his legs and folding his arms, "but I can't quite understand his being so partial to drunken scamps and vagabonds, black sheep and ne'er-do-wells. He's got a tremendous sympathy for drunks. He's do anything to help a drunken man. Ain't it marvellous? It's my private opinion that Peter must have been an awful boozer and scamp in his time."

The other two only thought. Mitchell was privileged. He was a young man of freckled, sandy complexion, and quizzical grey eyes. "Sly Joker" "could take a rise out of anyone on the quiet;" "You could never tell when he was getting at you;" "Face of a born comedian," as bushmen said of Mitchell. But he would probably have been a dead and dismal failure on any other stage than that of wide Australia.

Peter came back and they sat and smoked, and maybe they reflected along four very different back-tracks for a while.

The surveyor started to sing again:

> I have heard the mavis singing
> Her love-song to the morn.
> I have seen the dew-drop clinging
> To the rose just newly born.

They smoked and listened in silence all through to the end. It was very still. The full moon was high. The long white slender branches of a box-tree stirred gently overhead; the she-oaks in the creek sighed as they are always sighing, and the southern peak seemed ever so far away.

> That has made me thine for ever!
> Bonny Mary of Argyle.

"Blarst my pipe!" exclaimed Mitchell, suddenly. "I beg your pardon, Peter. My pipe's always getting stuffed up," and he proceeded to shell out and clear his pipe.

The breeze had changed and strengthened. They heard the violin playing "Annie Laurie."

"They must be having a Scotch night in that camp tonight," said Mitchell. The voice came again:

> Maxwelton Braes are bonny—
> Where early fa's the dew,
> For 'twas there that Annie Laurie
> Gie me her promise true—

Mitchell threw out his arm impatiently.

"I wish they wouldn't play and sing those old songs," he said. "They make you think of damned old things. I beg your pardon, Peter."

Peter sat leaning forward, his elbows resting on his knees and his hands fingering his cold pipe nervously. His sad eyes had grown haggard and haunted. It is in the hearts of exiles in new lands that the old songs are felt.

"Take no thought of the morrow, Mitchell," said Peter, abstractedly. "I beg your pardon, Mitchell. I mean——"

"That's all right, Peter," said Mitchell. "You're right; to-morrow is the past, as far as I'm concerned."

Peter blinked down at him as if he were a new species.

"You're an odd young man, Mitchell," he said. "You'll have to take care of that head of yours or you'll be found hanging by a saddle-strap to a leaning tree on a lonely track, or find yourself in a lunatic asylum before you're forty-five."

"Or else I'll be a great man," said Mitchell. "But—ah, well!"

Peter turned his eyes to the fire and smiled sadly.

"Not enjoyment and not sorrow, is our destined end or way," he repeated to the fire.

"But we get there just the same," said Mitchell, "destined or not."

> But to live, that each to-morrow,
> Finds us further than to-day!

"Why, that just fits my life, Peter," said Mitchell. "I might have to tramp two or three hundred miles before I get a cut* or a job, and if to-morrow didn't find me nearer than to-day I'd starve or die of thirst on a dry stretch."

"Why don't you get married and settle down, Mitchell?" asked Peter, a little tired. "You're a teetotaller."

"If I got married I couldn't settle down," said Mitchell. "I reckon I'd be the loneliest man in Australia." Peter gave him a swift glance. "I reckon I'd be single no matter how much married I might be. I couldn't get the girl I wanted, and—ah, well!"

Mitchell's expression was still quaintly humorous round the lower part of his face, but there was a sad light in his eyes. The strange light as of the old dead days, and he was still young.

The cornet had started in the surveyors' camp.

• Cut—a pen, or "stand" in a shearing-shed.

"Their blooming tunes seem to fit in just as if they knew what we were talking about," remarked Mitchell.

The cornet:

> You'll break my heart, you little bird,
> That sings upon the flowering thorn—
> Thou mind'st me of departed joys,
> Departed never to return.

"Damn it all," said Mitchell, sitting up, "I'm getting sentimental." Then, as if voicing something that was troubling him, "Don't you think a woman pulls a man down as often as she lifts him up, Peter?"

"Some say so," said Peter.

"Some say so, and they write it, too," said Mitchell. "Sometimes it seems to me as if women were fated to drag a man down ever since Adam's time. If Adam hadn't taken his wife's advice—but there, perhaps he took her advice a good many times and found it good, and, just because she happened to be wrong this time, and to get him into a hole, the sons of Adam have never let the daughters of Eve hear the last of it. That's human nature."

Jack Barnes, the young husband, who was suffering a recovery, had been very silent all the evening. "I think a man's a fool to always listen to his wife's advice," he said, with the unreasonable impatience of a man who wants to think while others are talking. "She only messes him up, and drives him to the devil as likely as not, and gets a contempt for him in the end."

Peter gave him a surprised, reproachful look, and stood up. He paced backwards and forwards on the other side of the fire, with his hands behind his back for a while; then he came and settled himself on the log again and filled his pipe.

"Yes," he said, "a man can always find excuses for himself when his conscience stings him. He puts mud on the sting. Man at large is beginning all over the world to rake up excuses for himself; he disguises them as 'Psychological studies,' and thinks he is clean and clever and cultured, or he calls 'em problems—the sex problem, for instance, and thinks he is brave and fearless."

Danny was in trouble again, and Peter went to him. He complained that when he lay down he saw the faces worse, and he wanted to be propped up somehow, so Peter got a pack-saddle and propped the old man's shoulders up with that.

"I remember," Peter began, when he came back to the fire, "I remember a young man who got married——"

Mitchell hugged himself. He knew Jack Barnes. He knew that Jack had a girl-wife who was many times too good for him; that Jack had been wild, and had nearly broken her heart, and he had guessed at once that Jack had broken out again, and that Peter M'Laughlan was shepherding him home. Mitchell had worked as mates with Jack, and liked him because of the good heart that was in him in spite of all; and, because he liked him, he was glad that Jack was going to get a kicking, so to speak, which might do him good. Mitchell saw it coming, as he said afterwards, and filled his pipe, and settled himself comfortably to listen.

"I remember the case of a naturally selfish young man who got married," said Peter. "He didn't know he was selfish; in fact, he thought he was too much the other way—but that doesn't matter now. His name was—well, we'll call him—we'll call him, 'Gentleman Once.'"

"Do you mean Gentleman Once that we saw drinking back at Thomas's shanty?" asked Joe.

"No," said Peter, "not him. There have been more than one in the bush who went by the nickname of 'Gentleman Once.' I knew one or two. It's a big clan, the clan of Gentleman Once, and scattered all over the world."

"By the way," said Mitchell—"excuse me for interrupting, Peter—but wasn't old Danny, there, a gentleman once? I've heard chaps say he was."

"I know he was," said Peter.

"Gentleman Once! Who's talking about Gentleman Once?" said an awful voice, suddenly and quickly. "About twenty or thirty years ago I was called Gentleman Once or Gentleman Jack, I don't know which—Get out! *Get out*, I say! It's all lies, and you're the devil. There's four devils sitting by the fire. I see them."

Two of the four devils by the fire looked round, rather startled. Danny was sitting up, his awful bloodshot eyes glaring in the firelight, and his ruined head looking like the bloated head of a hairy poodle that had been drowned and dried. Peter went to the old man and soothed him by waving off the snakes and devils with his hands, and telling them to go.

"I've heard Danny on the Gentleman Once racket before," remarked Mitchell. "Seems funny, doesn't it, for a man to be proud of the fact that he was called 'Gentleman Once' about twenty years ago?"

"Seems more awful than funny to me," said Joe.

"You're right, Joe," said Mitchell. "But the saddest things are often funny."

When Peter came back he went on with his story, and was only interrupted once or twice by Danny waking up and calling him to drive off the snakes, and green and crimson dogs with crocodile heads, and devils with flaming tails, and those unpleasant sorts of things that force their company on boozers and madmen.

"Gentleman Once," said Peter, "he came from the old country with a good education and no character. He disgraced himself and family once too often and came, or was sent, out to Australia to reform. It's a great mistake. If a man is too far gone, or hasn't the strength to live the past down and reform at home, he won't do it in a new country, unless a combination of circumstances compels him to it. A man rises by chance; just as often he falls by chance. Some men fall into the habit of keeping steady and stick to it, for the novelty of it, until they are on their feet and in their sane minds and can look at the past, present and future sensibly. I knew one case— But that's got nothing to do with the story.

"Gentleman Once came out on the remittance system. That system is fatal in nine cases out of ten. The remittance system is an insult to any manhood that may be left in the black sheep, and an insult to the land he is sent to. The cursed quarterly allowance is a stone round his neck which will drag him down deeper in a new land than he would have fallen at home. You know that remittance men are regarded with such contempt in the bush that a man seldom admits he is one, save when he's drunk and reckless and wants money or credit. When a ne'er-do-well lands in Melbourne or Sydney without a penny he will probably buck-up and do something for himself. When he lands with money he will probably spend it all in the first few months and then straighten up, because he has to. But when he lands on the remittance system he drinks, first to drown homesickness. He decides that he'll wait till he gets his next quarter's allowance and then look round. He persuades himself that it's no use trying to do anything: that, in fact, he can't do anything until he gets his money. When he gets it he drifts into one 'last' night with chums he has picked up in second- and third-rate hotels. He drinks from pure selfishness. No matter what precautions his friends at home take, he finds means of getting credit or drawing on his allowance before it is due—until he is two or three quarters behind. He drinks because he feels happy and jolly and clever and good-natured and brave and honest while he is drinking. Later on he drinks because he feels the reverse of all these things when he is sober. He drinks to drown the past and repentance. He doesn't know that a healthy-minded man doesn't waste time in repenting. He doesn't know how easy it is to reform, and is too weak-willed to try.

He gets a muddled idea that the past can't be mended. He finds it easy to get drink and borrow money on the strength of his next quarter's allowance, so he soon gets a quarter or two behind, and sometimes gets into trouble connected with borrowed money. He drifts to the bush and drinks, to drown the past only. The past grows blacker and blacker until it is a hell without repentance; and often the black sheep gets to that state when a man dreads his sober hours. And the end? Well, you see old Danny there, and you saw old Awful Example back at Thomas's shanty—he's worse than Danny, if anything. Sometimes the end comes sooner. I saw a young new-land-new-leaf man dying in a cheap lodging-house in Sydney. He was a schoolmate of mine, by the way. For six weeks he lay on his back and suffered as I never saw a man suffer in this world; and I've seen some bad cases. They had to chloroform him every time they wanted to move him. He had affected to be hard and cynical, and I must say that he played it out to the end. It was a strong character, a strong mind sodden and diseased with drink. He never spoke of home and his people except when he was delirious. He never spoke, even to me, of his mental agony. That was English home training. You young Australians wouldn't understand it; most bushmen are poets and emotional.

"My old schoolmate was shifted to the Sydney Hospital at last, and consented to the amputation of one leg. But it was too late. He was gone from the hips down. Drink—third-rate hotel and bush shanty drink—and low debauchery."

Jack Barnes drew up his leg and rubbed it surreptitiously. He had "pins and needles." Mitchell noticed and turned a chuckle into a grunt.

"Gentleman Once was a remittance man," continued Peter. "But before he got very far he met an Australian girl in a boarding-house. Her mother was the landlady. They were bush people who had drifted to the city. The girl was pretty, intelligent and impulsive. She pitied him and nursed him. He wasn't known as Gentleman Once then, he hadn't got far enough to merit the nickname."

Peter paused. Presently he jerked his head, as if he felt a spasm of pain, and leaned forward to get a stick from the fire to light his pipe.

"Now, there's the girl who marries a man to reform him, and when she has reformed him never lets him hear the last of it. Sometimes, as a woman, she drives him back again. But this was not one of that sort of girls. I once held a theory that sometimes a girl who has married a man and reformed him misses in the reformed man the something which attracted her in the careless scamp, the something which made her love him—and so she ceases to love him, and their married life is a far more miserable one than it would have been had he continued drinking. I hold no theory of that kind now. Such theories ruin many married lives."

Peter jerked his head again as if impatient with a thought, and reached for a fire-stick.

"But that's got nothing to do with the story. When Gentleman Once reformed his natural selfishness came back. He saw that he had made a mistake. It's a terrible thing for a young man, a few months, perhaps a few weeks after his marriage, to ask himself the question, 'Have I made a mistake?' But Gentleman Once wasn't to be pitied. He discovered that he had married beneath him in intellect and education. Home training again. He couldn't have discovered that he had married beneath him as far as birth was concerned, for his wife's father had been a younger son of an older and greater family than his own— But Gentleman Once wouldn't have been cad enough to bother about birth. I'll do him that much justice. He discovered, or thought he did, that he and his wife could never have one thought in common; that she couldn't possibly understand him. I'll tell you later on whether he was mistaken or not. He was gloomy most times, and she was a bright, sociable, busy little body. When she tried to draw him out of himself he grew irritable. Besides, having found that they couldn't have a thought in common he ceased to bother to talk to her. There are many men who don't bother talking to their wives; they don't think their wives feel it—because the wives cease to complain after a while; they grow tired of trying to make the man realize how they suffer. Gentleman Once tried his best—according to his lights—and weakness. Then he went in for self-pity and all the problems. He liked to brood, and his poor little wife's energy and cheerfulness were wearying to him. He wanted to be left alone. They were both high-spirited, in different ways; she was highly strung and so was he—because of his past life mostly. They quarrelled badly sometimes. Then he drank again and she stuck to him. Perhaps the only time he seemed cheerful and affectionate was when he had a few drinks in him. It was a miserable existence—a furnished room in a cheap lodging-house, and the use of the kitchen.

"He drank alone.

"Now a dipsomaniac mostly thinks he is in the right—except, perhaps, after he has been forced to be sober for a week. The noblest woman in the world couldn't save him—everything she does to reform him irritates him; but a strong friend can save him sometimes—a man who has been through it himself. The poor little wife of Gentleman Once went through it all. And she stuck to him. She went into low pubs after him."

Peter shuddered again.

"She went through it all. He swore promises. He'd come home sober and fill her with hope of future happiness, and swear that he'd never take another glass. 'And we'll be happy yet, my poor boy,' she'd say, 'we'll be happy yet. I believe you, I trust you' (she used to call him her 'bonny boy' when they were first married). And next night he'd come home worse than ever. And one day he—he struck her!"

Peter shuddered, head and shoulders, like a man who had accidentally smashed his finger.

"And one day he struck her. He was sober when he did it—anyhow he had not taken drink for a week. A man is never sober who gets drunk more than once a week, though he might think he is. I don't know how it happened, but anyway he struck her, and that frightened him. He got a billet in the Civil Service up-country. No matter in what town it was. The little wife hoped for six months.

"I think it's a cruel thing that a carelessly selfish young man cannot realize how a sensitive young wife suffers for months after he has reformed. How she hopes and fears, how she dreads the moment he has to leave her, and frets every hour he is away from home—and suffers mental agony when he is late. How the horror of the wretched old past time grows upon her until she dares not think of it. How she listens to his step and voice and watches his face, when he comes home, for a sign of drink. A young man, a mate of mine, who drank hard and reformed, used to take a delight in pretending for a few minutes to be drunk when he came home. He was good-hearted, but dense. He said he only did it to give his wife a pleasant surprise afterwards. I thought it one of the most cruel things I had ever seen.

"Gentleman Once found that he could not stand the routine of office work and the dull life in that place. He commenced to drink again, and went on till he lost his billet. They had a little boy, a bright little boy, yet the father drank.

"The last spree was a terrible one. He was away from home a fortnight, and in that fortnight he got down as deep as a man could get. Then another man got hold of him and set him on his feet, and straightened him up. The other man was a ruined doctor, a wreck whose devil was morphia. I don't hold that a man's salvation is always in his own hands; I've seen mates pull mates out of hell too often to think that.

"Then Gentleman Once saw the past as he had never seen it

before—he saw hope for the future with it. And he swore an oath that he felt he would keep.

"He suffered from reaction on his way home, and, as he neared the town, a sudden fear, born of his nervous state, no doubt, sent a cold, sick emptiness through him: 'Was it too late?'

"As he turned into the street where he lived, he noticed a little group of bush larrikins standing at the corner. And they moved uneasily when they caught sight of him, and, as he passed, they touched and lifted their hats to him. Now he knew that he had lost the respect even of bush larrikins; and he knew enough of the bush to know that a bushman never lifts his hat to a man—only to death, and a woman sometimes. He hurried home and read the truth in his wife's eyes. His little boy was dead. He went down under the blow, and she held his head to her breast and kept saying, 'My poor boy, my poor boy!'

"It was he that she meant, not the boy she had lost. She knew him, she understood him better than he did himself, and, heart-broken as she was, she knew how he was going to suffer, and comforted him. 'My poor boy, my poor, foolish boy!'

"He mended the past, as far as he could, during the next two years, and she seemed happy. He was very gentle, he was very kind to her. He was happy, too, in a new, strange way. But he had learned what it was to suffer through his own fault, and now he was to learn what it was to suffer through no fault of his own, and without the consolation of saying 'I was wrong! I was to blame!' At the end of the two years there was another child, and his wife died."

The four sat silently smoking until Jack Barnes asked:

"And what did he do then, Peter?"

"Who?" said Peter, abstractedly.

"Why, Gentleman Once."

Peter roused himself.

"Well, I've told the story, and it is about time to turn in," he said. "I can't say exactly what Gentleman Once did when his wife died. He might have gone down to a deeper depth than Danny's. He might have risen higher than he had ever been before. From what I knew of his character he would never have gone down an easy slope as Danny has done. He might have dropped plump at first and then climbed up. Anyway, he had the memory of the last two years to help him.

"Then there's the reformed drunkard who has trained himself to take a drink when he needs it, to drink in moderation—he's the strongest character of all, I think—but it's time to turn in."

The cornet up the creek was playing a march.

Peter walked across and looked at Danny, who seemed to be sleeping as peacefully as could be expected of him.

Jack Barnes got up and walked slowly down the creek in the moonlight. He wanted to think.

Peter rolled out his blankets on the grass and arranged his saddle-bags for a pillow. Before he turned in Mitchell shook hands with him, a most unusual and unnecessary proceeding in camp. But there's something in the bush grip which means "I know," or "I understand."

Joe Wilson rolled out his blankets close to Mitchell's camp; he wanted to enjoy some of Mitchell's quiet humour before he went to sleep, but Mitchell wasn't in a philosophical mood. He wanted to reflect.

"I wonder who Gentleman Once was?" said Joe to Mitchell. "Could he have been Danny, or old Awful Example back there at the shanty?"

"Dunno," said Mitchell. He puffed three long puffs at his pipe, and then said, reflectively:

"I've heard men tell their own stories before to-night, Joe."

It was Joe who wanted to think now.

About four o'clock Mitchell woke and stood up. Peter was lying rolled in his blanket with his face turned to the west. The moon was low, the shadows had shifted back, and the light was on Peter's face. Mitchell stood looking at him reverently, as a grown son night who sees his father asleep for the first time. Then Mitchell quietly got some boughs and stuck them in the ground at a little distance from Peter's head, to shade his face from the bright moonlight; and then he turned in again to sleep till the sun woke him.

THE GHOSTS OF MANY CHRISTMASES

Did you ever trace back your Christmas days?—right back to the days when you were innocent and Santa Claus was real. At times you thought you were very wicked, but you never realize how innocent you were until you've grown up and knocked about the world.

Let me think!

Christmas in an English village, with bare hedges and trees, and leaden skies that lie heavy on our souls as we walk, with overcoat and umbrella, sons of English exiles and exiles in England, and think of bright skies and suns overhead, and sweeps of country disappearing into the haze, and blue mountain ranges melting into the azure of distant lower skies, and curves of white and yellow sand beaches, and runs of shelving yellow sandstone sea-walls—and the glorious Pacific! Sydney Harbour at sunrise, and the girls we took to Manly Beach.

Christmas in a London flat. Gloom and slush and soot. It is not the cold that affects us Australians so much, but the horrible gloom. We get heart-sick for the sun.

Christmas at sea—three Christmases, in fact—one going saloon from Sydney to Westralia early in the Golden Nineties with funds; and one, the Christmas after next, coming back steerage with nothing but the clothes we'd slept in. All of which was bad judgment on our part—the order and manner of our going and coming should have been reversed.

Christmas in a hessian tent in "th' Western," with so many old mates from the East that it was just old times over again. We had five pounds of corned beef and a kerosene-tin to boil it in; and while we were talking of old things the skeleton of a kangaroo-dog grabbed the beef out of the boiling water and disappeared into the scrub—which made it seem more like old times than ever.

Christmas going to New Zealand, with experience, by the s.s. *Tasmania*. We had plum duff, but it was too "soggy" for us to eat. We dropped it overboard, lest it should swamp the boat—and it sank to the ooze. The *Tasmania* was saved on that occasion, but she foundered next year outside Gisborne. Perhaps the cook had made more duff. There was a letter from a sweetheart of mine amongst her mails when she went down; but that's got nothing to do with it, though it made some difference in my life.

Christmas on a new telegraph line with a party of lining gangmen in New Zealand. There was no duff nor roast because there was no firewood within twenty miles. The cook used to pile armfuls of flax-sticks under the billies, and set light to them when the last man arrived in camp.

Christmas in Sydney, with a dozen invitations out to dinner. The one we accepted was to a sensible Australian Christmas dinner; a typical one, as it should be, and will be before the Commonwealth is many years old. Everything cold except the vegetables, the hose playing on the veranda and vines outside, the men dressed in sensible pyjama-like suits, and the women and girls fresh and cool and jolly, instead of being hot and cross and looking like boiled

carrots, and feeling like boiled rags, and having headaches after
dinner, as would have been the case had they broiled over the fire in
a hot kitchen all the blazing forenoon to cook a scalding indigestible
dinner, as many Australian women do, and for no other reason than
that it was the fashion in England. One of those girls was very pretty
and—ah, well!—

Christmas dinner in a greasy Sydney sixpenny restaurant, that
opened a few days before with brass band going at full blast at the
door by way of advertisement. "Roast-beef, one! Cabbage and
potatoes, one! Plum pudding, two!" (That was the first time I dined
to music.) The Christmas dinner was a good one, but my appetite
was spoilt by the expression of the restaurant keeper, a big man with
a heavy jowl, who sat by the door with a cold eye on the sixpences,
and didn't seem to have much confidence in human nature.

Christmas—no, that was New Year—on the Warrego River, out
back (an alleged river with a sickly stream that looked like bad
milk). We spent most of that night hunting round in the dark and
feeling on the ground for camel and horse droppings with which to
build fires and make smoke round our camp to keep off the
mosquitoes. The mosquitoes started at sunset and left off at
daybreak, when the flies got to work again.

Christmas dinner under a brush shearing-shed. Mutton and plum
pudding—and fifty miles from beer!

An old bush friend of mine, one Jimmy Nowlett, who ranked as a
bullock-driver, told me of a Christmas time he had. He was cut off
by the floods with his team, and had nothing to eat for four days but
potatoes and honey. He said potatoes dipped in honey weren't so
bad; but he had to sleep on bullock yokes laid on the ground to keep
him out of the water, and he got a toothache that paralysed him all
down one side.

And speaking of plum pudding, I consider it one of the most
barbarous institutions of the British. It is a childish, silly, savage
superstition; it must have been a savage inspiration, looking at it all
round—but then it isn't so long since the British were savages.

I got a letter last year from a mate of mine in Western
Australia—prospecting the awful desert out beyond White
Feather—telling me all about a "perish" he did on plum pudding.
He and his mates were camped at the Boulder Soak with some three
or four hundred miles—mostly sand and dust—between them and
the nearest grocer's shop. They ordered a case of mixed canned
provisions from Perth to reach them about Christmas. They didn't
believe in plum pudding—there are a good many British institutions
that bushmen don't believe in—but the cook was a new chum, and

he said he'd go home to his mother if he didn't have plum pudding for Christmas, so they ordered a can for him. Meanwhile, they hung out on kangaroo and damper and the knowledge that it couldn't last for ever. It was in a terrible drought, and the kangaroos used to come into the "Soak" for water, and they were too weak to run. Later on, when wells were dug, the kangaroos used to commit suicide in them—there was generally a kangaroo in the well in the morning.

The storekeeper packed the case of tinned dog, etc., but by some blunder he or his man put the label on the wrong box, and it went per rail, per coach, per camel, and the last stage per boot, and reached my friends' camp on Christmas Eve, to their great joy. My friend broke the case open by the light of the camp-fire.

"Here, Jack!" he said, tossing out a can, "here's your plum pudding."

He held the next can in his hand a moment longer and read the label twice.

"Why! he's sent two," he said, "and I'm sure I only ordered one. Never mind—Jack'll have a tuck-out."

He held the next can close to the fire and blinked at it hard.

"I'm damned if he hasn't sent three tins of plum pudding. Never mind, we'll manage to scoff some of it between us. You're in luck's way this trip, Jack, and no mistake."

He looked harder still at the fourth can; then he read the labels on the other tins again to see if he'd made a mistake.

He didn't tell me what he said then, but a milder mate suggested that the storekeeper had sent half a dozen tins by mistake. But when they reached the seventh can the language was not even fit to be written down on a piece of paper and handed up to the magistrate. The storekeeper had sent them an unbroken case of canned plum pudding, and probably by this time he was wondering what had become of that blanky case of duff.

The kangaroos disappeared about this time and my friend tells me that he and his mates had to live for a mortal fortnight on canned plum pudding. They tried it cold and they tried it boiled, they tried it baked, they had it fried, and they had it toasted, they had it for breakfast, dinner and tea. They had nothing else to think, or talk, or argue and quarrel about; and they dreamed about it every night, my friend says. It wasn't a joke—it gave them the nightmare and day-horrors.

They tried it with salt. They picked as many of the raisins out as they could and boiled it with salt kangaroo. They tried to make Yorkshire pudding out of it; but it was too rich.

My friend was experimenting and trying to discover a simple process for separating the ingredients of plum pudding when a fresh supply of provisions came along. He says he was never so sick of anything in his life, and he has had occasion to be sick of a good many things.

The new-chum jackeroo is still alive, but he won't ever eat plum pudding any more, he says. It cured him of home-sickness. He wouldn't eat it even if his bride made it.

Christmas on the goldfields in the last of the roaring days, in the palmy days of Gulgong and those fields. Let's see! it must be nearly thirty years ago! Oh, how the time goes by!

Santa Claus, young, fresh-faced and eager; Santa Claus, blonde and flaxen; Santa Claus, dark; Santa Claus with a brogue and Santa Claus speaking broken English; Santa Claus as a Chinaman (Sun Tong Lee & Co. storekeepers), with strange, delicious sweets that melted in our mouths, and rum toys and Chinese dolls for the children.

Lucky diggers who were with difficulty restrained from putting pound notes and nuggets and expensive lockets and things into the little ones' stockings. Santa Claus in flannel shirt and clay-covered moleskins. Diggers who bought lollies by the pound and sent the little ones home with as much as they could carry.

Diggers who gave a guinea or more for a toy for a child that reminded them of some other child at home. Diggers who took as many children as they could gather on short notice into a store, slapped a five-pound note down on the counter and told the little ones to call for whatever they wanted. Who set a family of poor children side by side on the counter and called for a box of mixed children's boots—the best—and fitted them on with great care and anxiety and frequent inquiries as to whether they pinched. Who stood little girls and boys on the counter and called for the most expensive frocks, the latest and best in sailor suits, and the brightest ribbons; and things came long distances by bullock dray and were expensive in those days. Impressionable diggers—and most of them were—who threw nuggets to singers, and who, sometimes, slipped a parcel into the hands of a little boy or girl, with instructions to give it to an elder sister (or young mother, perhaps) whom the digger had never spoken to, only worshipped from afar off. And the elder sister or young mother, opening the parcel, would find a piece of jewellery or a costly article of dress, and wonder who sent it.

Ah, the wild generosity of luck-intoxicated diggers of those days!

and the reckless generosity of the drinkers. "We thought it was going to last for ever!"

"If I don't spend it on the bairns I'll spend it on the drink," Sandy Burns used to say. "I ha' nane o' me own, an' the lass who was to gi' me bairns, she couldn't wait."

Sandy had kept steady and travelled from one end of the world to the other, and roughed it and toiled for five years, and the very day he bottomed his golden hole on the Brown Snake Lead at Happy Valley he got a letter from his girl in Scotland to say she had grown tired of waiting and was married. Then he drank, and drink and luck went together.

Gulgong on New Year's Eve! Rows and rows of lighted tents and camp-fires, with a clear glow over it all. Bonfires on the hills and diggers romping round them like big boys. Tin kettling—gold dishes and spoons, and fiddles, and hammers on pointing anvils, and sticks and empty kerosene-tins (*they* made a row); concertinas and cornets, shot-guns, pistols and crackers, all sorts of instruments, and "Auld Lang Syne" in one mighty chorus.

And now—a wretched little pastoral town; a collection of glaring corrugated-iron hip-roofs, and maybe a rotting propped-up bark or weather-board humpy or two—relics of the roaring days; a dried-up storekeeper and some withered hags; a waste of caved-in holes with rain-washed mullock heaps and quartz and gravel glaring in the sun; thistles and burrs where old bars were; drought, dryness, desolation and goats.

Lonely graves in the bush and grey old diggers here and there, anywhere in the world, doing anything for a living, lonely yet because of the girls who couldn't wait, but prospecting and fossicking here and there, and dreaming still.

They thought it was going to last for ever.

Christmas at Eurunderee Creek, amongst the old selection farms in the western spurs of the Blue Mountains. They used to call it "Th' Pipeclay" thirty years ago, but the old black names have been restored. They make plum puddings yet, weeks beforehand, and boil them for hours and hang them in cloths to the rafters to petrify; then they take them down and boil them again. On Christmas Eve the boys cut boughs or young pines on the hills, and drag them home and lash them to the veranda-posts.

Ted has turned up with his wife and children from his selection out back. The wheat is in and shearing is over on the big stations. Tom—steady-going old Tom—clearing or fencing or dam-sinking up-country, hides his tools in the scrub and gets his horse and rides home. Aunt Emma (to everyone's joy) has arrived from Sydney with presents (astonishing bargains in frocks, etc.) and marvellous descriptions of town life.

Joe, "poor" Mary's husband, who has been droving in Queensland since the Christmas before last—while poor Mary, who is afraid to live alone, shared a skillion and the family quarrels at home—Joe rides day and night and reaches home at sunrise on Christmas morning, tired and dusty, gaunt and haggard, but with his last cheque intact. He kisses his wife and child and throws himself on the bed to sleep till dinner-time, while Mary moves round softly, hushes the baby, dresses it and herself, lays out Joe's clean things, and bends over him now and then, and kisses him, perhaps, as he sleeps.

In the morning the boys and some of the men go down to the creek for a swim in the big shady pool under the she-oaks and take their Sunday clothes with them and dress there.

Some of them ride into town to church, and some of the women and children drive in in spring-carts—the children to go to Sunday school, leaving mother and the eldest daughter—usually a hard-worked, disappointed, short-tempered girl—at home to look after the cooking.

There is some anxiety (mostly on mother's part) about Jim, who is "wild," and is supposed to be somewhere out back. There was "a piece of blue paper" out for Jim on account of sweating (illegally using) a horse, but his mother or father has got a hint—given in a kindly way by the police-sergeant—that Jim is free to come home and stay at home if he behaves himself. (There is usually a horse missing when Jim goes out back.)

Jim turns up all right—save that he has no money—and is welcomed with tearful affection by his favourite sister Mary, shakes hands silently with his father, and has a long whispered conversation with his mother, which leaves him very subdued. His brothers forbear to sneer at him, partly because it is Christmas, partly on mother's account, and thirdly, because Jim can use his hands. Aunt Emma, who is fond of him, cheers him up wonderfully.

The family sit down to dinner. "An old mate of your father's"—a bearded old digger—has arrived and takes the place of honour. ("I knowed yer father, sonny, on the diggings long afore any of you was ever thought on.")

The family have only been a few hours together, yet there is an undercurrent of growling, that, to the stranger, mysterious yet evident undercurrent of nastiness and resentment which goes on in ll families and drags many a promising young life down. But Aunt Emma and the old mate make things brighter, and so the dinner—of hot roast and red-hot plum pudding—passes off fairly well.

The men sleep the afternoon away and wake up bathed in perspiration and helpless; some of the women have headaches. After tea they gather on the veranda in the cool of the evening, and that's the time when the best sides of their natures and the best parts of the past have a chance of coming uppermost, and perhaps they begin to feel a bit sorry that they are going to part again.

The local races or "sports" on Boxing Day. There is nothing to keep the boys home over New Year. Ted and his wife go back to their lonely life on their selection; Tom returns to his fencing or tank-sinking contract; Jim, who has borrowed "a couple of quid" from Tom, goes out back with strong resolutions for the New Year, and shears "stragglers," breaks in horses, cooks and clerks for survey parties, and gambles and drinks, and gets into trouble again. Maybe Joe "knocks about" the farm a bit before going into the Great North-West with another mob of cattle.

The last time I saw the Old Year out at Eurunderee the bush-fires were burning all over the ranges, and looked like great cities lighted up. No need for bonfires then Christmas in Bourke, the metropolis of the great pastoral scrubs and plains, five hundred miles west, with the thermometer one-hundred-and-something-scarey in the shade. The rough, careless shearers come in from stations many dusty miles out in the scrubs to have their Christmas sprees, to drink and "shout" and fight—and have the horrors some of them—and be run in and locked up with difficulty, within sound of a church-going bell.

The Bourke Christmas is a very beery and exciting one. The hotels shut up in front on Christmas Day to satisfy the law (or out of consideration for the feelings of the sergeant in charge of the police station), and open behind to satisfy the public, who are supposed to have made the law.

Sensible cold dinners are the fashion in Bourke, I think, with the nose going, and free-and-easy costumes.

The free males take their blankets and sleep in the "park;" the women sleep with doors and windows open, and the married men on mattresses on the verandas across the open doors—in case of accidents.

Christmas in Sydney, though Christmas holidays are not so popular as Easter, or even Anniversary Day, in the Queen city of the South. Buses, electric, cable and the old steam trams crowded with holiday-makers with baskets. Harbour boats loaded down to the water's edge with harbour picnic-parties. "A trip round the harbour

and to the head of Middle Harbour one shilling return!" Strings o
tourist trains running over the Blue Mountains and the Grea
Zigzag, and up the coast to Gosford and Brisbane Water, and dow
the south coast to beautiful Illawarra, until after New Year
Hundreds of young fellows going out with tents to fish in lonely bay
or shoot in the mountains, and rough it properly like bushmen—no
with deck chairs, crockery, a piano and servants. For you can cam
in the grand and rugged solitude of the bush within a stone's throw
of the city, so to speak.

Jolly camps and holiday parties all round the beautiful bays of th
harbour, and up and down the coast, and all close to home. Camp
in the moonlight on sandy beaches under great dark bluffs an
headlands, where yellow, shelving, sandstone cliffs run, broken onl
by sandy-beached bays, and where the silver-white breakers lea
and roar.

And Manly Beach on a holiday! Thousands of people in fresl
summer dress, hundreds of bare-legged, happy children running
where the "blue sea over the white sand rolls," racing in and ou
with the rollers, playing with the glorious Pacific. Manly—"Ou
Village"—Manly Beach, where we used to take our girls, with th
most beautiful harbour in the world on one side, and the width of th
grandest ocean on the other. Ferny gullies and "fairy dells" to nortl
and south, and every shady nook its merry party or happy couple

Manly Beach—I remember five years ago (oh, how the time goe
by!)—and two names that were written together in the sand whe
the tide was coming in.

And the boat home in the moonlight, past the Heads, where w
felt the roll of the ocean, and the moonlit harbour—and the harbou
lights of Sydney—the grandest of them all.

THE RISING OF THE COURT

THE RISING OF THE COURT

Oh, then tell us, Kings and Judges, where our meeting is to be,
When the laws of men are nothing, and our spirits all are free—
When the laws of men are nothing, and no wealth can hold the fort,
There'll be thirst for mighty brewers at the Rising of the Court.

The same dingy court room, deep and dim, like a well, with the clock high up on the wall, and the doors low down in it; with the bench, which, with some gilding, might be likened to a gingerbread imitation of a throne; the royal arms above it and the little witness box to one side, where so many honest poor people are bullied, insulted and laughed at by third-rate blackguardly little "lawyers," and so many pitiful, pathetic and noble lies are told by pitiful sinners and disreputable heroes for a little liberty for a lost self, or for the sake of a friend—of a "pal" or a "cobber." The same overworked and underpaid magistrate trying to keep his attention fixed on the same old miserable scene before him; as a weary, overworked and underpaid journalist or author strives to keep his attention fixed on his proofs. The same row of big, strong, healthy, good-natured policemen trying not to grin at times; and the police-court solicitors ("the place stinks with 'em," a sergeant told me) wrangling over some miserable case for a crust, and the "reporters," shabby some of them, eager to get a brutal joke for their papers out of the accumulated mass of misery before them, whether it be at the expense of the deaf, blind, or crippled man, or the alien.

And opposite the bench, the dock, divided by a partition, with the women to the left and the men to the right, as it is on the stairs or the block in polite society. They bring children here no longer. The same shaking, wild-eyed, blood-shot-eyed and blear-eyed drunks and disorderlies, though some of the women have nerves yet; and the same decently dressed, but trembling and conscience-stricken little wretch up for petty larceny or something, whose motor car bosses of a big firm have sent a solicitor, "manager," or some understrapper here to prosecute and give evidence.

But, over there, on a form to one side of the bench—opposite the witness box—and as the one bright spot in this dark, and shameful, and useless scene—and in a patch of sunlight from the skylight as it happens—sit representatives of the Prisoners' Aid Society, Prison Gate and Rescue Brigades, etc. (one or two of the ladies in nurses' uniforms), who are come to help us and to fight for us against the Law of their Land and of ours, God help us!

Mrs Johnson, of Red Rock Lane, is here, and her rival in revolution, One-Eyed Kate, and Cock-Eyed Sal, and one or two of the other aristocrats of the alley. And the weeping bedraggled remains of what was once, and not so long ago, a pretty, slight, fair-haired and blue-eyed Australian girl. She is up for inciting One-Eyed Kate to resist the police. Also, Three-Pea Ginger, Stousher, and Wingy, for some participation in the row amongst the aforementioned ladies. (Wingy, by the way, is a ratty little one-armed man, whose case is usually described in the head-line, as "A 'Armless Case," by one of our great dailies.) And their pals are waiting outside in the vestibule—Frowsy Kate (The Red Streak), Boko Bill, Pincher and his "piece," etc., getting together the stuff for the possible fines, and the ten-bob fee for the lawyer, in one case, and ready to swear to anything, if called upon. And I myself— though I have not yet entered Red Rock Lane Society—on bail, on a charge of "plain drunk." It was "drunk and disorderly" by the way, but a kindly sergeant changed it to plain drunk—(though I always thought my drunk was ornamental).

Yet I am not ashamed—only comfortably dulled and a little tired—dully interested and observant, and hopeful for the sunlight presently. We low persons get too great a contempt for things to feel much ashamed at any time; and this very contempt keeps many of us from "reforming." We hear too many lies sworn that we *know* to be lies, and see too many unjust and brutal things done that we know to be brutal and unjust.

But let us go back a bit, and suppose we are still waiting for the magistrate, and think of Last Night. "Silence!"—but from no human voice this time. The whispering, shuffling, and clicking of the court typewriter ceases, the scene darkens, and the court is blotted out as a scene is blotted out from the sight of a man who has thrown himself into a mesmeric trance. And:

Drink—lurid recollection of being "searched"—clang of iron cell door, and I grope for and crawl on to the slanting plank. Period of oblivion—or the soul is away in some other world. Clang of cell door again, and soul returns in a hurry to take heed of another soul, belonging to a belated drunk on the plank by my side. Other soul says:

"Gotta match?"

So we're not in hell yet.

We fumble and light up. They leave us our pipes, tobacco and matches; presently, one knocks with his pipe on the iron trap of the door and asks for water, which is brought in a tin pint-pot. Then follow intervals of smoking, incoherent mutterings that pass for conversation, borrowings of matches, knockings with the pannikin on the cell door wicket or trap for more water, matches, and bail; false and fitful starts into slumber perhaps—or wild attempts at flight on the part of our souls into that other world that the sober and sane know nothing of; and, gradually, suddenly it seems, reason (if this world is reasonable) comes back.

"What's your trouble?"

"Don't know. Bomb outrage, perhaps."

"Drunk?"

"Yes."

"What's yours?"

"Same boat."

But presently he is plainly uneasy (and I am getting that way, too, to tell the truth), and, after moving about, and walking up and down in the narrow space as well as we can, he "rings up" another policeman, who happens to be the fat one who is to be in charge all night.

"Wot's up here?"

"What have I been up to?"

"Killin' a Chinaman. Go to sleep."

Policeman peers in at me inquiringly, but I forbear to ask questions.

Blankets are thrown in by a friend of mine in the force, though we are not entitled to them until we are bailed or removed to the "paddock" (the big drunks' dormitory and dining cell at the Central), and we proceed to make ourselves comfortable. My mate wonders whether he asked them to send to his wife to get bail, and hopes he didn't.

They have left our wicket open, seeing, or rather hearing, that we are quiet. But they have seemingly left some other wickets open also, for from a neighbouring cell comes the voice of Mrs Johnson holding forth. The locomotive has apparently just been run into the cleaning sheds, and her fires have not had time to cool. They say that Mrs Johnson was a "lady once," like many of her kind; that she is not a "bad woman"—that is, not a woman of loose character—but gets money sent to her from somewhere—from her "family," or her husband, perhaps. But when she lets herself loose—or, rather, when the beer lets her loose—she is a tornado and a terror in Red Rock Lane, and it is only her fierce, practical kindness to her unfortunate or poverty-stricken sisters in her sober moments that keeps her forgiven in that classic thoroughfare. She can certainly speak "like a lady" when she likes, and like an intelligent, even a clever, woman—not like a "woman of the world," but as a woman who knew and knows the world, and is in hell. But now her language is the language of a rough shearer in a "rough shed" on a blazing hot day.

After a while my mate calls out to her:

"Oh! for God's sake give it a rest!"

Whereupon Mrs Johnson straightway opens on him and his ancestry, and his mental, moral, and physical condition—especially the latter. She accuses him of every crime known to Christian countries and some Asiatic and ancient ones. She wants to know how long he has been out of jail for kicking his wife to pieces that time when she was up as a witness against him, and whether he is in for the same thing again? (She has never set eyes on him, by the way, nor he on her.)

He calls back that she is not a respectable woman, and he knows all about her.

Thereupon she shrieks at him and bangs and kicks at her door, and demands his name and address. It would appear that she *is* a respectable woman, and hundreds can prove it, and she is going to make him prove it in open court.

He calls back that his name is Percy Reginald Grainger, and his town residence is "The Mansions," Macleay Street, next to Mr Isaacs, the magistrate, and he also gives her the address of his solicitor.

She bangs and shrieks again, and states that she will get his name from the charge sheet in the morning and have him up for criminal libel, and have his cell mate up as a witness—and hers, too. But just here a policeman comes along and closes her wicket with a bang and cuts her off, so that her statements become indistinct, or come only as shrieks from a lost soul in an underground dungeon. He also threatens to cut us off and smother us if we don't shut up. I wonder whether they've got her in the padded cell.

We settle down again, but presently my fellow captive nudges me and says: "Listen!" From another cell comes the voice of a woman singing—the girl who is in for "inciting to resist, your worship," in fact. "Listen!" he says, "that woman could sing once." Her voice is low and sweet and plaintive, as of a woman who had been a singer but had lost her voice. And what do you think it is?

> The crowd in accents hushed reply—
> "Jesus of Nazareth passeth by."

Mrs Johnson's cell is suddenly silent. Then, not mimickingly, mockingly, or scornfully, but as if the girl is a champion of Jesus of Nazareth, and is hurt at the ignorance of the multitude, and pities *Him*:

> Now who is this Jesus of Nazareth, say?

The policeman, coming along the passage, closes the wicket in her door, but softly this time, and not before we catch the plaintive words again.

> The crowd in accents hushed reply—
> "Jesus of Nazareth passeth by."

My fellow felon throws the blanket off him impatiently, sits up with a jerk, and gropes for his pipe.

"God!" he says. "But this is red hot! Have you got another match?"

I wonder what the Nazarene would have to say about it.

Sleep for a while. I wonder whether they'll give us time, or we'll be able to sleep some of our sins off in the end, as we sleep our drink off here? Then "The Paddock" and daylight; but there's little time for the Paddock here, for we must soon be back in court. The men borrow and lend and divide tobacco, lend even pipes, while some break up hard tobacco and roll cigarettes with bits of newspaper. If it is Sunday morning, even those who have no hope for bail, and have a long horrible day and night before them, will sometimes join in a cheer as the more fortunate are bailed. But the others have tea and bread and butter brought to them by one of the Prisoners' Aid Societies, who ask for no religion in return. They come to save bodies, and not to fish for souls. The men walk up and down and to and fro, and cross and recross incessantly, as caged men and animals always do—and as some uncaged men do too.

"Any of you gentlemen want breakfast?" Those who have money and appetites order; some order for the sake of the tea alone; and some "shout" two or three extra breakfasts for those who had nothing on them when they were run in. We low people can be very kind to each other in trouble. But now it's time to call us out by the lists, marshal us up in the passage, and draft us into court. Ladies first. But I forgot that I am out on bail, and that the foregoing belongs to another occasion. Or was it only imagination, or hearsay? Journalists have got themselves run in before now, in order to see and hear and feel and smell for themselves—and write.

"Silence! Order in the Court." I come like a shot out of my nightmare, or trance, or what you will, and we all rise as the magistrate takes his seat. None of us noticed him come in, but he's there, and I've a quaint idea that he bowed to his audience. Kindly, humorous Mr Isaacs, whom we have lost, always gave me that idea. And, while he looks over his papers, the women seem to group themselves, unconsciously as it were, with Mrs Johnson as front centre, as though they depended on her in some vague way. She has slept it off and tidied, or been tidied, up, and is as clear-headed as she ever will be. Crouching directly behind her, supported and comforted on one side by One-Eyed Kate, and on the other by Cock-Eyed Sal, is the poor bedraggled little resister of the Law, sobbing convulsively, her breasts and thin shoulders heaving and shaking under her openwork blouse—the girl who seemed to pity Jesus of Nazareth last night in her cell. There's very little inciting to resist about her now. Most women can cry when they like, I know, and many have cried men to jail and the gallows; but *here* in *this place*, if a woman's tears can avail her anything, who, save perhaps a police-court solicitor and gentleman-by-Act-of-Parliament, would, or dare, raise a sneer.

I wonder what the Nazarene would have to say about it if He came in to speak for her. But probably they'd send Him to the receiving house as a person of unsound mind, or give Him worse punishment for drunkenness and contempt of court.

His Worship looks up.

Mrs Johnson (from the dock): "Good morning, Mr Isaacs. How do you do? You're looking very well this morning, Mr Isaacs."

His Worship (from the Bench): "Thank you, Mrs Johnson. I'm feeling very well this morning."

There's a pause, but there is no "laughter." The would-be satellites don't know whom the laugh might be against. His Worship bends over the papers again, and I can see that he is having trouble with that quaintly humorous and kindly smile, or grin, of his. He has as hard a job to control his smile and get it off his face as some magistrates have to get a smile on to theirs. And there's a case

coming by and by that he'll have to look a bit serious over.
However—

"Jane Johnson!"

Mrs Johnson is here present, and reminds the Sergeant that she is.

Then begins, or does begin in most courts, the same dreary old
drone, like the giving out of a hymn, of the same dreary old charge:
"You — Are — Charged — With — Being — Drunk — And —
Disorderly — In — Such — And — Such — A — Street — How
— Do — You — Plead — Guilty — Or — Not — Guilty?" But
they are less orthodox here. The "disorderly" has dropped out of
Mrs Johnson's charge somehow, on the way from the charge room.
I don't know what has been going on behind the scenes, but,
anyway, it is Christmas-time, and the Sergeant seems anxious to
let Mrs Johnson off lightly. It means anything from twenty-four
hours or five shillings to three months on the Island for her. The
lawyers and the police—especially the lawyers—are secretly afraid
of Mrs Johnson.

However, again—

The Sergeant: "This woman has not been here for six weeks, your
Worship."

Mrs Johnson (who has him set and has been waiting for him for a
year or so): "It's a damned lie, Mr Isaacs. I was here last
Wednesday!" Then, after a horrified pause in the Court: "But I beg
your pardon, Mr Isaacs."

His Worship's head goes down again. The "laughter" doesn't
come here, either. There is a whispered consultation, and (it being
Christmas-time) they compromise with Mrs Johnson for "five
shillings or the risin'," and she thanks his Worship and is escorted
out, rather more hurriedly than is comportable with her dignity, for
she remarks about it.

The members of the Johnsonian sisterhood have reason to be
thankful for the "lift" she has given them, for they all get off lightly,
and even the awful resister of Law-an'-order is forgiven.
Mrs Johnson has money and is waiting outside to stand beers for
them; she always shouts for the boys when she has it. And—what
good does it all do?

It is very hard to touch the heart of a woman who is down, though
they are intensely sympathetic amongst themselves. It is nearly as
hard as it is to combat the pride of a hard-working woman in
poverty. It was such women as Mrs Johnson, One-Eyed Kate, and
their sisters who led Paris to Versailles, and a King and a Queen

died for it. It is such women as Mrs Johnson and One-Eyed Kate and their sisters who will lead a greater Paris to a greater Versailles some day, and many "Trust" kings and queens, and their princes and princesses shall die for it. And that reminds me of two reports in a recent great daily:

Miss Angelina De Tapps, the youngest daughter of the well-known great family of brewers, was united in the holy bonds of matrimony to Mr Reginald Wells—(here follows a long account of the smart society wedding). The happy pair leave *en route* for Europe per the —— next Friday.

Jane Johnson, an old offender, again faced the music before Mr Isaacs, S.M., at the Central yesterday morning—(here follows a "humorous" report of the case).

Next time poor Mrs Johnson will leave *en route* for "Th' Island" and stay there three months.

The sisters join Mrs Johnson, who has some money and takes them to a favourite haunt and shouts for them—as she does for the boys sometimes. Their opinions on civilization are not to be printed.

Ginger and Wingy get off with the option, and, though the fine is heavy, it is paid. They adjourn with Boko Bill, and their politics are lurid.

Squinny Peters (plain drunk—five bob or the risin'), who is peculiar for always paying his fine, elects to take it out this time. It appears that the last time Squinny got five bob or the risin' he ante'd up the splosh like a man, and the court rose immediately, to Squinny's intense disgust. He isn't taking any chances this time.

Wild-Flowers-Charley, who recently did a fortnight, and has been out on bail, has had a few this morning, and, in spite of warnings from and promises to friends, insists on making a statement, though by simply pleading guilty he might get off easily. The statement lasts some ten minutes. Mr Isaacs listens patiently and politely and remarks:

"Fourteen days."

Charley saw the humour of it afterwards, he says.

But what good does it all do?

I had no wish to treat drunkenness frivolously in beginning this sketch; I have seen women in the horrors—that ought to be enough.

"ROLL UP AT TALBRAGAR"

Jack Denver died at Talbragar when Christmas Eve began,
And there was sorrow round the place, for Denver was a man;
Jack Denver's wife bowed down her head—her daughter's grief was wild,
And big Ben Duggan by the bed stood sobbing like a child.
But big Ben Duggan saddled up, and galloped fast and far,
To raise the longest funeral ever seen on Talbragar.

                                                        —*Ben Duggan.*

Both funerals belonged to Big Ben Duggan in a way, though Jack Denver was indirectly the cause of both.

Jack Denver was reckoned the most popular man in the district (outside the principal township)—a white man and a straight man—a white boss and a straight sportsman. He was a squatter, though a small one; a real squatter who lived on his run and worked with his men—no dummy, super, manager for a bank, or swollen cockatoo about Jack Denver. He was on the committees at agricultural shows and sports, great at picnics and dances, beloved by school children at school feasts (I wonder if they call them feasts still), giver of extra or special prizes, mostly sovs. and half-sovs., for foot races, etc.; leading spirit for the scrub district in electioneering campaigns—they went as right as men could go in the politics of those days who watched and went the way Jack Denver went; header of subscription lists for burnt-out, flooded-out, sick, hurt, dead or killed or otherwise knocked-out selectors and others, or their families; barracker and agitator for new provisional schools, assister of his Reverence and little bush chapels, friend of all manner of wanderers—careless, good-hearted scamps in trouble, broken-hearted new chums, wrecks and failures and outcasts of any colour or creed, and especially of old King Jimmy and the swiftly vanishing remnant of his tribe. His big slab-and-shingle and brick-floored kitchen, with its skillions, built on more generous plans and specifications than even the house itself, was the wanderer's goal and home in bad weather. And—yes, owner, on a small scale, of racehorses, and a keen sportsman.

Jack Denver and Big Ben Duggan were boys together on the old selections, and at the new provisional bark school at Pipeclay; they went into the Great North-West together—"where all the rovers go"—stock-riding and droving and over-landing, and came back after a few years bronzed and seasoned and with wild yarns.

Jack married and settled down on a small run his father had bought near Talbragar, and his generous family of tall, straight bush boys and tall, straight bush girls grew up and had their sweethearts. But, when Jack married, Big Ben Duggan went back again, up into Queensland and the Great North-West, with a makeshift mate who had also lost his mate through marriage. Ever and again, after one, and two, and three years—the periods of absence lengthening as the years went on—Big Ben Duggan would come back home, and stay a while (till the Great North-West began to call insistently) at Denver's, where he would be welcomed jubilantly by all—even the baby who had never seen him—for there was "something about the man." And, until late on the night of his return, he and Jack would sit by the fire in winter, or outside on the wood-heap in summer, and yarn long and fondly about the Wide Places, and strange things they knew and understood.

How sudden things are! Ben was back (just in time for the holidays and the Mudgee races) out of the level lands, where distance dwells in her halls of shimmering haze, after following her for five years.

They were riding home from the races, the women and children in carts and buggies, the men and boys on horseback—of course. They raced each other along the road, across short cuts, through scrub and timber, and back to the slow-coming overloaded vehicles again, some riding wildly and recklessly. Jack Denver was amongst them, his heart warmed with good luck at the races, good whisky to wet it, and the return of his old mate. "We're as good as the best of the young 'uns yet, Ben!" he cried, as they swung through the trees. "Ain't we, you old ——?"

And then and there it happened.

A new chum suggested that Jack had more than he thought aboard and was thrown from his horse; but the new chum was repudiated with scorn and bad words and indignation by bushmen and bushwomen alike—as indeed he would be by any bushman who had seen a drunken rider ride.

"I learnt him to ride when he was a kiddy about so high," said old Break-the-News Fosbery, resentfully gasping and gulping, "and Jack wasn't thrown." It was thought at first that his horse had shied and run him against a tree, or under an overhanging branch; but Ben Duggan had seen it, and explained the thing to the doctor with that strange calmness or quietness that comes to men in the midst of a life's grief. Jack was riding loosely, and swung forward just as the filly, a fresh young thing, threw back her head; and it struck him with sledge-hammer force, full in the face.

He was dead, even before they got him to Anderson's Halfway Inn. There was wild racing back to town for doctors, and some accidents; one horse was killed and another ridden to death. Others went as a forlorn hope in search of Doc. Wild, eccentric Yankee bush "quack," who had once saved one of Denver's little girls from diphtheria; others, again, for Peter M'Laughlan, bush missionary, to face the women—for they couldn't.

Big Ben Duggan, blubbering unashamed by the bedside, put his hand on Mrs Denver's shoulder, as she crouched there, wild-eyed, like a hunted thing. "Nev—never mind, Mrs Denver!" he blurted out, with a note as of indignation and defiance—just for all the world as if Jack Denver had done a wrong thing and the district was down on him—"he'll have the longest funeral ever seen in these parts! Leave that to me." Then some of the women took her out to her daughter's. Big Ben Duggan gave terse instructions to some of the young riders about, and then, taking the best and freshest horse, the cross-country scrub swallowed him—west. The young men jumped on their horses and rode, fan-like, east.

They took Jack Denver home. They always took their dead home first, whenever possible, and no matter the distance, before taking them to their last long home; and they do it yet, I suppose. They are not always so particular about it in cities, from what I've seen.

But this was a strange funeral. They had arranged mattress and sheet in the bottom of a four-wheeler, and covered him with sheet, blanket, and quilt, though the weather was warm; and over the body, from side to side of the trap, they had stretched the big dark-green table-cloth from Anderson's dinning-room. The long, ghostly, white, cleared government road between the dark walls of timber in the moonlight. The buggies and carts behind, and the dead-white faces and glistening or despairingly staring eyes of the women—wife, daughters, and nieces, and those who had come to help and comfort. The men—sons and brothers, and few mates and chums and sweethearts—riding to right and left like a bodyguard, to comfort and be comforted who needed comfort.

Now and again a brother or son—mostly a brother—riding close to the wheel, would suddenly throw out his arm on the mud splasher of buggy or cart, and, laying his head on it, sob as he rode, careless of tyre and spokes, till a woman pushed him off gently:

"Take care of the wheel, Jim—mind the wheel."

The eldest son held the most painful position, by his mother's side in the first buggy, supported by an aunt on the other side, while somebody led his horse. In the next buggy, between two daughters, sat a young fellow who was engaged to one of them—they were to be married after the holidays. The poor girls were white and worn out; he had an arm round each, and now and again they rested their heads on his shoulders. The younger girl would sleep by fits and starts, the sleep of exhaustion, and start up half laughing and happy, to be stricken wild-eyed the next moment by terrible reality. Some couldn't realize it at all—and to most of them all things were very dreamy, unreal and far away on that lonely, silent road in the moonlight—silent save for the slow, stumbling hoofs of tired horses, and the deliberate, half-hesitating clack-clack of wheel-boxes on the axles.

Ben Duggan rode hard, as grief-stricken men ride—and walk. At Cooyal he woke up the solitary storekeeper and told him the news; then along that little-used old road for some miles both ways, and back again, rousing prospectors and fossickers, the butcher of the neighbourhood, clearers, fencers, and timber-getters, in hut and tent.

"Who's that?"

"What's up?"

"What's the matter?"

"Ben Duggan! Jack Denver's dead! Killed ridin' home from the races! Funeral's to-morrow. Roll up at Talbragar or the nearest point you can get to on the government road. Tell the neighbours and folks."

"Good God! How did it happen?"

But the hoofs of Ben's horse would be clattering or thudding away into the distance.

He struck through to Dunne's selection—his brother-in-law, who had not been to the races; then to Ross's farm—Old Ross was against racing, but struck a match at once and said something to his auld wife about them black trousers that belonged to the black coat and vest.

Then Ben swung to the left and round behind the spurs to the school at Old Pipeclay, where he told the schoolmaster. Then west again to Morris's and Schneider's lonely farms in the deep estuary of Long Gully, and through the gully to the Mudgee-Gulgong road at New Pipeclay. The long, dark, sullenly-brooding gully through which he had gone to school in the glorious bush sunshine with Jack Denver, and his sweetheart—now but three hours his hopelessly-stricken widow; Bertha Lambert, Ben's sweetheart—married now, and newly a grandmother; Harry Dale—drowned in the Lachlan; Lucy Brown—Harry's school-day and boy-and-girl sweetheart—

dead; and—and all the rest of them. Far away, far away—and near away: up in Queensland and out on the wastes of the Never-Never. Riding and camping, hardship and comfort, monotony and adventure, drought, flood, blacks, and fire; sprees and—the rest of it. Long dry stretches on Dead Man's Track. Cutting across the country in No Man's Land where there were no tracks into the Unknown. Chancing it and damning it. Ill luck and good luck. Laughing at it afterwards and joking at it always; he and Jack—always he and Jack—till Jack got married. The children used to say Long Gully was haunted, and always hurried through it after sunset. It was haunted enough now all right.

But, raising the gap at the head of the gully, he woke suddenly and came back from the hazy, lazy plains; the

> Level lands where Distance hides in her halls of shimmering haze,
> And where her toiling dreamers ride towards her all their days;

where "these things" are ever far away, and Distance ever near—and whither he had drifted, the last hour, with Jack Denver, from the old Slab School.

"I wonder whether old Fosbery's got through yet?" he muttered, with nervous anxiety, as he looked down on the cluster of farms and scattered fringe of selections in the broad moonlight. "I wonder if he's got there yet?" Then, as if to reassure himself: "He must have started an hour before me, and the old man can ride yet." He rode down towards a farm on Pipeclay Creek, about the centre of the cluster of farms, vineyards, and orchards.

Old Fosbery—otherwise Break-the-News—was a character round there. If he was handy and no woman to be had, he was always sent to break the news to the wife of a digger or bushman who had met with an accident. He was old, and world-wise, and had great tact—also great experience in such matters. Bad news had been broken to him so many times that he had become hardened to it, and he had broken bad news so often that he had come to take a decided sort of pleasure in it—just as some bushmen are great at funerals and will often travel miles to advise, and organize, and comfort, and potter round a burying and are welcomed. They had broken the news to old Fosbery when his boy went wrong and was "taken" ("when they took Jim"). They had broken the news to old Fosbery when his daughter, Rose, went wrong, and bolted with Flash Jack Redmond. They had broken the news to the old man when young Ted was thrown from his horse and killed. They had broken the news to the old man when the unexpected child of his old age and hopes was accidentally burnt to death. So the old man knew how it felt.

The farm was the home of one of Jack Denver's married sisters, and, as there was no woman to go so far in the night, they had sent old Fosbery to tell her. Folks were most uneasy and anxious, by the way, when they saw old Fosbery coming unexpectedly, and sometimes some of them got a bad start—but it helped break the news.

"Well, if he ain't there, I suppose I'll have to do it," thought Ben as he passed quietly through the upper sliprails and neared the house. "The old man might have knocked up or got drunk after all. Anyway, no one might come in the morning till it's too late—it always happens that way—and—besides, the women'll want time to look up their black things."

But, turning the corner of the cow-yard, he gave a sigh of relief as he saw old Fosbery's horse tied up. They were up, and the big kitchen lighted; he caught a glimpse of a shock of white hair and bushy white eyebrows that could have belonged to no one except old Break-the-News. They were sitting at the table, the tearful wife pouring out tea, and by the tokens Ben knew that old Fosbery had been very successful. He rode quietly to the lower sliprails, let them down softly, led his horse carefully over them, put them up cautiously, and stood in a main road again. He paused to think, leaning one arm on his saddle and tickling the nape of his neck with his little finger; his jaw dropped, reflecting and grief forgotten in the business on hand, and the horse "gave" to him, thinking he was about to mount. He was tired—weary with that strange energetic weariness that cannot rest. It was five miles from Mudgee and the news was known there and must have spread a bit already; but the bulk of the Gulgong and Gulgong Road race-goers had passed here before the accident. Anyway, he thought he might as well go over and tell old Buckolts, of the big vineyard, across the creek, who was a great admirer of Jack Denver and had been drinking with him at the races that day. Old Buckolts was a man of weight in the district, and was always referred to by all from his old wife down, as "der boss," and by no other term. The old slab farmhouse and skillions and out-houses, and the new square brick house built in front, were all asleep in the moonlight. The dogs woke the old man first (as was generally the case), as Ben opened the big white home gate and passed through without dismounting.

"Who's dat? Who voss die [there]?" shouted the old man as the horse's hoofs crunched on the white creek-bed gravel between the two houses.

"Ben Duggan!"

"Vot voss der matter?"

"Jack Denver's dead—killed riding home from the races."

"Vot dat you say?"

Ben repeated.

"Go avay! Go home and go to sleep! You voss shoking—and trunk. Vat for you gum by my house mit a seely cock mit der bull shtory at dis hour of der night?"

"It's only too true, Mr Buckolts," said Ben. "I wish to God it wasn't."

"You've got der yoomps, Pen. Go to der poomp and poomp on your head and den turn in someveers till ter morning. I tells von of der poys to gif you a nip and show you a poonk. Vy! I trink mit Shack Denver not twelf hour ago!"

But Ben persisted: "I'm not drunk, Mr Buckolts, and I ain't got the horrors—I wish to God I was an' had. Poor Jack was killed near Anderson's, riding home, about six o'clock."

Though Ben couldn't see him, he could feel and hear by his tones, that old Buckolts sat up in bed suddenly.

"*Mein Gott!* How did it happen, Pen?"

Ben told him.

"Ven and veer voss der funeral?"

Ben told him.

"Frett! Shonny! Villie! Sharley!" shouted the old man at the top of his voice to the boys sleeping in the old house. "Get up and pring all der light horses in from der patticks, and gif dem a goot feet mit plenty corn; and get der double-parreled puggy ant der sinkle puggy and der three spring carts retty. Dere vill pe peoples vanting lifts to-morrow. Ant get der harnesses and sattles retty. Vake up, olt vomans!" (Mrs Buckolts must have been awake by this time.) "Call der girls ant see to dere plack tresses. Py Gott, ve *moost* do dis thing in style. Does his poor sister know over dere across the creeks, Pen? Durn out! you lazy, goot-for-noddings, or I will chain you up on an ants' bed mit a rope like a tog; do you not hear that Shack Denver voss dett?"

"I vill sent some of der girls over dere first thing in der morning. Holt on, Pen, ant I vill sent you out some vine."

Ben rode with the news to Lee's farm where Maurice Lee—at feud with Buckolts and a silent man—was, for he had known Denver all his life, and had gone, in his young days, on a long droving trip with him and Ben Duggan.

A little later Ben returned to the main road on a fresh horse. He turned towards Gulgong, and rode hard, past the new bark provisional school and along the sidings. He left the news at Con O'Donnell's lonely tin grocery and sly-grog shop, perched on the hillside—("God forgive us all!" said Con O'Donnell). He left the news at the tumble-down public-house, among the huts and thistles and goats that were left of the Log Paddock Rush. There were goats on the veranda and the place seemed dead; but there were startled replies and inquiries and matches struck. He left the news at Newton's selection, and Old Bones Farm, and at Foley's at the foot of Lowe's Peak, close under the gap between Peak and Granite Ridge. Then he turned west, at right angles to the main road, and took a track that was deserted except for one farm and on every alternate Sunday. He passed the lonely little slab bush "chapel" of the locality, that broke startlingly out of the scrub by the track side as he reached it; and left the news at Southwick's farm at the end of the blind track. At more than one farm he left the bushwoman hurriedly looking up her "black things," and at more than one, one of the boys getting his bridle to catch his horse and ride elsewhere with the news.

Ben rode back, through the moonlight and the moon-shadow haunted paddocks, and the naked, white, ringbarked trees, along Snakes Creek, parallel with the main road he had recently travelled till he struck Pipeclay Creek again lower down. He turned down the track towards the river, and at the junction left word at Lowe's—one of the old land-grant families. The dogs woke an old handy man (who had been "sent out" in past ages for "knocking a donkey off a hen-roost"—as most of them were) and Ben told him to tell the family.

At Belinfante's Bridge across the Cudgegong Ben struck a big camp of bullock-drivers, some going down with wool and some going back for more.

"Hold on, Ben," cried Jimmy Nowlett, from his hammock under his wagon as Ben was riding off—"Hold on a minute! I want to look at yer."

Jimmy got his head out of his bunk very cautiously and carefully, and his body after it—there were nut ends of bolts, a heavy axle, and extremely hard projections, points, and corners within a very few short inches of his chaff-filled sugar-bag pillow. Slipping cannily on to his hands and knees, he crawled out under the tail-board, dragging his "moles" after him, and stood outside in the moonlight shaking himself into his trousers.

Jimmy was a little man who always wore a large size in mole-skins—for some reason best known to himself—or more probably for no reason at all; or because of a habit he'd got into accidentally years ago—or because of the motherly trousers his mother used to build for him when he was a boy. And he always shook himself into his pants after the manner of a woman shaking a pillow into a clean slip; his chin down on his chest and his jaw dropped, as if he'd take himself in his teeth, after the manner of the woman with a pillow, were he not prevented by sound anatomical reasons.

"You look reg'lerly tuckered out, Ben," he said, "an' yer horse could do with a spell too. Git down, man, and have a pint er tea and a bite."

Ben got down wearily and knew at once how knocked up he was. He sat right down on the hard ground, embracing and drawing up his knees, and felt as if he'd like never to get up again: while Jimmy shook some chaff and corn that he carried for his riding hack into a box for the horse, and his travelling mate, Billy Grimshaw, lifted his big namesake half full of cold tea, on to the glowing coals by the burning log—looking just like an orang-outang in a Crimean shirt.

Ben got a fresh horse at Alfred Gentle's farm under the shadow of Granite Ridge, and then on to Canadian (th' Canadian Lead of the roaring days), which had been saved from the usual fate by becoming a farming township. Here he roused and told the storekeeper. Then up the creek to Home Rule, dreariest of deserted diggings.

He struck across the ages-haunted bush, and up Chinaman's Creek, past "the Chinamen's Graves," and through the scrub and over the ridges for the Talbragar Road. For he had to see Jack Denver home from start to finish.

Glaring, hot and dusty, lay the long, white road; coated with dust that felt greasy to the touch and taste. The coffin was in a four-wheeled trap, for the solitary hearse that Mudgee boasted then was to meet them some three miles ou beldown—at the racecourse, as it happened, by one of those eternal ironies of fate. (Johns, the undertaker, had had another job that morning.) The long string of buggies and carts and horsemen; other buggies and carts and horsemen drawn respectfully back amongst the trees here and there along the route; male hats off and held rigidly vertical with right ears as the coffin passed; and drivers waiting for a chance to draw into the line.

Think of it; up early on the first morning, a long day at the races, a long journey home, awake and up all night with grief and sympathy. Some of the men had ridden till daylight; the women, worn out and exhausted, had perhaps an hour or so of sleep towards morning—yet they were all there, except Ben Duggan, on the long, hot, dusty road back, heads swimming in the heat and faces and hands coated with perspiration and dust—and never, never once breaking out of a slow walk. It would have been the same had it been pouring with rain. I have seen funerals trotting fast in London, and they are trotting more and more in Australian cities, with only "the time" for an excuse. But in the bush I have never seen a funeral faster than the slowest of walks no matter who or what might wait, or what might happen or be lost. They stood by their dead well out there. Maybe some of the big, simple souls had a sort of vague idea that the departed would stand a better show if accompanied as far as possible by the greatest possible number of friends—"barrackers," so to speak.

Here all the shallow and involuntary sham of it, the shirking of a dull and irksome duty—a bore, though the route be only a mile or so. The satisfied undertaker, and the hard-up professional mutes and mourners in seedy, mouldy, greeny-black, and with boozers' faces and noses and a constant craving for beer to help them bear up against their grief and keep their mock solemn faces. Out there you were carried to the hearse or trap from your home, and from the hearse or trap to your grave—and with infinite carefulness and gentleness—on the shoulders of men, and of men who had known and loved you.

There had been wonder and waiting in the morning for Ben Duggan; and the women especially, on the way home, when free from restraint, were greatly indignant against him. To think that he should break out and go on the drunk on this day of all days, when his oldest mate and friend was being carried to his grave. The men, knowing how he had ridden all night, found great excuses; but later on some grew anxious and wondered what could have become of him.

Some, returning home by a short cut, passed over Dead Man's Gap beyond Lowe's Peak.

"Wonder what could have become of Ben Duggan," mused one, as they rode down.

There and then their wonders ceased.

A party of road-clearers had been at work along the bottom, and there was much smoke from the burning-off, which must have made the track dim and vague and uncertain at night. Just at the foot of the gap, clear of the rough going, a newly-fallen tree lay across the track. It was stripped—had been stripped late the previous afternoon, in fact; and, well, you won't know what a log like that is when the sap is well up until you have stepped casually on to it to take a look round. A confident skip, with your boot soles well greased, on to the ice in a glaciarium for the first time would be nothing to it in its results, I fancy. (I remember we children used to scrape the sap off, and eat it with satisfaction, if not with relish—white box I think the trees were.)

Ben must have broken into a canter as he reached the level, as indeed his horse's tracks showed he did, and the horse must have blundered in the smoke, or jumped too long or too short; anyway, his long slithering shoe marks were in the sap on the log, and he lay there with a broken leg and shoulder. He had struck it near the stump and the sharp edge of an outcrop of rock.

There was more breakneck riding, and they got a cart and some bedding and carried Ben to Anderson's, which was handiest, if not nearest, and there was more wild and reckless riding for the doctor.

One got a gun, and rode back to shoot the horse.

Ben's case was hopeless from the first. He was hurt close to that big heart of his, as well as having a fractured skull. He talked a lot of the selections and old John Tierney, of the old bark school, and the Never-Never country with Jack—and, later on, of the present. "What's Ben sayin' now, Jim?" asked one young bushman as another came out of the room with an awestruck face.

"He's sayin' that Jack Denver's dead, killed ridin' home from the races, an' that the funeral's to-morrow, an' we're to roll up at Talbragar!" answered the other, with wide eyes, a blank face and in an awed voice. "He's thinkin' to-day's yisterday."

But towards the end, under the ministrations of the doctor, Ben became conscious. He rolled his head a little on the pillow after he woke, and then, seeming to remember all that happened up to his stunning fall, he asked quietly:

"What sort of a funeral did Jack have?"

They told him it was the biggest ever seen in the district.

"Muster bin more'n a mile long," said one.

"Watcher talkin' about, Jim?" put in another. "Yer talkin' through yer socks. It was more'n a mile an' a half, Ben, if it was er inch. Some of the chaps timed it an' measured it an' compared notes as well as they could. Why, the head was at the Rececourse when the tail was at Old——"

Ben sank back satisfied and a little later took the track that Jack Denver had taken.

WANTED BY THE POLICE

Could it have been the Soul of Man and none higher that gave spoken and written word to the noblest precepts of human nature? For the deeper you sound it the more noble it seems, in spite of all the wrong, injustice, sin, sorrow, pain, religion, atheism, and cynics in the world. We make (or are supposed to make, or allow others to make) laws for the protection of society, or property, or religion, or what you will; and we pay thousands of men like ourselves to protect those laws and see them carried out; and we build and maintain expensive offices, police stations, court-houses and jails for the protecting and carrying out of those laws, and the punishing of men—like ourselves—who break them. Yet, in our heart of hearts we are antagonistic to most of the laws, and to the Law as a whole (which we regard as an ass), and to the police magistrates and the judges. And we hate lawyers and loathe spies, pimps, and informers of all descriptions and the hangman with all our soul. For the Soul of Man says: Thou shalt not refuse refuge to the outcast, and thou shalt not betray the wanderer.

And those who do it we make outcast.

So we form Prisoners' Aid Societies, and Prisoners' Defence Societies, and subscribe to them and praise them and love them and encourage them to protect or defend men from the very laws that we pay so dearly to maintain. And how many of us, in the case of a crime against property—and though the property be public and ours—would refuse tucker to the hunted man, and a night's shelter from the pouring rain and the scowling, haunting, threatening, and terrifying darkness? Or show the police in the morning the track the poor wretch had taken? I know I couldn't.

The Heart of Man says: Thou shalt not.

At country railway stations, where the trains stop for refreshments, when a prisoner goes up or down in charge of a policeman, a native delicacy prevents the local loafers from seeming to notice him; but at the last moment there is always some hand to thrust in a clay pipe and cake of tobacco, and maybe a bag of sandwiches to the policeman.

And, when a prisoner escapes, in the country at least—unless he be a criminal maniac in for a serious offence, and therefore a real danger to society—we all honestly hope that they won't catch him, and we don't hide it. And, if put in a corner, most of us would help them not to catch him.

The thing came down through the ages and survived through the dark Middle Ages, as all good things come down through the ages and survive through the blackest ages. The hunted man in the tree, or cave, or hole, and strangers creeping to him with food in the darkness, and in fear and trembling; though he was, as often happened, an enemy to their creed, country, or party. For he was outcast, and hungry, and a wanderer whom men sought to kill.

These were mostly poor people or peasants; but it was so with the rich and well-to-do in the bloody Middle Ages. The Catholic country gentleman helping the Protestant refugee to escape disguised as a manservant (or a maidservant), and the Protestant country gentleman doing likewise by a hunted Catholic in his turn, as the battles went. Rebel helping royalist, and royalist helping rebel. And always, here and there, down through those ages, the delicate girl standing with her back to a door and her arms outstretched across it, and facing, with flashing eyes, the soldiers of the king or of the church—or entertaining and bluffing them with beautiful lies—to give some poor hunted devil time to hide or escape, though she a daughter of royalists and the church, and he a rebel to his king and a traitor to his creed. For they sought to kill him.

There was sanctuary in those times, in the monkeries and the churches, where the soldiers of the king dared not go, for fear of God. There has been sanctuary since, in London and other places, where His or Her Majesty's police dared not go because of the fear of man. The "Rocks" was really sanctuary, even in my time—also Woolloomooloo. Now the only sanctuary is the jail.

And, not so far away, my masters! Down close to us in history, and in Merrie England, during Judge Jeffreys's "Bloody Assize," which followed on the Monmouth rebellion and formed the blackest page in English history, "a worthy widow named Elizabeth Gaunt was burned alive at Tyburn, for having sheltered a wretch who himself gave evidence against her. She settled the fuel about herself with her own hands, so that the flames should reach her quickly; and nobly said, with her last breath, that she had obeyed the sacred command of God, to give refuge to the outcast and not to betray the wanderer." (Charles Dickens's *History of England*.)

Note, I am not speaking of rebel to rebel, or loyalist to loyalist, or comrade to comrade, or clansman to clansman in trouble—that goes without saying—but of *man and woman to man and woman in trouble*, the highest form of clannishness, the clannishness that embraces the whole of this wicked world—the Clan of Mankind!

French people often helped English prisoners of war to escape to the coast and across the water, and English people did likewise by the French; and none dared raise the cry of "traitors." It was the highest form of patriotism on both sides. And, by the way, it was, is, and shall always be the women who are first to pity and help the rebel refugee or the fallen enemy.

Succour thine enemy.

There must have been a lot of human kindness under the smothering, stifling cloud of the "System" and behind the iron clank and swishing "cat" strokes of brutality—a lot of soul light in the darkness of our dark past—a page that has long since been closed down—when innocent men and women were transported to shame, misery, and horror; when mere boys were sent out on suspicion of stealing a hare from the squire's preserves, and mere girls on suspicion of lifting a ribband from the merchant's counter. But the many kindly and self-sacrificing and even noble things that free and honest settlers did, in those days of loneliness and hardship, for wretched runaway convicts and others, are closed down with the pages too. My old grandmother used to tell me tales, but—well, I don't suppose a wanted man (or a man that wasn't wanted, for that matter) ever turned away from her huts, far back in the wild bush, without a quart of coffee and a "feed" inside his hunted carcass, or went short of a bit of bread and meat to see him on, and a gruff but friendly hint, maybe, from the old man himself. And they were a type of the early settlers, she an English lady and the daughter of a clergyman. Ah! well——

Do you ever seem to remember things that you could not possibly remember? Something that happened in your mother's life, maybe, if you are a girl, or your father's if you are a boy—that happened *to* your mother or father some years, perhaps, before you were born. I have many such haunting memories—as of having once witnessed a murder, or an attempt at murder, for instance, and once seeing a tree fall on a man—and as a child I had a memory of having been a man myself once before. But here is one of the pictures.

A hut in a dark gully; slab and stringy-bark, two rooms and a detached kitchen with the boys' room roughly partitioned off it. Big clay fire-place with a big log fire in it. The settler, or selector, and his wife; another man who might have been "uncle," and a younger woman who might have been "aunt;" two little boys and the baby. It was raining heavens hard outside, and the night was as black as pitch. The uncle was reading a report in a paper (that seemed to have come, somehow, a long way from somewhere) about two men who were wanted for sheep- and cattle-stealing in the district. I decidedly remember it was during the reign of the squatters in the nearer west. There came a great gust that shook the kitchen and caused the mother to take up the baby out of the rough gin-case cradle. The father took his pipe from his mouth and said: "Ah, well! poor devils." "I hope they're not out in a night like this, poor fellows," said the mother, rocking the child in her arms. "And I hope they'll never catch 'em," snapped her sister. "The squatters has enough."

"I wonder where poor Jim is?" the mother moaned, rocking the baby, and with two of those great, silent tears starting from her haggard eyes.

"Oh don't start about Jim again, Ellen," said her sister impatiently. "He can take care of himself. You were always rushing off to meet trouble half-way—time enough when they come, God knows."

"Now, look here, Ellen," put in Uncle Abe, soothingly, "he was up in Queensland doing well when we last heerd of him. Ain't yer never goin' to be satisfied?"

Jim was evidently another and a younger uncle, whose temperament from boyhood had given his family constant cause for anxiety.

The father sat smoking, resting his elbow on his knee, bunching up his brush of red whiskers, and looking into the fire—and back into his own foreign past in his own foreign land perhaps: and, it may be, thinking in his own language.

Silence and smoke for a while; then the mother suddenly straightened up and lifted a finger:

"Hush! What's that? I thought I heard someone outside."

"Old Poley coughin'," said Uncle Abe, after they'd listened a space. "She must be pretty bad—oughter give her a hot bran mash." (Poley was the best milker.)

"But I fancied I heard horses at the sliprails," said the mother.

"Old Prince," said Uncle Abe. "Oughter let him into the shed."

"Hush!" said the mother, "there's someone outside." There *was* a step, as of someone retreating after peeping through a crack in the door, but it was not old Poley's step; then, from farther off, a cough that was like old Poley's cough, but had a rack in it.

"See who it is, Peter," said the mother. Uncle Abe, who was dramatic and an ass, slipped the old double-barrelled muzzle-loader from its leathers on the wall and stood it in the far corner and sat down by it. The mother, who didn't seem to realize anything, frowned at him impatiently. The coughing fit started again. It was a man.

"Who's there? Anyone outside there?" said the settler in a loud voice.

"It's all right. Is the boss there? I want to speak to him," replied a voice with no cough in it. The tone was reassuring, yet rather strained, as if there had been an accident—or it might be a cautious policeman or bushranger reconnoitring.

"Better see what he wants, Peter," said his sister-in-law quietly. "Something's the matter—it may be the police."

Peter threw an empty bag over his shoulders, took the peg from the door, opened it and stepped out. The racking fit of coughing burst forth again, nearer. "That's a churchyarder!" commented Uncle Abe.

The settler came inside and whispered to the others, who started up, interested. The coughing started again outside. When the fit was over the mother said:

"Wait a minute till I get the boys out of the road and then bring them in." The boys were bundled into the end room and told to go to bed at once. They knelt up on the rough bed of slabs and straw mattress, instead, and applied eyes and ears to the cracks in the partition.

The mother called to the father, who had gone outside again. "Tell them to come inside, Peter."

"Better bring the horses into the yard first and put them under the shed," said the father to the unknown outside in the rain and darkness. Clatter of sliprails let down and tired hoofs over them, and sliprails put up again; then they came in.

Wringing wet and apparently knocked up, a tall man with black curly hair and beard, black eyes and eyebrows that made his face seem the whiter; dressed in tweed coat, too small for him and short at the sleeves, strapped riding-pants, leggings, and lace-up boots, all sodden. The other a mere boy, beardless or clean shaven, figure and face of a native, but lacking in something; dressed like his mate—like drovers or stockmen. Arms and legs of riders, both of them; cabbage-tree hats in left hands—as though the right ones had to be kept ready for something (and looking like it)—pistol butts probably. The young man had a racking cough that seemed to wrench and twist his frame as the settler steered him to a seat on a stool by the fire. (In the intervals of coughing he glared round like a watched and hunted sneak-thief—as if the cough was something serious against the law, and he must try to stop it.)

"Take that wet coat off him at once, Peter," said the settler's wife, "and let me dry it." Then, on second thoughts: "Take this candle and take him into the house and get some dry things on him."

The dark man, who was still standing in the doorway, swung aside to let them pass as the settler steered the young man into the "house;" then swung back again. He stood, drooping rather, with one hand on the door-post; his big, wild, dark eyes kept glancing round and round the room and even at the ceiling, seeming to overlook or be unconscious of the faces after the first keen glance, but always coming back to rest on the door in the partition of the boys' room opposite.

"Won't you sit down by the fire and rest and dry yourself?" asked the settler's wife, rather timidly, after watching him for a moment.

He looked at the door again, abstractedly it seemed, or as if he had not heard her.

Then Uncle Abe (who, by the way, was supposed to know more than he should have been supposed to know) spoke out.

"Set down, man! Set down and dry yerself. There's no one there except the boys—that's the boys' room. Would yer like to look through?"

The man seemed to rouse himself from a reverie. He let his arm and hand fall from the doorpost to his side like dead things. "Thank you, missus," he said, apparently unconscious of Uncle Abe, and went and sat down in front of the fire.

"Hadn't you better take your wet coat off and let me dry it?"

"Thank you." He took off his coat, and, turning the sleeves inside out, hung it from his knees with the lining to the fire; then he leaned forward, with his hands on his knees, and stared at the burning logs and steam. He was unarmed, or, if not, had left his pistols in the saddle-bag outside.

Andy Page, general handy-man (who was there all the time, but has not been mentioned yet, because he didn't mention anything himself which seemed necessary to this dark picture), now remarked to the stranger, with a wooden-face expression but a soft heart, that the rain would be a good thing for the grass, mister, and make it grow; a safe remark to make under the present, or, for the matter of that, under any circumstances.

The stranger said, "Yes, it would."

"It will make it spring up like anything," said Andy.

The stranger admitted that it would.

Uncle Abe joined in, or, rather, slid in, and they talked about the drought and the rain and the state of the country, in monosyllables mostly, with "Jesso," and "So it is," and "You're right there," till the settler came back with the young man dressed in rough and patched, but dry, clothes. He took another stool by his mate's side at the fire, and had another fit of coughing. When it was over, Uncle Abe remarked:

"That's a regular churchyarder yer got, young feller."

The young fellow, too exhausted to speak, even had he intended doing so, turned his head in a quick, half-terrified way and gave it two short jerky nods.

The settler had brought a bottle out—it was gin they kept for medicine. They gave him some hot, and he took it in his sudden, frightened, half-animal way, like a dog that was used to ill-usage.

"He ought to be in the hospital," said the mother.

"He ought to be in bed right now at once," snapped the sister. "Couldn't you stay till morning, or at least till the rain clears up?" she said to the elder man. "No one ain't likely to come near this place in this weather."

"If we did he'd stand a good chance to get both hospital and a bed pretty soon, and for a long stretch, too," said the dark man grimly. "No, thank you all the same, miss—and missus—I'll get him fixed up all right and safe before morning."

The father came into the end room with a couple of small feed boxes and both boys tumbled under the blankets. The father emptied some chaff, from a bag in the corner, into the boxes, and then dished some corn from another bag into the chaff and mixed it well with his hands. Then he went out with the boxes under his arms, and the boys got up again.

The mother had brought two chairs from the front room (I remember the kind well: black painted hardwood that were always coming to pieces and with apples painted on the backs). She stood them with their backs to the fire and, taking up the young man's wet clothes, which the settler had brought out under his arm and thrown on a stool, arranged them over the backs of chairs and the stool to dry. He lost some of his nervousness or scared manner under the influence of the gin, and answered one or two questions with reference to his complaint.

The baby was in the cradle asleep. The sister drew boiling water from the old-fashioned fountain over one side of the fire and made coffee. The mother laid the coarse brownish cloth and set out the camp-oven bread, salt beef, tin plates, and pintpots. This was always called "setting the table" in the bush.

"You'd better have it by the fire," said the bush-wife to the dark man.

"Thank you, missus," he said, as he moved to a bench by the table, "but it's plenty warm enough here. Come on, Jack."

Jack, under the influence of another tot, was in a fit state to sit down to a table something like a Christian, instead of coming to his food like a beaten dog.

The hum of bush common-places went on. One of the boys fell across the bed and into deep slumber; the other watched on awhile, but must have dozed.

When he was next aware, he saw, through the cracks, the taller man putting on his dried coat by the fire; then he went to a rough "sofa" at the side of the kitchen, where the young man was sleeping—with his head and shoulders curled in to the wall and his arm over his face, like a possum hiding from the light—and touched him on the shoulder.

"Come on, Jack," he said, "wake up."

Jack sprang to his feet with a blundering rush, grappled with his mate, and made a break for the door.

"It's all right, Jack," said the other, gently yet firmly, holding and shaking him. "Go in with the boss and get into your own clothes—we've got to make a start." The other came to himself and went inside quietly with the settler. The dark man stretched himself, crossed the kitchen and looked down at the sleeping child; he returned to the fire without comment. The wildness had left his eyes. The bushwoman was busy putting some tucker in a sugar-bag. "There's tea and sugar and salt in these mustard tins, and they won't get wet," she said, "and there's some butter too; but I don't know how you'll manage about the bread—I've wrapped it up, but you'll have to keep it dry as well as you can."

"Thank you, missus, but that'll be all right. I've got a bit of oil-cloth," he said.

They spoke lamely for a while, against time; then the bushwoman touched the spring, and their voices became suddenly low and earnest as they drew together. The stranger spoke as at a funeral, but the funeral was his own.

"I don't care about myself so much," he said, "for I'm tired of it, and—and—for the matter of that I'm tired of everything; but I'd like to see poor Jack right, and I'll try to get clear myself, for his sake. You've seen him. I can't blame myself, for I took him from a life that was worse than jail. You know how much worse than animals some brutes treat their children in the bush. And he was an 'adopted.' You know what that means. He was idiotic with ill-treatment when I got hold of him. He's sensible enough when away with me, and true as steel. He's about the only living human thing I've got to care for, or to care for me, and I want to win out of this hell for his sake."

He paused, and they were all silent. He was measuring time, as his next words proved: "Jack must be nearly ready now." Then he took a packet from some inside pocket of his blue dungaree shirt. It was wrapped in oil-cloth, and he opened it and laid it on the table; there was a small Bible and a packet of letters—and portraits, maybe.

"Now, missus," he said, "you mustn't think me soft, and I'm neither a religious man nor a hypocrite. But that Bible was given to me by my mother, and her hand-writing is in it, so I couldn't chuck it away. Some of the letters are hers and some—someone else's. *You* can read them if you like. Now, I want you to take care of them for me and dry them if they are a little damp. If I get clear I'll send for them some day, and, if I don't—well, I don't want them to be taken with me. I don't want the police to know who I was, and what I was, and who my relatives are and where they are. You wouldn't have known, if you *do* know now, only your husband knew me on the diggings, and happened to be in the court when I got off on that first cattle-stealing charge, and recognized me again to-night. I can't thank you enough, but I want you to remember that I'll never forget. Even if I'm taken and have to serve my time I'll never forget it, and I'll live to prove it."

"We—we don't want no thanks, an' we don't want no proofs," said the bushwoman, her voice breaking.

The sister, her eyes suspiciously bright, took up the packet in her sharp, practical way, and put it in a work-box she had in the kitchen.

The settler brought the young fellow out dressed in his own clothes. The elder shook hands quietly all round, or, rather, they shook hands with him. "Now, Jack!" he said. They had fastened an oilskin cape round Jack's shoulders.

Jack came forward and shook hands with a nervous grip that he seemed to have trouble to take off. "I won't forget it," he said; "that's all I can say—I won't forget it." Then they went out with the settler. The rain had held up a little. Clatter of sliprails down and up, but the settler didn't come back.

"Wonder what Peter's doing?" said the wife.

"Showin' 'em down the short cut," said Uncle Abe.

But, presently, clatter of sliprails down again, and cattle driven over them.

"Wonder what he's doing with the cows," said the wife.

They waited in wonder, and with growing anxiety, for some quarter of an hour; then Abe and Andy, going out to see, met the settler coming back.

"What in thunder are you doing with the cows, Peter?" asked Uncle Abe.

"Oh, just driving them out and along a bit over those horse tracks; we might get into trouble," said Peter.

When the boys woke it was morning, and the mother stood by the bed. "You needn't get up yet, and don't say anyone was here last night if you're asked," she whispered, and went out. They were up on their knees at once with their eyes to the cracks, and got the scare of their young lives. Three mounted troopers were steaming their legs at the fire—their bodies had been protected by oilskin capes. The mother was busy about the table and the sister changing the baby. Presently the two younger policemen sat down to bread and bacon and coffee, but their senior (the sergeant) stood with his back to the fire, with a pint-pot of coffee in his hand, eating nothing, but frowning suspiciously round the room.

Said one of the young troopers to Aunt Annie, to break the lowering silence, "You don't remember me?"

"Oh yes, I do; you were at Brown's School at Old Pipeclay—but I was only there a few months."

"You look as if you didn't get much sleep," said the senior-sergeant, bluntly, to the settler's wife, "and your sister too."

"And so would you," said Aunt Annie, sharply, "if you were up with a sick baby all night."

"Sad affair that, about Brown the schoolmaster," said th
younger trooper to Aunt Annie.

"Yes," said Aunt Annie, "it was indeed."

The senior-sergeant stood glowering. Presently he said brutally—
"The baby don't seem to be very sick; what's the matter with it?"

The young troopers move uneasily, and one impatiently.

"You should have seen her" (the baby) "about twelve o'clock las
night," said Aunt Annie, "we never thought she would live till th
morning."

"Oh, didn't you?" said the senior-sergeant, in a half-and-ha[l]
tone.

The mother took the baby and held it so that its face was hidde[n]
from the elder policeman.

"What became of Brown's family, miss?" asked the youn[g]
trooper. "Do you remember Lucy Brown?"

"I really don't know," answered Aunt Annie, "all I know is tha[t]
they went to Sydney. But I think I heard that Lucy was married."

Just then Uncle Abe and Andy came in to breakfast. Andy sa[t]
down in the corner with a wooden face, and Uncle Abe, who was [a]
tall man, took up a position with his back to the fire, by the side [of]
the senior trooper, and seemed perfectly at home and at ease. H[e]
lifted up his coat behind, and his face was a study in bucoli[c]
unconsciousness. The settler passed through to the boy's room
(which was harness room, feed room, tool house, and several othe[r]
things), and as he passed out with a shovel the sergeant said, "S[o]
you haven't seen anyone along here for three days?"

"No," said the settler.

"Except Jimmy Marshfield that took over Barker's selection i[n]
Long Gully," put in Aunt Annie. "He was here yesterday. Do yo[u]
want him?"

"An' them three fellers on horseback as rode past the corner of th[e]
lower paddock the day afore yesterday," mumbled Uncle Abe, "bu[t]
one of 'em was one of the Coxes' boys, I think."

At the sound of Uncle Abe's voice both women started and pale[d]
and looked as if they'd like to gag him, but he was safe.

"What were they like?" asked the constable.

The women paled again, but Uncle Abe described them. He ha[d]
imagination, and was only slow where the truth was concerne[d].

"Which way were they going?" asked the constable.

"Towards Mudgee" (the police-station township), said Uncl[e]
Abe.

The constable gave his arm an impatient jerk and dropped Uncl[e]
Abe.

Uncle Abe looked as if he wanted badly to wink hard at someone, but there was no friendly eye in the line of wink that would be safe.

"Well, it's strange," said the sergeant, "that the men we're after didn't look up an out-of-the-way place like this for tucker, or horse-feed, or news, or something."

"Now, look here," said Aunt Annie, "we're neither cattle duffers nor sympathizers; we're honest, hard-working people, and God knows we're glad enough to see a strange face when it comes to this lonely hole; and if you only want to insult us you'd better stop it at once. I tell you there's nobody been here but old Jimmy Marshfield for three days, and we haven't seen a stranger for over a fortnight, and that's enough. My sister's delicate and worried enough without you." She had a masculine habit of putting her hand up on something when holding forth, and as it happened it rested on the work-box on the shelf that contained the cattle-stealer's mother's Bible; but if put to it, Aunt Annie would have sworn on the Bible itself.

"Oh well, no offence, no offence," said the constable. "Come on, men, if you've finished, it's no use wasting time round here."

The two young troopers thanked the mother for their breakfast, and strange to say, the one who had spoken to her went up to Aunt Annie and shook hands warmly with her. Then they went out, and mounting, rode back in the direction of Mudgee.

Uncle Abe winked long and hard and solemnly at Andy Page, and Andy winked back like a mechanical wooden image. The two women nudged and smiled and seemed quite girlish, not to say skittish, all the morning. Something had come to break the cruel hopeless monotony of their lives. And even the settler became foolishly cheerful.

Five years later: same hut, same yard, and a not much wider clearing in the gully, and a little more fencing—the women rather more haggard and tired looking, the settler rather more horny-handed and silent, and Uncle Abe rather more philosophical. The men had had to go out and work on the stations. With the settler and his wife it was, "If we only had a few pounds to get the farm cleared and fenced, and another good plough horse, and a few more cows." That had been the burden of their song for the five years and more.

Then, one evening, the mail boy left a parcel. It was a small parcel, in cloth-paper, carefully tied and sealed. What could it be? It couldn't be the Christmas number of a weekly they subscribed to, for it never came like that. Aunt Annie cut the discussion short by cutting the string with a table knife and breaking the wax.

And behold, a clean sugar-bag tightly folded and rolled.

And inside a strong whitey-brown envelope.

And on the envelope written or rather printed the words: "For horse-feed, stabling, and supper."

And underneath, in smaller letters, "Send Bible and portraits to —————." (Here a name and address.)

And inside the envelope a roll of notes.

"Count them," said Aunt Annie.

But the settler's horny and knotty hands trembled too much, and so did his wife's withered ones; so Aunt Annie counted them.

"Fifty pounds!" she said.

"Fifty pounds!" mused the settler, scratching his head in a perplexed way.

"Fifty pounds!" gasped his wife.

"Yes," said Aunt Annie sharply, "fifty pounds!"

"Well, you'll get it settled between yer some day!" drawled Uncle Abe.

Later, after thinking comfortably over the matter, he observed: "Cast yer coffee an' bread an' bacon upon the waters——" Uncle Abe never hurried himself or anybody else.

THE BATH

The moral should be revived. Therefore, this is a story with a moral. The lower end of Bill Street—otherwise William—overlooks Blue's Point Road, with a vacant wedge-shaped allotment running down from a Scottish church between Bill Street the aforesaid and the road, and a terrace on the other side of the road. A cheap, mean-looking terrace of houses, flush with the pavement, each with two windows upstairs and a large one in the middle downstairs, with a slit on one side of it called a door—looking remarkably skully in ghastly dawns, afterglows, and rainy afternoons and evenings. The slits look as if the owners of the skulls got it there from an upward blow of a sharp tomahawk, from a shorter man—who was no friend of theirs—just about the time they died. The slits open occasionally, and mothers of the nation, mostly holding their garments together at neck or bosom, lean out—at right angles almost—and peer up and down the road, as if they are casually curious as to what is keeping

he rent collector so late this morning. Then they shut up till late in
he day, when a boy or two comes home from work. The terrace
hould be called "Jim's Terrace" if the road is not "James's" Road,
because no bills ever seem to be paid there as they are in our
treet—and for other reasons. There are four houses, but seldom
more than two of them occupied at one time—often only one.
Tenants never shift in, or at least are never seen to, but they get
here. The sign is a furtive candle light behind an old table-cloth, a
kirt, or any rag of dark stuff tacked across the front bedroom
window, upstairs, and a shadow suggestive of a woman making up a
bed on the floor.

If more than two of the houses are occupied there is almost certain
o be an old granny with ragged grey hair, who folds her arms tight
under her ragged old breasts, and bends her tough old body, and
ticks her ragged grey old head out of the slit called a door, and
quints up and down the road, but not in the interests of
mischief-making—they are never here long enough—only out of
mild, ragged, grey-headed curiosity regarding the health or affairs of
he rent collector.

Perhaps there are no bills to be collected in Skull Terrace because
no credit is given. No jugs are put out, because there is no place to
but them, except on the pavement, or on the narrow window ledges,
where they would be in great and constant danger from the feet or
elbows of passers-by. There are no trademen's entrances to the
houses in Skull Terrace.

Tenants and sub-tenants often leave on Friday morning in the full
glare of the day. Granny throws down garments from the top
window to hurry things, and the wife below ties up much in an old
allegedly green or red table-cloth, on the pavement, at the last
moment. Van of the "bottle ho" variety. It is all done very quickly,
and nobody takes any notice—they are never there long enough.
Landlord, landlady, or rent collector—or whatever it is—calls later
on; maybe, knocks in a tired, even bored, way; makes inquiries next
door, and goes away, leaving the problem to take care of itself—all
kind of casual. The business people of North Sydney, especially
removers and labourers, are very casual. Down old Blue's Point
Road the folk get so casual that they just exist, but don't seem to
do so.

One thing I never could make out about Skull Terrace is that
when one house becomes vacant from a house agent's point of
view—there is a permanent atmosphere of vacancy about the whole
terrace—the people of another move into it. And there's not the

slightest difference between the houses. It is because the removal is such a small affair, I suppose, and the change is the main thing. I always do better for awhile in a new house—but then I always did seem to get on better somewhere else.

There are many points, or absence of points, about Skull Terrace that fit in with Jim's casualness as against Bill's character, therefore Blue's Point Road ought to be James's Street.

But just now, in the heat of summer, the terrace happens to be full, and all the blinds are decent—the two new-comers are newly come down to Skull Terrace, and the other blinds are looked up, washed, and fixed up by force of example or from very shame's sake.

All of which seems to have nothing whatever to do with the story, except that the scene is down opposite my balcony as I think and smoke, and it is a blur on one of the most beautiful harbour views in the world.

I had been working hard all day, mending the fence, putting up a fowl-house and some lattice work and wire netting, and limewashing and painting. Labours of love. I'd rather build a fowl-house than a "pome" or story any day. And when finished—the fowl-house, I mean—I sit and contemplate my handiwork with pure and unadulterated joy. And I take a candle out several times, after dark, to look at it again. I never got such pleasure out of rhyme, story, or first-class London Academy notice. I find it difficult to drag myself from the fowl-house, or whatever it is, to meals, and harder to this work, and I lie awake planning next day's work until I fall asleep in the sleep of utter happy weariness. And I'm up and at it, before washing, at daylight. But I was a carpenter and housepainter first.

Well, it had been a long, close day, and I was very dirty and tired, but with the energy and restlessness of healthy, happy tiredness, when work is unfinished. But I was out of two-inch nails, and the shops were shut.

Then it struck me to start up the copper and have a real warm bath after my own heart and ideas. The bathroom is outside, next the wash-house and copper. There were plenty of splinters and ends of softwood that were mine by right of purchase and labour. My landlady is, and always has been, sensitive on the subject of firewood. She'll buy anything else to make the house comfortable and beautiful. She has been known to buy a piano for one of her nieces and burn rubbish in the stove the same day. I knew she was uneasy about the softwood odds and ends, but I couldn't help that—she'd still be sentimental about them if she had a stack of firewood as big as the house. There's at least one thing that most folk hate to buy—mine's boot-laces or bone studs, so long as I can make pins or inked string do.

I put a bucket of water in the copper, started a fire under that sent sparks out of the wash-house flue at an alarming rate, filled the copper to the brim, and, in the absence of a lid, covered it with a piece of flattened galvanized iron I had.

I tacked the side edge of a strip of canvas to the matchboard wall along over the inner edge of the bath, fastened a short piece of gas-pipe to the outer edge, with pieces of string through holes made in it, and let it hang down over the bath, leaving a hole at the head for my head and shoulders. I was going to have a long, comfortable, and utterly lazy and drowsy hot water and steam bath, you know.

I fastened a piece of clothes-line round and over the head of the bath, and twisted an old toilet-table cover and a towel round it where it sagged into the bath, for a head rest—also to be soaped for where I couldn't get at my back with my hands.

I went up to my room for some things, and it struck me to arrange two chairs by the bed—candle and matches and tobacco on one side, and a pile of Jack London, Kipling, and Yankee magazines on the other, with the last *Lone Hand* and *Bulletin* on top.

Going down with pyjamas, towel, and soap, it struck me to have a kettle and a saucepan full of water on the stove to use as the water from the copper cooled.

I took a roomy, hard-bottomed kitchen chair into the bathroom; on it I placed a carefully scraped, cleared, and filled pipe, matches, more tobacco, tooth-brush, saucer with a lump of whiting and salt, piece of looking-glass—to see progress of the teeth—and knife for finger and toe nails. And I knocked up a few three-inch iron nails in the wall to hang things on. I placed a clean suit of pyjamas over the back of the chair, and over them the towels.

I arranged with the landlady to have a good cup of coffee made, as she knows how to make it, ready to hand in round the edge of the door when I should be in the bath. There's nothing in that. I've been with her for years, and on account of the canvas it would be just the same as if I were in bed. On second thought I asked her to hand in some toast—or bread and butter and bloater paste—at the same time. I fed the fire with judgment, and the copper boiled just as the last blaze died down. I got a pail and carried the water to the bath, pouring it in through the opening at the head. The last few pints I dipped into the pail with a cup. I covered the opening with a towel to keep the steam and heat in until I was ready. I got the boiling water from the kitchen into the bucket, covered it with another towel, and stood it in a handy corner in the bathroom.

I made an opening, turned on the cold water, and commenced to undress. I hung my clothes on the wall, till morning, for I intended to go straight from the bath to bed in my pyjamas and to lie there reading.

I turned off the cold water tap to be sure, lifted the towel off, and put my good right foot in to feel the temperature—into about three inches of cold water, and that was vanishing.

I'd forgotton to put in the plug.

I'm deaf, you know, and the landlady, hearing the water run, thought I was flushing out the bath (we were new tenants) and wondered vaguely why I was so long at it.

I dressed rather hurriedly in my working clothes, went inside, and spread myself dramatically on the old cane lounge and covered my face with my oldest hat, to show that it was come and I took it that way. But my landlady was so full of sympathy, condolence, and self-reproach (because she failed to draw my attention to the gurgling) that she let the coffee and toast burn.

I went up and lay on my bed, and was so tired and misty and far away that I went to sleep without undressing, or even washing my face and hands.

How many, in this life, forget the plug!

And how many, ah! how many, who passed through, and are passing through Skull Terrace, commenced life as confidently, carefree, and clear headed, and with such easily exercised, careful, intelligent, practised, and methodical attention to details as I did the bath business arrangements—and forgot to put in the plug.

And many because they were handicapped physically.

INSTINCT GONE WRONG

Old Mac used to sleep in his wagon in fine weather, when he had no load, on his blankets spread out on the feed-bags; but one time he struck Croydon, flush from a lucky and good back trip, and looked in at the (say) Royal Hotel to wet his luck—as some men do with their sorrow—and he "got there all right." Next morning he had breakfast in the dining-room, was waited on as a star boarder, and became thoroughly demoralized; and his mind was made up (independent of himself, as it were) to be a gentleman for once in his life. He went over to the store and bought the sloppiest suit of reach-me-downs of glossiest black, and the stiffest and stickiest white shirt they had to show—also four bone studs, two for the collar and two for the cuffs. Then he gave his worn "larstins" to the stable-boy (with half a crown) to clean, and—proceeded. He put the boots on during the day, one at a time between drinks, gassing all the time, and continued. He concluded about midnight, after a very noisy time and interviews with everyone on sight (slightly interrupted by drinks) concerning "his room." It was show time, you see, and all the rooms were as full as he was—he was too full even to share the parlour or billiard room with others; but he consented at last to a shake-down on the balcony, the barmaid volunteering to spread the couch with her own fair hands.

Towards daylight he woke, for one of the reasons why men do wake. It is well known, to people who know, that old campers-out (and young men new to it, too) will wake *once*—if in a party, each at different times—to tend to their cattle, or listen for the hobbles of their horses, or simply to rise on their elbows and have a look round—the last, I suppose, from an instinct born in old dangerous times. Mac woke up, and it was dark. He reached out and his hand fell, instinctively, on the rail of the balcony, which was to him (instinctively—and that shows how instinct errs) the rail of the side of his wagon, in which as I have said, he was wont to sleep. So he drew himself up on his knees and to his feet, with the instinctive intention of getting down to (say) put some chaff and corn in the feed-bags stretched across the shafts for the horses; for he intended, by instinct, to make an early start. Which shows how instinct can never be trusted to travel with memory, but will get ahead of it—or behind it. (Say it was instinct mixed with or adulterated by drink.) He got a long, hairy leg over and felt (instinctively) for the hub of the wheel; his foot found and rested on the projecting ledge of the balcony floor outside, and that, to him, was the hub all right. He swung his other leg over and expected to drop lightly on to the grass or dust of the camp; but, being instinctively rigid, he fell heavily some fifteen feet into a kerbed gutter.

As a result of his howls lights soon flickered in windows and fanlights; and with prompt, eager, anxious, and awed bush first-aid and assistance, they carried a very sober, battered and blasphemous driver inside and spread mattresses on the floor. And, some six weeks afterwards, an image, mostly of plaster-of-Paris and bandages, reclined, much against its will, on a be-cushioned cane lounge on the hospital veranda; and, from the only free and workable corner of its mouth, when the pipe was removed, came shockingly expressed opinions of them ————— newfangled —————! two-story —————! "night houses" (as it called them). And, thereafter, when he had a load on, or the weather was too bad for sleeping in or under his wagon, the veranda of a one-storied shanty (if he could get to it) was good enough for MacSomething, the carrier.

THE HYPNOTIZED TOWNSHIP

They said that Harry Chatswood, the mail contractor would do anything for Cobb & Co., even to stretching fencing-wire across the road in a likely place: but I don't believe that—Harry was too good-hearted to risk injuring innocent passengers, and he had a fellow feeling for drivers, being an old coach driver on rough out-back tracks himself. But he did rig up fencing-wire for old Mac, the carrier, one night, though not across the road. Harry, by the way, was a city-born bushman, who had been everything for some years. Anything from six-foot-six to six-foot-nine, fourteen stone, and a hard case. He is a very successful coach-builder now, for he knows the wood, the roads, and the weak parts in a coach.

It was in the good seasons when competition was keen and men's hearts were hard—not as it is in times of drought, when there is no competition, and men's hearts are soft, and there is all kindness and goodwill between them. He had had much opposition in fighting Cobb & Co., and his coaches had won through on the outer tracks. There was little malice in his composition, but when old Mac, the teamster, turned his teams over to his sons and started a light van for parcels and passengers from Cunnamulla—that place which always sounds to me suggestive of pumpkin pies—out in seeming opposition to Harry Chatswood, Harry was annoyed.

Perhaps Mac only wished to end his days on the road with parcels that were light and easy to handle (not like loads of fencing wire) and passengers that were sociable; but he had been doing well with his teams, and, besides, Harry thought he was after the mail contract: so Harry was annoyed more than he was injured. Mac was

mean with the money he had—not because of the money he had a
chance of getting; and he mostly slept in his van, in all weathers,
when away from home which was kept by his wife about half-way
between the half-way house and the next "township."

One dark, gusty evening, Harry Chatswood's coach dragged,
heavily though passengerless, into Cunnamulla, and, as he turned
into the yard of the local "Royal," he saw Mac's tilted four-wheeler
(which he called his "van") drawn up opposite by the kerbing round
the post office. Mac always chose a central position—with a vague
idea of advertisement perhaps. But the nearness to the P.O.
reminded Harry of the mail contracts, and he knew that Mac had
taken up a passenger or two and some parcels in front of him
(Harry) on the trip in. And something told Harry that Mac was
asleep inside his van. It was a windy night, with signs of rain, and
the curtains were drawn close.

Old Mac was there all right, and sleeping the sleep of a tired
driver after a long drowsy day on a hard box-seat, with little or no
back railing to it. But there was a lecture on, or an exhibition of
hypnotism or mesmerism—"a blanky spirit rappin' fake," they
called it, run by "some blanker" in "the hall;" and when old Mac
had seen to his horses, he thought he might as well drop in for half
an hour and see what was going on. Being a Mac, he was, of course,
theological, scientific, and argumentative. He saw some things
which woke him up, challenged the performer to hypnotize him, was
"operated" on or "fooled with" a bit, had a "numb sorter
light-headed feelin'," and was told by a voice from the back of the
hall that his "leg was being pulled, Mac," and by another buzzin'
far-away kind of "ventrillick" voice that he would make a good
subject, and that, if he only had the will power and knew how
(which he would learn from a book the professor had to sell for five
shillings) he would be able to drive his van without horses or
anything, save the pole sticking straight out in front. These weren't
the professor's exact words— But, anyway, Mac came to himself
with a sudden jerk, left with a great Scottish snort of disgust and the
sound of heavy boots along the floor; and after a resentful whisky at
the Royal, where they laughed at his scrooging bushy eyebrows,
fierce black eyes and his deadly-in-earnest denunciation of all
humbugs and imposters, he returned to the aforesaid van, let down
the flaps, buttoned the daft and "feekle" world out, and himself in,
and then retired some more and slept, as I have said, rolled in his
blankets and overcoats on a bed of cushions and chaff-bag.

Harry Chatswood got down from his empty coach, and was helping the yard boy take out the horses, when his eye fell on the remnant of a roll of fencing wire standing by the stable wall in the light of the lantern. Then an idea struck him unexpectedly, and his mind became luminous. He unhooked the swinglebar, swung it up over his "leader's" lump (he was driving only three horses that trip), and hooked it on to the horns of the hames. Then he went inside (there was another light there) and brought out a bridle and an old pair of spurs that were hanging on the wall. He buckled on the spurs at the chopping block, slipped the winkers off the leader and the bridle on, and took up the fencing-wire, and started out the gate with the horse. The boy gaped after him once, and then hurried to put up the other two horses. He knew Harry Chatswood, and was in a hurry to see what he would be up to.

There was a good crowd in town for the show, or the races, or a stock sale, or land ballot, or something; but most of them were tired, or at tea—or in the pubs—and the corners were deserted. Observe how fate makes time and things fit when she wants to do a good turn—or play a practical joke. Harry Chatswood, for instance, didn't know anything about the hypnotic business.

It was the corners of the main street or road and the principal short cross street, and the van was opposite the pub stables in the main street. Harry crossed the streets diagonally to the opposite corner, in a line with the van. There he slipped the bar down over the horse's rump, and fastened one end of the wire on to the ring of it. Then he walked back to the van, carrying the wire and letting the coils go wide, and, as noiselessly as possible, made a loop in the loose end and slipped it over the hooks on the end of the pole. ("Unnecessary detail!" my contemporaries will moan, "Overloaded with uninteresting details!" But that's because they haven't got the details—and it's the details that go.) Then Harry skipped back to his horse, jumped on, gathered up the bridle reins, and used his spurs. There was a swish and a clang, a scrunch and a clock-clock and rattle of wheels, and a surprised human sound; then a bump and a shout—for there was no underground drainage, and the gutters belonged to the Stone Age. There was a swift clocking and rattle, more shouts, another bump, and a yell. And so on down the longish main street. The stable-boy, who had left the horses in his excitement, burst into the bar, shouting, "The Hypnertism's on, the Mesmerism's on! Ole Mac's van's runnin' away with him without no horses all right!" The crowd scuffled out into the street; there were some unfortunate horses hanging up of course at the panel by the pub trough, and the first to get to them jumped on and rode; the rest ran. The hall— where they were clearing the willing professor out in favour of a "darnce"—and the other pubs decanted their contents, and chance souls skipped for the verandas of weather-board shanties out of which other souls popped to see the runaway. They saw a weird horseman, or rather, something like a camel (for Harry rode low, like Tod Sloan with his long back humped—for effect)—apparently fleeing for its life in a veil of dust, along the long white road, and some forty rods behind, an unaccountable tilted coach careered in its own separate cloud of dust. And from it came the shouts and yells. Men shouted and swore, women screamed for their children, and kids whimpered. Some of the men turned with an oath and stayed the panic with:

"It's only one of them flamin' motor-cars, you fools."

It might have been, and the yells the warning howls of a motorist who had burst or lost his honk-konk and his head.

"It's runnin' away!" or "The toff's mad or drunk!" shouted others. "It'll break its crimson back over the bridge."

"Let it!" was the verdict of some. "It's all the crimson carnal things are good for."

But the riders still rode and the footmen ran. There was a clatter of hoofs on the short white bridge looming ghostly ahead, and then, at a weird interval, the rattle and rumble of wheels, with no hoof-beats accompanying. The yells grew fainter. Harry's leader was a good horse, of the rather heavy coachhorse breed, with a little of the racing blood in her, but she was tired to start with, and only excitement and fright at the feel of the "pull" of the twisting wire kept her up to that speed; and now she was getting winded, so half a mile or so beyond the bridge Harry thought it had gone far enough, and he stopped and got down. The van ran on a bit, of course, and the loop of the wire slipped off the hooks of the pole. The wire recoiled itself roughly along the dust nearly to the heels of Harry's horse. Harry grabbed up as much of the wire as he could claw for, took the mare by the neck with the other hand, and vanished through the dense fringe of scrub off the road, till the wire caught and pulled him up; he stood still for a moment, in the black shadow on the edge of a little clearing, to listen. Then he fumbled with the wire until he got it untwisted, cast it off, and moved off silently with the mare across the soft rotten ground, and left her in a handy bush stockyard, to be brought back to the stables at a late hour that night—or rather an early hour next morning—by a jackeroo stable-boy who would have two half-crowns in his pocket and afterthought instructions to look out for that wire and hide it if possible.

Then Harry Chatswood got back quickly, by a roundabout way, and walked into the bar of the Royal, through the back entrance from the stables, and stared, and wanted to know where all the chaps had gone to, and what the noise was about, and whose trap had run away, and if anybody was hurt.

The growing crowd gathered round the van, silent and awe-struck, and some of them threw off their hats, and lost them, in their anxiety to show respect for the dead, or render assistance to the hurt, as men do, round a bad accident in the bush. They got the old man out, and two of them helped him back along the road, with great solicitude, while some walked round the van, and swore beneath their breaths, or stared at it with open mouths, or examined it curiously, with their eyes only, and in breathless silence. They muttered, and agreed, in the pale moonlight now showing, that the sounds of the horses' hoofs had only been "spirit-rappin' sounds;" and, after some more muttering, two of the stoutest, with subdued oaths, laid hold of the pole and drew the van to the side of the road, where it would be out of the way of chance night traffic. But they stretched and rubbed their arms afterwards, and then, and on the way back, they swore to admiring acquaintances that they felt the "blanky 'lectricity" runnin' all up their arms and "elbers" while they were holding the pole, which, doubtless, they did—in imagination.

They got old Mac back to the Royal, with sundry hasty whiskies on the way. He was badly shaken, both physically, mentally, and in his convictions, and, when he'd pulled himself together, he had little to add to what they already knew. But he confessed that, when he got under his possum rug in the van, he couldn't help thinking of the professor and his creepy (it was "creepy," or "uncanny," or "awful," or "rum" with 'em now)—his blanky creepy hypnotism; and he (old Mac) had just laid on his back comfortable, and stretched his legs out straight, and his arms down straight by his sides, and drew long, slow breaths, and tried to fix his mind on nothing—as the professor had told him when he was "operatin' on him" in the hall. Then he began to feel a strange sort of numbness coming over him, and his limbs went heavy as lead, and he seemed to be gettin' light-headed. Then, all on a sudden, his arms seemed to begin to lift, and just when he was goin' to pull 'em down the van started as they had heard and seen it. After a while he got on to his knees and managed to wrench a corner of the front curtain clear of the button and get his head out. And there was the van going helter-skelter, and feeling like Tam o'Shanter's mare (the old man said), and he on her barebacked. And there was no horses, but a cloud of dust—or a spook—on ahead, and the bare pole steering straight for it, just as the professor had said it would be. The old man thought he was going to be taken clear across the Never-Never country and left to roast on a sandhill, hundreds of miles from anywhere, for his sins, and he said he was trying to think of a prayer or two all the time he was yelling. They handed him more whisky from the publican's own bottle. Hushed and cautious inquiries for the Professor (with a big P now) elicited the hushed and cautious fact that he had gone to bed. But old Mac caught the awesome name and glared round, so they hurriedly filled out another for him, from the boss's bottle. Then there was a slight commotion. The housemaid hurried scaredly in to the bar behind and whispered to the boss. She had been startled nearly out of her wits by the Professor suddenly appearing at his bedroom door and calling upon her to have a stiff nobbler of whisky hot sent up to his room. The jackeroo yard-boy, aforesaid, volunteered to take it up, and while he was gone there were hints of hysterics from the kitchen, and the boss whispered in his turn to the crowd over the bar. The jackeroo just handed the tray and glass in through the partly opened door, had a glimpse of pyjamas, and, after what seemed an interminable wait, he came tiptoeing into the bar amongst its awe-struck haunters with an air of great mystery, and no news whatever.

They fixed old Mac on a shake-down in the Commercial Room, where he'd have light and some overflow guests on the sofas for company. With a last whisky in the bar, and a stiff whisky by his side on the floor, he was understood to chuckle to the effect that he knew he was all right when he'd won "the keystone o' the brig." Though how a wooden bridge with a level plank floor could have a keystone I don't know—and they were too much impressed by the event of the evening to inquire. And so, with a few cases of hysterics to occupy the attention of the younger women, some whimpering of frightened children and comforting or chastened nagging by mothers, some unwonted prayers muttered secretly and forgettingly, and a good deal of subdued blasphemy, Cunnamulla sank to its troubled slumbers—some of the sleepers in the commercial and billiard-rooms and parlours at the Royal, to start up in a cold sweat, out of their beery and hypnotic nightmares, to find Harry Chatswood making elaborate and fearsome passes over them with his long, gaunt arms and hands, and a flaming red table-cloth tied round his neck.

To be done with old Mac, for the present. He made one or two more trips, but always by daylight, taking care to pick up a swagman or a tramp when he had no passenger; but his "conveections" had had too much of a shaking, so he sold his turnout (privately and at a distance, for it was beginning to be called "the haunted van") and returned to his teams—always keeping one of the lads with him for company. He reckoned it would take the devil's own hypnotism to move a load of fencing-wire, or pull a wool-team of bullocks out of a bog; and before he invoked the ungodly power, which he let them believe he could—he'd stick there and starve till he and his bullocks died a "natural" death. (He was a bit Irish—as all Scots are—back on one side.)

But the strangest is to come. The Professor, next morning, proved uncomfortably unsociable, and though he could have done a roaring business that night—and for a week of nights after, for that matter—and though he was approached several times, he, for some mysterious reason known only to himself, flatly refused to give one more performance, and said he was leaving the town that day. He couldn't get a vehicle of any kind, for fear, love, or money, until Harry Chatswood, who took a day off, volunteered, for a stiff consideration, to borrow a buggy and drive him (the Professor) to the next town towards the then railway terminus, in which town the Professor's fame was not so awesome, and where he might get a lift to the railway. Harry ventured to remark to the Professor once or twice during the drive that "there was a rum business with old Mac's van last night," but he could get nothing out of him, so gave it best, and finished the journey in contemplative silence.

Now, the fact was that the Professor had been the most surprised and startled man in Cunnamulla that night; and he brooded over the thing till he came to the conclusion that hypnotism was a dangerous power to meddle with unless a man was physically and financially strong and carefree—which he wasn't. So he threw it up.

He learnt the truth, some years later, from a brother of Harry Chatswood, in a Home or Retreat for Geniuses, where "friends were paying," and his recovery was so sudden that it surprised and disappointed the doctor and his friend, the manager of the home. As it was, the Professor had some difficulty in getting out of it.

THE EXCISEMAN

Harry Chatswood, mail contractor (and several other things), was driving out from, say, Georgeville to Croydon, with mails, parcels, and only one passenger—a commercial traveller, who had shown himself unsociable, and close in several other ways. Nearly half-way to a place that was half-way between the half-way house and the town, Harry overhauled "Old Jack," a local character (there are many well-known characters named "Old Jack"), and gave him a lift as a matter of course.

"Hello! Is that you, Jack?" in the gathering dusk.

"Yes, Harry."

"Then jump up here."

Harry was good-natured and would give anybody a lift if he could.

Old Jack climbed up on the box-seat, between Harry and the traveller, who grew rather more stand- (or rather *sit*-) offish, wrapped himself closer in his overcoat, and buttoned his cloak of silence and general disgust to the chin button. Old Jack got his pipe to work and grunted, and chatted, an exchanged bush compliments with Harry comfortably. And so on to where they saw the light of a fire outside a hut ahead.

"Let me down here, Harry," said Old Jack uneasily, "I owe Mother Mac fourteen shillings for drinks, and I haven't got it on me, and I've been on the spree back yonder, and she'll know it, an' I don't want to face her. I'll cut across through the paddock and you can pick me up on the other side."

Harry thought a moment.

"Sit still, Jack," he said. "I'll fix that all right." He twisted and went down into his trouser-pocket, the reins in one hand, and brought up a handful of silver. He held his hand down to the coach lamp, separated some of the silver from the rest by a sort of sleight of hand—or rather sleight of fingers—and handed the fourteen shillings over to Old Jack.

"Here y'are, Jack. Pay me some other time."

"Thanks, Harry!" grunted Old Jack, as he twisted for *his* pocket.

It was a cold night, the hint of a possible shanty thawed the traveller a bit, and he relaxed with a couple of grunts about the weather and the road, which were received in a brotherly spirit. Harry's horses stopped of their own accord in front of the house, an old bark-and-slab whitewashed humpy of the early settlers' farm-house type, with a plank door in the middle, one bleary-lighted window on one side, and one forbiddingly blind one, as if death were there, on the other. It might have been. The door opened, letting out a flood of lamp-light and firelight which blindly showed the sides of the coach and the near pole horse and threw the coach lamps and the rest into the outer darkness of the opposing bush.

"Is that you, Harry?" called a voice and tone like Mrs Warren's of the Profession.

"It's me."

A stoutly aggressive woman appeared. She was rather florid, and looked, moved and spoke as if she had been something in the city in other years, and had been dumped down in the bush to make money in mysterious ways; had married, mated—or got herself to be supposed to be married—for convenience, and continued to make money by mysterious means. Anyway, she was "Mother Mac" to the bush, but, in the bank in the "town," and in the stores where she dealt, she was *Mrs* Mac, and there was always a promptly propped chair for her. She was, indeed, the missus of no other than old Mac, the teamster of hypnotic fame, and late opposition to Harry Chatswood. Hence, perhaps, part of Harry's hesitation to pull up, farther back, and his generosity to Old Jack.

Mrs or Mother Mac sold refreshments, from a rough bush dinner at eighteenpence a head to passengers, to fly-blown bottle of ginger-ale or lemonade, hot in hot weather from a sunny fly-specked window. In between there was cold corned beef, bread and butter, and tea, and (best of all if they only knew it) a good bush billy of coffee on the coals before the fire on cold wet nights. And outside of it all, there was cold tea, which, when confidence was established, or they knew one of the party, she served hushedly in cups without saucers; for which she sometimes apologized, and which she took into her murderous bedroom to fill, and replenish, in its darkest and most felonious corner from homicidal-looking pots, by candle-light. You'd think you were in a cheap place, where you shouldn't be, in the city.

Harry and his passengers got down and stretched their legs, and while Old Jack was guardedly answering a hurriedly whispered inquiry of the traveller, Harry took the opportunity to nudge Mrs Mac, and whisper in her ear:

"Look out, Mrs Mac!—Exciseman!"

"The devil he is!" whispered she.

"Ye-e-es!" whispered Harry.

"All right, Harry!" she whispered. "Never a word! I'll take care of him, bless his soul."

After a warm at the wide wood fire, a gulp of coffee and a bite or two at the bread and meat, the traveller, now thoroughly thawed, stretched himself and said:

"Ah, well, Mrs Mac, haven't you got anything else to offer us?"

"And what more would you be wanting?" she snapped. "Isn't the bread and meat good enough for you?"

"But—but—you know——" he suggested lamely.

"Know?—I know!—What do *I* know?" A pause, then, with startling suddenness, "Phwat d'y' mean?"

"No offence, Mrs Mac—no offence; but haven't you got something in the way of—of a drink to offer us?"

"Dhrink! Isn't the coffee good enough for ye? I paid two and six a pound for ut, and the milk new from the cow this very evenin'—an' th' water rain-water."

"But—but—you know what I mean, Mrs Mac."

"An' I *doan't* know what ye mean. *Phwat do ye mean?* I've asked ye that before. What are ye dhrivin' at, man—out with it!"

"Well, I mean a little drop of the right stuff," he said, nettled. Then he added: "No offence—no harm done."

"O-o-oh!" she said, illumination bursting in upon her brain. "It's the dirrty drink ye're afther, is it? Well, I'll tell ye, first for last, that we doan't keep a little drop of the right stuff nor a little drop of the wrong stuff in this house. It's a honest house, an' me husband's a honest harrd-worrkin' carrier, as he'd soon let ye know if he was at home this cold night, poor man. No dirrty drink comes into this house, nor goes out of it, I'd have ye know."

"Now, now, Mrs Mac, between friends, I meant no offence; but it's a cold night, and I thought you might keep a bottle for medicine—or in case of accident—or snake-bite, you know—they mostly do in the bush."

"Medicine! And phwat should we want with medicine? This isn't a five-guinea private hospital. We're clean, healthy people, I'd have ye know. There's a bottle of painkiller, if that's what ye want, and a packet of salts left—maybe they'd do ye some good. An' a bottle of eye-water, an' something to put in your ear for th' earache—maybe ye'll want 'em both before ye go much farther."

"But, Mrs Mac——"

"No, no more of it!" she said. "I tell ye that if it's a nip ye're afther, ye'll have to go on fourteen miles to the pub in the town. Ye're coffee's gittin' cowld, an' it's eighteenpence each to passengers

I charge on a night like this; Harry Chatswood's the driver an' welcome, an' Ould Jack's an ould friend." And she flounced round to clatter her feelings amongst the crockery on the dresser—just as men make a great show of filling and lighting their pipes in the middle of a barney. The table, by the way, was set on a brown holland cloth, with the brightest of tin plates for cold meals, and the brightest of tin pint-pots for the coffee (the crockery was in reserve for hot meals and special local occasions) and at one side of the wide fire-place hung an old-fashioned fountain, while in the other stood a camp-oven; and billies and a black kerosene-tin hung evermore over the fire from sooty chains. These, and a big bucket-handled frying-pan and a few rusty convict-time arms on the slab walls, were mostly to amuse jackeroos and jackerooesses, and let them think they were getting into the Australian-dontcherknow at last.

Harry Chatswood took the opportunity (he had a habit of taking opportunities of this sort) to whisper to Old Jack:

"Pay her the fourteen bob, Jack, and have done with it. She's got the needle to-night all right, and damfiknow what for. But the sight of your fourteen bob might bring her round." And Old Jack—as was his way—blundered obediently and promptly right into the hole that was shown him.

"Well, Mrs Mac," he said, getting up from the table and slipping his hand into his pocket. "I don't know what's come over yer to-night, but, anyway——" Here he put the money down on the table. "There's the money I owe yer for—for——"

"For what?" she demanded, turning on him with surprising swiftness for such a stout woman.

"The—the fourteen bob I owed for them drinks when Bill Hogan and me——"

"You don't owe me no fourteen bob for dhrinks, you dirty blaggard! Are ye mad? You got no drink off of me. Phwat d'ye mean?"

"Beg—beg pardin, Mrs Mac," stammered Old Jack, very much taken aback; "but the—yer know—the fourteen bob, anyway, I owed you when—that night when me an' Bill Hogan an' yer sister-in-law, Mary Don——"

"What? Well, I—Git out of me house, ye low blaggard! I'm a honest, respectable married woman, and so is me sister-in-law, Mary Donelly; and to think!—Git out of me door!" and she caught up the billy of coffee. "Git outside me door, or I'll let ye have it in ye'r ugly face, ye low woolscourer—an' it's nearly bilin'."

Old Jack stumbled dazedly out, and blind instinct got him on to the coach as the safest place. Harry Chatswood had stood with his long, gaunt figure hung by an elbow to the high mantel-shelf, all the time, taking alternate gulps from his pint of coffee and puffs from his pipe, and very calmly and restfully regarding the scene.

"An' now," she said, "if the *gentleman's* done, I'd thank him to pay—it's eighteenpence—an' git his overcoat on. I've had enough dirty insults this night to last me a lifetime. To think of it—the blaggard!" she said to the table, "an' me a woman alone in a place like this on a night like this!"

The traveller calmly put down a two-shilling piece, as if the whole affair was the most ordinary thing in the world (for he was used to many bush things) and comfortably got into his overcoat.

"Well, Mrs Mac, I never thought Old Jack was mad before," said Harry Chatswood. "And I hinted to him," he added in a whisper. "Anyway" (out loudly), "you'll lend me a light, Mrs Mac, to have a look at that there swingle-bar of mine?"

"With pleasure, Harry," she said, "for you're a white man, anyway. I'll bring ye a light. An' all the lights in heaven if I could, an'—an' in the other place if they'd help ye."

When he'd looked to the swingle-bar, and had mounted to his place and untwisted the reins from a side-bar, she cried:

"An' as for them two, Harry, shpill them in the first creek you come to, an' God be good to you! It's all they're fit for, the low blaggards, to insult an honest woman alone in the bush in a place like this."

"All right, Mrs Mac," said Harry, cheerfully. "Good night, Mrs Mac."

"Good night, Harry, an' God go with ye, for the creeks are risen after last night's storm." And Harry drove on and left her to think over it.

She thought over it in a way that would have been unexpected to Harry, and would have made him uneasy, for he was really good-natured. She sat down on a stool by the fire, and presently, after thinking over it a bit, two big, lonely tears rolled down the lonely woman's fair, fat, blonde cheeks in the firelight.

"An' to think of Old Jack," she said. "The very last man in the world I'd dreamed of turning on me. But—but I always thought Old Jack was goin' a bit ratty, an' maybe I was a bit hard on him. God forgive us all!"

Had Harry Chatswood seen her then he would have been sorry he did it. Swagmen and broken-hearted new chums had met worse women than Mother Mac.

But she pulled herself together, got up and bustled round. She put on more wood, swept the hearth, put a parcel of fresh steak and sausages—brought by the coach—on to a clean plate on the table, and got some potatoes into a dish; for Chatswood had told her that her first and longest and favourite stepson was not far behind him with the bullock team. Before she had finished the potatoes she heard the clock-clock of heavy wheels and the crack of the bullock whip coming along the dark bush track.

But the very next morning a man riding back from Croydon called, and stuck his head under the veranda eaves with a bush greeting, and she told him all about it.

He straightened up, and tickled the back of his head with his little finger, and gaped at her for a minute.

"Why," he said, "that wasn't no excise officer. I know him well—I was drinking with him at the Royal last night afore we went to bed, an' had a nip with him this morning afore we started. Why! that's Bobby Howell, Burns and Bridges' traveller, an' a good sort when he wakes up, an' willin' with the money when he does good biz, especially when there's a chanst of a drink on a long road on a dark night."

"That Harry Chatswood again! The infernal villain," she cried, with a jerk of her arm. "But I'll be even with him, the dirrty blaggard. An' to think—I always knew Old Jack was a white man an'—to think! There's fourteen shillin's gone that Old Jack would have paid me, an' the traveller was good for three shillin's f'r the nips, an'—but Old Jack will pay me next time, and I'll be even with Harry Chatswood, the dirrty mail carter. I'll take it out of him in parcels—I'll be even with him."

She never saw Old Jack again with fourteen shillings, but she got even with Harry Chatswood, and—— But I'll tell you about that some other time. Time for a last smoke before we turn in.

MATESHIP IN SHAKESPEARE'S ROME

How we do misquote sayings, or misunderstand them when quoted rightly! For instance, we "wait for something to turn up, like Micawber," careless or ignorant of the fact that Micawber worked harder than all the rest put together for the leading characters'

sakes; he was the chief or only instrument in straightening out of
the sadly mixed state of things—and he held his tongue till the
time came. Moreover—and "*Put a pin in that spot*, young man," as
Dr "Yark" used to say—when there came a turn in the tide of the
affairs of Micawber, he took it at the flood, and it led on to fortune.
He became a hard-working settler, a pioneer—a respected early
citizen and magistrate in this bright young Commonwealth of ours,
my masters!

And, by the way, and strictly between you and me, I have a
shrewd suspicion that Uriah Heep wasn't the only cad in David
Copperfield.

Brutus, the originator of the saying, took the tide at the flood,
and it led him and his friends on to death, or—well, perhaps,
under the circumstances, it was all the same to Brutus and his old
mate, Cassius.

> And this, my masters, brings me home,
> A Bush-born bard, to Ancient Rome.

And there's little difference in the climate, or the men—save in
the little matter of ironmongery— and no difference at all in the
women.

We'll pass over the accident that happened to Caesar. Such
accidents had happened to great and little Caesars hundreds of
times before, and have happened many times since, and will
happen until the end of time, both in "sport" (in plays) and in
earnest:

> *Cassius*: ....How many ages hence
>   Shall this our lofty scene be acted over
>   In states unborn and accents yet unknown?
> *Brutus*: How many times shall Caesar bleed in sport,
>   That now at Pompey's basis lies along
>   No worthier than the dust!

Shakespeare hadn't Australia and George Rignold in his mind's
eye when he wrote that.

> *Cassius*: So oft as that shall be,
>   So often shall the knot of us be call'd
>   The men that gave their country liberty.

Well, be that as it will, I'm with Brutus too, irrespective of the
merits of the case. Antony spoke at the funeral, with free and
generous permission, and see what he made of it. And why
shouldn't I? and see what I'll make of it.

Antony, after sending abject and uncalled-for surrender, and grovelling unasked in the dust to Brutus and his friends as no straight mate should do for another, dead or alive—and after taking the blood-stained hands of his alleged friend's murderers—got permission to speak. To speak for his own ends or that paltry, selfish thing called "revenge," be it for one's self or one's friend.

"Brutus, I want a word with you," whispered Cassius. "Don't let him speak! You don't know how he might stir up the mob with what he says."

But Brutus had already given his word:

> *Antony*: That's all I seek:
>   And am moreover suitor that I may
>   Produce his body to the market place,
>   And in the pulpit, as becomes a friend,
>   Speak in the order of his funeral.
> *Brutus*: You shall, Mark Antony.

And now, strong in his right, as he thinks, and trusting to the honour of Antony, he only stipulates that he (Brutus) shall go on to the platform first and explain things; and that Antony shall speak all the good he can of Caesar, but not abuse Brutus and his friends.

And Antony (mark you) agrees and promises and breaks his promise immediately afterwards. Maybe he was only gaining time for his good friend Octavius Caesar, but time gained by such foul means is time lost through all eternity. Did Mark think of these things years afterwards in Egypt when he was doubly ruined and doubly betrayed to his good friend Octavius by that hot, jealous, selfish, shallow, shifty, strumpet, Cleopatra, and Octavius was after his scalp with a certainty of getting it? He did—and he spoke of it, too.

Brutus made his speech, a straightforward, manly speech in prose, and the gist of the matter was that he did what he did (killed Caesar), not because he loved Caesar less, but because he loved Rome more. And I believe he told the simple honest truth.

Then he acts as Antony's chairman, or introducer, in a manly straightforward manner, and then he goes off and leaves the stage to him, which is another generous act; though it was lucky for Brutus, as it happened afterwards, that he *was* out of the way.

Mark Antony gets all the limelight and blank verse. He had the "gift of the gab" all right. Old Cassius referred to it later on in one of those "words-before-blows" barneys they had on the battlefield where they hurt each other a damned sight more with their tongues than they did with their swords afterwards.

We've all heard of Antony's speech:

> I come to bury Caesar, not to praise him.

Which was a lie to start with.

> The evil that men do lives after them,
> The good is oft interred with their bones.

Which is not so true in these days of newspapers and magazines. And so on. He says that Brutus and his friends are honourable men about nine times in his short speech. Now, was Mark Antony an honourable man?

And then the flap-doodle about dead Caesar's wounds, and their poor dumb mouths, and the people kissing them, and dipping their handkerchiefs in his sacred blood. All worthy of our Purves trying to pump tears out of a jury.

But it fetched the crowd; it always did, it always has done, it always does, and it always will do. And the hint of Caesar's will, and the open abuse of Brutus and Co. when he saw that he was safe, and the cheap anti-climax of the reading of the will. Nothing in this line can be too cheap for the crowd, as witness the melodramas of our own civilized and enlightened times.

Antony was a noble Purves.

And the mob rushed off to burn houses, as it has always done, and will always do when it gets a chance—it tried to burn mine more than once.

The quarrel scene between Brutus and Cassius is one of the best scenes in Shakespeare. It is great from the sublime to the ridiculous —you must read it for yourself. It seems that Brutus objected to Cassius's, or one of his off-side friends' methods of raising the wind—he reckoned it was one of the very things they killed Julius Caesar for; and Cassius, loving Brutus more than a brother, is very much hurt about it. I can't make out what the trouble really was about and I don't suppose either Cassius or Brutus was clear as to what it was all about either. It's generally the way when friends fall out. It seems also that Brutus thinks that Cassius refused to lend him a few quid to pay his legions; and, you know, it's an unpardonable crime for one mate to refuse another a few quid when he's in a hole; but it seems that the messenger was but a fool who brought Cassius's answer back. It is generally the messenger who is to blame, when friends make it up after a quarrel that was all their own fault. Messengers had an uncomfortable time in those days, as witness the case of the base slave who had to bring

Cleopatra the news of Antony's marriage with Octavia.

But the quarrel scene is great for its deep knowledge of the hearts of men in matters of man to man—of man friend to man friend—and it is as humanly simple as a barney between two old bush mates that threatens to end in a bloody fist-fight and separation for life, but chances to end in a beer. This quarrel threatened to end in the death of either Brutus or Cassius or a set-to between their two armies, just at the moment when they all should have been knit together against the forces of Mark Antony and Octavius Caesar; but it ended in a beer, or its equivalent, a bowl of wine.

Earlier in the quarrel, where Brutus asks why, after striking down the foremost man in all the world for supporting land agents and others, should they do the same thing and contaminate their fingers with base bribes?

> I'd rather be a dog and bay the moon,
> Than such a Roman.

Cassius says:—

> Brutus, bait not me
> I'll not endure it: you forget yourself,
> To hedge me in; I am a soldier, I,
> Older in practice, abler than yourself
> To make conditions.
> *Brutus*: Go to, you are not, Cassius.
> *Cassius*: I am.
> *Brutus*: I say you are not.

And so they get to it again until:

> *Cassius*: Is it come to this?
> *Brutus*: You say you are a better soldier:
> Let it appear so; make your vaunting true,
> And it shall please me well: for mine own part,
> I shall be glad to learn of noble men.
> *Cassius*: You wrong me every way; you wrong me, Brutus;
> I said, an elder soldier, not a better.
> Did I say better?

(What big boys they were—and what big boys we all are!)

> *Brutus*: If you did, I care not.
> *Cassius*: When Caesar lived he durst not thus have moved me.
> *Brutus*: Peace, peace! you durst not thus have tempted him.
> *Cassius*: I durst not!
> *Brutus*: No.
> *Cassius*: What! Durst not tempt him!

> *Brutus*: For your life you durst not.
> *Cassius*: Do not presume too much upon my love;
>   I may do that I shall be sorry for.
> *Brutus*: You have done that you should be sorry for.

And so on till he gets to the matter of the refused quids, which is cleared up at the expense of the messenger.

> *Cassius*: ....Brutus hath rived my heart:
>   A friend should bear his friend's infirmities,
>   But Brutus makes mine greater than they are.
> *Brutus*: I do not, till you practise them on me.
> *Cassius*: You love me not.
> *Brutus*: I do not like your faults.
> *Cassius*: A friendly eye could never see such faults.
> *Brutus*: A flatterer's would not, though they do appear
>   As huge as high Olympus.

Then Cassius lets himself go. He calls on Antony and young Octavius and all the rest of 'em to come and be revenged on him alone, for he's tired of the world ("Cassius is aweary of the world," he says). He's hated by one he loves (that's Brutus). He's braved by his "brother" (Brutus), checked like a bondman, and Brutus keeps an eye on all his faults and puts 'em down in a note-book, and learns 'em over and gets 'em off by memory to cast in his teeth. He offers Brutus his dagger and bare breast and wants Brutus to take out his heart, which, he says, is richer than all the quids—or rather gold—which Brutus said he wouldn't lend him. He wants Brutus to strike him as he did Caesar, for he reckons that when Brutus hated Caesar worst he loved him far better than ever he loved Cassius.

Remember these men were Southerners, like ourselves, not cold-blooded Northerners—and, in spite of the seemingly effeminate Italian temperament, as brave as our men were at Elands River. The reason of Brutus's seeming coldness and hardness during the quarrel is set forth in a startling manner later on, as only the greatest poet in this world could do it.

Brutus tells him kindly to put up his pig-sticker (and button his shirt) and he could be just as mad or good-tempered as he liked, and do what he liked, Brutus wouldn't mind him:

> ....Dishonour shall be humour.
> O Cassius, you are yoked with a lamb
> That carries anger as the flint bears fire,
> Who, much enforced, shows a hasty spark
> And straight is cold again.

Whereupon Cassius weeps because he thinks Brutus is laughing at him.

> Hath Cassius lived
> To be but mirth and laughter to his Brutus,
> When grief and blood ill-temper'd vexeth him.
> *Brutus*: When I spoke that, I was ill-temper'd too.
> *Cassius*: Do you confess so much? Give me your hand.
> *Brutus*: And my heart too.

Then Cassius explains that he got his temper from his mother (as I did mine).

> *Cassius*: O Brutus!
> *Brutus*: What's the matter? [Shakespeare should have added "now."]
> *Cassius*: Have not you love enough to bear with me,
> When that rash humour which my mother gave me
> Makes me forgetful?
> *Brutus*: Yes, Cassius, and from henceforth,
> When you are over-earnest with your Brutus,
> He'll think your mother chides, and leave you so.

And all this on the brink of disaster and death.

But here comes a rare touch, and we might as well quote it in full.

Mind you, I am following Shakespeare, and not history, which is mostly lies.

A great poet's instinct might be nearer the truth, after all. Of course scholars know that Macbeth (or Macbethad) reigned for upwards of twenty years in Scotland a wise and a generous king—so much so that he was called "Macbathad the Liberal," and it was Duncan who found his way to the throne by way of murder; but it didn't fit in with Shakespeare's plans, and—anyway that's only a little matter between the ghosts of Bill and Mac which was doubtless fixed up long ago. More likely they thought it such a one-millionth part of a trifle that they never dreamed of thinking of mentioning it.

> *(Noise within.)*
> *Poet* (within):   Let me go in to see the generals;
> There is some grudge between 'em—'tis not meet.
> They be alone.
> *Lucilius* (within): You shall not come to them.
> *Poet* (within):   Nothing but death shall stay me.

("Within" in this case is, of course, without—outside the tent where Lucilius and Titinius are on guard.)

Enter POET.

Cassius: How now! What's the matter?

Poet: For shame, you generals! What do you mean?
         Love, and be friends, as two such men should be:
         For I have seen more years, I'm sure, than ye.

Cassius: Ha, ha! how vilely doth this cynic rhyme!

Brutus: Get you hence, sirrah; saucy fellow, hence!

Cassius: Bear with him, Brutus; 'tis his fashion.

Brutus: I'll know his humour when he knows his time:
         What should the wars do with these jingling fools?
         Companion, hence!

Cassius: Away, away, be gone!

(*Exit* POET.)

Blessed are the peacemakers, for they shall inherit a black eye (*Lawson*). Shakespeare was ever rough on poets—but stay! Consider that this great world of Rome and all the men and women in it were created by a "jingling fool" and a master of bad—not to say execrable—rhymes, and his name was William Shakespeare. You need to sit down and think awhile after that.

Brutus sends Lucilius and Titinius to bid the commanders lodge their companies for the night, and then all come to him. Then he gives Cassius a shock and strikes him to the heart for his share in the quarrel. It is almost directly after the row, when they have kicked out the "jingling fool" of a poet. Cassius does not know that Brutus has to-day received news of the death, in Rome, of his good and true wife Portia, who, during a fit of insanity, brought on by her grief and anxiety for Brutus, and in the absence of her attendant, has poisoned herself—or "swallowed fire," as Shakespeare has it.

Brutus (to Lucius, his servant): Lucius, a bowl of wine!

Cassius: I did not think you could have been so angry.

Brutus: O Cassius, I am sick of many griefs.

Cassius: Of your philosophy you make no use,
         If you give place to accidental evils.

Brutus: No man bears sorrow better:—Portia is dead.

Cassius: Ha! Portia!

Brutus: She is dead.

Cassius: How 'scaped I killing when I cross'd you so?
         O insupportable and touching loss!
         Upon what sickness?

Brutus: Impatient of my absence,
         And grief that young Octavius with Mark Antony
         Have made themselves so strong: for with her death
         That tidings came; with this she fell distract,
         And, her attendants absent, swallowed fire.

> *Cassius*: And died so?
> *Brutus*: Even so.
> *Cassius*: O, ye immortal gods!
>   (*Enter Lucius, with a jar of wine, a goblet, and a taper.*)
> *Brutus*: Speak no more of her. Give me a bowl of wine:
>   In this I bury all unkindness, Cassius.
>
>   (*Drinks.*)
>
> *Cassius*: My heart is thirsty for that noble pledge.
>   Fill, Lucius, till the wine o'erswell the cup;
>   I cannot drink too much of Brutus' love.
>
>   (*Drinks.*)

You ought to read that scene carefully. It will do no one any harm. It did me a lot of good one time, when I was about to quarrel with a friend whose heart was sick with many griefs that I knew nothing of at the time. You never know what's behind.

Titinius and Messala come in, and proceed to discuss the situation.

> *Brutus*: Come in, Titinius! Welcome, good Messala.
>   Now sit we close about this taper here,
>   And call in question our necessities.
> *Cassius*: (on whom the wine seems to have taken some effect):
>   Portia, art thou gone?
> *Brutus*: No more, I pray you.
>   Messala, I have here received letters,
>   That young Octavius and Mark Antony
>   Come down upon us with a mighty power,
>   Bending their expedition towards Philippi.

Messala has also letters to the same purpose, and they have likewise news of the murder, or execution, of upwards of a hundred senators in Rome.

> *Cassius*: Cicero one!
> *Messala*: Cicero is dead.

Poor Brutus! His heart had cause to be sick of many griefs that day. Messala thinks he has news to break, and Brutus draws him out. How many and many a man and woman, with a lump in the throat, have broken sad and bad news since that day, and started out to do it in the same old gentle way:

> *Messala*: Had you your letters from your wife, my lord?
> *Brutus*: No, Messala.
> *Messala*: Nor nothing in your letters writ of her?
> *Brutus*: Nothing, Messala.
> *Messala*: That, methinks, is strange.
> *Brutus*: Why ask you? Hear you aught of her in yours?

Maybe it strikes Messala like a flash that Brutus is in no need of any more bad news just now, and it had better be postponed till after the battle:

> *Messala*: No, my lord.
> *Brutus*: Now, as you are a Roman, tell me true.
> *Messala*: Then like a Roman bear the truth I tell:
> For certain she is dead, and by strange manner.
> *Brutus*: Why, farewell, Portia. We must die, Messala:
> With meditating that she must die once
> I have the patience to endure it now.

Poor Messala comes to the scratch again rather lamely with a little weak flattery: "Even so great men great losses should endure;" and Cassius says, rather mixedly—it might have been the wine—that he has as much strength in bearing trouble as Brutus has, and yet he couldn't bear it so.

> I have as much of this in art as you,
> But yet my nature could not bear it so.
> *Brutus*: Well, to our work alive. What do you think
> Of marching on Philippi presently?

Brutus was a strong man. Portia's spirit must bide a while. They discuss a plan of campaign. Cassius is for waiting for the enemy to seek them and so get through his tucker and knock his men up, while they rest in a good position; but Brutus argues that the enemy will gather up the country people between Philippi and their camp and come on refreshed with added numbers and courage, and it would be better for them to meet him at Philippi with these people at their back. The politics or inclination of the said country people didn't matter in those days. "There is a tide in the affairs of men"—and so they decide to take it at the flood and float high on to the rocks at Philippi. Ah well, it led on to immortality, if it didn't to fortune.

Well, there's no more to say. Brutus thinks that the main thing now is a little rest—in which you'll agree with him; and he sends for his night-shirt.

> Good night, Titinius: noble, noble Cassius,
> Good night, and good repose!

That old fool of a Cassius—remorseful old smooth-bore—is still a bit maudlin—maybe he had another swig at the wine when Shakespeare wasn't looking.

> *Cassius*: O my dear brother!

> This was an ill beginning of the night:
> Never come such division 'tween our souls!
> Let it not, Brutus.

Brutus: Everything is well.
Cassius: Good night, my lord.
Brutus: Good night, good brother.
Titinius and *Messala*: Good night, Lord Brutus.
Brutus: Farewell, every one.

And Cassius is the man whom Caesar denounced as having a lean and hungry look: "Let me have men about me that are fat ... such men are dangerous." (Mr Archibald held with that—and he had a lean, if not a hungry, look too.) When Antony put in a word for Cassius, Caesar said that he wished he was fatter anyhow. "He thinks too much," Caesar said to Antony. He read a lot; he could look through men; he never went to the theatre, and heard no music; he never smiled except as if grinning sarcastically at himself for "being moved to smile at anything." Caesar said that such men were never at heart's ease while they could see a bigger man than themselves, and therefore such men were dangerous. "Come on my right hand, for this ear is deaf, and tell me truly what thou think'st of him." (That's a touch, for deafness in people affected that way is usually greater in the left ear.)

When Lucilius returned from taking a message from Brutus to Cassius *re* the loan of the fivers aforementioned and other matters—and before the arrival of Cassius with his horse and foot, and the quarrel—Brutus asked Lucilius what sort of a reception he had, and being told "With courtesy and respect enough," he remarked, "Thou hast described a hot friend cooling," and so on. But Cassius will cool no more until death cools him to-morrow at Philippi.

The rare gentleness of Brutus's character—and of the characters of thousands of other bosses in trouble—is splendidly, and ah! so softly, pictured in the tent with his servants after the departure of the others. It is a purely domestic scene without a hint of home, women, or children—save that they themselves are big children. The scene now has the atmosphere of a soft, sad nightfall, after a long, long, hot and weary day full of toil and struggle and trouble—though it is really well on towards morning.

Lucius comes in with the gown. Brutus says, "Give me the gown," and asks where his (Lucius's) musical instrument is, and Lucius replies that it's here in the tent. Brutus notices that he speaks drowsily. "Poor knave, I blame thee not, thou are o'er-watched." He tells him to call Claudius and some other of his men: "I'd have them sleep on cushions in my tent." They come. He tells them he might have to send them on business by and by to his "brother" Cassius, and bids them lie down and sleep, calling them sirs. They say they'll stand and watch his pleasure. "I will not have it so; lie down, good sirs." He finds, in the pocket of his gown, a book he'd been hunting high and low for—and had evidently given Lucius a warm time about—and he draws Lucius's attention to the fact:

> Look, Lucius, here's the book I sought for so:
> I put it in the pocket of my gown.
> *Lucius:* I was sure your lordship did not give it to me.
> *Brutus:* Bear with me, good boy, I am much forgetful, etc.

He asks Lucius if he can hold up his heavy eyes and touch his instrument a strain or two. But better give it all—it's not long:

> *Lucius:* Ay, my lord, an't please you.
> *Brutus:* It does, my boy:
> I trouble thee too much, but thou art willing.
> *Lucius:* It is my duty, sir.
> *Brutus:* I should not urge thy duty past thy might;
> I know young bloods look for a time of rest.
> *Lucius:* I have slept, my lord, already.
> *Brutus:* It was well done; and thou shalt sleep again;
> I will not hold thee long: if I do live,
> I will be good to thee. (*Music, and a song.*)
> This is a sleepy tune. O murderous slumber,
> Lay'st thou thy leaden mace upon my boy
> That plays thee music? Gentle knave, good-night;
> I will not do thee so much wrong to wake thee:
> If thou dost nod, thou break'st thy instrument;
> I'll take it from thee; and, good boy, good-night.
> Let me see, let me see; is not the leaf turn'd down
> Where I left reading? Here it is, I think.
>
> (*He sits down.*)

A man for all time! How natural it all reads! You must remember that he is a tired man after a long, strenuous day such as none of us ever know. The fate of Rome and his—a much smaller matter—are hanging on the balance, and tomorrow will decide; but he is so mind-dulled and shoulder-weary under the tremendous burden of great things and of many griefs that he is almost apathetic; and over all is the cloud of a loss that he has not yet had time to realize. He is self-hypnotized, so to speak, and his mind mercifully dulled for the moment on the Sea of Fatalism.

> *Enter* GHOST of CAESAR
> *Brutus:* How ill this taper burns! Ha! who comes here?
> I think it is the weakness of mine eyes

> That shapes this monstrous apparition.
> It comes upon me. Art thou any thing?
> Art thou some god, some angel, or some devil
> That makest my blood cold, and my hair to stare?
> Speak to me what thou art?

His very "scare," or rather his cold blood and staring hair are as things apart, to be analysed and explained quickly and put aside.

> *Ghost*: Thy evil spirit, Brutus.

That was frank enough, anyway.

> *Brutus*: Why comest thou?
> *Ghost*: To tell thee thou shalt see me at Philippi.
> *Brutus*: Well; then I shall see thee again?
> *Ghost*: Ay, at Philippi.
>
> > *(Vanishes.)*

That was very satisfactory, so far. But Brutus, having taken heart, as he says, would hold more talk with the "ill spirit." A ghost always needs to be taken quietly—it's no use getting excited and threshing round. But Caesar's, being a new-chum ghost and bashful, was doubtless embarrassed by his cool, matter-of-fact reception, and left. It didn't matter much. They were to meet soon, above Philippi, on more level terms.

But I cannot get away from the idea that Caesar's ghost's visit was made in a friendly spirit. Who knows? Perhaps Portia's spirit had sent it to comfort Brutus: her own being prevented from going for some reason only known to the immortal gods.

Then Brutus wakes them all.

> *Lucius*: The strings, my lord, are false.
> *Brutus*: He thinks he is still at his instrument.
> Lucius, awake!

And after questioning them as to whether they cried out in their sleep, or saw anything, he bids the boy sleep again (it is easy for tired boys to sleep at will in camp) and sends two of the others to Cassius to bid him get his forces on the way early and he would follow.

> *Brutus*: Go and commend me to my brother Cassius;
> Bid him set on his powers betimes before,
> And we will follow.
> *Varro* and *Claudius*: It shall be done, my lord.

For, being a wise soldier, as well as a brave and gentle one, he reckoned, no doubt, that it would be best to have a strong man in the rear until the field was actually reached, for the benefit of

would-be deserters, and unconsidered trifles of country people—
and maybe for another reason not totally disconnected with his
erratic friend Cassius.

Just one more scene, and a very different one, before we hurry
on to the end, as they have done to Philippi. It's the only scene in
which those two unlucky Romans, Cassius and Brutus, seem to
score.

It is during the barney, or as Shakespeare calls it, the "parley"
before the battle. Those parleys never seemed to do any good—
except to make matters worse, if I might put it like that: it's the
same, under similar circumstances, right up to to-day. Enter on
one side Octavius Caesar, Mark Antony, and their pals and army;
and, on the other, Brutus and Cassius and the friends and followers
of their falling fortunes.

> *Brutus*: Words before blows: is it so, countrymen?
> *Octavius*: Not that we love words better, as you do.

You see, Octavius starts it.
Brutus lays himself open:

> *Brutus*: Good words are better than bad strokes, Octavius.
> *Antony*: In your bad strokes, Brutus, you give good words:
>   Witness the hole you made in Caesar's heart,
>   Crying, "Long live! hail, Caesar!"

This is one for Brutus, though it contains a lie. But Cassius comes
to the rescue:

> *Cassius*: Antony,
>   The posture of your blows are yet unknown,
>   But, for your words, they rob the Hybla bees
>   And leave them honeyless.
> *Antony*: Not stingless too.
> *Brutus*: O, yes, and soundless too;
>   For you have stol'n their buzzing, Antony,
>   And very wisely threat before you sting.

That was one for Antony, and he gets mad. "Villains!" he yells,
and he abuses them about their vile daggers hacking one another
in the sides of Caesar (a little matter that ought to be worn threadbare by now), and calls them apes and hounds and bondmen and
curs, and O, flatterers (which seems to be worst of all in his opinion
—for he isn't one, you know), and damns 'em generally.

Old Cassius remarks, "Flatterers!"

Then Octavius breaks loose, and draws his Roman chopper and
waves it round, and spreads himself out over Caesar's three-and-

thirty wounds—which ought to be given a rest by this time, but only seem to be growing in number—and swears that he won't put up said chopper till said wounds are avenged,

> Or till another Caesar
> Have added slaughter to the sword of traitors.

Brutus says quietly that he cannot die by traitors unless he brings 'em with him. (He sent one to Egypt later on.) Octavius says he hopes he wasn't born to die on Brutus's sword; and Brutus says, in effect, that even if he was any good he couldn't die more honourably.

> *Brutus*: O, if thou wert the noblest of thy strain,
>   Young man, thou couldst not die more honourable.
> *Cassius*: A peevish schoolboy, worthless of such honour,
>   Join'd with a masker and a reveller!

Octavius calls off his dogs, and tells them to come on to-day if they dare, or if not, when they have stomachs.

> *Cassius*: Why, now, blow wind, swell billow, and swim bark!
>   The storm is up, and all is on the hazard.

Yes, I reckon old Cassius ("old" in an affectionate sense) and Brutus came out top dogs from that scrap anyway. And, yes, Antony *was* good at orating. He was great at orating over dead men—especially dead "friends" (as he called his rivals) and dead enemies. Brutus was "the noblest Roman of them all" when Antony came across him stiff later on. Now when I die——

Octavius, by the way, orated over Antony and his dusky hussy later on in Egypt, and they were the most "famous pair" in the world. I wonder whether the grim humour of it struck Octavius *then*: but then that young man seemed to have but little brains and less humour.

But now they go to see about settling the matter with iron-mongery. You can imagine the fight; the heat and the dust, for it was spring in a climate like ours. The bullocking, sweating, grunting, slaughter, the crack and clash and rattle as of fire-irons in a fender. The bad Latin language; the running away and chasing *en masse* and by individuals. The mutual pauses, the truces or spells—"smoke-ho's" we'd call 'em—between masses and individuals. The battered-in, lost, discarded or stolen helmets; the blood-stained, dinted, and loosened armour with bits missing, and the bloody and grotesque bandages. The confusion amongst the soldiers, as it is to-day—the ignorance of one wing as to the fate of the other, of one party as to the fate of the other, of one individual as to the fate of another:

> *Brutus*: Ride, ride, Messala, ride, and give these bills [directions to officers]
> Unto the legions on the other side:

Poor Cassius, routed and in danger of being surrounded, and thinking Brutus is in the same plight, or a prisoner or dead—and that Titinius is taken or killed—gets his bondman, whose life he once saved, to kill him in return for his freedom.

> Stand not to answer: here, take thou the hilts;
> And when my face is cover'd, as 'tis now,
> Guide thou the sword.
> Caesar, thou art revenged,
> Even with the sword that kill'd thee.

Good-bye, Cassius, old chap!

Titinius and Messala, coming too late, find Cassius dead; and Titinius, being left alone while Messala takes the news to Brutus, kills himself with Cassius's sword. Titinius, farewell!

Come Brutus and those that are left.

> *Brutus*: Where, where, Messala, doth his body lie?
> *Messala*: Lo, yonder, and Titinius mourning it.
> *Brutus*: Titinius' face is upward.
> *Cato*: He is slain.

Grim mates in a grim day in a grim hour. Then the cry of Brutus:

> O Julius Caesar, thou art mighty yet!

But if he were, perhaps he only gathered old Cassius and Titinius to be sure of their company with him and Brutus amongst the gods a little later.

> *Brutus*: Friends, I owe more tears
> To this dead man than you shall see me pay.
> I shall find time, Cassius, I shall find time.

And, after making arrangements for the removal of Cassius's body, they go to try their fortunes in a second fight.

Young Cato is killed and good Lucilius taken. Comes Brutus beaten, with Dardanius his last friend, and his three servants, Clitus, Strato, and Volumnius.

> *Brutus*: Come, poor remains of friends, rest on this rock.

Strato, exhausted, goes to sleep, as man can sleep during a battle; and Brutus whispers the others, one after another, to kill him; but they are shocked and refuse: "I'll rather kill myself," "I do such a deed?" etc. He begs Volumnius, his old schoolmate, to hold his sword-hilt while he runs on it, for their love of old.

> *Volumnius*: That's not the office for a friend, my lord.

There are alarums, and they urge him to fly, for it's no use stopping there.

> *Brutus*: Farewell to you; and you; and you, Volumnius.
> Strato, thou hast been all this while asleep;
> Farewell to thee too, Strato! Countrymen,
> My heart doth joy that yet in all my life
> I found no man but he was true to me.

Ye gods! but it's grand. I wish to our God that I could say as much—or that man or woman ever found me untrue. Could Antony say as much, afterwards, in Egypt—or Octavius? with Antony then on his mind? Even Antony's last man and servant failed him in the end, killing himself rather than kill his master. But Strato——
There are more alarums and voices calling to them to run. They urge Brutus again, and he tells them to go and he'll follow. They all run except Strato, who hesitates.

> *Brutus*: I prithee, Strato, stay thou by thy lord:
> Thou art a fellow of a good respect;
> Thy life hath had some snatch of honour in it:
> Hold then my sword, and turn away thy face,
> While I do run upon it. Wilt thou, Strato?
> *Strato*: Give me your hand first: fare you well, my lord.
> *Brutus*: Farewell, good Strato. Caesar, now be well:
> I kill'd not thee with half so good a will.

Brutus, good night!
I like Shakespeare's servants. They seem to show that he sprang from servants or common people rather than from lords and masters, for he deals with them very gently. It must be understood that servants, bond and free, were born unto the same house and served it for generations; and so down to modern England, where the old nurse and the tottering old gardener often nursed and played with "Master Will," when his father, the dead and gone old squire, was a young man.

See where Timon's servants stand in the only patch of sun-light in that black and bitter story:

> *Enter* FLAVIUS, *with two or three* SERVANTS.

1 Serv.: Hear you, master steward, where's our master?
     Are we undone? cast off? nothing remaining?

Flav.: Alack, my fellows, what should I say to you?
     Let me be recorded by the righteous gods,
     I am as poor as you.

1 Serv.: Such a house broke!
     So noble a master fall'n! All gone! and not
     One friend to take his fortune by the arm,
     And go along with him!

2 Serv.: As we do turn our backs
     From our companion thrown into his grave,
     So his familiars to his buried fortunes
     Slink all away; leave their false vows with him,
     Like empty purses pick'd; and his poor self,
     A dedicated beggar to the air,
     With his disease of all-shunn'd poverty,
     Walks, like contempt, alone. More of our fellows.

              Enter other SERVANTS

Flav.: All broken implements of a ruin'd house.

3 Serv.: Yet do our hearts wear Timon's livery;
     That see I by our faces; we are fellows still,
     Serving alike in sorrow: leak'd is our bark,
     And we, poor mates, stand on the dying deck,
     Hearing the surges threat; we must all part
     Into this sea of air.

Flav.: Good fellows all,
     The latest of my wealth I'll share amongst you.
     Wherever we shall meet, for Timon's sake
     Let's yet be fellows; let's shake our heads, and say,
     As 'twere a knell unto our master's fortunes,
     "We have seen better days." Let each take some.

                      (*Giving them money.*)

     Nay, put out all your hands. Not one word more:
     Thus part we rich in sorrow, parting poor.

SEND ROUND THE HAT

SEND ROUND THE HAT

Now this is the creed from the Book of the Bush—
Should be simple and plain to a dunce:
"If a man's in a hole you must pass round the hat—
Were he jail-bird or gentleman once."

"Is it any harm to wake yer?"

It was about nine o'clock in the morning, and, though it was Sunday morning, it was no harm to wake me; but the shearer had mistaken me for a deaf jackeroo, who was staying at the shanty and was something like me, and had good-naturedly shouted almost at the top of his voice, and he woke the whole shanty. Anyway he woke three or four others who were sleeping on beds and stretchers, and one on a shake-down on the floor, in the same room. It had been a wet night, and the shanty was full of shearers from Big Billabong Shed which had cut out the day before. My room mates had been drinking and gambling overnight, and they swore luridly at the intruder for disturbing them.

He was six-foot-three or thereabout. He was loosely built, bony, sandy-complexioned and grey eyed. He wore a good-humoured grin at most times, as I noticed later on; he was of a type of bushman that I always liked—the sort that seem to get more good-natured the longer they grow, yet are hard-knuckled and would accommodate a man who wanted to fight, or thrash a bully in a good-natured way. The sort that like to carry somebody's baby round, and cut wood, carry water and do little things for overworked married bushwomen. He wore a saddle-tweed sac suit two sizes too small for him, and his face, neck, great hands and bony wrists were covered with sunblotches and freckles.

"I hope I ain't disturbin' yer," he shouted, as he bent over my bunk, "but there's a cove——"

"You needn't shout!" I interrupted, "I'm not deaf."

"Oh—I beg your pardon!" he shouted. "I didn't know I was yellin'. I thought you was the deaf feller."

"Oh, that's all right," I said. "What's the trouble?"

"Wait till them other chaps is done swearin' and I'll tell yer," he said. He spoke with a quiet, good-natured drawl, with something of the nasal twang, but tone and drawl distinctly Australian—altogether apart from that of the Americans.

"Oh, spit it out for Christ's sake, Long'un!" yelled One-eyed Bogan, who had been the worst swearer in a rough shed, and he fell back on his bunk as if his previous remarks had exhausted him.

"It's that there sick jackeroo that was pickin'-up at Big Billabong," said the Giraffe. "He had to knock off the first week, an' he's been here ever since. They're sendin' him away to the hospital in Sydney by the speeshall train. They're just goin' to take him up in the wagonette to the railway station, an' I thought I might as well go round with the hat an' get him a few bob. He's got a missus and kids in Sydney."

"Yer always goin' round with yer gory hat!" growled Bogan. "Yer'd blanky well take it round in hell!"

"That's what he's doing, Bogan," muttered Gentleman Once, on the shake-down, with his face to the wall.

The hat was a genuine "cabbage-tree," one of the sort that "last a lifetime." It was well coloured, almost black in fact with weather and age, and it had a new strap round the base of the crown. I looked into it and saw a dirty pound note and some silver. I dropped in half a crown, which was more than I could spare, for I had only been a green-hand at Big Billabong.

"Thank yer!" he said. "Now then, you fellers!"

"I wish you'd keep your hat on your head, and your money in your pockets and your sympathy somewhere else," growled Jack Moonlight as he raised himself painfully on his elbow and felt under his pillow for two half-crowns. "Here," he said, "here's two half-casers. Chuck 'em in and let me sleep for God's sake!"

Gentleman Once, the gambler, rolled round on his shakedown, bringing his good-looking, dissipated face from the wall. He had turned in in his clothes and, with considerable exertion, he shoved his hand down into the pocket of his trousers, which were a tight fit. He brought up a roll of pound notes and could find no silver.

"Here," he said to the Giraffe, "I might as well lay a quid. I'll chance it anyhow. Chuck it in."

"You've got rats this mornin', Gentleman Once," growled the Bogan. "It ain't a blanky horse race."

"P'r'aps I have," said Gentleman Once, and he turned to the wall again with his head on his arm.

"Now, Bogan, yer might as well chuck in somethin'," said the Giraffe.

"What's the matter with the —— jackeroo?" asked the Bogan, tugging his trousers from under the mattress.

Moonlight said something in a low tone.

"The —— he has!" said Bogan. "Well, I pity the ——! Here, I'll chuck in half a —— quid!" and he dropped half a sovereign into the hat.

The fourth man, who was known to his face as "Barcoo-Rot," and behind his back as "The Mean Man," had been drinking all night, and not even Bogan's stump-splitting adjectives could rouse him. So Bogan got out of bed, and calling on us (as blanky female cattle) to witness what he was about to do, he rolled the drunkard over, prospected his pockets till he made up five shillings (or a "caser" in bush language), and "chucked" them into the hat.

And Barcoo-Rot is probably unconscious to this day that he was ever connected with an act of charity.

The Giraffe struck the deaf jackeroo in the next room. I heard the chaps cursing "Long-'un" for waking them, and "Deaf-'un" for being, as they thought at first, the indirect cause of the disturbance. I heard the Giraffe and his hat being condemned in other rooms and cursed along the veranda where more shearers were sleeping; and after a while I turned out.

The Giraffe was carefully fixing a mattress and pillows on the floor of a wagonette, and presently a man, who looked like a corpse, was carried out and lifted into the trap.

As the wagonette started, the shanty-keeper—a fat, soulless-looking man—put his hand in his pocket and dropped a quid into the hat which was still going round, in the hands of the Giraffe's mate, little Teddy Thompson, who was as far below medium height as the Giraffe was above it.

The Giraffe took the horse's head and led him along on the most level parts of the road towards the railway station, and two or three chaps went along to help get the sick man into the train.

The shearing-season was over in that district, but I got a job of house-painting, which was my trade, at the Great Western Hotel (a two-storey brick place), and I stayed in Bourke for a couple of months.

The Giraffe was a Victorian native from Bendigo. He was well known in Bourke and to many shearers who came through the great dry scrubs from hundreds of miles round. He was stakeholder, drunkard's banker, peacemaker where possible, referee or second to oblige the chaps when a fight was on, big brother or uncle to most of the children in town, final court of appeal when the youngsters had a dispute over a foot-race at the school picnic, referee at their fights, and he was the stranger's friend.

"The feller as knows can battle around for himself," he'd say. "But I always like to do what I can for a hard-up stranger cove. I was a green-hand jackeroo once meself, and I know what it is."

"You're always bothering about other people, Giraffe," said Tom Hall, the shearers' union secretary, who was only a couple of inches shorter than the Giraffe. "There's nothing in it, you can take it from me—I ought to know."

"Well, what's a feller to do?" said the Giraffe. "I'm only hangin' round here till shearin' starts agen, an' a cove might as well be doin' something. Besides, it ain't as if I was like a cove that had old people or a wife an' kids to look after. I ain't got no responsibilities. A feller can't be doin' nothin'. Besides, I like to lend a helpin' hand when I can."

"Well, all I've got to say," said Tom, most of whose screw went in borrowed quids, etc. "All I've got to say is that you'll get no thanks, and you might blanky well starve in the end."

"There ain't no fear of me starvin' so long as I've got me hands about me; an' I ain't a cove as wants thanks," said the Giraffe.

He was always helping someone or something. Now it was a bit of a "darnce" that we was gettin' up for the girls; again it was Mrs Smith, the woman whose husban' was drowned in the flood in the Bogan River lars' Crismas, or that there poor woman down by the billabong—her husband cleared out and left her with a lot o' kids. Or Bill Something, the Bullocky, who was run over by his own wagon, while he was drunk, and got his leg broke.

Toward the end of his spree One-eyed Bogan broke loose and smashed nearly all the windows of the Carriers' Arms, and next morning he was fined heavily at the police court. About dinner-time I encountered the Giraffe and his hat, with two half-crowns in it for a start.

"I'm sorry to trouble yer," he said, "but One-eyed Bogan carn't pay his fine, an' I thought we might fix it up for him. He ain't half a bad sort of feller when he ain't drinkin'. It's only when he gets too much booze in him."

After shearing, the hat usually started round with the Giraffe's own dirty crumpled pound note in the bottom of it as a send-off, later on it was half a sovereign, and so on down to half a crown and a shilling, as he got short of stuff; till in the end he would borrow a "few bob"—which he always repaid after next shearing—"just to start the thing goin'."

There were several yarns about him and his hat. 'Twas said that the hat had belonged to his father, whom he resembled in every respect, and it had been going round for so many years that the crown was worn as thin as paper by the quids, half-quids, casers, half-casers, bobs and tanners or sprats—to say nothing of the scrums—that had been chucked into it in its time and shaken up.

They say that when a new governor visited Bourke the Giraffe happened to be standing on the platform close to the exit, grinning good-humouredly, and the local toady nudged him urgently and said in an awful whisper, "Take off your hat! Why don't you take off your hat?"

"Why?" drawled the Giraffe, "he ain't hard up, is he?"

And they fondly cherish an anecdote to the effect that, when the One-Man-One-Vote Bill was passed (or Payment of Members, or when the first Labour Party went in—I forget on which occasion they said it was) the Giraffe was carried away by the general enthusiasm, got a few beers in him, "chucked" a quid into his hat, and sent it round. The boys contributed by force of habit, and contributed largely, because of the victory and the beer. And when the hat came back to the Giraffe, he stood holding it in front of him with both hands and stared blankly into it for a while. Then it dawned on him.

"Blowed if I haven't bin an' gone an' took up a bloomin' collection for meself!" he said.

He was almost a teetotaller, but he stood his shout in reason. He mostly drank ginger beer.

"I ain't a feller that boozes, but I ain't got nothin' agen chaps enjoyin' themselves, so long as they don't go too far."

It was common for a man on the spree to say to him:

"Here! here's five quid. Look after it for me, Giraffe, will yer, till I git off the booze."

His real name was Bob Brothers, and his bush names, "Long-'un," "The Giraffe," "Send-round-the-hat," "Chuck-in-a-bob," and "Ginger-ale."

Some years before, camels and Afghan drivers had been imported to the Bourke distict; the camels did very well in the dry country, they went right across country and carried everythink from sardines to flooring-boards. And the teamsters loved the Afghans nearly as much as Sydney furniture makers love the cheap Chinese in the same line. They love 'em even as union shearers on strike love blacklegs brought up-country to take their places.

Now the Giraffe was a good, straight unionist, but in cases of sickness or trouble he was as apt to forget his unionism, as all bushmen are, at all times (and for all time), to forget their creed. So, one evening, the Giraffe blundered into the Carriers' Arms—of all places in the world—when it was full of teamsters; he had his hat in his hand and some small silver and coppers in it.

"I say, you fellers, there's a poor, sick Afghan in the camp down there along the——"

A big, brawny bullock-driver took him firmly by the shoulders, or, rather by the elbows, and ran him out before any damage was done. The Giraffe took it as he took most things, good-humouredly; but, about dusk, he was seen slipping down towards the Afghan camp with a billy of soup.

"I believe," remarked Tom Hall, "that when the Giraffe goes to heaven—and he's the only one of us, as far as I can see, that has a ghost of a show—I believe that when he goes to heaven, the first thing he'll do will be to take his infernal hat round amongst the angels—getting up a collection for this damned world that he left behind."

"Well, I don't think there's so much to his credit, after all," said Jack Mitchell, shearer. "You see, the Giraffe is ambitious; he likes public life, and that accounts for him shoving himself forward with his collections. As for bothering about people in trouble, that's only common curiosity; he's one of those chaps that are always shoving their noses into other people's troubles. And, as for looking after sick men—why! there's nothing the Giraffe likes better than pottering round a sick man, and watching him and studying him. He's awfully interested in sick men, and they're pretty scarce out here. I tell you there's nothing he likes better—except, maybe, it's pottering round a corpse. I believe he'd ride forty miles to help and sympathize and potter round a funeral. The fact of the matter is that the Giraffe is only enjoying himself with other people's troubles—that's all it is. It's only vulgar curiosity and selfishness. I set it down to his ignorance; the way he was brought up."

A few days after the Afghan incident the Giraffe and his hat had a run of luck. A German, one of a party who were building a new wooden bridge over the Big Billabong, was helping unload some girders from a truck at the railway station, when a big log slipped on the skids and his leg was smashed badly. They carried him to the Carriers' Arms, which was the nearest hotel, and into a bedroom behind the bar, and sent for the doctor. The Giraffe was in evidence as usual.

"It vas not that at all," said German Charlie, when they asked him if he was in much pain. "It vas not that at all. I don't cares a damn for der bain; but dis is der tird year—und I vas going home dis year—after der gontract—und der gontract yoost commence!"

That was the burden of his song all through, between his groans.

There were a good few chaps sitting quietly about the bar and veranda when the doctor arrived. The Giraffe was sitting at the end of the counter, on which he had laid his hat while he wiped his face, neck, and forehead with a big speckled "sweat-rag." It was a very hot day.

The doctor, a good-hearted young Australian, was heard saying something. Then German Charlie, in a voice that rung with pain:

"Make that leg right, doctor—quick! Dis is der tird pluddy year—und I must go home!"

The doctor asked him if he was in great pain.

"Neffer mind der pluddy bain, doctor! Neffer mind der pluddy bain! Dot vas nossing. Make dat leg well quick, doctor. Dis vas der last gontract, and I vas going home dis year." Then the words jerked out of him by physical agony: "Der girl was vaiting dree year, und—by Got! I must go home."

The publican—Watty Braithwaite, known as "Watty Broadweight," or, more familiarly, "Watty Bothways"—turned over the Giraffe's hat in a tired, bored sort of way, dropped a quid into it, and nodded resignedly at the Giraffe.

The Giraffe caught up the hint and the hat with alacrity. The hat went all round town, so to speak; and, as soon as his leg was firm enough not to come loose on the road German Charlie went home.

It was well known that I contributed to the Sydney *Bulletin* and several other papers. The Giraffe's bump of reverence was very large, and swelled especially for sick men and poets. He treated me with much more respect than is due from a bushman to a man, and with an odd sort of extra gentleness I sometimes fancied. But one day he rather surprised me.

"I'm sorry to trouble yer," he said in a shamefaced way. "I don't know as you go in for sportin', but One-eyed Bogan an' Barcoo-Rot is goin' to have a bit of a scrap down the Billy-bong this evenin', an'——".

"A bit of a what?" I asked.

"A bit of fight to a finish," he said apologetically. "An' the chaps is tryin' to fix up a fiver to put some life into the thing. There's bad blood between One-eyed Bogan and Barcoo-Rot, an' it won't do them any harm to have it out."

It was a great fight, I remember. There must have been a couple

of score blood-soaked handkerchiefs (or "sweat-rags") buried in a
hole on the field of battle, and the Giraffe was busy the rest of the
evening helping to patch up the principals. Later on he took up a
small collection for the loser, who happened to be Barcoo-Rot in
spite of the advantage of an eye.

The Salvation Army lassie, who went round with the *War Cry*,
nearly always sold the Giraffe three copies.

A new-chum parson, who wanted a subscription to build or
enlarge a chapel, or something, sought the assistance of the Giraffe's
influence with his mates.

"Well," said the Giraffe, "I ain't a churchgoer meself. I ain't what
you might call a religious cove, but I'll be glad to do what I can to
help yer. I don't suppose I can do much. I ain't been to church since
I was a kiddy."

The parson was shocked, but later on he learned to appreciate the
Giraffe and his mates, and to love Australia for the bushman's sake,
and it was he who told me the above anecdote.

The Giraffe helped fix some stalls for a Catholic Church bazaar
and some of the chaps chaffed him about it in the union office.

"You'll be taking up a collection for a joss-house down in the
Chinamen's camp next," said Tom Hall in conclusion.

"Well, I ain't got nothin' agen the Roming Carflics," said the
Giraffe. "An' Father O'Donovan's a very decent sort of cove. He
stuck up for the unions all right in the strike anyway." ("He
wouldn't be Irish if he wasn't," someone commented.) "I carried
swags once for six months with a feller that was a Carflick, an' he
was a very straight feller. And a girl I knowed turned Carflick to
marry a chap that had got her into trouble, an' she was always jes
the same to me after as she was before. Besides, I like to help
everything that's goin' on."

Tom Hall and one or two others went out hurriedly to have a
drink. But we all loved the Giraffe.

He was very innocent and very humorous, especially when he
meant to be most serious and philosophical.

"Some of them bush girls is regular tomboys," he said to me
solemnly one day. "Some of them is too cheeky altogether. I
remember once I was stoppin' at a place—they was sort of relations
o' mine—an' they put me to sleep in a room off the verander, where
there was a glass door an' no blinds. An' the first mornin' the
girls—they was sort o' cousins o' mine—they come gigglin' and
foolin' round outside the door on the verander, an' kep' me in bed
till nearly ten o'clock. I had to put me trowsis on under the

bed-clothes in the end. But I got back on 'em the next night," he reflected.

"How did you do that, Bob?" I asked.

"Why, I went to bed in me trowsis!"

One day I was on a plank, painting the ceiling of the bar of the Great Western Hotel. I was anxious to get the job finished. The work had been kept back most of the day by chaps handing up long beers to me, and drawing my attention to the alleged fact that I was putting on the paint wrong side out. I was slapping it on over the last few boards when:

"I'm very sorry to trouble yer; I always seem to be troublin' yer; but there's that there woman and them girls——"

I looked down—about the first time I had looked down on him—and there was the Giraffe, with his hat brim up on the plank and two half-crowns in it.

"Oh, that's all right, Bob," I said, and I dropped in half a crown.

There were shearers in the bar, and presently there was some barracking. It appeared that that there woman and them girls were strange women, in the local as well as the Biblical sense of the word, who had come from Sydney at the end of the shearing-season, and had taken a cottage on the edge of the scrub on the outskirts of the town. There had been trouble this week in connection with a row at their establishment, and they had been fined, warned off by the police, and turned out by their landlord.

"This is a bit too red-hot, Giraffe," said one of the shearers. "Them ——s has made enough out of us coves. They've got plenty of stuff, don't you fret. Let 'em go to ——! I'm blanked if I give a sprat."

"They ain't got their fares to Sydney." said the Giraffe. "An', what's more, the little 'un is sick, an' two of them has kids in Sydney."

"How the —— do you know?"

"Why, one of 'em come to me an' told me all about it."

There was an involuntary guffaw.

"Look here, Bob," said Billy Woods, the rouseabouts' secretary, kindly. "Don't you make a fool of yourself. You'll have all the chaps laughing at you. Those girls are only working you for all you're worth. I suppose one of 'em came crying and whining to you. Don't you bother about 'em. *You* don't know 'em; they can pump water at a moment's notice. You haven't had any experience with women yet, Bob."

"She didn't come within' and cryin' to me," said the Giraffe, dropping his twanging drawl a little. "She looked me straight in the face an' told me all about it."

"I say, Giraffe," said Box-o'-Tricks, "what have you been doin'? You've bin down there on the nod. I'm surprised at yer, Giraffe."

"An' he pretends to be so gory soft an' innocent, too," growled the Bogan. "We know all about you, Giraffe."

"Look here, Giraffe," said Mitchell the shearer. "I'd never have thought it of you. We all thought you were the only virgin youth west the river; I always thought you were a moral young man. You mustn't think that because your conscience is pricking you everyone else's is."

"I ain't had anythin' to do with them," said the Giraffe, drawling again. "I ain't a cove that goes in for that sort of thing. But other chaps has, and I think they might as well help 'em out of their fix."

"They're a rotten crowd," said Billy Woods. "You don't know them, Bob. Don't bother about them—they're not worth it. Put your money in your pocket. You'll find a better use for it before next shearing."

"Better shout, Giraffe," said Box-o'-Tricks.

Now in spite of the Giraffe's softness he was the hardest man in Bourke to move when he'd decided on what he thought was "the fair thing to do." Another peculiarity of his was that on occasion, such for instance as "sayin' a few words" at a strike meeting, he would straighten himself, drop the twang, and rope in his drawl, so to speak.

"Well, look here, you chaps," he said now. "I don't know anything about them women. I s'pose they're bad, but I don't suppose they're worse than men has made them. All I know is that there's four women turned out, without any stuff, and every woman in Bourke, an' the police, an' the law agen 'em. An' the fact that they is women is agenst 'em most of all. You don't expect 'em to hump their swags to Sydney! Why, only I ain't got the stuff I wouldn't trouble yer. I'd pay their fares meself. Look," he said, lowering his voice, "there they are now, an' one of the girls is cryin'. Don't let 'em see yer lookin'."

I dropped softly from the plank and peeped out with the rest.

They stood by the fence on the opposite side of the street, a bit up towards the railway station, with their portmanteaux and bundles at their feet. One girl leant with her arms on the fence rail and her face buried in them, another was trying to comfort her. The third girl and the woman stood facing our way. The woman was good-looking; she had a hard face, but it might have been made hard. The third girl seemed half defiant, half inclined to cry. Presently she went to the other side of the girl who was crying on the fence and put her arm round her shoulder. The woman suddenly turned her back on us and stood looking away over the paddocks.

The hat went round. Billy Woods was first, then Box-o'-Tricks, and then Mitchell.

Billy contributed with eloquent silence. "I was only jokin', Giraffe," said Box-o'-Tricks, dredging his pockets for a couple of shillings. It was some time after the shearing, and most of the chaps were hard up.

"Ah, well," sighed Mitchell. "There's no help for it. If the Giraffe would take up a collection to import some decent girls to this God-forgotten hole there might be some sense in it.... It's bad enough for the Giraffe to undermine our religious prejudices, and tempt us to take a morbid interest in sick Chows and Afghans, and blacklegs and widows; but when he starts mixing us up with strange women it's time to buck." And he prospected his pockets and contributed two shillings, some odd pennies, and a pinch of tobacco dust.

"I don't mind helping the girls, but I'm damned if I'll give a penny to help the old ——," said Tom Hall.

"Well, she was a girl once herself," drawled the Giraffe.

The Giraffe went round to the other pubs and to the union offices, and when he returned he seemed satisfied with the plate, but troubled about something else.

"I don't know what to do for them for to-night," he said. "None of the pubs or boardin'-houses will hear of them, an' there ain't no empty houses, an' the women is all agen 'em."

"Not all," said Alice, the big, handsome barmaid from Sydney. "Come here, Bob." She gave the Giraffe half a sovereign and a look for which some of us would have paid him ten pounds—had we had the money, and had the look been transferable.

"Wait a minute, Bob," she said, and she went in to speak to the landlord.

"There's an empty bedroom at the end of the store in the yard," she said when she came back. "They can camp there for to-night if they behave themselves. You'd better tell 'em, Bob."

"Thank yer, Alice," said the Giraffe.

Next day, after work, the Giraffe and I drifted together and down by the river in the cool of the evening, and sat on the edge of the steep, drought-parched bank.

"I heard you saw your lady friends off this morning, Bob," I said, and was sorry I said it, even before he answered.

"Oh, they ain't no friends of mine," he said. "Only four poor devils of women. I thought they mightn't like to stand waitin' with the crowd on the platform, so I jest offered to get their tickets an' told 'em to wait round at the back of the station till the bell rung.... An' what do yer think they did, Harry?" he went on, with an exasperatingly unintelligent grin. "Why, they wanted to kiss me."

"Did they?"

"Yes. An' they would have done it, too, if I hadn't been so long.... Why, I'm blessed if they didn't kiss me hands."

"You don't say so."

"God's truth. Somehow I didn't like to go on the platform with them after that; besides, they was cryin', and I can't stand women cryin'. But some of the chaps put them into an empty carriage." He thought a moment. Then:

"There's some terrible good-hearted fellers in the world," he reflected.

I thought so too.

"Bob," I said, "you're a single man. Why don't you get married and settle down?"

"Well," he said, "I ain't got no wife an' kids, that's a fact. But it ain't my fault."

He may have been right about the wife. But I thought of the look that Alice had given him, and——

"Girls seem to like me right enough," he said, "but it don't go no further than that. The trouble is that I'm so long, and I always seem to get shook after little girls. At least there was one little girl in Bendigo that I was properly gone on."

"And wouldn't she have you?"

"Well, it seems not."

"Did you ask her?"

"Oh, yes, I asked her right enough."

"Well, and what did she say?"

"She said it would be rediculus for her to be seen trottin alongside of a chimbley like me."

"Perhaps she didn't mean that. There are any amount of little women who like tall men."

"I thought of that too—afterwards. P'r'aps she didn't mean it that way. I s'pose the fact of the matter was that she didn't cotton on to me, and wanted to let me down easy. She didn't want to hurt me feelin's, if yer understand—she was a very good-hearted little girl.

There's some terrible tall fellers where I come from, and I know two as married little girls."

He seemed a hopeless case.

"Sometimes," he said, "sometimes I wish that I wasn't so blessed long."

"There's that there deaf jackeroo," he reflected presently. "He's something in the same fix about girls as I am. He's too deaf and I'm too long."

"How do you make that out?" I asked. "He's got three girls, to my knowledge, and, as for being deaf, why, he gasses more than any man in the town, and knows more of what's going on than old Mother Brindle the washerwoman."

"Well, look at that now!" said the Giraffe, slowly. "Who'd have thought it? He never told me he had three girls, an' as for hearin' news, I always tell him anything that's goin' on that I think he doesn't catch. He told me his trouble was that whenever he went out with a girl people could hear what they was sayin'—at least they could hear what she was sayin' to him, an' draw their own conclusions, he said. He said he went out one night with a girl, and some of the chaps foxed 'em an' heard her sayin' 'don't' to him, an' put it all round town."

"What did she say 'don't' for?" I asked.

"He didn't tell me that, but I s'pose he was kissin' her or huggin' her or something."

"Bob," I said presently, "didn't you try the little girl in Bendigo a second time?"

"No," he said. "What was the use. She was a good little girl, and I wasn't goin' to go botherin' her. I ain't the sort of cove that goes hangin' round where he isn't wanted. But somehow I couldn't stay about Bendigo after she gave me the hint, so I thought I'd come over an' have a knock round on this side for a year or two."

"And you never wrote to her?"

"No. What was the use of goin' pesterin' her with letters? I know what trouble letters give me when I have to answer one. She'd have only had to tell me the straight truth in a letter an' it wouldn't have done me any good. But I've pretty well got over it by this time."

A few days later I went to Sydney. The Giraffe was the last I shook hands with from the carriage window, and he slipped something in a piece of newspaper into my hand.

"I hope yer won't be offended," he drawled, "but some of the chaps thought you mightn't be too flush of stuff—you've been shoutin' a good deal; so they put a quid or two together. They thought it might help yer to have a bit of a fly round in Sydney."

I was back in Bourke before next shearing. On the evening of my arrival I ran against the Giraffe; he seemed strangely shaken over something, but he kept his hat on his head.

"Would yer mind takin' a stroll as fur as the Billerbong?" he said. "I got something I'd like to tell yer."

His big, brown, sunburnt hands trembled and shook as he took a letter from his pocket and opened it.

"I've just got a letter," he said. "A letter from that little girl at Bendigo. It seems it was all a mistake. I'd like you to read it. Somehow I feel as if I want to talk to a feller, and I'd rather talk to you than any of them other chaps."

It was a good letter, from a big-hearted little girl. She had been breaking her heart for the great ass all these months. It seemed that he had left Bendigo without saying good-bye to her. "Somehow I couldn't bring meself to it," he said, when I taxed him with it. She had never been able to get his address until last week; then she got it from a Bourke man who had gone south. She called him "an awful long fool," which he was, without the slightest doubt, and she implored him to write, and come back to her.

"And will you go back, Bob?" I asked.

"My oath! I'd take the train to-morrer only I ain't got the stuff. But I've got a stand in Big Billerbong Shed an' I'll soon knock a few quid together. I'll go back as soon as ever shearin's over. I'm goin' to write away to her to-night."

The Giraffe was the "ringer" of Big Billabong Shed that season. His tallies averaged a hundred and twenty a day. He only sent his hat round once during shearing, and it was noticed that he hesitated at first and only contributed half a crown. But then it was a case of a man being taken from the shed by the police for wife desertion.

"It's always that way," commented Mitchell. "Those soft, good-hearted fellows always end by getting hard and selfish. The world makes 'em so. It's the thought of the soft fools they've been that finds out sooner or later and makes 'em repent. Like as not the Giraffe will be the meanest man out back before he's done."

When Big Billabong cut out, and we got back to Bourke with our dusty swags and dirty cheques, I spoke to Tom Hall:

"Look here, Tom," I said. "That long fool, the Giraffe, has been breaking his heart for a little girl in Bendigo ever since he's been out back, and she's been breaking her heart for him, and the ass didn't know it till he got a letter from her just before Big Billabong started. He's going to-morrow morning."

That evening Tom stole the Giraffe's hat. "I s'pose it'll turn up in the mornin'," said the Giraffe. "I don't mind a lark," he added, "but it does seem a bit red hot for the chaps to collar a cove's hat and a feller goin' away for good, p'r'aps, in the mornin'."

Mitchell started the thing going with a quid.

"It's worth it," he said, "to get rid of him. We'll have some peace now. There won't be so many accidents or women in trouble when the Giraffe and his blessed hat are gone. Anyway, he's an eyesore in the town, and he's getting on my nerves for one.... Come on, you sinners! Chuck 'em in; we're only taking quids and half-quids."

About daylight next morning Tom Hall slipped into the Giraffe's room at the Carriers' Arms. The Giraffe was sleeping peacefully. Tom put the hat on a chair by his side. The collection had been a record one, and, besides the packet of money in the crown of the hat, there was a silver-mounted pipe with case—the best that could be bought in Bourke, a gold brooch, and several trifles—besides an ugly valentine of a long man in his shirt walking the room with a twin on each arm.

Tom was about to shake the Giraffe by the shoulder, when he noticed a great foot, with about half a yard of big-boned ankle and shank, sticking out at the bottom of the bed. The temptation was too great. Tom took up the hair-brush, and, with the back of it, he gave a smart rap on the point of an in-growing toe-nail, and slithered.

We heard the Giraffe swearing good-naturedly for a while, and then there was a pregnant silence. He was staring at the hat we supposed.

We were all up at the station to see him off. It was rather a long wait. The Giraffe edged me up to the other end of the platform. He seemed overcome.

"There's—there's some terrible good-hearted fellers in this world," he said. "You mustn't forgit 'em, Harry, when you make a big name writin'. I'm—well, I'm blessed if I don't feel as if I was jist goin' to blubber!"

I was glad he didn't. The Giraffe blubberin' would have been a spectacle. I steered him back to his friends.

"Ain't you going to kiss me, Bob?" said the Great Western's big, handsome barmaid, as the bell rang.

"Well, I don't mind kissin' you, Alice," he said, wiping his mouth. "But I'm goin' to be married, yer know." And he kissed her fair on the mouth.

"There's nothin' like gettin' into practice," he said, grinning round.

We thought he was improving wonderfully; but at the last moment something troubled him.

"Look here, you chaps," he said, hesitatingly, with his hand in his pocket, "I don't know what I'm going to do with all this stuff. There's that there poor washerwoman that scalded her legs liftin' the boiler of clothes off the fire——"

We shoved him into the carriage. He hung—about half of him—out the window, wildly waving his hat, till the train disappeared in the scrub.

And, as I sit here writing by lamplight at midday, in the midst of a great city of shallow social sham, of hopeless, squalid poverty, of ignorant selfishness, cultured or brutish, and of noble and heroic endeavour frowned down or callously neglected, I am almost aware of a burst of sunshine in the room, and a long form leaning over my chair, and:

"Excuse me for troublin' yer; I'm always troubin' yer; but there's that there poor woman...."

And I wish I could immortalize him!

THAT PRETTY GIRL IN THE ARMY

Now I often sit at Watty's, when the night is very near,
With a head that's full of jingles—and the fumes of bottled beer;
For I always have a fancy that, if I am over there
When the Army prays for Watty, I'm included in the prayer.
It would take a lot of praying, lots of thumping on the drum,
To prepare our sinful, straying, erring souls for Kingdom Come.
But I love my fellow-sinners! and I hope, upon the whole,
That the Army gets a hearing when it prays for Watty's soul.
                          —When the World was Wide.

The Salvation Army does good business in some of the outback towns of the great pastoral wastes of Australia. There's the thoughtless, careless generosity of the bushman, whose pockets don't go far enough down his trousers (that's what's the matter with him), and who contributes to anything that comes along, without troubling to ask questions, like long Bob Brothers of Bourke, who, chancing to be "a Protestant by rights," unwittingly subscribed towards the erection of a new Catholic church, and, being chaffed for his mistake, said:

"Ah, well, I don't suppose it'll matter a hang in the end, anyway it goes. I ain't got nothink agenst the Roming Carflicks."

There's the shearer, fresh with his cheque from a cut-out shed, gloriously drunk and happy, in love with all the world, and ready to subscribe towards any creed and shout for all hands—including Old Nick if he happened to come along. There's the shearer, half-drunk and inclined to be nasty, who has got the wrong end of all things with a tight grip, and who flings a shilling in the face of out-back conventionality (as he thinks) by chucking a bob into the Salvation Army ring. Then he glares round to see if he can catch anybody winking behind his back. There's the cynical joker, a queer mixture, who contributes generously and tempts the reformed boozer afterwards. There's the severe-faced old station-hand—in clean shirt and neckerchief and white moleskins—in for his annual or semiannual spree, who contributes on principle, and then drinks religiously until his cheque is gone and the horrors are come. There's the shearer, feeling mighty bad after a spree, and in danger of seeing things when he tries to go to sleep. He has dropping ten or twenty pounds over bar counters and at cards, and he now "chucks" a repentant shilling into the ring, with a very private and rather vague sort of feeling that something might come of it. There's the stout, contented, good-natured publican, who tips the Army as if it were a barrel-organ. And there are others and other reasons—black sheep and ne'er-do-weels—and faint echoes of other times in Salvation Army tunes.

Bourke, the metropolis of the Great Scrubs, on the banks of the Darling River, about five hundred miles from Sydney, was suffering from a long drought when I was there in ninety-two; and the heat may or may not have been another cause contributing to the success, from a business point of view, of the Bourke garrison. There was much beer boozing—and, besides, it was vaguely understood (as most things are vaguely understood out there in the drought-haze) that the place the Army came to save us from was hotter than Bourke. We didn't hanker to go to a hotter place than Bourke. But that year there was an extraordinary reason for the Army's great financial success there.

She was a little girl, nineteen or twenty, I should judge, the prettiest girl I ever saw in the Army, and one of the prettiest I've ever seen out of it. She had the features of an angel, but her expression was wonderfully human, sweet and sympathetic. Her big grey eyes were sad with sympathy for sufferers and sinners, and her poke bonnet was full of bunchy, red-gold hair. Her first appearance was somewhat dramatic—perhaps the Army arranged it so.

The Army used to pray, and thump the drum, and sing, and take up collections every evening outside Watty Bothways' Hotel, the Carriers' Arms. They performed longer and more often outside Watty's than any other pub in town—perhaps because Watty was considered the most hopeless publican and his customers the hardest crowd of boozers in Bourke. The band generally began to play about dusk. Watty would lean back comfortably in a basket easy-chair on his wide veranda, and clasp his hands, in a calm, contented way, while the Army banged the drum and got steam up, and whilst, perhaps, there was a barney going on in the bar, or a bloodthirsty fight in the backyard. On such occasions there was something like an indulgent or fatherly expression on his fat and usually emotionless face. And by and by he'd move his head gently and doze. The banging and the singing seemed to soothe him, and the praying, which was often very personal, never seemed to disturb him in the least.

Well, it was about dusk one day; it had been a terrible day, a hundred and something startling in the shade, but there came a breeze after sunset. There had been several dozen of buckets of water thrown on the veranda floor and the ground outside. Watty was seated in his accustomed place when the Army arrived. There was no barney in the bar because there was a fight in the backyard, and that claimed the attention of all the customers.

The Army prayed for Watty and his clients; then a reformed drunkard started to testify against publicans and all their works. Watty settled himself comfortably, folded his hands, and leaned back and dozed.

The fight was over, and the chaps began to drop round to the bar. The man who was saved waved his arms, and danced round and howled.

"Ye-es!" he shouted hoarsely. "The publicans, and boozers, and gamblers, and sinners may think that Bourke is hot, but hell is a thousand times hotter! I tell you——"

"Oh, Lord!" said Mitchell, the shearer, and he threw a penny into the ring.

"Ye-es! I tell you that hell is a million times hotter than Bourke! I tell you——"

"Oh, look here," said a voice from the background, "that won't wash. Why, don't you know that when the Bourke people die they send back for their blankets?"

The saved brother glared round.

"I hear a freethinker speaking, my friends," he said. Then, with sudden inspiration and renewed energy, "I hear the voice of a freethinker. Show me the face of a freethinker," he yelled, glaring round like a hunted, hungry man. "Show me the face of a freethinker, and I'll tell you what he is."

Watty hitched himself into a more comfortable position and clasped his hands on his knee and closed his eyes again.

"Ya-a-a-s!" shrieked the brand. "I tell you, my friends, I can tell a freethinker by his face. Show me the face of a——"

At this point there was an interruption. One-eyed, or Wall-eyed, Bogan, who had a broken nose, and the best side of whose face was reckoned the ugliest and most sinister—One-eyed Bogan thrust his face forward from the ring of darkness into the torchlight of salvation. He had got the worst of a drawn battle; his nose and mouth were bleeding, and his good eye was damaged.

"Look at my face!" he snarled, with dangerous earnestness. "Look at my face! That's the face of a freethinker, and I don't care who knows it. Now! what have you got to say against my face, 'Man-without-a-Shirt?'"

The brother drew back. He had been known in the north-west in his sinful days as "Man-without-a-Shirt," *alias* "Shirty," or "The Dirty Man," and was flabbergasted at being recognized in speech. Also, he had been in a shearing-shed and in a shanty orgie with One-eyed Bogan, and knew the man.

Now most of the chaps respected the Army, and, indeed, anything that looked like religion, but the Bogan's face, as representing free-thought, was a bit too sudden for them. There were sounds on the opposite side of the ring as from men being smitten repeatedly and rapidly below the belt, and long Tom Hall and one or two others got away into the darkness in the background, where Tom rolled helplessly on the grass and sobbed.

It struck me that Bogan's face was more the result of free speech than anything else.

The Army was about to pray when the Pretty Girl stepped

forward, her eyes shining with indignation and enthusiasm. She had arrived by the evening train, and had been standing shrinkingly behind an Army lass of fifty Australian summers, who was about six feet high, flat and broad, and had a square face, and a mouth like a joint in boiler plates.

The Pretty Girl stamped her pretty foot on the gravel, and her eyes flashed in the torchlight.

"You ought to be ashamed of yourselves," she said. "Great big men like you to be going on the way you are. If you were ignorant or poor, as I've seen people, there might be some excuse for you. Haven't you got any mothers, or sisters, or wives to think of? What sort of a life is this you lead? Drinking, and gambling, and fighting, and swearing your lives away! Do you ever think of God and the time when you were children? Why don't you make homes? Look at that man's face!" (she pointed suddenly at Bogan, who collapsed and sidled behind his mates out of the light). "Look at that man's face! Is it a face for a Christian? And you help and encourage him to fight. You're worse than he is. Oh, it's brutal. It's—it's wicked. Great big men like you, you ought to be ashamed of yourselves."

Long Bob Brothers—about six-foot-four—the longest and most innocent there, shrunk down by the wall and got his inquiring face out of the light. The Pretty Girl fluttered on for a few moments longer, greatly excited, and then stepped back, seemingly much upset, and was taken under the wing of the woman with the boiler-plate mouth.

It was a surprise, and very sudden. Bogan slipped round to the backyard, and was seen bathing his battered features at the pump. The rest wore the expression of men who knew that something unusual has happened, but don't know what, and are waiting vacantly for developments.—Except Tom Hall, who had recovered and returned. He stood looking over the head of the ring of bushmen, and apparently taking the same critical interest in the girl as he would in a fight—his expression was such as a journalist might wear who is getting exciting copy.

The Army had it all their own way for the rest of the evening, and made a good collection. The Pretty Girl stood smiling round with shining eyes as the bobs and tanners dropped in, and then, being shoved forward by the flat woman, she thanked us sweetly, and said we were good fellows, and that she was sorry for some things she'd said to us. Then she retired, fluttering and very much flushed, and hid herself behind the hard woman—who, by the way, had an excrescence on her upper lip which might have stood for a rivet.

Presently the Pretty Girl came from behind the big woman and stood watching things with glistening eyes. Some of the chaps on the opposite side of the ring moved a little to one side and all were careful not to meet her eye—not to be caught looking at her—lest she should be embarrassed. Watty had roused himself a little at the sound of a strange voice in the Army (and such a clear, sweet voice too!) and had a look; then he settled back peacefully again, but it was noticed that he didn't snore that evening.

And when the Army prayed, the Pretty Girl knelt down with the rest on the gravel. One or two tall bushmen bowed their heads as if they had to, and One-eyed Bogan, with the blood washed from his face, stood with his hat off, glaring round to see if he could catch anyone sniggering.

Mitchell, the shearer, said afterwards that the whole business made him feel for the moment like he felt sometimes in the days when he used to feel things.

The town discussed the Pretty Girl in the Army that night and for many days thereafter, but no one could find out who she was or where she belonged to—except that she came from Sydney last. She kept her secret, if she had one, very close—or else the other S.A. women were not to be pumped. She lived in skillion-rooms at the back of the big weather-board Salvation Army barracks with two other "lassies," who did washing and sewing and nursing, and went shabby, and half starved themselves, and were baked in the heat, like scores of women in the bush, and even as hundreds of women, suffering from religious mania, slave and stint in city slums, and neglect their homes, husbands and children—for the glory of Booth.

The Pretty Girl was referred to as Sister Hannah by the Army people, and came somehow to be known by sinners as "Miss Captain." I don't know whether that was her real name or what rank she held in the Army, if indeed she held any.

She sold *War Crys*, and the circulation doubled in a day. One-eyed Bogan, being bailed up unexpectedly, gave her "half a caser" for a *Cry*, and ran away without the paper or the change. Jack Mitchell bought a *Cry* for the first time in his life, and read it. He said he found some of the articles intensely realistic, and many of the statements were very interesting. He said he read one or two things in the *Cry* that he didn't know before. Tom Hall, taken unawares, bought three *Crys* from the Pretty Girl, and blushed to find it fame.

Little Billy Woods, the Labourers' Union secretary—who had a poetic temperament and more than the average bushman's reverence for higher things—Little Billy Woods told me in a burst of confidence that he generally had two feelings, one after the other, after encountering that girl. One was that unfathomable far-away feeling of loneliness and longing, that comes at odd times to the best of married men, with the best of wives and children—as Billy had. The other feeling, which came later on, and was a reaction in fact, was the feeling of a man who thinks he's been twisted round a woman's little finger for the benefit of somebody else. Billy said that he couldn't help being reminded by the shy, sweet smile and the shy, sweet "thank you" of the Pretty Girl in the Army, of the shy, sweet smile and the shy, sweet gratitude of a Sydney private barmaid, who had once roped him in, in the days before he was married. Then he'd reckon that the Army lassie had been sent out back to Bourke as a business speculation.

Tom Hall was inclined to reckon so too—but that was after he'd been chaffed for a month about the three *War Crys*.

The Pretty Girl was discussed from psychological points of view; not forgetting the sex problem. Donald Macdonald—shearer, union leader and labour delegate to other colonies on occasion—Donald Macdonald said that whenever he saw a circle of plain or ugly, dried-up women or girls round a shepherd, evangelist or a Salvation Army drum, he'd say "sexually starved!" They were hungry for love. Religious mania was sexual passion dammed out of its course. Therefore he held that morbidly religious girls were the most easily seduced.

But this couldn't apply to Pretty Girl in the Army. Mitchell reckoned that she'd either had a great sorrow—a lot of trouble, or a disappointment in love (the "or" is Mitchell's); but they couldn't see how a girl like her could possibly be disappointed in love—unless the chap died or got into jail for life. Donald decided that her soul had been starved somehow.

Mitchell suggested that it might be only a craving for notoriety, the same things that makes women and girls go amongst lepers, and out to the battlefield, and nurse ugly pieces of men back to life again; the same thing that makes some women and girls swear ropes round men's necks. The Pretty Girl might be the daughter of well-to-do people—even aristocrats, said Mitchell—she was pretty enough and spoke well enough. "Every woman's a barmaid at heart," as the *Bulletin* puts it, said Mitchell.

But not even one of the haggard women of Bourke ever breathed a suspicion of scandal against her. They said she was too good and too pretty to be where she was. You see it was not as in an old settled town where hags blacken God's world with their tongues. Bourke was just a little camping town in a big land, where free, good-hearted democratic Australians, and the best of black sheep from the old world, were constantly passing through; where husbands were often obliged to be away from home for twelve months, and the storekeepers had to trust the people, and mates trusted each other, and the folks were broad-minded. The mind's eye had a wide range.

After her maiden speech the Pretty Girl seldom spoke, except to return thanks for collections—and she never testified. She had a sweet voice and used to sing.

Now, if I were writing pure fiction, and were not cursed with an obstinate inclination to write the truth, I might say that, after the advent of the Pretty Girl, the morals of Bourke improved suddenly and wonderfully. That One-eyed Bogan left off gambling and drinking and fighting and swearing, and put on a red coat and testified and fought the devil only; that Mitchell dropped his mask of cynicism; that Donald Macdonald ate no longer of the tree of knowledge and ceased to worry himself with psychological problems, and was happy; and that Tom Hall was no longer a scoffer. That no one sneaked round through the scrub after dusk to certain necessary establishments in weather-board cottages on the outskirts of the town; and that the broad-minded and obliging ladies thereof became Salvation Army lassies.

But none of these things happened. Drunks quieted down or got out of the way if they could when the Pretty Girl appeared on the scene, fights and games of "headin' 'em" were adjourned, and weak, ordinary language was used for the time being, and that was about all.

Nevertheless, most of the chaps were in love with that Pretty Girl in the Army—all those who didn't *worship* her privately. Long Bob Brothers hovered round in hopes, they said, that she'd meet with an accident—get run over by a horse or something—and he'd have to carry her in; he scared the women at the barracks by dropping firewood over the fence after dark. Barcoo-Rot, the meanest man in the back country, was seen to drop a threepenny bit into the ring, and a rumour was industriously circulated (by Tom Hall) to the effect that One-eyed Bogan intended to shave and join the Army disguised as a lassie.

Handsome Jake Boreham (*alias* Bore-'em), a sentimental shearer from New Zealand, who had read Bret Harte, made an elaborate attempt for the Pretty Girl, by pretending to be going to the dogs headlong, with an idea of first winning her sorrowful interest and sympathy, and then making an apparently hard struggle to straighten up for her sake. He related his experience with the

cheerful and refreshing absence of reserve which was characteristic
of him, and is of most bushmen.

"I'd had a few drinks," he said, "and was having a spell under a
gum by the river, when I saw the Pretty Girl and another Army
woman coming down along the bank. It was a blazing hot day. I
thought of Sandy and the Schoolmistress in Bret Harte, and I
thought it would be a good idea to stretch out in the sun and pretend
to be helpless; so I threw my hat on the ground and lay down, with
my head in the blazing heat, in the most graceful position I could get
at, and I tried to put a look of pained regret on my face, as if I was
dreaming of my lost boyhood and me mother. I thought, perhaps,
the Girl would pity me, and I felt sure she'd stoop and pick up my
hat and put it gently over my poor troubled head. Then I was going
to become conscious for a moment, and look hopelessly round, and
into her eyes, and then start and look sorrowful and ashamed, and
stagger to my feet, taking off my hat like the Silver King does to the
audience when he makes his first appearance drunk on the stage;
and then I was going to reel off, trying to talk as straight as I could.
And next day I was going to clean up my teeth and nails and put on
a white shirt, and start to be a new man henceforth.

"Well, as I lay there with my eyes shut, I heard the footsteps come
up and stop, and heard 'em whisper, and I thought I heard the
Pretty Girl say 'Poor fellow!' or something that sounded like that;
and just then I got a God-almighty poke in the ribs with an
umbrella—at least I suppose it was aimed for my ribs; but women
are bad shots, and the point of the umbrella caught me in the side,
just between the bottom rib and the hip-bone, and I sat up with a
click, like the blade of a pocket-knife.

"The other lassie was the big square-faced woman. The Pretty
Girl looked rather more frightened and disgusted than sentimental,
but she had plenty of pluck, and soon pulled herself together. She
said I ought to be ashamed of myself, a great big man like me, lying
there in the dust like a drunken tramp—an eyesore and a disgrace to
all the world. She told me to go to my camp, wherever that was, and
sleep myself sober. The square-jawed woman said I looked like a
fool sitting there. I did feel ashamed, and I reckon I did look like a
fool—a man generally does in a fix like that. I felt like one, anyway. I
got up and walked away, and it hurt me so much that I went over to
West Bourke and went to the dogs properly for a fortnight, and lost
twenty quid on a game of draughts against a blindfold player. Now
both those women had umbrellas, but I'm not sure to this day which
of 'em it was that gave me the poke. It wouldn't have mattered much

anyway. I haven't borrowed one of Bret Harte's books since."

Jake reflected a while.

"The worst of it was," he said ruefully, "that I wasn't sure that the girl or the woman didn't see through me, and that worried me a bit. You never can tell how much a woman suspects, and that's the worst of 'em. I found that out after I got married."

The Pretty Girl in the Army grew pale and thin and bigger-eyed. The women said it was a shame, and that she ought to be sent home to her friends, wherever they were. She was laid up for two or three days, and some of the women cooked delicacies and handed 'em over the barracks fence, and offered to come in and nurse her; but the square woman took washing home and nursed the girl herself.

The Pretty Girl still sold *War Crys* and took up collections, but in a tired, listless, half shamed-faced way. It was plain that she was tired of the Army, and growing ashamed of the Salvationists. Perhaps she had come to see things too plainly.

You see, the Army does no good out back in Australia—except from a business point of view. It is simply there to collect funds for hungry headquarters. The bushmen are much too intelligent for the Army. There was no poverty in Bourke—as it is understood in the city; there was plenty of food; and camping out and roughing it come natural to the bushmen. In cases of sickness, accident, widows or orphans, the chaps sent round the hat, without banging a drum or testifying, and that was all right. If a chap was hard up he borrowed a couple of quid from his mate. If a strange family arrived without a penny, someone had to fix 'em up, and the storekeepers helped them till the man got work. For the rest, we work out our own salvation, or damnation—as the case is—in the bush, with no one to help us, except a mate, perhaps. The Army can't help us, but a fellow-sinner can, sometimes, who has been through it all himself. The Army is only a drag on the progress of Democracy, because it attracts many who would otherwise be aggressive Democrats—and for other reasons.

Besides, if we all reformed the Army would get deuced little from us for its city mission.

The Pretty Girl went to service for a while with the stock inspector's wife, who could get nothing out of her concerning herself or her friends. She still slept at the barracks, stuck to the Army, and attended its meetings.

It was Christmas morning, and there was peace in Bourke and goodwill towards all men. There hadn't been a fight since yesterday evening, and that had only been a friendly one, to settle an argument concerning the past ownership, and, at the same time, to decide as to the future possession of a dog.

It had been a hot, close night, and it ended in a suffocating sunrise. The free portion of the male population were in the habit of taking their blankets and sleeping out in "the Park," or town square, in hot weather; the wives and daughters of the town slept, or tried to sleep, with bedroom windows and doors open, while husbands lay outside on the verandas. I camped in a corner of the park that night, and the sun woke me.

As I sat up I caught sight of a swagman coming along the white, dusty road from the direction of the bridge, where the cleared road ran across west and on, a hundred and thirty miles, through the barren, broiling mulga scrubs, to Hungerford, on the border of Sheol. I knew that swagman's walk. It was John Merrick (Jack Moonlight), one-time Shearers' Union secretary at Coonamble, and generally "Rep" (shearers' representative) in any shed where he sheared. He was a "better-class shearer," one of those quiet, thoughtful men of whom there are generally two or three in the roughest of rough sheds, who have great influence, and give the shed a good name from a Union point of view. Not quiet with the resentful or snobbish reserve of the educated Englishman, but with a sad or subdued sort of quietness that has force in it—as if they fully realized that their intelligence is much higher than the average, that they have suffered more real trouble and heartbreak than the majority of their mates, and that their mates couldn't possibly understand them if they spoke as they felt and couldn't see things as they do—yet men who understand and are intensely sympathetic in their loneliness and sensitive reserve.

I had worked in a shed with Jack Moonlight, and had met him in Sydney, and to be mates with a bushman for a few weeks is to know him well—anyway, I found it so. He had taken a trip to Sydney the Christmas before last, and when he came back there was something wanting. He became more silent, he drank more, and sometimes alone, and took to smoking heavily. He dropped his mates, took little or no interest in Union matters, and travelled alone, and at night.

The Australian bushman is born with a mate who sticks to him through life—like a mole. They may be hundreds of miles apart sometimes, and separated for years, yet they are mates for life. A bushman may have many mates in his roving, but there is always one *his* mate, "my mate;" and it is common to hear a bushman, who is, in every way, a true mate to the man he happens to be travelling with, speak of *his mate's mate*—"Jack's mate"—who might be in Klondyke or South Africa. A bushman has always a mate to comfort him and argue with him, and work and tramp and drink with him, and lend him quids when he's hard up, and call him a b—— fool, and fight him sometimes; to abuse him to his face and defend his name behind his back; to bear false witness and perjure his soul for his sake; to lie to the girl for him if he's single, and to his wife if he's married; to secure a "pen" for him at a shed where he isn't on the spot, or, if the mate is away in New Zealand or South Africa, to write and tell him if it's any good coming over this way. And each would take the word of the other against all the world, and each believes that the other is the straightest chap that ever lived—"a white man!" And next best to your old mate is the man you're tramping, riding, working, or drinking with.

About the first thing the cook asks you when you come along to a shearers' hut is, "Where's your mate?" I travelled alone for a while one time, and it seemed to me sometimes, by the tone of the inquiry concerning the whereabouts of my mate, tht the bush had an idea that I might have done away with him and that the thing ought to be looked into.

When a man drops mateship altogether and takes to "hatting" in the bush, it's a step towards a convenient tree and a couple of saddle-straps buckled together.

I had an idea that I, in a measure, took the place of Jack Moonlight's mate about his time.

"'Ullo, Jack!" I hailed as he reached the corner of the park.

"Good morning, Harry!" said Jack, as if he'd seen me last yesterday evening instead of three months ago. "How are you getting on?"

We walked together towards the Union Office, where I had a camp in the skillion-room at the back. Jack was silent. But there's no place in the world where a man's silence is respected so much (within reasonable bounds) as in the Australian bush, where every man has a past more or less sad, and every man a ghost—perhaps from other lands that we know nothing of, and speaking in a foreign tongue. They say in the bush, "Oh, Jack's only thinking!" And they let him think. Generally you want to think as much as your mate; and when you've been together some time it's quite natural to travel all day without exchanging a word. In the morning Jim says, "Well, I think I made a bargain with that horse, Bill," and some time late in the afternoon, say twenty miles farther on, it occurs to Bill to "rejoin," "Well, I reckon the blank as sold it to you had yer proper!"

I like a good thinking mate, and I believe that thinking in company is a lot more healthy and more comfortable, as well as less risky, than thinking alone.

On the way to the Union Office Jack and I passed the Royal Hotel, and caught a glimpse, through the open door, of a bedroom off the veranda, of the landlord's fresh, fair, young Sydney girl-wife, sleeping prettily behind the mosquito-net, like a sleeping beauty, while the boss lay on a mattress outside on the veranda, across the open door. (He wasn't necessary for publication, but an evidence of good faith.)

I glanced at Jack for a grin, but didn't get one. He wore the pained expression of a man who is suddenly hit hard with the thought of something that might have been.

I boiled the billy and fried a pound of steak.

"Been travelling all night, Jack?" I asked.

"Yes," said Jack. "I camped at Emus yesterday."

He didn't eat. I began to reckon that he was brooding too much for his health. He was much thinner than when I saw him last, and pretty haggard, and he had something of the hopeless, haggard look that I'd seen in Tom Hall's eyes after the last big shearing strike, when Tom had worked day and night to hold his mates up all through the hard, bitter struggle, and the battle was lost.

"Look here, Jack!" I said at last. "What's up?"

"Nothing's up, Harry," said Jack. "What made you think so?"

"Have you got yourself into any fix?" I asked. "What's the Hungerford track been doing to you?"

"No, Harry," he said, "I'm all right. How are you?" And he pulled some string and papers and a roll of dusty pound notes from his pocket and threw them on the bunk.

I was hard up just then, so I took a note and the billy to go to the Royal and get some beer. I thought the beer might loosen his mind a bit.

"Better take a couple of quid," said Jack. "You look as if you want some new shirts and things." But a pound was enough for me, and I think he had reason to be glad of that later on, as it turned out.

"Anything new in Bourke?" asked Jack as we drank the beer.

"No," I said, "not a thing—except there's a pretty girl in the Salvation Army."

"And it's about time," growled Jack.

"Now, look here, Jack," I said presently, "what's come over you lately at all? I might be able to help you. It's not a bit of use telling me that there's nothing the matter. When a man takes to brooding and travelling alone it's a bad sign, and it will end in a leaning tree and a bit of clothes-line as likely as not. Tell me what the trouble is. Tell us all about it. There's a ghost, isn't there?"

"Well, I suppose so," said Jack. "We've all got our ghosts for that matter. But never you mind, Harry; I'm all right. I don't go interfering with your ghosts, and I don't see what call you've got to come haunting mine. Why, it's as bad as kicking a man's dog." And he gave the ghost of a grin.

"Tell me, Jack," I said, "is it a woman?"

"Yes," said Jack, "it's a woman. Now, are you satisfied?"

"Is it a girl?" I asked.

"Yes," he said.

So there was no more to be said. I'd thought it might have been a lot worse than a girl. I'd thought he might have got married somewhere, sometime, and made a mess of it.

We had dinner at Billy Woods's place, and a sensible Christmas dinner it was—everything cold, except the vegetables, with the hose going on the veranda in spite of the by-laws, and Billy's wife and her sister, fresh and cool-looking and jolly, instead of being hot and brown and cross like most Australian women who roast themselves over a blazing fire in a hot kitchen on a broiling day, all the morning, to cook scalding plum pudding and red-hot roasts, for no other reason than that their grandmothers used to cook hot Christmas dinners in England.

And in the afternoon we went for a row on the river, pulling easily up the anabranch and floating down with the stream under the shade of the river timber—instead of going to sleep and waking up helpless and soaked in perspiration, to find the women with headaches, as many do on Christmas Day in Australia.

Mrs Woods tried to draw Jack out, but it was no use, and in the evening he commenced drinking, and that made Billy uneasy. "I'm afraid Jack's on the wrong track," he said.

After tea most of us collected about Watty's veranda. Most things that happened in Bourke happened at Watty's pub, or near it.

If a horse bolted with a buggy or cart, he was generally stopped outside Watty's, which seemed to suggest, as Mitchell said, that most of the heroes drank at Watty's—also that the pluckiest men were found amongst the hardest drinkers. (But sometimes the horse fetched up against Watty's sign and lamppost—which was a stout one of "iron-bark"—and smashed the trap.) Then Watty's was the Carriers' Arms, a union pub; and Australian teamsters are mostly hard cases: while there was something in Watty's beer which made men argue fluently, and the best fights came off in his backyard. Watty's dogs were the most quarrelsome in town, and there was a dog-fight there every other evening, followed as often as not by a man-fight. If a bushman's horse ran away with him the chances were that he'd be thrown on to Watty's veranda, if he wasn't pitched into the bar; and victims of accidents, and sick, hard-up shearers, were generally carried to Watty's pub, as being the most convenient and comfortable for them. Mitchell denied that it was generosity or good nature on Watty's part, he said it was all business—advertisement. Watty knew what he was doing. He was very deep, was Watty. Mitchell further hinted that if he was sick *he* wouldn't be carried to Watty's, for Watty knew what a thirsty business a funeral was. Tom Hall reckoned that Watty bribed the Army on the quiet.

I was sitting on a stool along the veranda wall with Donald Macdonald, Bob Brothers (the Giraffe) and Mitchell, and one or two others, and Jack Moonlight sat on the floor with his back to the wall and his hat well down over his eyes. The Army came along at the usual time, but we didn't see the Pretty Girl at first—she was a bit late. Mitchell said he liked to be at Watty's when the Army prayed and the Pretty Girl was there; he had no objection to being prayed for by a girl like that, though he reckoned that nothing short of a real angel could save him now. He said his old grandmother used to pray for him every night of her life and three times on Sunday, with Christmas Day extra when Christmas Day didn't fall on a Sunday; but Mitchell reckoned that the old lady couldn't have had much influence because he become more sinful every year, and went deeper in ways of darkness, until finally he embarked on a career of crime.

The Army prayed, and then a thin "ratty" little woman bobbed up in the ring; she'd gone mad on religion as women do on woman's rights and hundreds of other things. She was so skinny in the face, her jaws so prominent, and her mouth so wide, that when she opened it to speak it was like a ventriloquist's dummy and you could almost see the cracks open down under her ears.

"They say I'm cracked!" she screamed in a shrill, cracked voice. "But I'm not cracked—I'm only cracked on the Lord Jesus Christ! That's all I'm cracked on——." And just then the Amen man of the Army—the Army groaner we called him, who was always putting both feet in it—just then he blundered forward, rolled up his eyes, threw his hands up and down as if he were bouncing two balls, and said, with deep feeling:

"Thank the Lord she's got a crack in the right place!"

Tom Hall doubled up, and most of the other sinners seemed to think there was something very funny about it. And the Army, too, seemed struck with an idea that there was something wrong somewhere, for they started a hymn.

A big American negro, who'd been a night watchman in Sydney, stepped into the ring and waved his arms and kept time, and as he got excited he moved his hands up and down rapidly, as if he was hauling down a rope in a great hurry through a pulley block above, and he kept saying, "Come down, Lord!" all through the hymn, like a bass accompaniment, "Come down, Lord; come down, Lord; come down, Lord; come down, Lord!" and the quicker he said it the faster he hauled. He was as good as a drum. And, when the hymn was over, he started to testify.

"My frens!" he said, "I was once black as der coals in der mined! I was once black as der ink in der ocean of sin! But now—thank an' bless the Lord!—I am whiter dan der dribben snow!"

Tom Hall sat down on the edge of the veranda and leaned his head against a post and cried. He had contributed a bob this evening, and he was getting his money's worth.

Then the Pretty Girl arrived and was pushed forward into the ring. She looked thinner and whiter than I'd ever seen her, and there was a feverish brightness in her eyes that I didn't like.

"Men!" she said, "this is Christmas Day——." I didn't hear any more for, at the sound of her voice, Jack Moonlight jumped up as if he'd sat on a baby. He started forward, stared at her for a moment as if he couldn't believe his eyes, and then said, "Hannah!" short and sharp. She started as if she was shot, gave him a wild look, and stumbled forward; the next moment he had her in his arms and was steering for the private parlour.

I heard Mrs Bothways calling for water and smelling-salts; she was as fat as Watty, and very much like him in the face, but she was emotional and sympathetic. Then presently I heard, through the open window, the Pretty Girl say to Jack, "Oh, Jack, Jack! Why did you go away and leave me like that? It was cruel!"

"But you told me to go, Hannah," said Jack.

"That—that didn't make any difference. Why didn't you write?" she sobbed.

"Because you never wrote to me, Hannah," he said.

"That—that was no excuse!" she said. "It was so k-k-k-cruel of you, Jack."

Mrs Bothways pulled down the window. A new-comer asked Watty what the trouble was, and he said that the Army girl had only found her chap, or husband, or long-lost brother or something, but the missus was looking after the business; then he dozed again.

And then we adjourned to the Royal and took the Army with us.

"That's the way of it," said Donald Macdonald. "With a woman it's love or religion; with a man its love or the devil."

"Or with a man," said Mitchell, presently, "it's love and the devil both, sometimes, Donald."

I looked at Mitchell hard, but for all his face expressed he might only have said, "I think it's going to rain."

"LORD DOUGLAS"

> They hold him true, who's true to one,
> However false he be.
>
> —*The Rouseabout of Rouseabouts.*

The Imperial Hotel was rather an unfortunate name for an out-back town pub, for out back is the stronghold of Australian democracy; it was the out-back vote and influence that brought about "One Man One Vote," "Payment of Members," and most of the democratic legislation of late years, and from out back came the overwhelming vote in favour of Australian as Imperial Federation.

The name Royal Hotel is as familiar as that of the Railway Hotel, and passes unnoticed and ungrowled at, even by bush republicans. The Royal Hotel at Bourke was kept by an Irishman, one O'Donohoo, who was Union to the backbone, loudly in favour of "Australia for the Australians," and, of course, against even the democratic New South Wales Government of the time. He went round town all one St Patrick's morning with a bunch of green ribbon fastened to his coat-tail with a large fish-hook, and wasn't aware of the fact till he sat down on the point of it. But that's got nothing to do with it.

The Imperial Hotel at Bourke was unpopular from the first. It was said that the very existence of the house was the result of a swindle. It had been built with money borrowed on certain allotments in the centre of the town and on the understanding that it should be built on the mortgaged land, whereas it was erected on a free allotment. Which fact was discovered, greatly to its surprise, by the building society when it came to foreclose on the allotments some years later. While the building was being erected the Bourke people understood, in a vague way, that it was to be a convent (perhaps the building society thought so, too), and when certain ornaments in brick and cement in the shape of a bishop's mitre were placed over the corners of the walls the question seemed decided. But when the place was finished a bar was fitted up, and up went the sign, to the disgust of the other publicans, who didn't know a licence had been taken out—for licensing didn't go by local option in those days. It was rumoured that the place belonged to, and the whole business was engineered by, a priest. And priests are men of the world.

The Imperial Hotel was patronized by the pastoralists, the civil servants, the bank manager and clerks—all the scrub aristocracy; it was the headquarters of the Pastoralists' Union in Bourke; a barracks for blacklegs brought up from Sydney to take the place of Union shearers on strike; and the new Governor, on his inevitable visit to Bourke, was banqueted at the Imperial Hotel. The editor of the local "capitalistic rag" stayed there; the pastoralists' member was elected mostly by dark ways and means devised at the Imperial Hotel, and one of its managers had stood as a dummy candidate to split the Labour vote; the management of the hotel was his reward. In short, it was there that most of the plots were hatched to circumvent Freedom, and put away or deliver into the clutches of law and order certain sons of Light and Liberty who believed in converting blacklegs into jellies by force of fists when bribes, gentle persuasion and pure Australian language failed to convert them to clean Unionism. The Imperial Hotel was called the "Squatters' Pub," the "Scabbery," and other and more expressive names.

The hotel became still more unpopular after Percy Douglas had managed it for a while. He was an avowed enemy of Labour Unionists. He employed Chinese cooks, and that in the height of the anti-Chinese agitation in Australia, and he was known to have kindly feelings towards the Afghans who, with their camels, were running white carriers off the roads. If an excited Unionist called a man a "blackleg" or "scab" in the Imperial bar he was run out—sometimes with great difficulty, and occasionally as far as the lock-up.

Percy Douglas was a fine-looking man, "wid a chest on him an' well hung—a fine fee-*gure* of a man," as O'Donohoo pronounced it. He was tall and erect, he dressed well, wore small side-whiskers, had an eagle nose, and looked like an aristocrat. Like many of his type, who start sometimes as billiard-markers and suddenly become hotel managers in Australia, nothing was known of hs past. Jack Mitchell reckoned, by the way he treated his employees and spoke to workmen, that he was the educated son of an English farmer—gone wrong and sent out to Australia. Someone called him "Lord Douglas," and the nickname caught on.

He made himself well hated. He got One-eyed Bogan "three months' hard" for taking a bottle of whisky off the Imperial bar counter because he (Bogan) was drunk and thirsty and had knocked down his cheque, and because there was no one minding the bar at the moment.

Lord Douglas dismissed the barmaid, and, as she was leaving, he had her boxes searched and gave her in charge for stealing certain articles belonging to the hotel. The chaps subscribed to defend the case, and subsequently put a few pounds together for the girl. She proved her gratitude by bringing a charge of a baby against one of one chaps—but that was only one of the little ways of the world, as Mitchell said. She joined a Chinese camp later on.

Lord Douglas employed a carpenter to do some work about the hotel, and because the carpenter left before the job was finished, Lord Douglas locked his tools in an outhouse and refused to give them up; and when the carpenter, with the spirit of an Australian workman, broke the padlock and removed his tool-chest, the landlord gave him in charge for breaking and entering. The chaps defended the case and won it, and hated Lord Douglas as much as if he were their elder brother. Mitchell was the only one to put in a word for him.

"I've been puzzling it out," said Mitchell, as he sat nursing his best leg in the Union Office, "and, as far as I can see, it all amounts to this—we're all mistaken in Lord Douglas. We don't know the man. He's all right. We don't understand him. He's really a sensitive, good-hearted man who's been shoved a bit off the track by the world. It's the world's fault—he's not to blame. You see, when he was a youngster he was the most good-natured kid in the school; he was always soft, and, consequently, he was always being imposed upon, and bullied, and knocked about. Whenever he got a penny to buy lollies he'd count 'em out carefully and divide 'em round amongst his schoolmates and brothers and sisters. He was the only one that worked at home, and consequently they all hated him. His father respected him, but didn't love him, because he wasn't a younger son, and wasn't bringing his father's grey hairs down in sorrow to the grave. If it was in Australia, probably Lord Douglas was an elder son and had to do all the hard graft, and teach himself at night, and sleep in a bark skillion while his younger brothers benefited—they were born in the new brick house and went to boarding-schools. His mother had a contempt for him because he wasn't a black sheep and a prodigal, and, when the old man died, the rest of the family got all the stuff and Lord Douglas ws kicked out because they could do without him now. And the family hated him like poison ever afterwards (especially his mother), and spread lies about him—because they had treated him shamefully and because his mouth was shut—they knew he wouldn't speak. Then probably he went in for Democracy and worked for Freedom, till Freedom trod on him once too often with her hob-nailed boots. Then the chances are, in the end, he was ruined by a girl or woman, and driven, against his will, to take refuge in pure individualism. He's all right, only we don't appreciate him. He's only fighting against his old ideals—his old self that comes up sometimes—and that's what makes him sweat his barmaids and servants, and hate us, and run us in; and perhaps when he cuts up extra rough it's because his conscience kicks him when he thinks of the damned soft fool he used to be. He's all right—take my word for it. It's all a mask. Why, he might be one of the kindest hearted men in Bourke underneath."

Tom Hall rubbed his head and blinked, as if he was worried by an idea that there might be some facts in Mitchell's theories.

"You're allers findin' excuses for blacklegs an' scabs, Mitchell," said Barcoo-Rot, who took Mitchell seriously (and who would have taken a laughing jackass seriously). "Why, you'd find a white spot on a squatter. I wouldn't be surprised if you blacklegged yourself in the end."

This was an unpardonable insult, from a Union point of view, and the chaps half-unconsciously made room on the floor for Barcoo-Rot to fall after Jack Mitchell hit him. But Mitchell took the insult philosophically.

"Well, Barcoo-Rot," he said, nursing the other leg, "for the matter of that, I did find a white spot on a squatter once. He lent me a quid when I was hard up. There's white spots on the blackest characters if you only drop prejudice and look close enough. I suppose even Jack-the-Ripper's character was speckled. Why, I can even see spots on your character, sometimes, Barcoo-Rot. I've known white spots to spread on chaps' characters until they were little short of saints. Sometimes I even fancy I can feel my own wings sprouting. And as for turning blackleg—well, I suppose I've got a bit of the crawler in my composition (most of us have), and a man never knows what might happen to his principles."

"Well," said Barcoo-Rot, "I beg yer pardon—ain't that enough?"

"No," said Mitchell, "you ought to wear a three-bushel bag and ashes for three months, and drink water; but since the police would send you to an asylum if you did that, I think the best thing we can do is to go out and have a drink."

Lord Douglas married an Australian girl somewhere, somehow, and brought her to Bourke, and there were two little girls—regular little fairies. She was a gentle, kind-hearted little woman, but she didn't seem to improve him much, save that he was very good to her.

"It's mostly that way," commented Mitchell. "When a boss gets married and has children he thinks he's got a greater right to grind his fellowmen and rob their wives and children. I'd never work for a boss with a big family—it's hard enough to keep a single boss nowadays in this country."

After one stormy election, at the end of a long and bitter shearing strike, One-eyed Bogan, his trusty enemy, Barcoo-Rot, and one or two other enthusiastic reformers were charged with rioting, and got from one to three months' hard. And they had only smashed three windows of the Imperial Hotel and chased the Chinese cook into the river.

"I used to have some hopes for Democracy," commented Mitchell, "but I've got none now. How can you expect Liberty, Equality or Fraternity—how can you expect Freedom and Universal Brotherhood and Equal Rights in a country where Sons of Light get three months' hard for breaking windows and bashing a Chinaman? It almost makes me long to sail away in a gallant barque."

There were other cases in connection with the rotten-egging of Capitalistic candidates on the Imperial Hotel balcony, and it was partly on the evidence of Douglas and his friends that certain respectable Labour leaders got heavy terms of imprisonment for rioting and "sedition" and "inciting," in connection with organized attacks on blacklegs and their escorts.

Retribution, if it was retribution, came suddenly and in a most unexpected manner to Lord Douglas.

It seems he employed a second carpenter for six months to repair and make certain additions to the hotel, and put him off under various pretences until he owed him a hundred pounds or thereabout. At last, immediately after an exciting interview with Lord Douglas, the carpenter died suddenly of heart disease. The widow, a strong-minded bushwoman, put a bailiff in the hotel on a very short notice—and against the advice of her lawyer, who thought the case hopeless—and the Lord Douglas bubble promptly burst. He had somehow come to be regarded as the proprietor of the hotel, but now the real proprietors or proprietor—he was still said to be a priest—turned Douglas out and put in a new manager. The old servants were paid after some trouble. The local storekeepers and one or two firms in Sydney, who had large accounts against the Imperial Hotel (and had trusted it, mainly because it was patronized by Capitalism and Fat), were never paid.

Lord Douglas cleared out to Sydney, leaving his wife and children, for the present, with her brother, a hay-and-corn storekeeper, who also had a large and hopeless account against the hotel; and when the brother went broke and left the district she rented a two-roomed cottage and took in dressmaking.

Dressmaking didn't pay so well in the bush then as it did in the old diggings days when sewing-machines were scarce and the possession of one meant an independent living to any girl—when diggers paid ten shillings for a strip of "flannen" doubled over and sewn together, with holes for arms and head, and called a shirt. Mrs Douglas had a hard time, with her two little girls, who were still better and more prettily dressed than any other children in Bourke. One grocer still called on her for orders and pretended to be satisfied to wait "till Mr Douglas came back," and when she would no longer order what he considered sufficient provisions for her and the children, and commenced buying sugar, etc., by the pound, for cash, he one day sent a box of groceries round to her. He pretended it was a mistake.

"However," he said, "I'd be very much obliged if you could use 'em, Mrs Douglas. I'm overstocked now; haven't got room for another tin of sardines in the shop. Don't you worry about bills, Mrs Douglas; I can wait till Douglas comes home. I did well enough out of the Imperial Hotel when your husband had it, and a pound's worth of groceries won't hurt me now. I'm only too glad to get rid of some of the stock."

She cried a little, thought of the children, and kept the groceries.

"I suppose I'll be sold up soon meself if things don't git brighter," said that grocer to a friend, "so it doesn't matter much."

The same with Foley the butcher, who had a brogue with a sort of drawling groan in it, and was a cynic of the Mitchell school.

"You see," he said, "she's as proud as the devil, but when I send round a bit o' rawst, or porrk, or the undercut o' the blade-bawn, she thinks o' the little gur-r-rls before she thinks o' sendin' it back to me. That's where I've got the pull on her."

The Giraffe borrowed a horse and tip-dray one day at the beginning of winter and cut a load of firewood in the bush, and next morning, at daylight, Mrs Douglas was nearly startled out of her life by a crash at the end of the cottage, which made her think that the chimney had fallen in, or a tree fallen on the house; and when she slipped on a wrapper and looked out, she saw a load of short-cut wood by the chimney, and caught a glimpse of the back view of the Giraffe, who stood in the dray with his legs wide apart and was disappearing into the edge of the scrub; and soon the rapid clock-clock-clock of the wheels died away in the west, as if he were making for West Australia.

The next we heard of Lord Douglas he had got two years' hard for embezzlement in connection with some canvassing he had taken up. Mrs Douglas fell ill—a touch of brain-fever—and one of the labourers' wives took care of the children while two others took turns in nursing. While she was recovering, Bob Brothers sent round the hat, and, after a conclave in the Union Office—as mysterious as any meeting ever called with the object of downing bloated Capitalism—it was discovered that one of the chaps—who didn't wish his name to be mentioned—had borrowed just twenty-five pounds from Lord Douglas in the old days and now wished to return it to Mrs Douglas. So the thing was managed, and if she had any suspicions she kept them to herself. She started a little fancy goods shop and got along fairly comfortable.

Douglas, by the way, was, publicly, supposed, for her sake and because of the little girls, to be away in West Australia on the goldfields.

Time passes without much notice out back, and one hot day, when the sun hung behind the fierce sandstorms from the northwest as dully lurid as he ever showed in a London fog, Lord Douglas got out of the train that had just finished its five-hundred-miles' run, and not seeing a new-chum porter, who started forward by force of habit to take his bag, he walked stiffly off the platform and down the main street towards his wife's cottage.

He was very gaunt, and his eyes, to those who passed him closely, seemed to have a furtive, hunted expression. He had let his beard grow, and it had grown grey.

It was within a few days of Christmas—the same Christmas that we lost the Pretty Girl in the Salvation Army. As a rule the big shearing-sheds within a fortnight of Bourke cut out in time for the shearers to reach the town and have their Christmas dinners and sprees—and for some of them to be locked up over Christmas Day—within sound of a church-going bell. Most of the chaps gathered in the Shearers' Union Office on New Year's Eve and discussed Douglas amongst other things.

"I vote we kick the cow out of the town!" snarled One-eyed Bogan, viciously.

"We can't do that," said Bob Brothers (the Giraffe), speaking more promptly than usual. "There's his wife and youngsters to consider, yer know."

"He something well deserted his wife," snarled Bogan, "an' now he comes crawlin' back to her to keep him."

"Well," said Mitchell, mildly, "but we ain't all got as much against him as you have, Bogan."

"He made a crimson jail-bird of me!" snapped Bogan.

"Well," said Mitchell, "that didn't hurt you much, anyway; it rather improved your character if anything. Besides, he made a jail-bird of himself afterwards, so you ought to have a fellow-feeling—a feathered feeling, so to speak. Now you needn't be offended, Bogan, we're all jail-birds at heart, only we haven't all got the pluck."

"I'm in favour of blanky well tarrin' an' featherin' him an' kickin' him out of the town!" shouted Bogan. "It would be a good turn to his wife, too; she'd be well rid of the ——."

"Perhaps she's fond of him," suggested Mitchell; "I've known such cases before. I saw them sitting together on the veranda last night when they thought no one was looking."

"He deserted her," said One-eyed Bogan, in a climbing-down tone, "and left her to starve."

"Perhaps the police were to blame for that," said Mitchell. "You know you deserted all your old mates once for three months, Bogan, and it wasn't your fault."

"He seems to be a crimson pet of yours, Jack Mitchell," said Bogan, firing up.

"Ah, well, all I know," said Mitchell, standing up and stretching himself wearily, "all I know is that he looked like a gentleman once, and treated us like a gentleman, and cheated us like a gentleman, and ran some of us in like a gentleman, and, as far as I can see, he's served his time like a gentleman and come back to face us and live himself down like a man. I always had a sneaking regard for a gentleman."

"Why, Mitchell, I'm beginning to think you are a gentleman yourself," said Jake Boreham.

"Well," said Mitchell, "I used to have a suspicion once that I had a drop of blue blood in me somewhere, and it worried me a lot; but I asked my old mother about it one day, and she scalded me—God bless her!—and father chased me with a stockwhip, so I gave up making inquiries."

"You'll join the bloomin' Capitalists next," sneered One-eyed Bogan.

"I wish I could, Bogan," said Mitchell. "I'd take a trip to Paris and see for myself whether the Frenchwomen are as bad as they're made out to be, or go to Japan. But what are we going to do about Douglas?"

"Kick the skunk out of town, or boycott him!" said one or two. "He ought to be tarred and feathered and hanged."

"Couldn't do worse than hang him," commented Jake Boreham, cheerfully.

"Oh, yes, we could," said Mitchell, sitting down, resting his elbows on his knees, and marking his points with one fore-finger on the other. "For instance, we might boil him slow in tar. We might skin him alive. We might put him in a cage and poke him with sticks, with his wife and children in another cage to look on and enjoy the fun."

The chaps, who had been sitting quietly listening to Mitchell, and grinning, suddenly became serious and shifted their positions uneasily.

"But I can tell you what would hurt his feelings more than anything else we could do," said Mitchell.

"Well, what is it, Jack?" said Tom Hall, rather impatiently.

"Send round the hat and take up a collection for him," said Mitchell, "enough to let him get away with his wife and children and start life again in some less respectable town than Bourke. You needn't grin, I'm serious about it."

There was a thoughtful pause, and one or two scratched their heads.

"His wife seems pretty sick," Mitchell went on in a reflective tone. "I passed the place this morning and saw him scrubbing out the floor. He's been doing a bit of house-painting for old Heegard to-day. I suppose he learnt it in jail. I saw him at work and touched my hat to him."

"What!" cried Tom Hall, affecting to shrink from Mitchell in horror.

"Yes," said Mitchell, "I'm not sure that I didn't take my hat off. Now I know it's not bush religion for a man to touch his hat, except to a funeral, or a strange roof or woman sometimes; but when I meet a braver man than myself I salute him. I've only met two in my life."

"And who were they, Jack?" asked Jake Boreham.

"One," said Mitchell—"one is Douglas, and the other—well, the other was the man I used to be. But that's got nothing to do with it."

"But perhaps Douglas thought you were crowing over him when you took off your hat to him—sneerin' at him, like, Mitchell," reflected Jake Boreham.

"No, Jake," said Mitchell, growing serious suddenly. "There are ways of doing things that another man understands."

They all thought for a while.

"Well," said Tom Hall, "supposing we do take up a collection for him, he'd be too damned proud to take it."

"But that's where we've got the pull on him," said Mitchell, brightening up. "I heard Dr Morgan say that Mrs Douglas wouldn't live if she wasn't sent away to a cooler place, and Douglas knows it; and, besides, one of the little girls is sick. We've got him in a corner and he'll have to take the stuff. Besides, two years in jail takes a lot of the pride out of a man."

"Well, I'm damned if I'll give a sprat to help the man who tried his best to crush the Unions!" said One-eyed Bogan.

"Damned if I will either!" said Barcoo-Rot.

"Now, look here, One-eyed Bogan," said Mitchell, "I don't like to harp on old things, for I know they bore you, but when you returned to public life that time no one talked of kicking you out of the town. In fact, I heard that the chaps put a few pounds together to help you get away for a while till you got over your modesty."

No one spoke.

"I passed Douglas's place on my way here from my camp to-night," Mitchell went on musingly, "and I saw him walking up and down in the yard with his sick child in his arms. You remember that little girl, Bogan? I saw her run and pick up your hat and give it to you one day when you were trying to put it on with your feet. You remember, Bogan? The shock nearly sobered you."

There was a very awkward pause. The position had become too psychological altogether and had to be ended somehow. The awkward silence had to be broken, and Bogan broke it. He turned up Bob Brothers's hat, which was lying on the table, and "chucked" in a "quid," qualifying the hat and the quid, and disguising his feelings with the national oath of the land.

"We've had enough of this gory, maudlin, sentimental tommy-rot," he said. "Here, Barcoo, stump up or I'll belt it out of your hide! I'll—I'll take yer to pieces!"

But Douglas didn't leave the town. He sent his wife and children to Sydney until the heat wave was past, built a new room on to the cottage, and started a book and newspaper shop, and a poultry farm in the back paddock, and flourished.

They called him Mr Douglas for a while, then Douglas, then Percy Douglas, and now he is well-known as Old Daddy Douglas, and the Sydney *Worker, Truth,* and *Bulletin,* and other democratic rags are on sale at his shop. He is big with schemes for locking the Darling River, and he gets his drink at O'Donohoo's. He is scarcely yet regarded as a straight-out democrat. He was a gentleman once, Mitchell said, and the old blood was not to be trusted. But, last elections, Douglas worked quietly for Unionism, and gave the leaders certain hints, and put them up to various electioneering dodges which enabled them to return, in the face of Monopoly, a Labour member who is as likely to go straight as long as any other Labour member.

THE BLINDNESS OF ONE-EYED BOGAN

They judge not and they are not judged—'tis their philosophy—
(There's something wrong with every ship that sails upon the sea).
    —*The Ballad of the Rouseabout.*

"And what became of One-eyed Bogan?" I asked Tom Hall when I met him and Jack Mitchell down in Sydney with their shearing cheques the Christmas before last.

"You'd better ask Mitchell, Harry," said Tom. "He can tell you about Bogan better than I can. But first, what about the drink we're going to have?"

We turned out of Pitt Street into Hunter Street, and across George Street, where a double line of fast electric tramway was running, into Margaret Street and had a drink at Pfahlert's Hotel, where a counter lunch—as good as many dinners you get for a shilling—was included with a sixpenny drink. "Get a quiet corner," said Mitchell, "I like to hear myself cackle." So we took our beer out in the fernery and got a cool place at a little table in a quiet corner amongst the fern boxes.

"Well, One-eyed Bogan was a hard case, Mitchell," I said. "Wasn't he?"

"Yes," said Mitchell, putting down his "long-beer" glass, "he was."

"Rather a bad egg?"

"Yes, a regular bad egg," said Mitchell, decidedly.

"I heard he got caught cheating at cards," I said.

"Did you?" said Mitchell. "Well, I believe he did. Ah, well," he added reflectively, after another long pull, "One-eyed Bogan won't cheat at cards any more."

"Why?" I said. "Is he dead then?"

"No," said Mitchell, "he's blind."

"Good God!" I said, "how did that happen?"

"He lost the other eye," said Mitchell, and he took another drink. "Ah, well, he won't cheat at cards any more—unless there's cards invented for the blind."

"How did it happen?" I asked.

"Well," said Mitchell, "you see, Harry, it was this way. Bogan went pretty free in Bourke after the shearing before last, and in the end he got mixed up in a very ugly-looking business: he was accused of doing two new-chum jackeroos out of their stuff by some sort of confidence trick."

"Confidence trick," I said. "I'd never have thought that One-eyed Bogan had the brains to go in for that sort of thing."

"Well, it seems he had, or else he used somebody else's brains; there's plenty of broken-down English gentlemen sharpers knocking about out back, you know, and Bogan might have been taking lessons from one. I don't know the rights of the case, it was hushed up, as you'll see presently; but, anyway, the jackeroos swore that Bogan had done 'em out of ten quid. They were both Cockneys and I suppose they reckoned themselves smart, but bushmen have more time to think. Besides, Bogan's one eye was in his favour. You see he always kept his one eye fixed strictly on whatever business he had in hand; if he'd had another eye to rove round and distract his attention and look at things on the outside, the chances are he would never have got into trouble."

"Never mind that, Jack," said Tom Hall. "Harry wants to hear the yarn."

"Well, to make it short, one of the jackeroos went to the police and Bogan cleared out. His character was pretty bad just then, so there was a piece of blue paper out for him. Bogan didn't seem to think the thing was so serious as it was, for he only went a few miles down the river and camped with his horses on a sort of island inside an anabranch, till the thing should blow over or the new chums leave Bourke.

"Bogan's old enemy, Constable Campbell, got wind of Bogan's camp, and started out after him. He rode round the outside track and came in on to the river just below where the anabranch joins it, at the lower end of the island and right opposite Bogan's camp. You know what those billabongs are: dry gullies till the river rises from the Queensland rains and backs them up till the water runs round into the river again and makes anabranches of 'em—places that you thought were hollows you'll find above water, and you can row over places you thought were hills. There's no water so treacherous and deceitful as you'll find in some of those billabongs. A man starts to ride across a place where he thinks the water is just over the grass, and blunders into a deep channel—that wasn't there before—with a steady undercurrent with the whole weight of the Darling River funnelled into it; and if he can't swim and his horse isn't used to it—or sometimes if he can swim—it's a case with him, and the Darling River cod hold an inquest on him, if they have time, before he's buried deep in Darling River mud for ever. And somebody advertises in the missing column for Jack Somebody who was last heard of in Australia."

"Never mind that, Mitchell, go on," I said.

"Well, Campbell knew the river and saw that there was a stiff current there, so he hailed Bogan.

" 'Good day, Campbell,' shouted Bogan.

" 'I want you, Bogan,' said Campbell. 'Come across and bring your horses.'

" 'I'm damned if I will,' says Bogan. 'I'm not going to catch me death o' cold to save your skin. If you want me you'll have to bloody well come and git me.' Bogan was a good strong swimmer, and he had good horses, but he didn't try to get away—I suppose he reckoned he'd have to face the music one time or another—and one time is as good as another out back.

"Campbell was no swimmer; he had no temptation to risk his life—you see it wasn't as in war with a lot of comrades watching ready to advertise a man as a coward for staying alive—so he argued with Bogan and tried to get him to listen to reason, and swore at him. 'I'll make it damned hot for you, Bogan,' he said, 'if I have to come over for you.'

" 'Two can play at that game,' says Bogan.

" 'Look here, Bogan," said Campbell, 'I'll tell you what I'll do. If you give me your word that you'll come up to the police station to-morrow I'll go back and say nothing about it. You can say you didn't know a warrant was out after you. It will be all the better for you in the end. Better give me your word, man.'

"Perhaps Campbell knew Bogan better than any of us.

" 'Now then, Bogan,' he said, 'don't be a fool. Give your word like a sensible man, and I'll go back. I'll give you five minutes to make up your mind.' And he took out his watch.

"But Bogan was nasty and wouldn't give his word, so there was nothing for it but for Campbell to make a try for him.

"Campbell had plenty of pluck, or obstinacy, which amounts to the same thing. He put his carbine and revolver under a log, out of the 'rain that was coming on, saw to his handcuffs, and then spurred his horse into the water. Bogan lit his pipe with a stick from his camp-fire—so Campbell said afterwards—and sat down on his heels and puffed away, and waited for him.

"Just as Campbell's horse floundered into the current Bogan shouted to go back, but Campbell thought it was a threat and kept on. But Bogan had caught sight of a log coming down the stream, end on, with a sharp, splintered end, and before Campbell knew where he was, the sharp end of the log caught the horse in the flank. The horse started to plunge and struggle sideways, with all his legs, and Campbell got free of him as quick as he could. Now, you know, in some of those Darling River reaches the current will seem to run steadily for a while, and then come with a rush. (I was caught in one of those rushes once, when I was in swimming, and would have been drowned if I hadn't been born to be hanged.) Well, a rush came along just as Campbell got free from his horse, and he went down-stream one side of a snag and his horse the other. Campbell's pretty stout, you know, and his uniform was tight, and it handicapped him.

"Just as he was being washed past the lower end of the snag he caught hold of a branch that stuck out of the water and held on. He swung round and saw Bogan running down to the point opposite him. Now, you know there was always a lot of low cunning about Bogan, and I suppose he reckoned that if he pulled Campbell out he'd stand a good show of getting clear of his trouble; anyway, if he didn't save Campbell it might be said that he killed him—besides, Bogan was a good swimmer, so there wasn't any heroism about it anyhow. Campbell was only a few feet from the bank, but Bogan started to strip—to make the job look as big as possible, I suppose. He shouted to Campbell to say he was coming, and to hold on. Campbell said afterwards that Bogan seemed an hour undressing. The weight of the current was forcing down the bough that Campbell was hanging on to, and suddenly, he said, he felt a great feeling of helplessness take him by the shoulders. He yelled to Bogan and let go.

"Now, it happened that Jake Boreham and I were passing away

the time between shearings, and we were having a sort of fishing and shooting loaf down the river in a boat arrangement that Jake had made out of boards and tarred canvas. We called her the *Jolly Coffin*. We were just poking up the bank in the slack water, a few hundred yards below the billabong, when Jake said, 'Why, there's a horse or something in the river.' Then he shouted, 'No, by God, it's a man,' and we poked the *Coffin* out into the stream for all she was worth. 'Looks like two men fighting in the water,' Jake shouts presently. 'Hurry up, or they'll drown each other.'

"We hailed 'em, and Bogan shouted for help. He was treading water and holding Campbell up in front of him now in real professional style. As soon as he heard us he threw up his arms and splashed a bit—I reckoned he was trying to put as much style as he could into that rescue. But I caught a crab, and, before we could get to them, they were washed past into the top of a tree that stood well below flood-mark. I pulled the boat's head round and let her stern down between the branches. Bogan had one arm over a limb and was holding Campbell with the other, and trying to lift him higher out of the water. I noticed Bogan's face was bleeding—there was a dead limb stuck in the tree with nasty sharp points on it, and I reckoned he'd run his face against one of them. Campbell was gasping like a codfish out of water, and he was the whitest man I ever saw (except one, and *he'd* been drowned for a week). Campbell had the sense to keep still. We asked Bogan if he could hold on, and he said he could, but he couldn't hold Campbell any longer. So Jake took the oars and I leaned over the stern and caught hold of Campbell, and Jake ran the boat into the bank, and we got him ashore; then we went back for Bogan and landed him.

"We had some whisky and soon brought Campbell round; but Bogan was bleeding like a pig from a nasty cut over his good eye, so we bound wet handkerchiefs round his eyes and led him to a log and he sat down for a while, holding his hand to his eye and groaning. He kept saying, 'I'm blind, mates, I'm blind! I've lost me other eye!' but we didn't dream it was so bad as that: we kept giving him whisky. We got some dry boughs and made a big fire. Then Bogan stood up and held his arms stiff down to his sides, opening and shutting his hands as if he was in great pain. And I've often thought since what a different man Bogan seemed without his clothes and with the broken bridge of his nose and his eyes covered by the handkerchiefs. He was clean shaven, and his mouth and chin are his best features, and he's clean limbed and well hung. I often thought afterwards that there was something of a blind god about him as he stood there naked by the fire on the day he saved Campbell's life—something that reminded me of a statue I saw once in the Art Gallery. (Pity the world isn't blinder to a man's worst points.)

"Presently Jake listened and said, 'By God, that's lucky!' and we heard a steamer coming up-river and presently we saw her coming round the point with a couple of wool-barges in tow. We got Bogan aboard and got some clothes on him, and took him ashore at Bourke to the new hospital. The doctors did all they knew, but Bogan was blind for life. He never saw anything again—except 'a sort of dull white blur,' as he called it—or his past life sometimes, I suppose. Perhaps he saw that for the first time. Ah, well!

"Bogan's old enemy, Barcoo-Rot, went to see him in the hospital, and Bogan said, 'Well, Barcoo, I reckon we've had our last fight. I owe you a hiding, but I don't see how I'm going to pay you.' 'Never mind that, Bogan, old man,' says Barcoo. 'I'll take it from anyone yer likes to appoint, if that worries yer; and, look here, Bogan, if I can't fight you I can fight for you—and don't you forget it!' And Barcoo used to lead Bogan round about town in his spare time and tell him all that was going on; and I believe he always had an ear cocked in case someone said a word against Bogan—as if any of the chaps would say a word against a blind man.

"Bogan's case was hushed up. The police told us to fix it up the best way we could. One of the jackeroos, who reckoned that Bogan had swindled him, was a gentleman, and he was the first to throw a quid in the Giraffe's hat when it went round for Bogan, but the other jackeroo was a cur: he said he wanted the money that Bogan had robbed him of. There were two witnesses, but we sent 'em away, and Tom Hall, there, scared the jackeroo. You know Tom was always the best hand we had at persuading witnesses in Union cases to go home to see their mothers."

"How did you scare that jackeroo, Tom?" I asked.

"Tell you about it some other time," said Tom.

"Well," said Mitchell, "Bogan was always a good wool-sorter, so, next shearing, old Baldy Thompson—(you know Baldy Thompson, Harry, of West-o'-Sunday Station)—Baldy had a talk with some of the chaps, and took Bogan out in his buggy with him to West-o'-Sunday. Bogan would sit at the end of the rolling tables, in the shearing-shed, with a boy to hand him the fleeces, and he'd feel a fleece and tell the boy what bin to throw it into; and by and by he began to learn to throw the fleeces into the bins himself. And sometimes Baldy would have a sheep brought to him and get him to feel the fleece and tell him the quality of it. And then again Baldy would talk, just loud enough for Bogan to overhear, and swear that he'd sooner have Bogan, blind as he was, than half a dozen scientific jackeroo experts with all their eyes about them.

"Of course Bogan wasn't worth anything much to Baldy, but Baldy gave him two pounds a week out of his own pocket, and another quid that we made up between us; so he made enough to pull him through the rest of the year.

"It was curious to see how soon he learned to find his way about the hut and manage his tea and tucker. It was a rough shed, but everybody was eager to steer Bogan about—and, in fact, two of them had a fight about it one day. Baldy and all of us—and especially visitors when they came—were mighty interested in Bogan; and I reckon we were rather proud of having a blind wool-sorter. I reckon Bogan had thirty or forty pairs of eyes watching out for him in case he'd run against something or fall. It irritated him to be messed round too much—he said a baby would never learn to walk if it was held all the time. He reckoned he'd learn more in a year than a man who'd served a lifetime to blindness; but we didn't let him wander much—for fear he'd fall into the big rocky water-hole there, by accident.

"And after the shearing-season Bogan's wife turned up in Bourke——"

"Bogan's wife!" I exclaimed. "Why, I never knew Bogan was married."

"Neither did anyone else," said Mitchell. "But he was. Perhaps that was what accounted for Bogan. Sometimes, in his sober moods, I used to have an idea that there must have been something behind the Bogan to account for him. Perhaps he got trapped—or got married and found out that he'd made a mistake—which is about the worst thing a man can find out——"

"Except that his wife made the mistake, Mitchell," said Tom Hall.

"Or that both did," reflected Mitchell. "Ah, well!—never mind—Bogan had been married two or three years. Maybe he got married when he was on the spree—I knew that he used to send money to someone in Sydney and I suppose it was her. Anyway, she turned up after he was blind. She was a hard-looking woman—just the sort that might have kept a third-rate pub or a sly-grog shop. But you can't judge between husband and wife, unless you've lived in the same house with them—and under the same roofs with their parents right back to Adam for that matter. Anyway, she stuck to Bogan all right; she took a little two-roomed cottage and made him comfortable—she's got a sewing-machine and a mangle and takes in washing and sewing. She brought a carrotty-headed youngster with her, and the first time I saw Bogan sitting on the veranda with that youngster on his knee I thought it was a good thing that he was blind."

"Why?" I asked.

"Because the youngster isn't his," said Mitchell.

"How do you know that?"

"By the look of it—and by the look on her face, once, when she caught me squinting from the kid's face to Bogan's."

"And whose was it?" I asked, without thinking.

"How am I to know?" said Mitchell. "It might be yours for all I know—it's ugly enough, and you never had any taste in women. But you mustn't speak of that in Bourke. But there's another youngster coming, and I'll swear that'll be Bogan's all right.

"A curious thing about Bogan is that he's begun to be fidgety about his personal appearance—and you know he wasn't a dood. He wears a collar now, and polishes his boots; he wears elastic-sides, and polishes 'em himself—the only thing is that he blackens over the elastic. He can do many things for himself, and he's proud of it. He says he can see many things that he couldn't see when he had his eyes. You seldom hear him swear, save in a friendly way; he seems much gentler, but he reckons he would stand a show with Barcoo-Rot even now, if Barcoo would stand up in front of him and keep yelling——"

"By the way," I asked, "how did Bogan lose the sight of his other eye?"

"Sleeping out in the rain when he was drunk," said Mitchell. "He got a cold in his eye." Then he asked, suddenly:

"Did you ever see a blind man cry?"

"No," I said.

"Well, I have," said Mitchell. "You know Bogan wears goggles to hide his eyes—his wife made him do that. The chaps often used to drop round and have a yarn with Bogan and cheer him up, and one evening I was sitting smoking with him, and yarning about old times, when he got very quiet all of a sudden, and I saw a tear drop from under one of his shutters and roll down his cheek. It wasn't the eye he lost saving Campbell—it was the old wall-eye he used to use in the days before he was called 'One-eyed Bogan.' I suppose he thought it was dark and that I couldn't see his face. (There's a good many people in this world who think you can't see because they can't.) It made me feel like I used to feel sometimes in the days when I felt things——"

"Come on, Mitchell," said Tom Hall, "you've had enough beer."

"I think I have," said Mitchell. "Besides, I promised to send a wire to Jack Boreham to tell him that his mother's dead. Jake's shearing at West-o'-Sunday; shearing won't be over for three or four weeks, and Jake wants an excuse to get away without offending old Baldy and come down and have a fly round with us before the holidays are over."

Down at the telegraph-office Mitchell took a form and filled it in very carefully:—"Jacob Boreham. West-o'-Sunday Station. Bourke. Come home at once. Mother is dead. In terrible trouble. Father dying.—Mary Boreham."

"I think that will do," said Mitchell. "It ought to satisfy Baldy, and it won't give Jake too much of a shock, because he hasn't got a sister or sister-in-law, and his father and mother's been dead over ten years."

"Now, if I was running a theatre," said Mitchell, as we left the office, "I'd give five pounds a night for the face Jake'll have on him when he takes that telegram to Baldy Thompson."

TWO SUNDOWNERS

Sheep stations in Australia are any distance from twenty to a hundred miles apart, to keep well within the boundaries of truth and the great pastoral country. Shearing at any one shed only lasts a few weeks in the year; the number of men employed is according to the size of the shed—from three to five men in the little bough-covered shed of the small "cockatoo," up to a hundred and fifty or two hundred hands all told in the big corrugated iron machine shed of a pastoral company.

Shearing starts early up in northern Queensland, where you can get a "January shed;" and further south, in February, March or April sheds, and so on down into New South Wales, where shearing often lasts over Christmas. Shearers travel from shed to shed; some go a travel season without getting a pen, and an unlucky shearer might ride or tramp for several seasons and never get hands in wool; and all this explains the existence of the "footman" with his swag and the horseman with his packhorse. They have a rough life, and the Australian shearers are certainly the most democratic and perhaps the most independent, intelligent and generous body of workmen in the world.

Shearers at a shed elect their own cook, pay him so much a head, and they buy their rations in the lump from the station store; and "travellers," i.e. shearers and rouseabouts travelling for work, are invited, as a matter of course, to sit down to the shearers' table. Also a certain allowance of tea, sugar, flour or meat is still made to travellers at most Western station stores; so it would be rather surprising if there weren't some who travelled on the game. The swagman loafer, or "bummer," times himself, especially in bad weather, to arrive at the shed just about sundown; he is then sure of "tea," shelter for the night, breakfast, and some tucker from the cook to take him on along the track. Brummy and Swampy were sundowners.

Swampy was a bummer born—and proud of it. Brummy had drifted down to loaferdom, and his nature was soured and his spirit revengeful against the world because of the memory of early years wasted at hard work and in being honest. Both were short and stout, and both had scrubby beards, but Brummy's beard was a dusty black and Swampy's fiery red—he indulged in a monkey-shave sometimes, but his lower face was mostly like a patch of coarse stubble with a dying hedge round it. They had travelled together for a long time. They seemed at times to hate each other with a murderous hatred, but they were too lazy to fight. Sometimes they'd tramp side by side and growl at each other by the hour, other times they'd sulk for days; one would push on ahead and the other drop behind until there was a mile or two between them; but one always carried the billy, or the sugar, or something that was necessary to the comfort of the other, so they'd come together at sundown. They had travelled together a long time, and perhaps that was why they hated each other. They often agreed to part and take different tracks, and sometimes they parted—for a while. They agreed in cadging, and cadged in turn. They carried a spare set of tucker-bags, and if, for instance, they were out of sugar and had plenty flour and tea, Brummy or Swampy would go to the store, boundary-rider's hut, or selector's, with the sugar-bag in his hand and the other bags in his shirt front on spec. He'd get the sugar first, and then, if it looked good enough, the flour-bag would come out, then the tea-bag. And before he left he'd remark casually that he and his mate hadn't had a smoke for two days. They never missed a chance. And when they'd cadged more tucker than they could comfortably carry, they'd camp for a day or two and eat it down. Sometimes they'd have as much as a pound of tobacco, all in little "borrowed" bits, cut from the sticks or cakes of honest travellers. They never missed a chance. If a stranger gave Swampy his cake of tobacco with instructions to "cut off a pipeful," Swampy would cut off as much as he thought judicious, talking to the stranger and watching his eye all the time, and hiding his palm as much as possible—and sometimes, when he knew he'd cut off more than he could cram into his pipe, he'd put his hand in his pocket for the pipe and drop some of the tobacco there. Then he'd hand the plug to his mate, engage the stranger in conversation and try to hold his eye or detract his attention from Brummy so as to give Brummy a chance of cutting off a couple of pipefuls, and, maybe, nicking off a corner of the cake and slipping it into his pocket. I once heard a bushman say that no one but a skunk would be guilty of this tobacco trick—that it is about the meanest trick a man could be capable of—*because it spoils the chances of the next hard-up swaggy who asks the victim for tobacco.*

When Brummy and Swampy came to a shed where shearing was in full swing, they'd inquire, first thing, and with some show of anxiety, if there was any chance of gettin' on; if the shed was full-handed they'd growl about hard times, wonder what the country was coming to; talk of their missuses and kids that they'd left in Sydney, curse the squatters and the Government, and, next morning, get a supply of rations from the cook and depart with looks of gloom. If, on the other hand, there was room in the shed for one or both of them, and the boss told them to go to work in the morning, they'd keep it quiet from the cook if possible, and depart, after breakfast, unostentatiously.

Sometimes, at the beginning of a drought, when the tall dead grass was like tinder for hundreds of miles and a carelessly-dropped match would set the whole country on fire, Swampy would strike a hard-faced squatter, manager or overseer with a cold eye, and the conversation would be somewhat as follows:

Swampy: "Good day, boss!"

Boss (shortly): " 'Day."

Swampy: "Any chance of a job?"

Boss: "Naw. Got all I want and we don't start for a fortnight."

Swampy: "Can I git a bit o' meat?"

Boss: "Naw! Don't kill till Saturday."

Swampy: "Pint o' flour?"

Boss: "Naw. Short ourselves."

Swampy: "Bit o' tea or sugar, boss?"

Boss: "Naw—what next?"

Swampy: "Bit o' baccer, boss. Ain't had a smoke for a week."

Boss: "Naw. Ain't got enough for meself till the wagon comes out."

Swampy: "Ah, well! It's hot, ain't it, boss?"

Boss: "Yes—it's hot."

Swampy: "Country very dry?"

Boss: "Yes. Looks like it."

Swampy: "A fire 'ud be very bad just now?"

Boss: "Eh?"

Swampy: "Yes. Now I'm allers very careful with matches an' fire when I'm on the track."

Boss: "Are yer?"

Swampy: "Yes. I never lights a fire near the grass—allers in the middle of the track—it's the safest place yer can get. An' I allers puts the fire out afore I leaves the camp. If there ain't no water ter spare I covers the ashes with dirt. An' some fellers are so careless with matches lightin' their pipes." (Reflective pause.)

Boss: "Are they?"

Swampy: "Yes. Now, when I lights me pipe on the track in dry weather I allers rubs the match head up an' drops it in the dust. I never drops a burnin' match. But some travellers is so careless. A chap might light his pipe an' fling the match away without thinkin' an' the match might fall in a dry tuft, an'—there yer are!" (with a wave of his arms). "Hundreds of miles o' grass gone an' thousands o' sheep starvin'. Some fellers is so careless—they never thinks. . . . An' what's more, they don't care if they burn the whole country."

Boss (scratching his head reflectively): "Ah—umph!—You can go up to the store and get a bit of tucker. The storekeeper might let yer have a bit o' tobacco."

On one occasion, when they were out of flour and meat, Brummy and Swampy came across two other pilgrims camped on a creek, who were also out of flour and meat. One of them had tried a surveyors' camp a little further down, but without success. The surveyors' cook had said that he was short of flour and meat himself. Brummy tried him—no luck. Then Swampy said *he'd* go and have a try. As luck would have it, the surveyors' cook was just going to bake; he had got the flour out in the dish, put in the salt and baking powder, mixed it up, and had gone to the creek for a billy of water when Swampy arrived. While the cook was gone Swampy slipped the flour out of the dish into his bag, *wiped* the dish, set it down again, and planted the bag behind a tree at a little distance. Then he stood waiting, holding a spare empty bag in his hand. When the cook came back he glanced at the dish, lowered the billy of water slowly to the ground, scratched his head, and looked at the dish again in a puzzled way.

"Blanked if I didn't think I got that flour out!" he said.

"What's that, mate?" asked Swampy.

"Why! I could have sworn I got the flour out in the dish and mixed it before I went for the water," said the cook, staring at the dish again. "It's rum what tricks your memory plays on you sometimes."

"Yes," said Swampy, showing interest, while the cook got some more flour out into the dish from a bag in the back of the tent. "It is strange. I've done the same thing meself. I suppose it's the heat that makes us all a bit off at times."

"Do you cook, then?" asked the surveyors' cook.

"Well, yes. I've done a good bit of it in me time; but it's about played out. I'm after stragglers now." (Stragglers are stray sheep missed in the general muster and found about the out paddocks and shorn after the general shearing.)

They had a yarn and Swampy "bit the cook's ear" for a "bit o' meat an' tea an' sugar," not forgetting "a handful of flour if yer can spare it."

"Sorry," said the cook, "but I can only let you have about a pint. We're very short ourselves."

"Oh, that's all right!" said Swampy, as he put the stuff into his spare bags. "Thank you! Good day!"

"Good day," said the cook.

The cook went on with his work and Swampy departed, catching up the bag of flour from behind the tree as he passed it, and keeping the clump of timber well between him and the surveyors' camp, lest the cook should glance round, and, noticing the increased bulk of his load, get some new ideas concerning mental aberration.

Nearly every bushman has at least one superstition, or notion, that lasts his time—as nearly every bushman has at least one dictionary word which lasts him all his life. Brummy had a gloomy notion—Lord knows how he got it!—that he should 'a' gone on the boards if his people hadn't been so ignorant. He reckoned that he had the face and cut of an actor, could mimic any man's voice, and had wonderful control over his features. They came to a notoriously "hungry" station, where there was a Scottish manager and storekeeper. Brummy went up to "government house" in his own proper person, had a talk with the storekeeper, spoke of a sick mate, and got some flour and meat. They camped down the creek, and next morning Brummy started to shave himself.

"Whatever are you a-doin' of, Brummy?" gasped Swampy in great astonishment.

"Wait and see," growled Brummy, with awful impressiveness, as if he were going to cut Swampy's throat after he'd finished shaving. He shaved off his beard and whiskers, put on a hat and coat belonging to Swampy, changed his voice, dropped his shoulders, and went limping up to the station on a game leg. He saw the cook and got some "brownie," a bit of cooked meat and a packet of baking powder. Then he saw the storekeeper and approached the tobacco question. Sandy looked at him and listened with some slight show of interest, then he said:

"Oh that's all right now! But ye needn't ha' troublt shavin' yer beard—the cold weather's comin' on! An' yer mate's duds don't suit ye—they're too sma'; an' yer game leg doesn't fit ye either—it takes a lot o' practice. Ha' ye got ony tea an' sugar?"

Brummy must have touched something responsive in that old Scot somewhere, but *his* lack of emotion upset Brummy somewhat, or else an old deep-rooted superstition had been severely shaken. Anyway he let Swampy do the cadging for several days thereafter.

But one bad season they were very hard up indeed—even for Brummy and Swampy. They'd tramped a long hungry track, and had only met a few wretched jackeroos, driven out of the cities by hard times, and tramping hopelessly west. They were out of tobacco, and their trousers were so hopelessly "gone" behind that when they went to cadge at a place where there was a woman they were moved to back and sidle and edge away again—and neither Brummy nor Swampy was over fastidious in matters of dress or personal appearance. It was absolutely necessary to earn a pound or two, so they decided to go to work for a couple of weeks. It wouldn't hurt them, and then there was the novelty of it.

They struck West-o'-Sunday Station, and the boss happened to want a rouseabout to pick up wool and sweep the floor for the shearers.

"I can put *one* of you on," he said. "Fix it up between yourselves and go to work in the morning."

Brummy and Swampy went apart to talk it over.

"Look here! Brum, old man," said Swampy, with great heartiness, "we've been mates for a long while now, an' shared an' shared alike. You've allers acted straight to me an' I want to do the fair thing by you. *I* don't want to stand in *your* light. You take the job an' I'll be satisfied with a pair of pants out of it and a bit o' tobacco now an' agen. There yer are! I can't say no fairer than that."

"Yes," said Brummy, resentfully, "an' you'll always be throwin' it up to me afterwards that I done you out of a job!"

"I'll swear I won't," said Swampy, hurriedly. "But since you're so blasted touchy and suspicious about it, *you* take this job an' I'll take the next that turns up. How'll that suit you?"

Brummy thought resentfully.

"Look here!" he said presently, "let's settle it and have done with this damned sentimental tommy-rot. I'll tell you what I'll do—I'll give you the job and take my chance. The boss might want another man to-morrow. Now, are you satisfied?"

But Swampy didn't look grateful or happy.

"Well," growled Brummy, "of all the —— I ever travelled with you're the ——. What do you want anyway? What'll satisfy you? That's all I want to know. Hey?—can't yer speak?"

"Let's toss up for it," said Swampy, sulkily.

"All right," said Brummy, with a big oath, and he felt in his pocket for two old pennies he had. But Swampy had got a suspicion somehow that one of those pennies had two heads on it, and he wasn't sure that the other hadn't two tails—also, he suspected Brummy of some skill in "palming," so he picked up a chip from the wood-heap, spat on it, and spun it into the air. "Sing out!" he cried, "wet or dry?"

"Dry," said Brummy, promptly. He had a theory that the wet side of the chip, being presumably heaviest, was more likely to fall downwards; but this time it was "wet" up three times in succession. Brummy ignored Swampy's hand thrown out in hearty congratulation; and next morning he went to work in the shed. Swampy camped down the river, and Brummy supplied him with a cheap pair of moleskin trousers, tucker and tobacco. The shed cut out within three weeks and the two sundowners took the track again, Brummy with two pounds odd in his pocket—he having negotiated his cheque at the shed.

But now there was suspicion, envy, and distrust in the hearts of those two wayfarers. Brummy was now a bloated capitalist, and proud, and anxious to get rid of Swampy—at least Swampy thought so. He thought that the least that Brummy might have done was to have shared the "stuff" with him.

"Look here, Brummy," he said reproachfully, "we've shared and shared alike, and——"

"We never shared money," said Brummy, decidedly.

"Do you think I want yer blasted money?" retorted Swampy, indignantly. "When did I ever ask yer for a sprat? Tell me that!"

"You wouldn't have got it if you had asked," said Brummy, uncompromisingly. "Look here!" with vehemence. "Didn't I keep yer in tobacco and buy yer gory pants? What are you naggin' about anyway?"

"Well," said Swampy, "all I was goin' to say was that yer might let me carry one of them quids in case you lost one—yer know you're careless and lose things; or in case anything happened to you."

"I ain't going to lose it—if that's all that's fretting you," said Brummy, "and there ain't nothing going to happen to me—and don't you forget it."

"That's all the thanks I get for givin' yer my gory job," said Swampy, savagely. "I won't be sich a soft fool agen, I can tell yer."

Brummy was silent, and Swampy dropped behind. He brooded darkly, and it's a bad thing for a man to brood in the bush. He was reg'lar disgusted with Brummy. He'd allers acted straight to him, and Brummy had acted like a "cow." He'd stand it no longer; but he'd have some satisfaction. He wouldn't be a fool. If Brummy was mean skunk enough to act to a mate like that, Swampy would be even with him; he would wait till Brummy was asleep, collar the stuff, and clear. It was his job, anyway, and the money was his by rights. He'd have his rights.

Brummy, who carried the billy, gave Swampy a long tramp before he camped and made a fire. They had tea in silence, and smoked moodily apart until Brummy turned in. They usually slept on the ground, with a few leaves under them, or on the sand where there was any, each wrapped in his own blankets, and with their spare clothes, or rags rather, for pillows. Presently Swampy turned in and pretended to sleep, but he lay awake watching, and listening to Brummy's breathing. When he thought it was safe he moved cautiously and slipped his hand under Brummy's head, but Brummy's old pocket-book—in which he carried some dirty old letters in a woman's handwriting—was not there. All next day Swampy watched Brummy sharply every time he put his hands into his pockets, to try and find out in which pocket he kept his money. Brummy seemed very cheerful and sociable, even considerate, to his mate all day, and Swampy pretended to be happy. They yarned more than they had done for many a day. Brummy was a heavy sleeper, and that night Swampy went over him carefully and felt all his pockets, but without success. Next day Brummy seemed in high spirits—they were nearing Bourke, where they intended to loaf round the pubs for a week or two. On the third night Swampy waited till about midnight, and then searched Brummy, every inch of him he could get at, and tickled him with a straw of grass till he turned over, and ran his hands over the other side of him, and over his feet (Brummy slept with his socks on), and looked in his boots, and in the billy and in the tucker-bags, and felt in every tuft of grass round the camp, and under every bush, and down a hollow stump, and up a hollow log: but there was no pocket-book. Brummy couldn't have lost the money and kept it dark—he'd have gone back to look for it at once. Perhaps he'd thrown away the book and sewn the money in his clothes somewhere. Swampy crept back to him and felt the lining of his hat, and was running his hand over Brummy's chest when Brummy suddenly started to snore, and Swampy desisted without loss of time. He crept back to bed, breathing short, and thought hard. It struck him that there was something aggressive about that snore. He began to suspect that Brummy was up to his little game, and it pained him.

Next morning Brummy was decidedly frivolous. At any other time Swampy would have put it down to a "touch o' the sun," but now he felt a growing conviction that Brummy knew what he'd been up to the last three nights, and the more he thought of it the more it pained him—till at last he could stand it no longer.

"Look here, Brummy," he said frankly, "where the hell do you keep that flamin' stuff o' yourn? I been tryin' to git at it ever since we left West-o'-Sunday."

"I know you have, Swampy," said Brummy, affectionately—as if he considered that Swampy had done his best in the interests of mateship.

"I *knowed* yer knowed!" exclaimed Swampy, triumphantly. "But where the blazes did yer put it?"

"Under *your* head, Swampy, old man," said Brummy, cheerfully.

Swampy was hurt now. He commented in the language that used to be used by the bullock-punchers of the good days as they pranced up and down by their teams and lammed into the bullocks with saplings and crow-bars, and called on them to lift a heavy load out of a bog in the bed of a muddy creek.

"Never mind, Swampy!" said Brummy, soothingly, as his mate paused and tried to remember worse oaths. "It wasn't your fault."

But they parted at Bourke. Swampy had allers acted straight ter Brummy—share 'n' share alike. He'd do as much for a mate as any other man, an' put up with as much from a mate. He had put up with a lot from Brummy: he'd picked him up on the track and learned him all he knowed; Brummy would have starved many a time if it hadn't been for Swampy; Swampy had learned him how to "battle." He'd stick to Brummy yet, but he couldn't stand ingratitude. He hated low cunnin' an' suspicion, and when a gory mate got suspicious of his own old mate and wouldn't trust him, an' took to plantin' his crimson money—it was time to leave him.

A SKETCH OF MATESHIP

Bill and Jim, professional shearers, were coming into Bourke from the Queensland side. They were horsemen and had two packhorses. At the last camp before Bourke Jim's packhorse got disgusted and home-sick during the night and started back for the place where he was foaled. Jim was little more than a new-chum jackeroo; he was no bushman and generally got lost when he went down the next gully. Bill was a bushman, so it was decided that he should go back to look for the horse.

Now Bill was going to sell his packhorse, a well-bred mare, in Bourke, and he was anxious to get her into the yards before the horse sales were over; this was to be the last day of the sales. Jim was the best "barracker" of the two; he had great imagination; he was a very entertaining story-teller and conversationalist in social life, and a glib and a most impressive liar in business, so it was decided that he should hurry on into Bourke with the mare and sell her for Bill. Seven pounds, reserve.

Next day Bill turned up with the missing horse and saw Jim standing against a veranda-post of the Carriers' Arms, with his hat down over his eyes, and thoughtfully spitting in the dust. Bill rode over to him.

" 'Ullo, Jim."

" 'Ullo, Bill. I see you got him."

"Yes, I got him."

Pause.

"Where'd yer find him?"

" 'Bout ten mile back. Near Ford's Bridge. He was just feedin' along."

Pause. Jim shifted his feet and spat in the dust.

"Well," said Bill at last. "How did you get on, Jim?"

"Oh, all right," said Jim. "I sold the mare."

"That's right," said Bill. "How much did she fetch?"

"Eight quid;" then, rousing himself a little and showing some emotion, "An' I could 'a' got ten quid for her if I hadn't been a dam' fool."

"Oh, that's good enough," said Bill.

"I could 'a' got ten quid if I'd 'a' waited."

"Well, it's no use cryin'. Eight quid is good enough. Did you get the stuff?"

"Oh, yes. They parted all right. If I hadn't been such a dam' fool an' rushed it, there was a feller that would 'a' given ten quid for that mare."

"Well, don't break yer back about it," said Bill. "Eight is good enough."

"Yes. But I could 'a' got ten," said Jim, languidly, putting his hand in his pocket.

Pause. Bill sat waiting for him to hand over the money; but Jim withdrew his hand empty, stretched, and said:

"Ah, well, Bill, I done it in. Lend us a couple o' notes."

Jim had been drinking and gambling all night and he'd lost the eight pounds as well as his own money.

Bill didn't explode. What was the use? He should have known that Jim wasn't to be trusted with money in town. It was he who had been the fool. He sighed and lent Jim a pound, and they went in to have a drink.

Now it strikes me that if this had happened in a civilized country (like England) Bill would have had Jim arrested and jailed for larceny as a bailee, or embezzlement, or whatever it was. And would Bill or Jim or the world have been any better for it?

ON THE TUCKER TRACK

A STEELMAN STORY

Steelman and Smith, professional wanderers from New Zealand, took a run over to Australia one year to have a look at the country, and drifted out back, and played cards and "headin'- 'em" at the shearing-sheds (while pretending to be strangers to each other), and sold eye-water and unpatented medicine, and worked the tucker tracks. They struck a streak of bad luck at West-o'-Sunday Station, where they were advised (by the boss and about fifty excited shearers) to go east, and not to stop till they reached the coast. They were tramping along the track towards Bourke; they were very hard up and had to "battle" for tucker and tobacco along the track. They came to a lonely shanty, about two camps west of Bourke.

"We'll turn off into the scrub and strike the track the other side of the shanty and come back to it," said Steelman. "You see, if they see us coming into Bourke they'll say to themselves, 'Oh, we're never likely to see these chaps again,' and they won't give us anything, or, perhaps, only a pinch of tea or sugar in a big lump of paper. There's some women that can never see a tucker-bag, even if you hold it right under their noses. But if they see us going out back they'll reckon that we'll get a shed likely as not, and we'll be sure to call there with our cheques coming back. I hope the old man's got the lumbago, or sciatica, or something."

"Why?" asked Smith.

"Because whenever I see an old man poking round the place on a stick I always make for him straight and inquire about his trouble; and no matter what complaint he's got, my old man suffered from it for years. It's pretty hard graft listening to an old man with a pet leg, but I find it pays; and I always finish up by advising him to try St Jacob's oil. Perhaps he's been trying it for years, but that doesn't matter; the consultation works out all right all the same, and there's never been a remedy tried yet but I've got another.

"I've got a lot of Maori and blackfellow remedies in my mind, and when they fail I can fall back on the Chinese; and if that isn't enough I've got a list of my grandmother's remedies that she wrote down for me when I was leaving home, and I kept it for a curiosity. It took her three days to write them, and I reckon they'll fill the bill.

"You don't want a shave. You look better with that stubble on. You needn't say anything; just stand by and wear your usual expression, and if they ask me what's the matter with my mate I'll fix up a disease for you to have, and get something extra on your account, poor beggar!

"I wish we had a chap with us that could sing a bit and run the gamut on a fiddle or something. With a sickly-looking fish like you to stand by and look interesting and die slowly of consumption all the time, and me to do the talking, we'd be able to travel from one end of the bush to the other and live on the fat of the land. I wouldn't cure you for a hundred pounds."

They reached the shanty, and there, sure enough, was an old man pottering round with a list to starboard. He was working with a hoe inside a low paling fence round a sort of garden. Steelman and Smith stopped outside the fence.

"Good day, boss!"

" 'Day."

"It's hot."

"It's hot."

So far it was satisfactory.

He was a little man, with a wiry, red beard. He might have been a Scandinavian.

"You seem to be a bit lame," said Steelman. "Hurt your foot?"

"Naw," said the old man. "It's an old thing."

"Ah!" said Steelman, "lumbago, I suppose? My father suffered cruel from it for years."

"Naw," said the old man, moving closer to the fence. "It ain't in me back; the trouble's with me leg."

"Oh!" said Steelman. "One a bit shorter than the other?"

"Well, yes. It seems to be wearin' a bit shorter. I must see to it."

"Hip disease, perhaps?" said Steelman. "A brother o' mine had——"

"Naw, it's not in the hip," said the old man. "My leg's gone at the knee."

"Oh! stiff joint; I know what that is. Had a touch of it once myself. An uncle of mine was nearly crippled with it. He used to use St Jacob's oil. Ever try St Jacob's oil?"

"Naw," said the old man, "not that I know of. I've used linseed oil though."

"Linseed oil!" said Steelman; "I've never heard of that for stiff knee. How do you use it?"

"Use it raw," said the old man. "Raw linseed oil; I've rubbed it in, and I've soaked me leg in it."

"Soaked your leg in it!" said Steelman. "And did it do it any good?"

"Well, it seems to preserve it—keeps it from warping, and it wears better—and it makes it heavier. It seemed a bit too light before."

Steelman nudged Smith under cover of the palings. The old man was evidently a bit ratty.

"Well, I hope your leg will soon be all right, boss," said Steelman.

"Thank you," said the old man, "but I don't think there's much hope. I suppose you want some tucker?"

"Well, yes," said Steelman, rather taken aback by the old man's sudden way of putting it. "We're hard up."

"Well, come along to the house and I'll see if I can get yer something," said the old man; and they walked along outside the fence, and he hobbled along inside, till he came to a little gate at the corner. He opened the gate and stumped out. He had a wooden leg. He wore his trouser-leg down over it, and the palings had hidden the bottom from Steelman and Smith.

He wanted them to stay to dinner, but Steelman didn't feel comfortable, and thanked him, and said they'd rather be getting on (Steelman always spoke for Smith); so the old man gave them some cooked meat, bread, and a supply of tea and sugar. Steelman watched his face very close, but he never moved a muscle. But when they looked back he was leaning on his hoe, and seemed to be shaking.

"Took you back a bit, Steely, didn't it?" suggested Smith.

"How do you make that out?" snorted Steelman, turning on him suddenly. "I knew a carpenter who used to soak his planes in raw linseed oil to preserve them and give them weight. There's nothing funny about that."

Smith rubbed his head.

A BUSH PUBLICAN'S LAMENT

> . . . For thirst is long and throats is short
> Among the sons o' men.
>
> M. J. C.

I wish I was spifflicated before I ever seen a pub!

You see, it's this way. Suppose a cove comes along on a blazin' hot day in the drought—an' *you* ought to know how hell-hot it can be out here—an' he dumps his swag in the corner of the bar; an' he turns round an' he ses ter me, "Look here boss, I ain't got a lonely steever on me, an' God knows when I'll git one. I've tramped ten mile this mornin', an' I'll have ter tramp another ten afore to-night. I'm expectin' ter git on shearin' with ol' Baldy Thompson at West-o'-Sunday nex' week. I got a thirst on me like a sun-struck bone, an', for God sake, put up a couple o' beers for me an' my mate, an' I'll fix it up with yer when I come back after shearin'."

An' what's a feller ter do? I bin there meself, an'—I put it to you! I've known what it is to have a thirst on me.

An' suppose a poor devil comes along in the jim-jams, with every inch on him jumpin' an' a look in his eyes like a man bein' murdered an' sent ter hell, an' a whine in his voice like a whipped cur, an' the snakes a-chasing of him; an' he hooks me with his finger ter the far end o' the bar—as if he was goin' ter tell me that the world was ended—an' he hangs over the bar an' chews me lug, an' tries to speak, an' breaks off inter a sort o' low shriek, like a terrified woman, an' he says, "For Mother o' Christ's sake, giv' me a drink!" An' what am I to do? I bin there meself. I knows what the horrors is. He mighter blued his cheque at the last shanty. But what am I ter do? I put it ter you. If I let him go he might hang hisself ter the nex' leanin' tree.

What's a drink? yer might arst—I don't mind a drink or two; but when it comes to half a dozen in a day it mounts up, I can tell yer.

Drinks is sixpence here—I have to pay for it, an' pay carriage on it. It's all up ter me in the end. I used sometimes ter think it was lucky I wasn't west o' the sixpenny line, where I'd lose a shillin' on every drink I give away.

An' supposen a sundowner comes along smokin' tea-leaves, an' ses ter me, "Look her, boss! me an' my mate ain't had a smoke for three days!" What's a man ter do? I put it ter you! I'm a heavy smoker meself, an' I've known what it is to be without a smoke on the track. But "nail-rod" is ninepence a stick out here, an' I have ter pay carriage. It all mounts up, I can tell yer.

An' supposen Ole King Billy an' his ole black gin comes round at holiday time and squats on the verander, an' blarneys an' wheedles and whines and argues like a hundred Jews an' ole Irishwomen put tergether, an' accuses me o' takin' his blarsted country from him, an' makes me an' the missus laugh; an' we gives him a bottl'er rum an' a bag of grub ter get rid of him an' his rotten ole scarecrow tribe—It all tells up. I was allers soft on the blacks, an', beside, a ole gin nursed me an' me mother when I was born, an' saved me blessed life—not that that mounts to much. But it all tells up, an' I got me licence ter pay. An' some bloody skunk goes an' informs on me for supplyin' the haboriginalls with intossicatin' liquor, an' I have ter pay a fine an' risk me licence. But what's a man ter do?

An' three or four herrin'-gutted jackeroos comes along about dinner-time, when the table's set and the cookin' smellin' from the kichen, with their belts done up three holes, an' not the price of a feed on' em. What's man ter do? I've known what it is ter do a perish on the track meself. It's not the tucker I think on. I don't care a damn for that. When the shearers come every one is free to go inter the kitchin an' forage for hisself when he feels hungry—so long as he pays for his drink. But the jackeroos can't pay for drinks, an' I have ter pay carriage on the flour an' tea an' sugar an' groceries—an' it all tells up by the end o' the year.

An' a straight chap that knows me gets a job to take a flock o' sheep or a mob o' cattle ter the bloomin' Gulf, or South Australia, or somewheers—an' loses one of his horses goin' out ter take charge, an' borrers eight quid from me ter buy another. He'll turn up agen in a year or two an' most likely want ter make me take twenty quid for that eight—an' make everybody about the place blind drunk—but I've got ter wait, an' the wine an' sperit merchants an' the brewery won't. They know I can't do without liquor in the place.

An' lars' rains Jimmy Nowlett, the bullick-driver, gets bogged over his axle-trees back there on the Blacksoil Plains between two flooded billerbongs, an' prays till the country steams an' his soul's busted, an' his throat like a lime-kiln. He taps a keg o' rum or beer ter keep his throat in workin' order. I don't mind that at all, but him an' his mates git flood-bound for near a week, an' broach more kegs, an' go on a howlin' spree in ther mud, an' spill mor'n they swipe, an' leave a tarpaulin off a load, an' the flour gets wet, an' the sugar runs out of the bags like syrup, an'— What's a feller ter do? Do yer expect me to set the law onter Jimmy? I've knowed him all my life, an' he knowed my father afore I was born. He's been on the roads this forty year, till he's as thin as a rat, and as poor as a myall black; an' he's got a family ter keep back there in Bourke. No, I have ter pay for it in the end, an' it all mounts up, I can tell yer.

An' suppose some poor devil of a new-chum black sheep comes along, staggerin' from one side of the track to the other, and spoutin' poetry; dyin' o' heat or fever. or heartbreak an' home-sickness, or a life o' disserpation he'd led in England, an' without a sprat on him, an' no claim on the bush; an' I ketches him in me arms as he stumbles inter the bar, an' he wants me ter hold him up while he turns English inter Greek for me. An' I put him ter bed, an' he gits worse, an' I have ter send the buggy twenty mile for a doctor—an' pay him. An' the jackeroo gits worse, an' has ter be watched an' nursed an' held down sometimes; an' he raves about his home an' mother in England, an' the blarsted University that he was eddicated at—an' a woman—an' somethin' that sounds like poetry in French; an' he upsets my missus a lot, an' makes her blubber. An' he dies, an' I have ter pay a man ter bury him (an' knock up a sort o' fence round the grave arterwards ter keep the stock out), an' send the buggy agen for a parson, an'—Well, what's a man ter do? I couldn't let him wander away an' die like a dog in the scrub, an' be shoved underground like a dog, too, if his body was ever found. The Government might pay ter bury him, but there ain't never been a pauper funeral from my house yet, an' there won't be one if I can help it—except it be meself.

An' then there's the bother goin' through his papers to try an' find out who he was an' where his friends is. An' I have ter get the missus to write a letter to his people, an' we have ter make up lies about how he died ter make it easier for 'em. An' goin' through his letters, the missus comes across a portrait an' a locket of hair, an' letters from his mother an' sisters an' girl; an' they upset her, an' she blubbers agin, an' gits sentimental—like she useter long ago when we was first married.

There was one bit of poetry—I forgit it now—that that there

jackeroo kep' sayin' over an' over agen till it buzzed in me head; an', weeks after, I'd ketch the missus mutterin' it to herself in the kitchen till I thought she was goin' ratty.

An' we gets a letter from the jackeroo's friends that puts us to a lot more bother. I hate havin' anythin' to do with letters. An' someone's sure to say he was lambed down an' cleaned out an' poisoned with bad bush liquor at my place. It's almost enough ter make a man wish there *was* a recordin' angel.

An' what's the end of it? I got the blazin' bailiff in the place now! I can't shot him out because he's a decent, hard-up, poor devil from Bourke, with consumption or somethin', an' he's been talkin' to the missus about his missus an' kids; an' I see no chance of gittin' rid of him, unless the shearers come along with their cheques from West-o'-Sunday nex' week and act straight by me. Like as not I'll have ter roll up me swag an' take the track meself in the end. They say publicans are damned, an' I think so, too; an' I wish I'd bin operated on before ever I seen a pub.

THE SHEARER'S DREAM

Mitchell and I rolled up our swags after New Year and started to tramp west. It had been a very bad season after a long drought. Old Baldy Thompson had only shorn a few bales of grass-seed and burrs, so he said, and thought of taking the track himself; but we hoped to get on shearing stragglers at West-o'-Sunday or one of the stations of the Hungerford track.

It was very hot weather, so we started after sunset, intending to travel all night. We crossed the big billabong, and were ploughing through the dust and sand towards West Bourke, when a buggy full of city girls and swells passed by. They were part of a theatrical company on tour in the Back-Blocks, and some local Johnnies. They'd been driven out to see an artesian bore, or wool-shed, or something. The horses swerved, and jerked a little squawk out of one of the girls. Then another said:

"Ow-w! Two old swaggies. He! he! he!"

I glanced at Mitchell to see if he was hit, and caught his head down; but he pulled himself up and pretended to hitch his swag into an easier position.

About a hundred yards further on he gave me a side look and said: "Did that touch you, Harry?"

"No," I said, and I laughed.

"You see," reflected Mitchell, "they're more to be pitied than blamed. It's their ignorance. In the first place, we're not two old tramps, as they think. We are professional shearers; and the Australian shearers are about the most independent and intelligent class of men in the world. We've got more genius in one of our little fingers than there is in the whole of that wagonette-load of fiddle-daddle and fiddle-faddle and giggles. Their intellects are on a level with the rotten dramas they travel with, and their lives about as false. They are slaves to the public, and their home is the pub-parlour, with sickly, senseless Johnnies to shout suppers and drink for them and lend their men money. If one of those girls is above the average, how she must despise those Johnnies—and the life! She must feel a greater contempt for them than the private-barmaid does for the boozer she cleans out. He gets his drink and some enjoyment, anyhow. And how she must loathe the life she leads! And what's the end of it as often as not? I remember once, when I was a boy, I was walking out with two aunts of mine—they're both dead now. God rest their fussy, innocent old souls!—and one of 'em said suddenly, 'Look! Quick, Jack! There's Maggie So-and-So, the great actress.' And I looked and saw a woman training vines in a porch. It seemed like seeing an angel to me, and I never forgot her as she was then. The diggers used to go miles out of town to meet the coach that brought her, and take the horses out and drag it in, and throw gold in her lap, and worship her.

"The last time I was in Sydney I saw her sitting in the back parlour of a third-rate pub. She was dying of dropsy and couldn't move from her chair. She showed me a portrait of herself as I remembered her, and talked quite seriously about going on the stage again.

"Now, our home is about two thousand miles wide, and the world's our stage. If the worst comes to the worst we can always get tucker and wood and water for nothing. If we're camping at a job in a tent there's no house-cleaning to bother us. All we've got to do when the camp gets too dirty is to shift the tent to a fresh place. We've got time to think and—we're free.

"But then, agen," he reflected, "there's the world's point of view to be considered. Some day I might be flashing past in a buggy or saloon-carriage—or, the chances are it will be you—and you might look out the window and see an old swaggy tramping along in the dust, or camped under a strip of calico in the rain in the scrub. (And it might be me—old Mitchell—that really wrote your books, only the world won't know it.) And then you'll realize what a wretched, miserable life it was. We never realize the miseries of life till we look back—the mistakes and miseries that had to be and couldn't be helped. It's all luck—luck and chance."

But those girls seemed to have gravelled Mitchell, and he didn't seem able to talk himself round. He tramped on, brooding for a while, and then suddenly he said:

"Look here, Harry! Those girls are giving a dance to-night, and if I liked to go back to Bourke and tog up and go to the dance I could pick out the prettiest, dance with her all the evening, and take her for a stroll afterwards, old tramp as they thought me. I've lived—but it wouldn't be worth my while now."

I'd seen Jack in a mood like this before, and thought it best to say nothing. Perhaps the terrible heat had affected him a little. We walked on in silence until we came to the next billabong. "Best boil the billy here, Harry," said Mitchell, "and have some tea before we go any further."

I got some sticks together and made a fire and put the billy on. The country looked wretched—like the ghost of a burnt-out land—in the moonlight. The banks of the creek were like ashes, the thin, gnarled gum-bush seemed dry-rotting fast, and in many places the surface of the ground was cracked in squares where it had shrunk in the drought. In the bed of the creek was a narrow gutter of water that looked like bad milk.

Mitchell sat on his swag, with his pint of tea on the ground by his foot, and chewed his pipe.

"What's up, Jack?" I asked. "Have you got the blues?"

"Well, yes, Harry," he said. "I'm generally dull the first day on the track. The first day is generally the worst, anywhere or anytime—except, perhaps, when you're married.... I got—well, I got thinking of the time when a woman's word could have hurt me."

Just then one of the "travellers" who were camped a bit up the creek suddenly commenced to sing. It was a song called "The Shearer's Dream," and I suppose the buggy of girls, or the conversation they started, reminded him of it. He started his verses and most of his lines with a howl; and there were unexpected howls all through the song, and it wailed off, just as unexpectedly, in places where there was no pathos that I could see:

Oh, I dreamt I shore in a shearer's shed, and it was a dream of joy,
For every one of the rouseabouts was a girl dressed up as a boy—
Dressed up like a page in a pantomime, and the prettiest ever seen—
They had flaxen hair, they had coal-black hair—and every shade between.

"Every" with sudden and great energy, a long drop on to "shade," and a wail of intense sadness and regret running on into "between," the dirge reaching its wailsomest in the "tween" in every case.

The shed was cooled by electric fans that was over every "shoot";
The pens was of polished ma-ho-gany, and ev'rything else to suit;
The huts was fixed with spring-mattresses, and the tucker was simply grand,
And every night by the biller-bong we darnced to a German band.

    "Chorus, boys!"

There was short, plump girls, there was tall, slim girls, and the handsomest ever
    seen—
They was four-foot-five, they was six-foot high, and hevery size between.
Our pay was the wool on the jumbucks' backs, so we shore till all was blue—
The sheep was washed afore they was shore (and the rams was scented too);
And we all of us cried when the shed cut out, in spite of the long, hot days,
For hevery hour them girls waltzed in with whisky and beer on tr-a-a-a-ys!

    "Chorus! you ——!"

They had kind grey eyes, they had coal-black eyes, and the grandest ever seen—
They had plump pink hands, they had slim white hands, and hevery shape
    be-tw-e-e-n.
There was three of them girls to every chap, and as jealous as they could be—

    "Ow! you ——"

The singer's voice or memory seemed suddenly to have failed him at this point, but whether his mates hit him on the back of the head with a tomahawk, or only choked him, I do not know. Mitchell was inclined to think, from the sound of it, that they choked him.

THE LOST SOULS' HOTEL

Hungerford Road, February. One hundred and thirty miles of heavy reddish sand, bordered by dry, hot scrubs. Dense cloud of hot dust. Four wool-teams passing through a gate in a "rabbit proof" fence which crosses the road. Clock, clock, clock of wheels and rattle and clink of chains, crack of whips and explosions of Australian language. Bales and everything else coated with dust. Stink of old axle-grease and tarpaulins. Tyres hot enough to fry chops on: bows and chains so hot that it's a wonder they do not burn through the bullock's hides. Water lukewarm in blistered kegs slung behind the wagons. Bullocks dragging along as only bullocks do. Wheels ploughing through the deep sand, and the load lurching from side to side. Half-way on a "dry-stretch" of seventeen miles. Big "tank" full of good water through the scrub to the right, but it is a private tank and a boundary-rider is shepherding it. Mulga scrub and sparse, spiky undergrowth.

The carriers camp for dinner and boil their billies while the bullocks droop under their yokes in the blazing heat; one or two lie down and the leaders drag and twist themselves round under a dead tree, under the impression that there is shade there. The carriers look like Red Indians, with the masks of red dust "bound" with sweat on their faces, but there is an unhealthy-looking, whitish space round their eyes, caused by wiping away the blinding dust, sweat, and flies. The dry sticks burn with a pale flame and an almost invisible thin pale blue smoke. The sun's heat dancing and dazzling across every white fence-post, sandhill, or light-coloured object in the distance.

One man takes off his boot and sock, empties half a pint of sand out of them, and pulls up his trouser-leg. His leg is sheathed to the knee in dust and sweat; he absently scrapes it with his knife, and presently he amuses himself by moistening a strip with his forefinger and shaving it, as if he were vaguely curious to see if he is still a white man.

The Hungerford coach ploughs past in a dense cloud of dust.

The teams drag on again like a "wounded snake that dies at sundown," if a wounded snake that dies at sundown could revive sufficiently next morning to drag on again until another sun goes down.

Hopeless-looking swagmen are met with during the afternoon, and one carrier—he of the sanded leg—lends them tobacco; his mates contribute "bits o'" tea, flour, and sugar.

Sundown and the bullocks done up. The teamsters unyoke them and drive them on to the next water—five miles—having previously sent a mate to reconnoitre and see that boundary-rider is not round, otherwise, to make terms with him, for it is a squatter's bore. They hurry the bullocks down to the water and back in the twilight, and then, under cover of darkness, turn them into a clearing in the scrub off the road, where a sign of grass might be seen—if you look close.

But the "bullockies" are better off than the horse-teamsters, for bad chaff is sold by the pound and corn is worth its weight in gold.

Mitchell and I turned off the track at the rabbit-proof fence and made for the tank in the mulga. We boiled the billy and had some salt mutton and damper. We were making back for Bourke, having failed to get a cut in any of the sheds on the Hungerford track. We sat under a clump of mulga saplings, with our backs to the trunks, and got out our pipes. Usually, when the flies were very bad on the track, we had to keep twigs or wild-turkey-tail feathers going in front of our faces the whole time to keep the mad flies out of our eyes; and, when we camped, one would keep the feather going while the other lit his pipe—then the smoke would keep them away. But the flies weren't so bad in a good shade or in the darkened hut. Mitchell's pipe would have smoked out Old Nick; it was an ancient string-bound meerschaum, and strong enough to kill a blackfellow. I had one smoke out of it, once when I felt bad in my inside and wanted to be sick, and the result was very satisfactory.

Mitchell looked through his old pocket-book—more by force of habit than anything else—and turned up a circular from Tattersall's. And that reminded him.

"Do you know what I'd do, Harry," he said, "if I won Tattersall's big sweep, or was to come into fifty or a hundred thousand pounds, or, better still, a million?"

"Nothing, I suppose," I said, "except to get away to Sydney or some cooler place than this."

"I'll tell you what I'd do," said Mitchell, talking round his pipe. "I'd build a Swagman's Rest right here."

"A Swagman's Rest?"

"Yes. Right here on this very God-forsaken spot. I'd build a Swagman's Rest and call it the Lost Souls' Hotel, or the Sundowners' Arms, or the Half-way House to ——, or some such name that would take the bushmen's fancy. I'd have it built on the best plans for coolness in a hot country; bricks, and plenty of wide verandas with brick floors, and balconies, and shingles, in the old Australian style. I wouldn't have a sheet of corrugated iron about the place. And I'd have old-fashioned hinged sashes with small panes and vines round 'em; they look cooler and more homely and romantic than the glaring sort that shove up.

"And I'd dig a tank or reservoir for surface water as big as a lake, and bore for artesian water—and get it, too, if I had to bore right through to England; and I'd irrigate the ground and make it grow horse-feed and fruit, and vegetables too, if I had to cart manure from

Bourke. And every teamster's bullock or horse, and every shearer's hack, could burst itself free, but I'd make travelling stock pay—for it belongs to the squatters and capitalists. All carriers could camp for one night only. And I'd—no, I wouldn't have any flowers; they might remind some heart-broken, new-chum black sheep of the house where he was born, and the mother whose heart he broke—and the father whose grey hairs he brought down in sorrow to the grave—and break him up altogether."

"But what about the old-fashioned windows and the vines?" I asked.

"Oh!" said Mitchell, "I forgot them. On second thought, I think I *would* have some flowers; and maybe a bit of ivy-green. The new chum might be trying to work out his own salvation, and the sight of the roses and ivy would show him that he hadn't struck such a God-forgotten country after all, and help strengthen the hope for something better that's in the heart of every vagabond till he dies."

Puff, puff, puff, slowly and reflectively.

"Until he dies," repeated Mitchell. "And, maybe," he said, rousing himself, "I'd have a little room fixed up like a corner of a swell restaurant, with silver and napkins on the table, and I'd fix up a waiter, so that when a broken-down University wreck came along he might feel, for an hour or so, something like the man he used to be. But I suppose," Mitchell reflected, "he wouldn't feel completely his old self without a lady friend sitting opposite to him. I might fix up a black gin for him, but I suppose he'd draw the colour line. But that's nonsense.

"All teamsters and travellers could camp there for one night only. I'd have shower-baths; but I wouldn't force any man to have a bath against his will. They could sit down to a table and have a feed off a table-cloth, and sleep in sheets, and feel like they did before their old mothers died, or before they ran away from home."

"Who? The mothers?" I asked.

"Yes, in some cases," said Mitchell. "And I'd have a nice, cool little summer-house down near the artificial lake, out of earshot of the house, where the bullock-drivers could sit with their pipes after tea, and tell yarns, and talk in their own language. And I'd have boats on the lake, too, in case an old Oxford or Cambridge man, or an old sailor came along—it might put years on to his life to have a pull at the oars. You remember that old sailor we saw in charge of the engine back there at the government tank? You saw how he had the engine?—clean and bright as a new pin—everything spick-and-span and shipshape, and his hut fixed up like a ship's cabin. I believe he thinks he's at sea half his time, and shoving her through it, instead of pumping muddy water out of a hole in the baking scrubs for starving stock. Or maybe he reckons he's keeping her afloat."

"And would you have fish in this lake of yours?" I asked.

"Oh, yes," said Mithcell, "and any ratty old shepherd or sundowner, that's gone mad of heat and loneliness—like the old codger we met back yonder—he could sit by the lagoon in the cool of the evening and fish to his heart's content with a string and a bent pin, and dream he's playing truant from school and fishing in the brook near his native village in England about fifty years ago. It would seem more real than fishing in the dust as some mad old bushmen do."

"But you'd draw the line somewhere?" I asked.

"No," said Mitchell, "not even at poets. I'd try to cure them, too, with good wholesome food and plenty of physical exercise. The Lost Souls' Hotel would be a refuge for men who'd been jail-birds once as well as men who were gentlemen once, and for physical wrecks and ruined drunkards as well as healthy honest shearers. I'd sit down and talk to the boozer or felon just as if I thought he was as good a man as me—and he might be, for that matter—God knows.

"The sick man would be kept till he recovered, or died; and the boozer, suffering from a recovery, I'd keep him till he was on his legs again."

"Then you'd have to have a doctor," I said.

"Yes," said Mitchell, "I'd fix that up all right. I wouldn't bother much about a respectable medical practitioner from the city. I'd get a medical wreck who had a brilliant career before him once in England and got into disgrace, and cleared out to the colonies—a man who knows what the d.t.'s is—a man who's been through it all and knows it all."

"Then you'd want a manager, or a clerk or secretary," I suggested.

"I suppose I would," said Mitchell. "I've got no head for figures. I suppose I'd have to advertise for him. If an applicant came with the highest testimonials of character, and especially if one was signed by a parson, I'd tell him to call again next week; and if a young man could prove that he came of a good Christian family, and went to church regularly, and sang in the choir, and taught Sunday-school, I'd tell him that he needn't come again, that the vacancy was filled, for I couldn't trust him. The man who's been extra religious and honest and hard-working in his young days is most likely to go wrong afterwards. I'd sooner trust some poor old devil of a clerk who'd got into the hands of a woman or racing men when he was young, and went wrong, and served his time for embezzlement; anyway, I'd take him out and give him another chance."

"And what about woman's influence?" I asked.

"Oh, I suppose there'd have to be a woman, if only to keep the doctor on the line. I'd get a woman with a past, one that hadn't been any better than she should have been, they're generally the most kind-hearted in the end. Say an actress who'd come down in the world, or an old opera-singer who'd lost her voice but could still sing a little. A woman who knows what trouble is. And I'd get a girl to keep her company, a sort of housemaid, with a couple of black gins or half-castes to help her. I'd get hold of some poor girl who'd been deceived and deserted: and a baby or two wouldn't be an objection—the kids would amuse the chaps and help humanize the place."

"And what if the manageress fell in love with the doctor?" I asked.

"Well, I couldn't provide against love," said Mitchell. "I fell in love myself more than once—and I don't suppose I'd have been any worse off if I'd have stayed in love. Ah, well! But suppose she did fall in love with the doctor and marry him, or suppose she fell in love with him and didn't marry him, for that matter—and suppose the girl fell in love with the secretary? There wouldn't be any harm done; it would only make them more contented with the home and bind them to it. They'd be a happy family, and the Lost Souls' Hotel would be more cheerful and homelike than ever."

"But supposing they all fell in love with each other and cleared out," I said.

"I don't see what they'd have to clear out for," said Mitchell. "But suppose they did. There's more than one medical wreck in Australia, and more than one woman with a past, and more than one broken old clerk who went wrong and was found out, and who steadied down in jail, and there's more than one poor girl that's been deceived. I could easily replace 'em. And the Lost Souls' Hotel might be the means of patching up many wrecked lives in that way—giving people with pasts the chance of another future, so to speak."

"I suppose you'd have music and books and pictures?" I said.

"Oh, yes," said Mitchell. "But I wouldn't have any bitter or sex-problem books. They do no good. Problems have been the curse of the world ever since it started. I think one noble, kindly, cheerful character in a book does more good than all the clever villains or romantic adventurers ever invented. And I think a man ought to get rid of his maudlin sentiment in private, or when he's drunk. It's a pity that every writer couldn't put all his bitterness into one book and then burn it.

"No; I'd have good cheerful books of the best and brightest sides of human nature—Charles Dickens, and Mark Twain, and Bret Harte, and those men. And I'd have all Australian pictures— showing the brightest and best side of Australian life. And I'd have all Australian songs. I wouldn't have 'Swannie Ribber,' or 'Home, Sweet Home,' or 'Annie Laurie,' or any of those old songs sung at the Lost Souls' Hotel—they're the cause of more heartbreaks and drink and suicide in the bush than anything else. And if a jackeroo got up to sing, 'Just before the battle, mother,' or, 'Mother bit me in me sleep,' he'd find it was just before the battle all right. He'd have to go out and sleep in the scrub, where the mosquitoes and bulldog ants would bite him out of his sleep. I hate the man who's always whining about his mother through his nose, because, as a rule, he never cared a rap for his old mother, nor for anyone else, except his own paltry, selfish little self.

"I'd have intellectual and elevating conversation for those that——"

"Who'd take charge of that department?" I inquired hurriedly.

"Well," reflected Mitchell, "I did have an idea of taking it on myself for a while anyway; but, come to think of it, the doctor or the woman with the past would have more experience; and I could look after that part of the business at a pinch. Of course you're not in a position to judge as to my ability in the intellectual line; you see, I've had no one to practise on since I've been with you. But no matter—— There'd be intellectual conversation for the benefit of black-sheep new chums. And any broken-down actors that came along could get up a play if they liked—it would brighten up things and help elevate the bullock-drivers and sundowners. I'd have a stage fixed up and a bit of scenery. I'd do all I could to attract shearers to the place after shearing, and keep them from rushing to the next shanty with their cheques, or down to Sydney, to be cleaned out by barmaids.

"And I'd have the hero squashed in the last act for a selfish sneak, and marry the girl to the villain—he'd be more likely to make her happy in the end."

"And what about the farm?" I asked. "I suppose you'd get some expert from the agricultural college to manage that?"

"No," said Mitchell. "I'd get some poor drought-ruined selector and put him in charge of the vegetation. Only, the worst of it is," he reflected, "if you take a selector who has bullocked all his life to raise crops on dusty, stony patches in the scrubs, and put him on land, where there's plenty of water and manure, and where he's only got to throw the seed on the ground and then light his pipe and watch it grow, he's apt to get disheartened. But that's human nature.

"And, of course, I'd have to have a 'character' about the place—a sort of identity and joker to brighten up things. I wouldn't get a man who'd been happy and comfortable all his life; I'd get hold of some old codger whose wife had nagged him till she died, and who'd been sold off many times, and run in for drowning his sorrows, and who started as an undertaker and failed at that, and finally got a job pottering round—gardener, or gatekeeper, or something—in a lunatic asylum. I'd get him. He'd most likely be a humorist and a philosopher, and he'd help cheer up the Lost Souls' Hotel. I reckon the lost souls would get very fond of him."

"And would you have drink at Lost Souls'?" I asked.

"Yes," said Mitchell. "I'd have the best beer and spirits and wine to be had. After tea I'd let every man have just enough to make him feel comfortable and happy, and as good and clever, and innocent and honest as any other man, but no more. But if a poor devil came along in the horrors, with every inch of him jumping, and snakes, and green-eyed yahoos, and flaming-nosed bunyips chasing him, we'd take him in and give him soothing draughts, and nurse him, and watch him, and clear him out with purgatives, and keep giving him nips of good whisky, and, above all, we'd sympathize with him, and tell him that we were worse than he was many a time. We wouldn't tell him what a weak, selfish man he was, or harp on his ruined life. We'd try to make him out a good deal better morally than he really was. It's remorse that hurries most men to hell—especially in the Bush. When a man firmly believes he is a hopeless case, then there's no hope for him: but let him have doubts and there's a chance. Make him believe that there are far worse cases than his. We wouldn't preach the sin of dissipation to him, no—but we'd try to show him the *folly* of a wasted life. I ought to be able to preach that, God knows.

"And, above all, we'd try to drive out of his head the cursed old popular idea that it's hard to reform—that a man's got to fight a hard battle with himself to get away from drink—pity drunkards can't believe how easy it is. And we'd put it to him straight whether his few hours' enjoyment were worth the days he had to suffer hell for it."

"And, likely as not," I said, "when you'd put him on his feet he'd take the nearest track to the next shanty, and go on a howling spree, and come back to Lost Souls' in a week, raving and worse than ever. What would you do then?"

"We'd take him in again, and build him up some more; and a third or fourth time if necessary. I believe in going right on with a thing once I take it in hand. And if he didn't turn up after the last spree we'd look for him up the scrub and bring him in and let him die on a bed, and make his death as comfortable as possible. I've seen one man die on the ground, and found one dead in the bush. We'd bury him under a gum and put 'Sacred to the Memory of a Man who Died. (Let him R.I.P.)' over him. I'd have a nice little graveyard, with gums for tombstones—and I'd have some original epitaphs—I promise you."

"And how much gratitude would you expect to get out of the Lost Souls' Hotel?" I asked.

"None," said Mitchell, promptly. "It wouldn't be a Gratitude Discovery Syndicate. People might say that the Lost Souls' Hotel was a den for kidnapping women and girls to be used as decoys for the purpose of hocussing and robbing bushmen, and the law and retribution might come after me—but I'd fight the thing out. Or they might want to make a K.C.M.G., or a god of me, and worship me before they hung me. I reckon a philanthropist or reformer is lucky if he escapes with a whole skin in the end, let alone his character——But there!—— Talking of gratitude: it's the fear of ingratitude that keeps thousands from doing good. It's just as paltry and selfish and cowardly as any other fear that curses the world—it's rather more selfish than most fears, in fact—take the fear of being thought a coward, or being considered eccentric, or conceited, or affected, or too good, or too bad, for instance. The man that's always canting about the world's ingratitude has no gratitude owing to him as a rule—generally the reverse—he ought to be grateful to the world for being let live. He broods over the world's ingratitude until he gets to be a cynic. He sees the world like the outside of a window, as it were, with the blind drawn and the dead, cold moonlight shining on it, and he passes on with a sour face; whereas, if he took the trouble to step inside he'd most likely find a room full of ruddy firelight, and sympathy and cheerfulness, and kindness, and love, and gratitude. Sometimes, when he's right down on his uppers, and forced to go amongst people and hustle for bread, he gets a lot of surprises at the amount of kindness he keeps running against in the world—and in places where he'd never have expected to find it. But—ah, well! I'm getting maudlin."

"And you've forgot all about the Lost Souls' Hotel," I said.

"No, I haven't," said Mitchell; "I'd fix that up all right. As soon as I'd got things going smoothly under a man I could trust, I'd tie up every penny I had for the benefit of the concern; get some 'white men' for trustees, and take the track again. I'm getting too old to stay long in one place—(I'm a lost soul that always got along better in another place). I'm so used to the track that if I was shut up in a house I'd get walking up and down in my room of nights and disturb the folk; and, besides, I'd feel lost and light-shouldered without the swag."

"So you'd put all your money in the concern?"

"Yes—except a pound or two to go on the track with—for, who knows, I might come along there, dusty and tired, and ragged and hard up and old, some day, and be very glad of a night's rest at the Lost Souls' Hotel. But I wouldn't let on that I was old Mitchell, the millionaire, who founded Lost Souls'. They might be too officious, and I hate fuss.... But it's time to take the track, Harry."

There came a cool breeze with sunset; we stood up stiffly, shouldered our swags and tucker-bags, and pushed on, for we had to make the next water before we camped. We were out of tobacco, so we borrowed some from one of the bullock-drivers.

THE BOOZERS' HOME

"A dipsomaniac," said Mitchell, "needs sympathy and common-sense treatment. (Sympathy's a grand and glorious thing, taking it all round and looking at it any way you will: a little of it makes a man think that the world's a good world after all, and there's room and hope for sinners, and that life's worth living; enough of it makes him sure of it: and an overdose of sympathy makes a man *feel* weak and ashamed of himself, and so moves him to stop whining—and wining—and buck up.)

"Now, I'm not taking the case of a workman who goes on the spree on pay night and sweats the drink out of himself at work next day, nor a slum-bred brute who guzzles for the love of it; but a man with brains, who drinks to drown his intellect or his memory. He's generally a man under it all, and a sensitive, generous, gentle man with finer feelings as often as not. The best and cleverest and whitest men in the world seem to take to drink mostly. It's an awful pity. Perhaps it's because they're straight and the world's crooked and they can see things too plain. And I suppose in the bush the loneliness and the thoughts of the girl-world they left behind help to sink 'em.

"Now a drunkard seldom reforms at home, because he's always surrounded by the signs of the ruin and misery he has brought on the home; and the sight and thought of it sets him off again before he's had time to recover from the last spree. Then, again, the noblest wife in the world mostly goes the wrong way to work with a drunken husband—nearly everything she does is calculated to irritate him. If, for instance, he brings a bottle home from the pub, it shows that he wants to stay at home and not go back to the pub any more; but the first thing the wife does is to get hold of the bottle and plant it, or smash it before his eyes, and that maddens him in the state he is in then.

"No. A dipsomaniac needs to be taken away from home for a while. I knew a man that got so bad that the way he acted at home one night frightened him, and next morning he went into an inebriate home of his own accord—to a place where his friends had been trying to get him for a year past. For the first day or two he was nearly dead with remorse and shame—mostly shame; and he didn't know what they were going to do to him next—and he only wanted them to kill him quick and be done with it. He reckons he felt as bad as if he was in jail. But there were ten other patients there, and one or two were worse than he was, and that comforted him a lot. They compared notes and sympathized and helped each other. They discovered that all their wives were noble women. He struck one or two surprises too—one of the patients was a doctor who'd attended him one time, and another was an old boss of his, and they got very chummy. And there was a man there who was standing for Parliament—he was supposed to be having a rest down the coast. . . . Yes, my old mate felt very bad for the first day or two; it was all Yes, Nurse, and Thank you, Nurse, and Yes, Doctor, and No, Doctor, and Thank you, Doctor. But, inside a week, he was calling the doctor 'Ol' Pill-Box' behind his back, and making love to one of the nurses.

"But he said it was pitiful when women relatives came to visit patients the first morning. It shook the patients up a lot, but I reckon it did 'em good. There were well-bred old lady mothers in black, and hard-working, haggard wives and loving daughters—and the expressions of sympathy and faith and hope in those women's faces! My old mate said it was enough in itself to make a man swear off drink for ever. . . . Ah, God—what a world it is!

"Reminds me how I once went with the wife of another old mate of mine to see him. He was in a lunatic asylum. It was about the worst hour I ever had in my life, and I've had some bad ones. The way she tried to coax him back to his old self. She thought she could do it when all the doctors had failed. But I'll tell you about him some other time.

"The old mate said that the principal part of the treatment was supposed to be injection of bi-chloride of gold or something, and it was supposed to be a secret. It might have been water and sugar for all he knew, and he thought it was. You see, when patients got better they were allowed out, two by two, on their honour—one to watch the other—and it worked. But it was necessary to have an extra hold on them; so they were told that if they were a minute late for 'treatment,' or missed one injection, all the good would be undone. This was dinged into their ears all the time. Same as many things are done in the Catholic religion—to hold the people. My old mate said that, as far as the medical treatment was concerned, he could do all that was necessary himself. But it was the sympathy that counted, especially the sympathy between the patients themselves. They always got hold of a new patient and talked to him and cheered him up; he nearly always came in thinking he was the most miserable wretch in this world. And it comforts a man and strengthens him and makes him happier to meet another man who's worse off or sicker, or has been worse swindled than he has been. That's human nature. . . . And a man will take draughts from a nurse and eat for her when he wouldn't do it for his own wife—not even though she had been a trained nurse herself. And if a patient took a bad turn in the night at the Boozer's Home and got up to hunt the snakes out of his room, he wouldn't be sworn at, or laughed at, or held down; no, they'd help him shoo the snakes out and comfort him. My old mate said that, when he got better, one of the new patients reckoned that he licked St Pathrick at managing snakes. And when he came out he didn't feel a bit ashamed of his experience. The institution didn't profess to cure anyone of drink, only to mend up shattered nerves and build up wrecked constitutions; give them back some will-power if they weren't too far gone. And they set my old mate on his feet all right. When he went in his life seemed lost, he had the horror of being sober, he couldn't start the day without a drink or do any business without it. He couldn't live for more than two hours without a drink; but when he came out he didn't feel as if he wanted it. He reckoned that those six weeks in the institution were the happiest he'd ever spent in his life, and he wished the time had been longer; he says he'd never met with so much sympathy and genius, and humour and human nature under one roof before. And he said it was nice and novel to be looked after and watched and physicked and bossed by a pretty nurse in uniform—but I don't suppose he told his wife that. And when he came out he never took the trouble to hide the fact that he'd been in. If any of his friends had a drunkard in the family, he'd recommend the institution and do his best to get him into it. But when he came out he firmly believed that if he took one drink he'd be a lost man. He made a mania of that. One curious effect was that, for some time after he left the institution, he'd sometimes feel suddenly in high spirits—with nothing to account for it—something like he used to feel when he had half a dozen whiskies in him; then suddenly he'd feel depressed and sort of hopeless—with nothing to account for that either—just as if he was suffering a recovery. But those moods never lasted long and he soon grew out of them altogether. He didn't flee temptation. He'd knock round the pubs on Saturday nights with his old mates, but never drank anything but soft stuff—he was always careful to smell his glass for fear of an accident or trick. He drank gallons of ginger beer, milk-and-soda, and lemonade; and he got very fond of sweets, too—he'd never liked them before. He said he enjoyed the novelty of the whole thing and his mates amused him at first; but he found he had to leave them early in the evening, and, after a while, he dropped them altogether. They seemed such fools when they were drunk (they'd never seemed fools to him before). And, besides, as they got full, they'd get suspicious of him, and then mad at him, because he couldn't see things as they could. That reminds me that it nearly breaks a man's heart when his old drinking chum turns teetotaller—it's worse than if he got married or died. When two mates meet and one is drunk and the other sober there is only one of two things for them to do if they want to hit it together—either the drunken mate must get sober or the sober mate drunk. And that reminds me: Take the case of two old mates who've been together all their lives, say they always had their regular sprees together and went through the same stages of drunkenness together, and suffered their recoveries and sobered up together, and each could stand about the same quantity of drink and one never got drunker than the other. Each, when he's boozing, reckons his mate the cleverest man and the hardest case in the world—second to himself. But one day it happens, by a most extraordinary combination of circumstances, that Bill, being sober, meets Jim very drunk, and pretty soon Bill is the most disgusted man in this world. He never would have dreamed that his old mate could make such a fool and such a public spectacle of himself. And Bill's disgust intensifies all the time he is helping Jim home, and Jim arguing with him and wanting to fight him, and slobbering over him and wanting to love him by turns, until Bill swears he'll give Jim a hammering as soon as ever he's able to stand steady on his feet."

"I suppose your old boozing mate's wife was very happy when he reformed," I said to Mitchell.

"Well, no," said Mitchell, rubbing his head rather ruefully. "I suppose it was an exceptional case. But I knew her well, and the fact is that she got more discontented and thinner, and complained and nagged him worse than she'd ever done in his drinking days. And she'd never been afraid of him. Perhaps it was this way: She loved and married a careless, good-natured, drinking scamp, and when he reformed and became a careful, hard-working man, and an honest and respected fellow-townsman, she was disappointed in him. He wasn't the man that won her heart when she was a girl. Or maybe he was only company for her when he was half drunk. Or maybe lots of things. Perhaps he'd killed the love in her before he reformed—and reformed too late. I wonder how a man feels when he finds out for the first time that his wife doesn't love him any longer? But my old mate wasn't the nature to find out that sort of thing. Ah, well! If a woman caused all our trouble, my God! women have suffered for it since—and they suffer like martyrs mostly and with the patience of working bullocks. Anyway it goes, if I'm the last man in the world, and the last woman is the worst, and there's only room for one more in Heaven, I'll step down at once and take my chances in Blazes."

THE SEX PROBLEM AGAIN

It was Mitchell's habit to take an evening off now and then from yarning or reflecting, and proceed, in a most methodical manner, to wash his spare shirts and patch his pants. I was in the habit of contributing to some Sydney papers, and every man is an editor at heart, so, at other times, Mitchell would take another evening off, and root out my swag, and go through my papers in the same methodical manner, and make alterations and additions without comment or reference to me; and sometimes he'd read a little thing of my own which didn't meet his views, and accidentally drop it into the fire; and at other times he'd get hold of some rhyme or sketch that was troubling me, and wrap it up and give it to a passing mailman unbeknown to me. The unexpected appearance of such articles in the paper, as well as the effects of the involuntary collaboration in other pieces, gave me several big surprises.

It was in camp on a fencing contract west of Bourke. We had a book which we'd borrowed from a library at Bourke for a year or two—never mind the name of it—it was in ninety-one or ninety-two, and the sex problem was booming then.

I had been surreptitiously tearing some carefully-written slips of manuscript—leaves taken from an old pocket-book—into small pieces; I dropped them, with apparent carelessness, into the fire and stood with my back to it.

"I'll bet five pounds," said Mitchell, suddenly, "that you've been trying your hand on a sex-problem story."

I shifted uneasily and brought my hands from behind me into my pockets. "Well, to tell you the truth," I admitted, "I have."

"I thought so," exclaimed Mitchell. "We'll be put to the expense of sending you to Sydney for medical treatment yet. You've been having too easy times lately, plenty of hard graft and no anxiety about tucker or the future. What are the symptoms?"

"Well," I said, taking a hand out to scratch the back of my head, "the plot looked all right—at first sight."

"So there's a plot, is there? Well, in the first place, a plot is a problem. Well, what's the plot?... Come on, you needn't be frightened to tell an old mate like me."

"Well," I said, "the yarn looked all right at first sight; that article of 'T's' in the *Bulletin* turned me off it; listen and see what you think of it: There was a young fellow, a bit of a genius——"

"Just so, it's the geniuses that build the sex problems. It's an autobiography. Go on."

"Well, he married a girl."

Mitchell (*sotto voce*): "God help her."

"He loved her, and she loved him: but after they'd been married a while he found out that, although he understood her, she didn't and couldn't possibly ever understand him."

"Yes," commented Mitchell, "and if he hadn't caught the sex problem, nor been reading about it, he would never have found that out."

"It was a terrible disappointment," I continued—I had got into the habit of taking Mitchell's interruptions and comments as matters of course—"He saw that his life would be a hell with her——"

Mitchell: "Didn't strike him that her life would be a hell with him?"

"They had no thought in common."

Mitchell: "She was in her right mind then."

"But he couldn't leave her because he loved her, and because he knew that she loved him and would break her heart if he left her."

"Must have been a pretty cocksure sort of a fellow," remarked Mitchell, "but all geniuses are."

"When he was with her he saw all her obstinacy, unreason, and selfishness; but when he was away he only saw her good points."

Mitchell: "Pity such men don't stop away."

"He thought and thought, and brooded over it till his life was a' hell——"

Mitchell: "Jes-so: thanks to the problemaniacs."

"He thought of killing her and himself, and so taking her with him——"

"Where?" asked Mitchell. "He must have loved her a lot.... Good Lord! That shows the awful effects of the sex problem on the mind of a healthy young man like you;" and Mitchell stood up.

"He lay awake by her side at nights thinking and fighting the thing out."

"And you've been lying awake, thinking, with me and 'the Oracle' by your side. We'll have to plant the tommy-hawk, and watch you by turns at night till you get over this."

"One night he rested on his elbow, and watched her sleeping, and tried to reconstruct his ideal out of her, and, just when he was getting into a happier frame of mind, her mouth fell open, and she snored.... I didn't get any further than the snore," I said.

"No, of course you didn't," said Mitchell, "and none of the sex problemers ever will—unless they get as far as 'blanky.' You might have made the snore cure him; did it?"

"No, it was making things worse in my idea of the yarn. He fell back and lay staring at the ceiling in a hopeless kind of a way."

"Then he was a fit case for the lunatic asylum.... Now, look here, Harry, you're a good-natured, soft old fool when you're in your right mind; just you go on being a good-natured, soft old fool, and don't try to make a problem out of yourself or anybody else, or you'll come to a bad end. A pocket-book's to keep your accounts in, not to take notes in (you take them in your head and use 'em in your arms), not to write sex-problem rot in—that's spoilt many a good pocket-book, and many a good man. You've got a girl you're talking about going back to as soon as we've finished this contract. Don't you make a problem of her; make a happy wife and mother of her.... I was very clever when I was young"—and here

Mitchell's voice took a tinge of bitterness, or sadness. "I used to make problems out of things.... I ain't much to boast of now.... Seems to me that a good many men want to make angels of their wives without first taking trouble of making saints of themselves. We want to make women's ways our ways—it would be just as fair to make our ways theirs. Some men want to be considered gods in their own homes; you'll generally find that sort of men very small potatoes outside; if they weren't they wouldn't bother so much about being cocks on their own little dunghills.... And again, old mates seldom quarrel, because they understand each other's moods. Now, if you went brooding round for any length of time I'd say to you. 'Now then, Harry, what have I been doing to you? Spit it out, old man.' And you'd do the same by me; but how many men would take even that much trouble with their wives?"

A breeze stirred the mulga and brought the sound of a good voice singing in the surveyors' camp:

> Should old acquaintance be forgot
> And never brought to min'?
> Should old acquaintance be forgot
> And the days of Auld Lang Syne?

"That damned old tune will upset the Oracle* for the rest of the night," I said.

"Now, there's the Oracle," said Mitchell. "He was wronged by a woman as few men are wronged; his life was ruined—but he isn't the man to take any stock in sex problems on account of her. He thinks he's great on problems, but he isn't. It all amounts to this—that he's sorry for most men and all women and tries to act up to it to the best of his ability; and if he ain't a Christian, God knows what is—I don't. No matter what a woman does to you, or what you think she does to you, there come times, sooner or later, when you feel sorry for her—deep down in your heart—that is if you're a man. And, no matter what action or course you might take against her, and no matter how right or justified you might seem in doing it, there comes a time when, deep down in your heart, you feel mean and doubtful about your own part. You can take that as a general thing as regards men against women, and man against man, I think. And I believe that deep-down feeling of being doubtful, or mean, or sorry, that comes afterwards, when you are cooler and know more about the world, is a right and natural thing, and we ought to act more in accordance with it."

---

* *The Oracle*—See "The Story of the Oracle."

Came the refrain from the surveyors' camp:

> We twa hae run about the braes,
>   An' pu'd the gowans fine;
> But we've wandered mony a weary foot
>   Sin' Auld Lang Syne.

"We feel sorry for our quarrels with our worst enemy when we see him lying still and quiet—dead. Why can't we try and feel a bit sorry beforehand?"

> For Auld Lang Syne.
> We twa ha' padl't i' the burn,
>   Fra mornin' sun till dine;
> But seas between us braid ha' roar'd
>   Sin' Auld Lang Syne.

"I used to feel blazing bitter against things one time but it never hurt anybody but myself in the end. I argued and quarrelled with a girl once—and made a problem of the thing and went away. She's married to a brute now, and I'm what I am. I made a problem of a good home or the world once, and went against the last man in God's world that I should have gone against, and turned my back on his hand, and left him. His hand was very cold the next time I took it in mine. We don't want problems to make us more bitter against the world than we get sometimes."

> And here's a han' my trusty frien',
>   An' gie's a han' o' thine,
> We'll tak' a cup o' kindness yet
>   For Auld Lang Syne.

"And that song's the answer of all problems," said Mitchell. But it was I who lay awake and thought that night.

INDEX TO STORIES

INDEX TO STORIES